Other Books by Joey Green

Hellbent on Insanity

The Gilligan's Island Handbook

The Get Smart Handbook

The Partridge Family Album

Polish Your Furniture with Panty Hose

Hi Bob!

Selling Out

Paint Your House with Powdered Milk

Wash Your Hair with Whipped Cream

The Bubble Wrap Book

Joey Green's Encyclopedia of
Offbeat Uses for Brand-Name Products

The Zen of Oz

The Warning Label Book

Monica Speaks

The Official Slinky Book

You Know You've Reached
Middle Age If . . .

The Mad Scientist Handbook

Clean Your Clothes with Cheez Whiz

The Road to Success Is Paved with Failure

Clean It! Fix It! Eat It!

Joey Green's Magic Brands

The Mad Scientist Handbook 2

Senior Moments

Jesus and Moses: The Parallel Sayings

Joey Green's Amazing Kitchen Cures

Jesus and Muhammad:
The Parallel Sayings

Joey Green's Gardening Magic

How They Met

Joey Green's Incredible Country Store

Potato Radio, Dizzy Dice

Joey Green's Supermarket Spa

Weird Christmas

Contrary to Popular Belief

Marx & Lennon: The Parallel Sayings

Joey Green's Rainy Day Magic

The Jolly President

Champagne and Caviar Again?

Joey Green's Mealtime Magic

The Bathroom Professor:
Philosophy on the Go

Famous Failures

Joey Green's Fit-It Magic

Too Old for MySpace, Too Young for
Medicare

You Know You Need a Vacation If . . .

Sarah Palin's Secret Diary

Joey Green's Cleaning MAGIC

2,336 Ingenious Cleanups
Using Brand-Name Products

By Joey Green

RODALE

The author has compiled the information contained herein from a variety of sources, and neither the author, publisher, manufacturers, nor distributors can assume responsibility for the effectiveness of the suggestions. Caution is urged in the use of the cleaning solutions, folk medicine remedies, and pest control substances.

The brand-name products mentioned in this book are registered trademarks. The companies that own these trademarks and make these products do not endorse, recommend, or accept liability for any use of their products other than those uses indicated on the package labels or in current company brochures. This book should not be regarded as a substitute for professional medical treatment, and neither the author, publisher, manufacturers, nor distributors can accept legal responsibility for any problem arising out of the use of or experimentation with the methods described. For a full listing of trademarks, please see page 386.

Direct and trade editions are both being published in 2010.

Rodale books may be purchased for business or promotional use or for special sales. For information, please write to:
Special Markets Department, Rodale Inc., 733 Third Avenue, New York, NY 10017

Printed in the United States of America
Rodale Inc. makes every effort to use acid-free ♾, recycled paper ♻.

Book design by Christina Gaugler
Illustrations © 2010 by Terry LaBan

Library of Congress Cataloging-in-Publication Data

Green, Joey.
  Joey Green's cleaning magic : 2,336 ingenious cleanups using brand-name products / Joey Green.
      p. cm.
  Includes index.
  ISBN-13: 978-1-60529-744-6 (hardcover)
  ISBN-10: 1-60529-744-5 (hardcover)
  ISBN-13: 978-1-60529-745-3 (pbk.)
  ISBN-10: 1-60529-745-3 (pbk.)
  1. Home economics. 2. Brand name products—United States. 3. Cleaning. I. Title. II. Title: Cleaning magic.
  TX158.G678134   2009
  648—dc22   2009038157

Distributed to the trade by Macmillan

	4	6	8	10	9	7	5		hardcover
2	4	6	8	10	9	7	5	3	paperback

We inspire and enable people to improve their lives and the world around them

For more of our products visit **rodalestore.com** or call 800-848-4735

For my mother,
who spent my entire youth
telling me to clean my room

Contents

But First, a Word from Our Sponsor

Unless you're a neat freak like Felix Unger from *The Odd Couple*, Danny Tanner from *Full House*, or Monica Geller from *Friends*, you probably have no desire to spend any more time or money than absolutely necessary cleaning your house, doing the laundry, organizing clutter, or grooming yourself. Why? It's time-consuming and work-intensive. The task of cleaning up is overwhelming, painful, and downright annoying. If you're like most people, you do the best you can and let most of the cleaning chores pile up until they get beyond your control. But it doesn't have to be that way. Cleaning up can be an exciting adventure, a series of mad science experiments, a thrilling, spine-tingling game. Don't believe me?

Every day I receive an onslaught of letters and emails from people besieged by seemingly impossible cleaning problems. "How do I remove five years worth of baked-on grease and food from our stainless-steel stove top?" "How do I clean candle wax out of our linen tablecloth?" "How do you clean coffee stains from clothes?" "I've cleaned the entire refrigerator several times, but it still smells like sour milk. What should I do?" "My brand-new pot seems to be permanently scorched. Is there anything I can do to save it?"

At first, these dilemmas seem insurmountable, but in truth, the solutions are amazingly simple. You don't have to run out to the store to buy anything. You already have several brand-name products right now in your home that can do these jobs—easily and effortlessly. To clean baked-on grease from a stovetop, spritz Spray 'n Wash stain remover on the baked-on grease, let it set for a few minutes, and then wipe clean. To clean melted wax from a tablecloth, place a sheet of Bounty Paper Towels over the wax stain and press gently with a warm iron. (The heat from the iron melts the wax, and the quicker-picker-upper absorbs it.) To clean a wet coffee stain from clothes, saturate the stain with Canada Dry Club Soda, rinse, and launder as usual. To clean the pungent smell of sour milk from a refrigerator, simply make a paste from Arm & Hammer Baking Soda and water, scrub the interior of the refrigerator (and the drawers and shelves) with the paste, and rinse clean. To clean a scorched pot, just fill the pot with water, drop in two or three Efferdent denture cleansing tablets, and let the pot sit overnight. In the morning, use a sponge to wipe it clean. (You can also toss your dentures in the pot at the same time and kill two birds with one stone.)

Awestruck by the simplicity of these amazing tips, people just like you suddenly discover how easy it is to solve what they previously thought were hopeless household cleaning problems. Grease and grime, stains and scuffmarks, mold and mildew—they're problems that can all be simply remedied in ways that will inspire you to become your own cleaning machine.

And so, as a public service, I've put this book together, determined to share thousands of unusual cleaning tips, using hundreds of brand-name products we all know and love—such as L'eggs Sheer Energy Panty Hose, Bounce, Huggies Baby Wipes, Maxwell House Coffee, and Jell-O—in ways they were never intended to be used. I decided that the time had come for me to jam-pack this information kept secret from the public in one knock-your-socks-off book.

I plunged into my quest with wild abandon. I locked myself away in the public library, researching endlessly. I contacted companies to get their clandestine files. I combed through all those letters and emails I've received over the years. And I tested product after product, scrubbing the lime buildup off the tiles of our swimming pool with a Mr. Clean Magic Eraser, touching up a chip in our bathroom sink with Liquid Paper, and cleaning our brass doorknobs with ReaLemon lemon juice and Morton Salt.

I discovered some astonishing information. Coca-Cola cleans bloodstains from clothes. Lysol Disinfectant can be used to deodorize smelly shoes. Quaker Oats clean soiled suede. Old Spice prevents cats from scratching furniture. Bounce cleans inks stains from inside a dryer. Play-Doh cleans wallpaper. Tang cleans mineral deposits from a coffeemaker. But I had to know more. Who invented Easy-Off Oven Cleaner? Is everything really better with Blue Bonnet on it? Who invented Murphy Oil Soap? Was Lysol Disinfectant really once promoted as a contraceptive? Who invented Windex? Who is Mr. Clean? And why isn't he on speaking terms with Mrs. Butterworth?

The result of my full-body immersion into the quicksand of Americana? A decidedly quirky book that I'm proud to say reveals more than 2,500 cleaning tips using more than 200 brand-name products. I hope you enjoy the book. Otherwise, you can always use that Pepto-Bismol for its original purpose.

Automobiles

AIR FRESHENERS

- **Bounce.** Place a sheet of Bounce in the sun visor of your car or under the seat, inside a seat pocket, behind a visor, or inside the glove compartment to freshen the air.
- **Dial Soap.** To freshen the air in your car, place a wrapped bar of Dial Soap under the front seat.

BATTERY CORROSION

- **Arm & Hammer Baking Soda.** To clean corrosion from battery terminals, mix one-half cup Arm & Hammer Baking Soda and two cups warm water and use a clean, old toothbrush to scrub the terminals with the solution.

- **Vaseline Petroleum Jelly.** To protect clean battery terminals from corrosion, coat the terminals with Vaseline Petroleum Jelly.

BUMPER STICKERS

- **Conair 1875 Watt Hair Dryer** and **MasterCard.** To remove a bumper sticker, aim a Conair 1875 Watt Hair Dryer at the sticker to melt the adhesive backing, and then use the edge of an old MasterCard to peel up the sticker.

- **Cutex Nail Polish Remover.** To remove adhesive residue left behind by a peeled-off bumper sticker, saturate a cotton ball with Cutex Nail Polish Remover and rub the glue.

- **Star Olive Oil.** Saturate the bumper sticker with Star Olive Oil, let sit for five minutes to give the oil time to dissolve the adhesive, and peel off.

CARPETS

- **Heinz White Vinegar.** To clean imbedded salt residue from carpeting, mix one cup Heinz White Vinegar and two cups water and scrub with the solution.

CHROME

- **Arm & Hammer Baking Soda.** To clean chrome, sprinkle Arm & Hammer Baking Soda on a damp rag and scrub. Rinse clean.

- **Bounce.** After cleaning chrome, polish the metal with a clean, used sheet of Bounce.

- **Gold Medal Flour.** To clean chrome, sprinkle Gold Medal Flour on a damp sponge, scrub, rinse clean, and dry.

- **Heinz White Vinegar.** Saturate a sponge with Heinz White Vinegar and polish the chrome.

- **Murphy Oil Soap.** To clean chrome, mix one teaspoon Murphy Oil Soap and two cups water in a sixteen-ounce trigger-spray bottle. Spray the chrome with the solution and wipe with a soft, clean cloth. Rinse and dry.
- **ReaLemon.** Saturate a soft, clean cloth with ReaLemon lemon juice and wipe the chrome clean.
- **Reynolds Wrap.** To clean chrome, crumple up a sheet of Reynolds Wrap aluminum foil into a ball, dampen with water, and rub the chrome until it sparkles.
- **WD-40.** Spray WD-40 on a soft, clean cloth and rub the chrome until it shines like new.
- **Windex.** Spray the chrome with Windex and rub with a soft, clean cloth.

DASHBOARDS

- **Bounce.** Shine the dashboard with a clean, used sheet of Bounce. The antistatic elements in Bounce will help repel dust from the dashboard.

DEODORIZING

- **Lysol Disinfectant.** Is your automobile air conditioner blowing air that smells like mold or mildew? With the car parked outside, the engine running, and the air conditioner cooling on normal speed, spray Lysol Disinfectant into the air intake vent (found outside your car above the front hood, just below the windshield). Hold the can about ten inches away from the vent and spray for ten seconds. The air conditioning system will suck in the disinfectant and deodorize the entire system in seconds, killing any mold or mildew in the system. Be sure to turn off the car engine when you're finished.

DOORS

- **Pam Cooking Spray.** To prevent car doors from freezing shut, spray the black rubber gasket around the frame of the door with Pam Cooking

Spray. The vegetable oil simultaneously repels water and keeps the gaskets supple and clean.

FROST

- **MasterCard.** To clean frost off the inside of your car windshield, scrape it with a clean, old MasterCard.

HUBCAPS

- **Cascade.** To clean hubcaps, remove them from the tires, place them in the dish rack of your dishwasher, add Cascade in the soap receptacle dish, and run through the regular cycle.
- **Scrubbing Bubbles.** To clean dirt and grime from a hubcap, spray the hubcap with Scrubbing Bubbles, let sit for fifteen seconds, and rinse clean with a garden hose.

ICE

- **Glad Trash Bags.** To avoid having to clean ice from the windshield of your parked car, cut open a Glad Trash Bag along the seams, open the car doors, place the open plastic across the windshield, tuck the ends inside each door, and close the doors. The ice will form on the plastic sheet instead of the windshield. Be sure to remove the plastic before driving away.
- **Morton Salt.** To make cleaning ice off the windshield easier, rub Morton Salt on the ice, wait a few minutes, and then scrape. The salt melts the ice. Keep a canister of Morton Salt in your trunk.

INSECTS

- **Dr Pepper.** To clean insects off a car windshield, pour a can of Dr Pepper over the windshield and squeegee clean.

- **L'eggs Sheer Energy Panty Hose.** To scrape dead bugs off the windshield, ball up a pair of L'eggs Sheer Energy Panty Hose, saturate it with water, and wipe down the windshield. The nylon is a mild abrasive that works wonders.
- **Mr. Clean Magic Eraser.** To clean bugs from a car windshield, grille, and bumper, gently rub with a damp Mr. Clean Magic Eraser.
- **Pam Cooking Spray.** To prevent dead insects from sticking to the hood and grille of your car, spray the front of your car with Pam Cooking Spray before making a long trip. A fine coat of cooking spray allows you to wash off the insects with ease.

LEATHER UPHOLSTERY

- **Dove White Beauty Bar.** To clean the leather interior of a car, rub a Dove White Beauty Bar across a mildly damp, soft cloth and rub the cloth on the leather. Wipe dry with a fresh damp cloth and buff dry with a dry towel. After the leather dries, treat it with a leather conditioner. (For more ways to clean leather, see page 281.)

LOCKS

- **Glad Flexible Straws.** To defrost a frozen lock on a car door, insert a Glad Flexible Straw into the slot and blow warm air through the straw.

MAPS

- **Con-Tact Paper.** Cover those important road maps with clean Con-Tact Paper. Trace your route with a dry-erase marker that you can wipe off after the trip.

ODORS

- **Arm & Hammer Baking Soda.** To help minimize the smell of cigarette or cigar smoke in a car, pour a layer of Arm & Hammer Baking

Soda in the ashtray. Be sure to replace the baking soda once a month. If the upholstery and carpet smell like smoke, sprinkle Arm & Hammer Baking Soda on the upholstery and carpet, let sit for a few hours, and vacuum clean. Baking soda absorbs foul odors.

- **Bounce.** To mask the smell of cigarette or cigar smoke in a car, place a sheet of Bounce under the seat, behind a visor, in a seat pocket, or inside the glove compartment.

- **Jonny Cat Litter** and **L'eggs Sheer Energy Panty Hose.** To deodorize the interior of a car, cut off the two feet from a clean, used pair of L'eggs Sheer Energy Panty Hose, fill them both with Jonny Cat Litter, tie a knot in the open end, and place the sachets under the driver and passenger seats. The clay absorbs musty smells.

- **McCormick Pure Vanilla Extract.** To deodorize the smell of skunk from inside a car, saturate a rag with McCormick Pure Vanilla Extract and place it inside an open container on the floor of the backseat.

- **Parsons' Ammonia.** To kill cigarette odor in a car, pour one cup Parsons' Ammonia into a bowl, set it on the floor of the car, and lock the car shut for twenty-four hours. Remove the bowl, lower all the windows, and let the car air out thoroughly.

PAINT

- **Bon Ami.** To deoxidize dull paint on a car, sprinkle Bon Ami cleanser lightly onto the car while washing, rinse well, and wax the car.

POLISHING

- **Kingsford's Corn Starch.** After waxing your car, sprinkle some Kingsford's Corn Starch on the body and buff with a soft, clean cloth. The cornstarch absorbs excess polish.

SCUFFMARKS

- **Mr. Clean Magic Eraser.** To clean a paint scuffmark from a car, gently rub the scuffmark with a damp Mr. Clean Magic Eraser.

SPARK PLUGS

- **Easy-Off Oven Cleaner.** To clean dirty spark plugs, soak the tips of the spark plugs in Easy-Off Oven Cleaner for two hours in a well-ventilated area, rinse clean, and dry.

- **Forster Clothespins.** Before disconnecting the spark club cables to clean or replace the spark plugs, number Forster Clothespins with an indelible marker and clip to each cable.

STEERING WHEELS

- **Mr. Clean Magic Eraser.** To clean grime from the steering wheel of a car, gently rub the steering wheel with a damp Mr. Clean Magic Eraser and dry thoroughly.

STICKERS

- **Conair 1875 Watt Hair Dryer.** To remove a sticker from a car window, aim a Conair 1875 Watt Hair Dryer at the sticker to melt the adhesive backing and use a single-edge razor blade to peel up the sticker.

- **Cutex Nail Polish Remover.** To remove stickers from car windows, rub the stickers with a cotton ball saturated with Cutex Nail Polish Remover to dissolve the adhesive. Then carefully scrape off the sticker with a single-edge razor blade.

- **Star Olive Oil.** To remove stickers from car windows, saturate the sticker with Star Olive Oil and use care to scrape off the sticker with a single-edge razor blade.

TAR

- **Balmex.** To remove tar spots from car finishes without damaging the finish, apply Balmex to a cloth and rub until the tar glides off.

- **Nivea Creme.** To remove tar spots from a car's body, apply Nivea Creme to a cloth and rub until the tar glides off the finish.

- **Spray 'n Wash.** To clean tar from the side of a car or interior carpeting, spray the spot with Spray 'n Wash stain remover. Wait a few minutes, and then wipe clean with a soft, clean cloth. Wash off any residual Spray 'n Wash with soapy water, and rinse clean.

- **WD-40.** To remove tar from the body of a car, spray the tar with WD-40, let sit for two minutes, and wipe clean with a clean, soft cloth.

TIRES

- **Scrubbing Bubbles.** To clean dirt and grime from a tire, spray the tire with Scrubbing Bubbles, let sit for thirty seconds, and rinse clean with a garden hose.

TRUNKS

- **Pam Cooking Spray.** To prevent the trunk from freezing shut, spray the black rubber gasket around the frame of the trunk with Pam Cooking Spray. The vegetable oil simultaneously keeps the gaskets supple and repels any water that will freeze into ice.

UPHOLSTERY

- **Balmex.** To clean vinyl car upholstery, squeeze Balmex onto a soft cloth and wipe down the seats and other vinyl surfaces.

- **Nivea Creme.** To clean vinyl car upholstery, apply a dollop of Nivea Creme to a soft cloth and wipe down the seats and other vinyl surfaces.

WASHING

- **Jet-Dry.** After washing the car with a soapy solution and rinsing with a hose, mix one teaspoon Jet-Dry and two gallons water in a bucket, sponge the solution onto the car, and let dry. The surfactants in Jet-Dry will prevent streaking and spotting on the car.

- **Johnson's Baby Shampoo.** To wash a car, add two capfuls Johnson's Baby Shampoo to a bucket of water and soap up your car with the gentle suds.

- **Murphy Oil Soap.** Mix one-quarter teaspoon Murphy Oil Soap with two gallons water in a bucket, wash the car with a sponge saturated with suds, and rinse clean with a garden hose. Buff dry.

WAXING

- **Simple Green.** To remove wax from a car, mix one cup original Simple Green All-Purpose Cleaner and five cups hot water in a bucket. With the car parked in the shade, sponge the soapy mixture onto the car, let sit for five to ten minutes (without allowing it to dry), and rinse clean. Repeat if necessary to remove several coats of wax.

WHITEWALLS

- **Easy-Off Oven Cleaner.** To clean whitewalls, wet the tire, spray with Easy-Off Oven Cleaner (while wearing rubber gloves and protective eyewear), scrub with a brush for thirty seconds, and rinse clean with a hose. (Do not get Easy-Off on aluminum hubcaps.)

- **Mr. Clean Magic Eraser.** To clean the whitewalls on tires, gently rub the stains with a damp Mr. Clean Magic Eraser.

- **Purell Instant Hand Sanitizer.** Squirt Purell Instant Hand Sanitizer on whitewalls and scrub with a brush dipped in soapy water.

- **Scotch-Brite Heavy Duty Scrub Sponge.** To clean tire whitewalls, scrub with a damp Scotch-Brite Heavy Duty Scrub Sponge, and then rinse with a hose.

- **Scrubbing Bubbles.** To clean dirt and grime from whitewalls, spray the tire with Scrubbing Bubbles, let sit for fifteen seconds, and rinse clean with a garden hose.

- **Spray 'n Wash.** Spritz the whitewalls with Spray 'n Wash stain remover, let sit for five minutes, and rinse clean.

WINDSHIELDS AND WINDOWS

- **Arm & Hammer Baking Soda.** To clean the greasy film from a windshield and car windows, sprinkle Arm & Hammer Baking Soda on a damp rag and scrub. Rinse clean.

- **Gillette Foamy.** To prevent the inside of your car windshield from fogging up, apply Gillette Foamy shaving cream to the inside of the windshield with a sponge and then wipe clean with a soft, clean cloth. The residual soap film keeps the glass from fogging up.

- **Heinz White Vinegar.** To clean the greasy film from a windshield and car windows, mix equal parts Heinz White Vinegar and water and use the solution on a soft, clean, lint-free cloth to wipe the windshield clean.

Babies and Kids

ARTWORK

- **Alberto VO5 Hair Spray.** To prevent your kid's pastel artwork from smearing or rubbing off onto the carpet, furniture, or clothes, spray the artwork with Alberto VO5 Hair Spray, which works as a fixative to keep the pastels on the paper.

BABY BOTTLES

- **Arm & Hammer Baking Soda.** To deodorize the smell of sour milk or formula from a baby bottle, fill the bottle with warm water, add one teaspoon Arm & Hammer Baking Soda, shake well, and let sit overnight. In the morning, rinse well and let air dry.
- **ReaLemon.** To clean mineral deposits from baby bottles, add one tablespoon ReaLemon lemon juice when boiling the bottles.

Bandages

- **Johnson's Baby Oil.** Before pulling off that adhesive bandage, saturate the area with Johnson's Baby Oil, which dissolves the adhesive, making removal swift and painless.

Baseball Gloves

- **Vaseline Petroleum Jelly.** To clean baseball gloves and to keep the leather soft and supple, rub Vaseline Petroleum Jelly into the glove.

Bed Wetting

- **Canada Dry Club Soda** and **Arm & Hammer Baking Soda.** After blotting up as much urine as possible, pour Canada Dry Club Soda over the stained area and immediately blot. Let the spot dry completely, cover with Arm & Hammer Baking Soda, let sit for one hour, and then vacuum up. The baking soda will deodorize the smell of urine. (For more ways to clean urine from a mattress, see page 124.)

- **Glad Trash Bags.** To improvise a plastic sheet to waterproof a mattress for older children in beds (not babies or toddlers in cribs), cut a Glad Trash Bag down the sides and place it under the sheet. Or wrap the mattress in several Glad Trash Bags and secure the plastic in place with Scotch Packaging Tape.

- **Scotchgard Fabric Protector.** Protect the mattresses from urine by spraying it with Scotchgard Fabric Protector to make it waterproof.

Cards

- **Bounce.** To clean soiled plastic-coated playing cards, wipe the cards with a clean, used sheet of Bounce.

- **Huggies Baby Wipes.** To clean grease and grime from plastic-coated playing cards, wipe the cards with a Huggies Baby Wipe.

CHALK STAINS

- **Smirnoff Vodka.** To clean colored chalk from fabric, blot the stain with Smirnoff Vodka, and then launder as usual.

- **Soft Scrub Lemon Cleanser.** To clean chalk from floors, wall, tile, or countertops, put a few drops of Soft Scrub Lemon Cleanser on a damp sponge and rub. Rinse clean and dry.

CRAYON ON FABRIC

- **Bounty Paper Towels** and **Dawn Dishwashing Liquid.** To remove crayon from a garment made from washable fabric, place the stained garment on top of a sheet of Bounty Paper Towels, cover the stain with a second sheet of paper towel, and press the top sheet gently with a warm iron. The heat from the iron melts the crayon wax, and the quicker-picker-upper absorbs it. If any pigment from the crayon remains in the garment, rub a few drops of Dawn Dishwashing Liquid into the stain and launder as usual.

- **Spray 'n Wash, Ivory Soap,** and **Arm & Hammer Baking Soda.** To clean crayon from clothes, remove as much of the wax as possible, apply Spray 'n Wash stain remover to the stain, and launder with one-half cup Ivory Soap flakes (grate a bar of Ivory Soap through a cheese grater) and one cup Arm & Hammer Baking Soda.

- **WD-40** and **Dawn Dishwashing Liquid.** Spray WD-40 on crayon stains (both sides of the fabric), let sit for ten minutes, rub in a few drops of Dawn Dishwashing Liquid, and launder as usual in the hottest water possible for that fabric. (Do not use WD-40 on silk.)

CRAYON ON WALLS

- **Arm & Hammer Baking Soda.** To clean crayon marks from walls or wallpaper, sprinkle some Arm & Hammer Baking Soda on a damp sponge and rub gently.

- **Colgate Regular Flavor Toothpaste.** If you're seeing the writing on the wall, it's probably crayon. To clean it off, squeeze some Colgate Regular Flavor Toothpaste on an old toothbrush and scrub the marks.

- **Mr. Clean Magic Eraser.** To clean crayon marks from walls, dampen a Mr. Clean Magic Eraser with water and rub the crayon marks gently to avoid removing the shine from walls painted with satin, semi-gloss, and glossy paint.

- **Pledge.** Spritz crayon marks on wallpaper with Pledge furniture polish and wipe with a soft, clean cloth. The marks come right off.

- **S.O.S Steel Wool Soap Pads.** Gently rub crayon marks on wallpaper with a dry S.O.S Steel Wool Soap Pad.

- **Spray 'n Wash.** Spray a little Spray 'n Wash stain remover on the crayon mark, let sit for five minutes, and wipe clean.

- **WD-40, Bounty Paper Towels,** and **Dawn Dishwashing Liquid.** Spray crayon marks on walls with WD-40 and wipe off with Bounty Paper Towels. Then wash off the WD-40 with a soft cloth dampened with soapy water made with a few drops of Dawn Dishwashing Liquid.

DIAPER PAILS

- **Odorzout.** To control odors emanating from diaper pails, sprinkle some safe, nontoxic Odorzout into the diaper pail.

DIAPER PINS

- **Ivory Soap.** To keep diaper pins accessible—and lubricated to glide through diapers easily—stick them into a bar of Ivory Soap (kept well out of reach of children).

DIAPERS

- **Parsons' Ammonia.** To clean urine stains from diapers, mix one-quarter cup Parsons' Ammonia and one gallon water, soak the diaper in the solution for five minutes, and launder in the hottest water possible.

- **20 Mule Team Borax.** To clean cloth diapers, mix one-half cup 20 Mule Team Borax in a diaper pail filled with hot water. Soak the diapers in the solution for one hour, and then launder as usual.

DOLLS

- **Alberto VO5 Hair Spray.** To clean ink from the face of a plastic doll, spray the ink stains with Alberto VO5 Hair Spray and blot with a soft, clean cloth.

- **Crisco All-Vegetable Shortening.** To clean dirt and grime from the face of a plastic doll, apply a dab of Crisco All-Vegetable Shortening and wipe with a soft, clean cloth.

- **Land O Lakes Butter.** To clean ink from the face of a plastic doll, rub the ink stains with Land O Lakes Butter and let sit in the sun for several days. Then rinse clean and dry.

- **Revlon Gentle Cuticle Remover.** To clean a ballpoint ink or marker stain from a plastic doll's face, brush Revlon Gentle Cuticle Remover on the marks. Let sit for ten minutes, and then wipe off with a clean cloth dampened with soapy water. Buff dry with a soft, clean cloth.

- **Smirnoff Vodka.** To clean ballpoint ink and marker stains from a plastic doll's face, saturate a cotton ball with Smirnoff Vodka, apply it to the mark, and let soak for fifteen minutes. Rinse clean.

FORMULA STAINS

- **Adolph's Original Meat Tenderizer.** Cover the baby formula stain with a paste made from Adolph's Original Meat Tenderizer and cool water. Wait twenty minutes and sponge off with cool water. The enzymes in the meat tenderizer break up the proteins in the baby formula.

- **Arm & Hammer Baking Soda.** To clean a fresh formula stain, sprinkle some Arm & Hammer Baking Soda on a wet cloth and dab the stain. Then launder as usual.

- **Cascade.** To clean a stubborn formula stain from white clothes, wet the stain with water and rub in a few drops of Cascade Gel. Let sit overnight, and then launder as usual.

- **Clorox 2.** To clean a baby formula stain from colored clothes, rinse the stain with water, apply Clorox 2 (a non-chlorine bleach) directly to the stain, and rub in gently. Let sit for five minutes, and then launder as usual in your regular wash.

- **ReaLemon.** Saturate baby formula stains on white clothes with ReaLemon lemon juice and set the garment in the sun to bleach the stain away. Apply more lemon juice to the stain before laundering as usual.

Gum

- **Noxzema Original Deep Cleansing Cream.** To clean gum from hair, rub a dollop of Noxzema Original Deep Cleansing Cream into the gum, massage between your fingers, and then comb out. Shampoo several times to remove the cleansing cream from hair.

- **Shout.** To remove chewing gum from hair, shout it out by spraying the gum with Shout stain remover, making sure to avoid getting the stain remover in the child's eyes, nose, or mouth. Work in the stain remover to soften the gum, and then comb out. Shampoo hair and rinse.

- **Skippy Peanut Butter.** To clean gum from hair, rub a dollop of Skippy Peanut Butter into the gum, massage between your fingers, and then comb out. Shampoo.

- **Star Olive Oil.** To get gum out of hair, saturate the gum with Star Olive Oil, rub with your fingers to soften the gum, and comb out. Shampoo hair and rinse.

- **Vaseline Petroleum Jelly.** To clean gum from hair, rub a dollop of Vaseline Petroleum Jelly into the gum, massage between your fingers, and then comb out. Shampoo several times to get the petroleum jelly out of hair. (If necessary, use Dawn Dishwashing Liquid.)

Paint

- **Ivory Dishwashing Liquid.** To make cleaning up finger paint or tempera paint easier, add a few drops of Ivory Dishwashing Liquid to the paint and mix well. The dishwashing liquid does not harm the paint, but it makes cleaning up afterward effortless.

Playpens

- **Clorox Bleach, Dawn Dishwashing Liquid,** and **Playtex Living Gloves.** To clean the mesh screen on a playpen, remove the padding from the bottom of the playpen, remove all toys, and take the playpen outside. Mix three-quarters cup Clorox Bleach, one tablespoon Dawn Dishwashing Liquid, and one gallon hot water in a bucket. Put on a pair of Playtex Living Gloves and put an old sock over each glove. Dip the socks in the solution and rub the mesh. Rinse clean with a garden hose and let air dry.

Popsicles

- **Mr. Coffee Filters.** To avoid messy drips from Popsicles, punch the sticks through a Mr. Coffee Filter so it catches the drips as the Popsicle melts.

Rattles and Teething Rings

- **Cascade.** For a simple way to clean rattles and teething rings, secure them in place in the top rack of your dishwasher and wash with Cascade along with your regular dishes.

Shoes

- **Alberto VO5 Hair Spray.** After polishing white baby shoes, spray Alberto VO5 Hair Spray on the shoes to give them a protective coating.

- **Revlon Clear Nail Enamel.** Give spots on baby shoes that are easily · scuffed a protective coat of Revlon Clear Nail Enamel.

SILLY PUTTY

- **MasterCard, WD-40,** and **Dawn Dishwashing Liquid.** To clean Silly Putty from carpet or upholstered furniture, scrape off as much Silly Putty as possible with the edge of an old MasterCard, spray WD-40 on the affected area, let sit for fifteen minutes, and scrape again. Put a few drops of Dawn Dishwashing Liquid on a damp sponge and wipe the WD-40 stain. Rinse and blot well.

SPIT-UP

- **Canada Dry Club Soda.** To eliminate the odor of spit-ups on clothes, immediately rub the spot with a soft cloth dampened with Canada Dry Club Soda.

STUFFED ANIMALS

- **Arm & Hammer Baking Soda.** To clean and deodorize stuffed animals, dust the toy with a heavy coat of Arm & Hammer Baking Soda and let sit overnight. The next morning, brush off the baking soda, which will have absorbed liquids and stains.

- **Dawn Dishwashing Liquid** and **Downy Fabric Softener.** Mix one tablespoon Dawn Dishwashing Liquid, one half cup Downy Fabric Softener, and one quart warm water in a bucket. Apply the solution to the stuffed animal with a sponge, blot with a clean, soft towel, and let dry in the midday sun.

- **Kingsford's Corn Starch.** To clean stuffed animals, dust the toys with a heavy coat of Kingsford's Corn Starch and let sit overnight. The next morning, brush off the cornstarch, which will have absorbed all the liquids and stains.

THE DAWN OF DAWN

Scientists at Procter & Gamble invented Dawn Dishwashing Liquid with its proprietary grease-removing formula in 1972. Positioned as the dishwashing liquid that "takes grease out your way," Dawn quickly became the market leader. One of the many meanings of the word dawn is the onset of an amazing phenomenon, such as the dawn of a breakthrough dishwashing liquid.

In 2000, when the Colgate-Palmolive Company's expanded line of Palmolive Dishwashing Liquid, featuring a variety of fragrances in beautifully designed bottles, began to cut into Dawn's sales, Procter & Gamble developed its own line of fragranced Dawn in designer bottles.

Strange Facts

- In 1973, conservationists at the International Bird Rescue Research Center discovered that Dawn Dishwashing Liquid can be used to gently remove oil from aquatic birds, without harming the creatures' delicate feathers and skin. Since then, animal rescue groups have used thousands of donated bottles of Dawn in oil spill cleanups, raising the success rate for saving oiled wildlife from 3 percent to 90 percent.

- Randall W. Davis, head of the department of marine biology at Texas A&M University in Galveston, uses Dawn Dishwashing Liquid for bathing otters that have been coated with oil from a tanker spill.

- On April 30, 1998, a tanker truck flipped over on Interstate 74 in Cincinnati, Ohio, spilling four tons of inedible industrial animal fat. After workers tried unsuccessfully to clean up the spill with several industrial solvents, Cincinnati-based Procter & Gamble donated a tanker truck filled with Dawn Dishwashing Liquid to be sprayed over the oil slick and scrubbed with road sweeper brushes—in the largest demonstration of how well Dawn cuts through grease.

- On February 1, 2008, Dawn Direct Foam set a new Guinness World Record for "Largest Dish Ever Washed." In Phoenix, Arizona, legendary football star Emmitt Smith helped clean the giant plate, which measured ten feet in diameter.

- **L'eggs Sheer Energy Panty Hose.** To machine wash a machine-washable stuffed animal or toy with a head full of artificial hair, cut off one leg from a clean, old pair of L'eggs Sheer Energy Panty Hose and cover the hair with the nylon net to prevent the hair from getting knotted and tangled in the washing machine and dryer. Machine wash on the delicate cycle.

Toys

- **Con-Tact Paper.** To cover up stains and scuffs that you cannot clean off of old toys, redecorate the toys with different Con-Tact Paper patterns.

Training Pants

- **20 Mule Team Borax.** To whiten and deodorize plastic training pants, mix two tablespoons 20 Mule Team Borax and one gallon hot water in a bucket and soak the training pants in the solution for one hour. Launder as usual.

Traveling

- **Ziploc Storage Bags.** Before traveling with children, select the number of outfits the child will bring and place each outfit (along with socks and underwear) in its own Ziploc Storage Bag. This way, the child simply chooses a bag each morning, avoiding the hassle of picking out each individual item.

Watercolor Paint on Carpet or Fabric

- **Soft Scrub Lemon Cleanser.** To clean watercolor paint from furniture or clothing, put a few drops of Soft Scrub Lemon Cleanser on a damp sponge and gently rub around the stain, working into the center. Rinse clean and launder clothing as usual.

Barbecue Grills

CHARCOAL

- **Jonny Cat Litter.** To keep the bottom of a charcoal barbecue clean pour an even layer of Jonny Cat Litter to cover the bottom of the pan. The cat box filler insulates the metal bottom from the heat and absorbs grease and fat.

CLEANING

- **Bon Ami.** To clean burned-on grease and food from a barbecue grill rack, sprinkle Bon Ami on the cool rack and scrub with a wire brush dipped in water. Rinse clean.
- **Easy-Off Oven Cleaner** and **Glad Trash Bags.** Place the barbecue grill rack in a Glad Trash Bag, spray the rack with Easy-Off Oven Cleaner, seal the bag closed, and let it sit outside overnight. The next morning, remove the grill from the bag, hose it down well, and carefully dispose of the bag.

- **Maxwell House Coffee.** To clean a barbecue grill rack quickly, pour a pot of leftover Maxwell House Coffee on the cool rack and wipe dry.

- **Pam Cooking Spray.** To prevent food from sticking to the barbecue grill rack and make cleanup easier, spray the rack with Pam Cooking Spray before igniting the grill.

- **Parsons' Ammonia, Bounty Paper Towels,** and **Glad Trash Bags.** To clean a barbecue grill rack, unroll Bounty Paper Towels around the grill rack to wrap it in a paper tower, place the rack inside a Glad Trash

Keep It Clean

HOT TIPS FOR BARBECUES

How to Clean a Charcoal Grill

- Let cooking residue burn off the inside of your grill every time you use it. This minimizes the amount of scrubbing you'll have to do.

- Clean the cooking grate after each time you grill. After the coals burn out and while the grill is still warm (not hot), use a brass wire grill brush to brush off any baked-on food or grease from the grill. If the grill needs a more thorough cleaning, let cool and scrub gently with a wet, soapy, fine steel wool pad, rinse clean, and dry.

- Remove the cold ashes from the bottom of the kettle after each time you grill. Otherwise, the cold ashes will absorb moisture, which could rust the kettle. The pile of cold ashes also obstructs proper airflow.

- To get your grill shiny and sparkling, wash it inside and out with warm soapy water and a sponge.

How to Clean a Gas Grill

- Clean the cooking grate each time you grill. Before or after you use the grill, turn the flame on high and burn off any baked-on food or grease

Bag, saturate the paper towels with Parsons' Ammonia, and seal the bag shut. Let the bag sit overnight outside or in a well-ventilated garage. In the morning, open the bag carefully to avoid breathing the ammonia fumes, remove the rack, leaving the paper towels in the bag, and discard the bag. Wash the rack with soapy water, rinse clean, and dry.

- **Purell Instant Hand Sanitizer.** Clean the outside of a barbecue grill by rubbing Purell Instant Hand Sanitizer on the cool grill with a paper towel or old rag. Buff with a dry, clean rag.

. . . .

from the grill. When the smoke ceases, brush the grates with a brass wire grill brush. If the grates are cast-iron, leave any baked-on food or grease on the grates or griddle between barbecues to keep a protective coating on the cast iron. Burn-off just before you grill and brush off the charred flakes with a steel wire brush (not a brass wire brush).

- To clean rust from a cast-iron cooking grates or griddle, brush off the rust with a steel wire grill brush. Wash the grill with a mild dishwashing liquid, rinse with hot water, and dry thoroughly with a soft cloth or paper towel. Spread a thin coat of a solid vegetable shortening over the entire surface of the grill or griddle with a sheet of paper towel. Preheat the gas grill for 15 minutes, place the cast-iron grates or griddle in the grill, and heat on medium heat with the lid closed for one hour. Turn off all of the burners and let the grates or griddle cool.

- Change the drip pan under the bottom tray of the grill on a regular basis. This discourages animals from getting into your grill.

- To clean smoke stains from the grill lid, warming racks, and control panel, lightly rub the lid with a soapy, fine steel wool pad. Rinse clean. To clean a stainless steel lid, use warm, soapy water and a sponge.

- Remove the cool bottom tray from under the grill, place the tray over a trash can, and carefully scrape the inside with a putty knife or an old credit card, discarding the dregs. To deep clean the tray, use warm, soapy water and a soapy, fine steel wool pad.

- Never clean a gas grill with oven cleaner. It will remove the paint.

- **Reynolds Wrap.** To clean a barbecue grill rack coated with burned-on food and grease, wrap Reynolds Wrap aluminum foil around the rack with the shiny side facing inward, put the wrapped rack in place in the barbecue, and turn the heat on high for ten minutes or more. Let cool and remove the aluminum foil. The burned-on food and grease will fall off the rack.

- **Reynolds Wrap.** To clean a barbecue grill rack immediately after cooking the food and turning off the heat, crumple up a sheet of Reynolds Wrap aluminum foil into a ball and carefully scrub the warm rack.

- **Simple Green.** To clean a barbecue grill, mix one-half cup Simple Green All-Purpose Cleaner and five cups water in a bucket. Apply the solution to the grill; scrub well with a soft to medium bristle, nonabrasive brush; and rinse well.

- **Wesson Oil.** To polish the exterior of a barbecue grill, saturate a cloth with Wesson Oil and rub the oil into the outer surface of the warm barbecue. Buff with a dry cloth.

Glass Window

- **Easy-Off Oven Cleaner.** To clean the glass window on a barbecue grill, spray the inside of the glass window with Easy-Off Oven Cleaner, let sit for five minutes, scrub clean with soapy water, and rinse well.

- **Purell Instant Hand Sanitizer.** Clean the outside of a glass window on a barbecue grill by rubbing Purell Instant Hand Sanitizer on the glass with a paper towel or old rag. Buff with a dry, clean rag.

Pots and Pans

- **Ivory Soap.** Before placing a pot or pan on the barbecue grill, rub the bottom of the pot or pan with a bar of Ivory Soap. When you're finished cooking, the film of soap will make cleaning the bottom of the pot or pan much easier.

Bathrooms

BATHTUB DECALS

- **Conair 1875 Watt Hair Dryer** and **MasterCard.** To remove decals from the floor of a bathtub, make sure the bathtub water is turned off and use a Conair 1875 Watt Hair Dryer set on high to heat the decals. The heat melts the adhesive holding the decals to the tub, allowing you to pry the decals off using an old MasterCard.

- **Cutex Nail Polish Remover.** To remove the adhesive residue left by bathtub decals, saturate a cotton ball with Cutex Nail Polish Remover, rub the spot, and wipe clean.

- **Easy-Off Oven Cleaner.** To take off stubborn decals from the floor of a bathtub, spray the decals with Easy-Off Oven Cleaner (making sure the room is well ventilated), let sit for ten minutes, rinse thoroughly, and peel off the stickers.

- **Johnson's Baby Oil.** To remove decals from the floor of a bathtub, saturate the decal with Johnson's Baby Oil, let sit for an hour, and then peel off. Wash clean with soapy water to prevent someone from slipping on the oil in the bathtub.

- **Spray 'n Wash.** To make decals easier to remove, spray the decals with Spray 'n Wash stain remover, let sit for five minutes, fill the tub with water, and let soak for one hour. Using a single-edge razor blade, carefully scrape the decals off the tub floor. Rinse clean.

- **Vaseline Petroleum Jelly.** To remove the adhesive residue left by bathtub decals, cover the spot with Vaseline Petroleum Jelly, let sit for an hour, and wipe clean. Be sure to wash away the petroleum jelly with soapy water to prevent someone from slipping in the bathtub.

- **WD-40.** Saturate the decal with WD-40, let sit for an hour or longer, and peel off. Wash away the WD-40 with soapy water to prevent someone from slipping in the bathtub.

BATHTUB RING

- **Arm & Hammer Baking Soda.** To avoid getting a ring around your bathtub, add one-half cup Arm & Hammer Baking Soda to the bathwater, softening the water and giving you a luxurious bath at the same time.

- **Mr. Bubble Original Bubble Bath.** Taking a bubble bath using Mr. Bubble Original Bubble Bath simultaneously cleans the ring around your bathtub.

BATHTUB STAINS

- **Bon Ami.** To clean bathtub stains, sprinkle Bon Ami on a very wet sponge, scrub the stains, and rinse clean.

- **Easy-Off Oven Cleaner.** To clean a badly stained bathtub, spray the stain with Easy-Off Oven Cleaner (making sure the room is well ventilated), let sit for twenty minutes, rinse, wash clean with soapy water, and rinse again.

- **Hydrogen Peroxide** and **McCormick Cream of Tartar.** To clean stubborn stains from an enamel bathtub, make a paste from equal parts Hydrogen Peroxide and McCormick Cream of Tartar and apply the paste with a scrub brush, scouring well.

- **Mr. Clean Magic Eraser.** To clean soap scum from a bathtub, gently rub the stains with a damp Mr. Clean Magic Eraser, wash the tub thoroughly with soapy water, rinse clean, and dry.

- **ReaLemon** and **20 Mule Team Borax.** To clean stains from an enamel bathtub, make a paste from ReaLemon lemon juice and 20 Mule Team Borax and rub the stains with the paste.

CHROME FAUCETS

- **Arm & Hammer Baking Soda.** To clean chrome faucets, sprinkle Arm & Hammer Baking Soda on a damp sponge, scrub, rinse clean, and dry thoroughly.

- **Bounce.** After cleaning, polish chrome with a clean, used sheet of Bounce.

- **Gold Medal Flour.** To clean chrome faucets, sprinkle Gold Medal Flour on a damp sponge, scrub, rinse clean, and dry.

- **Heinz White Vinegar.** Dampen a sponge with Heinz White Vinegar to wipe soap scum and water spots from chrome. Dry with a soft, clean cloth.

- **Murphy Oil Soap.** To clean chrome, mix one teaspoon Murphy Oil Soap and two cups water in a sixteen-ounce trigger-spray bottle. Spray the chrome with the solution and wipe with a soft, clean cloth. Rinse and dry.

- **Reynolds Wrap.** To clean soap scum off chrome faucets, crumple a sheet of Reynolds Wrap aluminum foil into a ball and use it as a scrubber.

- **WD-40.** Spray WD-40 on a soft, clean cloth and rub the chrome faucets until they shine like new.

- **Windex.** Spray the chrome fixtures with Windex and rub with a soft, clean cloth.

CORNERS AND CREVICES

- **Oral-B Toothbrush.** To clean corners and crevices in the bathroom, use a clean, old Oral-B Toothbrush dipped in your favorite cleanser.

DEODORIZER

- **Bounce.** To keep the air fresh in your bathroom, insert a sheet of Bounce into the hollow cardboard tube inside a fresh roll of toilet paper before putting it on the toilet paper holder. (For more ways to deodorize a room, see page 305.)

- **ReaLemon.** To freshen the air in your bathroom, stand an open bottle of ReaLemon lemon juice in a corner.

DISINFECTANT

- **20 Mule Team Borax** and **Heinz White Vinegar.** To make your own disinfectant, mix one-quarter cup 20 Mule Team Borax, one ounce Heinz White Vinegar, and one gallon hot water. Mop or sponge the solution onto the surface, rinse clean, and let dry.

DRAINS

- **Arm & Hammer Baking Soda** and **Heinz White Vinegar.** To keep drains clean and open, pour one-half cup Arm & Hammer Baking Soda down the drain, and then pour one cup Heinz White Vinegar down the drain. The resulting foam clears the drain. Let sit thirty minutes, and then rinse clean with water. Repeat once a month.

- **Arm & Hammer Baking Soda** and **Morton Salt.** To open a clogged drain, pour one cup Arm & Hammer Baking Soda down the drain followed by one cup Morton Salt. Then pour one kettle of boiling water down the drain.

- **Arm & Hammer Super Washing Soda.** For a strong drain cleaner, dissolve two tablespoons Arm & Hammer Super Washing Soda in one quart hot water and pour the solution down the drain slowly. Let sit fifteen minutes and flush clean with hot water.

- **Heinz White Vinegar.** To clean mineral deposits from around drains, close the drain, pour enough Heinz White Vinegar in the shower, tub, or sink to cover the drain, and let sit overnight. In the morning, scrub with an abrasive sponge and rinse clean.

FAUCETS AND FIXTURES

- **Heinz White Vinegar.** Mix equal parts Heinz White Vinegar and water in a sixteen-ounce trigger-spray bottle, spray the faucets or fixture, and polish with a soft, clean cloth.

- **McCormick Alum** and **ReaLemon.** To clean mineral stains from faucets and fixtures, mix one teaspoon McCormick Alum and one-quarter cup ReaLemon lemon juice in a bowl. Saturate a soft, clean cloth with the solution, lay the wet cloth over the stain, let sit for one hour, and then scrub and rinse clean.

FIBERGLASS SHOWERS AND TUBS

- **Arm & Hammer Baking Soda.** Mix one-half cup Arm & Hammer Baking Soda and enough water to make a thick paste. Using a sponge, rub the paste on the fiberglass to clean it and rinse well.

- **Bon Ami.** To clean fiberglass showers, sprinkle Bon Ami on a wet sponge, scrub the fiberglass, and rinse clean.

- **Heinz White Vinegar.** Warm one cup Heinz White Vinegar in the microwave, pour it into a clean trigger-spray bottle, and spray the warm acetic acid (that's what vinegar is) on the fiberglass shower, bathtub, or hot tub. Let sit for fifteen minutes, and then dampen an abrasive sponge with more vinegar and scrub the tub. Rinse thoroughly with water.

- **20 Mule Team Borax** and **Heinz White Vinegar.** Mix one-half cup 20 Mule Team Borax and enough Heinz White Vinegar to make a thick paste. Using a sponge, rub the paste on the fiberglass to clean it and rinse thoroughly.

GROUT

- **Arm & Hammer Baking Soda** and **Clorox Bleach.** Make sure the room is well ventilated and, wearing rubber gloves, make a paste from Arm & Hammer Baking Soda and Clorox Bleach. Using a sponge, apply the paste to the grout. Let dry and rinse clean.

- **Arm & Hammer Baking Soda** and **20 Mule Team Borax.** Mix two cups Arm & Hammer Baking Soda, one cup 20 Mule Team Borax, and one cup hot water to make a thick paste. Apply the paste to the tile and grout and scrub with a brush. Rinse well.

- **Bon Ami.** To clean grout, sprinkle Bon Ami on the grout and scrub with a wet sponge.

- **Clorox Bleach.** To clean grout, mix five teaspoons Clorox Bleach and two cups warm water in a sixteen-ounce trigger-spray bottle. Wearing rubber gloves, goggles, and protective clothing (and making sure the room is well ventilated), spray the solution on the grout. Let sit three hours, rinse clean with water, and let dry.

- **Colgate Regular Flavor Toothpaste.** Squeeze a dollop of Colgate Regular Flavor Toothpaste on a clean, old toothbrush and scrub the grout. Rinse clean.

- **Mr. Clean Magic Eraser.** To clean grout, saturate a Mr. Clean Magic Eraser with water, squeeze out the excess water, and gently rub the stains in the grout until they come clean.

HAIRSPRAY BUILDUP

- **Bounce.** To remove hairspray from walls, mirrors, floors, or countertops, dampen a sheet of Bounce with water, wipe the area affected by the hairspray, and then wipe clean with a damp, clean cloth.

- **Downy Fabric Softener.** To remove hairspray from walls, mirrors, floors, or countertops, mix one part Downy Fabric Softener to two parts water in a clean trigger-spray bottle. Spray and wipe clean.
- **Mr. Clean Magic Eraser.** To clean hairspray buildup from bathroom walls, cabinet doors, and mirrors, gently rub the fixative spray with a damp Mr. Clean Magic Eraser.

HARD WATER STAINS

- **Arm & Hammer Baking Soda** and **20 Mule Team Borax.** Mix one cup Arm & Hammer Baking Soda and two ounces 20 Mule Team Borax and scrub the hard water stains with the powder on a damp sponge.
- **Heinz White Vinegar.** Saturate a cloth with Heinz White Vinegar, cover the hard water stains with the cloth, let sit overnight, and rinse clean in the morning.

MIRRORS

- **Gillette Foamy.** To clean and defog a mirror at the same time, squirt a dab of Gillette Foamy shaving cream on the mirror, smear it over the entire surface of the mirror, and wipe clean. The shaving cream leaves behind a thin film of soap and other emollients that prevent the mirror from steaming up.
- **Heinz White Vinegar.** To clean mirrors, mix equal parts Heinz White Vinegar and water in a trigger-spray bottle. Spray the solution on a clean, soft cloth, and wipe down the mirror.
- **Kingsford's Corn Starch.** Dissolve one cup Kingsford's Corn Starch in one gallon warm water. Dampen a sponge with the solution, wipe the mirror, and buff dry with a soft, clean, lint-free cloth.
- **Murphy Oil Soap** and **Heinz White Vinegar.** To clean a mirror, mix one-half teaspoon Murphy Oil Soap, three tablespoons Heinz White Vinegar, and two cups water in a sixteen-ounce trigger-spray bottle. Spray the solution on a clean, soft cloth and wipe the mirror.

Mold and Mildew

- **Arm & Hammer Baking Soda** and **20 Mule Team Borax.** To scrub mold or mildew from walls, tile, grout, or countertops, mix two-thirds cup Arm & Hammer Baking Soda and one-third cup 20 Mule Team Borax. Scour with a damp sponge and rinse well.

- **Clorox Bleach.** To clean stubborn mold from around the rim of a bathtub, mix five teaspoons Clorox Bleach and two cups warm water in a sixteen-ounce trigger-spray bottle. Wearing rubber gloves, goggles, and protective clothing (and making sure the room is well ventilated), spray the solution on the mold or mildew. Let sit until the color vanishes, rinse clean with water, and let dry.

- **Heinz White Vinegar**. To kill mold, saturate the affected area with Heinz White Vinegar, scrub with a sponge, and rinse clean.

- **Hydrogen Peroxide.** To kill mildew, mix two tablespoons Hydrogen Peroxide in one gallon water and wipe the surface with the solution. (Be sure to test the Hydrogen Peroxide on an inconspicuous spot first to make sure it doesn't bleach the surface.)

- **Jonny Cat Litter.** To prevent mold from growing, fill a bowl with Jonny Cat Litter and place it in damp areas to absorb moisture. Without moisture, mold cannot grow.

- **20 Mule Team Borax** and **Heinz White Vinegar.** To deter mold and mildew, mix one teaspoon 20 Mule Team Borax, three tablespoons Heinz White Vinegar, and two cups hot water in a sixteen-ounce trigger-spray bottle. Shake well, spray a fine mist of the solution on susceptible walls or counters in your bathroom, and let dry.

Plastic Showers

- **Turtle Wax.** To make cleaning a plastic shower trouble-free, apply a coat of Turtle Wax to the plastic (but not the floor) of the shower. The car wax prevents water from adhering to the walls.

PLUNGERS

- **Vaseline Petroleum Jelly.** To avoid making a mess when using a plunger to unclog a toilet or sink, apply Vaseline Petroleum Jelly around the rubber rim of the plunger to give the plunger better suction.

PORCELAIN BATHTUBS AND SINKS

- **Arm & Hammer Baking Soda.** To clean a porcelain tub or sink, sprinkle Arm & Hammer Baking Soda in the bathtub or sink, scrub with a damp sponge, and rinse well.

- **Bon Ami.** To clean a porcelain tub or sink, sprinkle Bon Ami in the tub or sink, rub with a wet sponge, and rinse clean.

- **Clorox Bleach.** To whiten a porcelain tub or sink, fill the tub or sink with warm water, add three-quarters cup Clorox Bleach, let sit for fifteen minutes, and rinse clean.

- **Colgate Regular Flavor Toothpaste.** To clean stubborn stains from a porcelain bathtub or sink, squeeze a dab of Colgate Regular Flavor Toothpaste on a soft, clean cloth and rub the stains. Rinse clean and dry.

- **Efferdent.** To clean stains from a porcelain sink, fill the sink with warm water, drop in two Efferdent denture cleansing tablets, let sit for thirty minutes, and rinse clean.

- **Liquid Paper.** To cover up an unsightly chip in the porcelain veneer of a bathtub or sink, paint over the spot with a touch of Liquid Paper.

- **McCormick Alum** and **ReaLemon.** To clean a stain from a porcelain bathtub or sink without removing the porcelain finish, make a paste from

McCormick Alum and ReaLemon lemon juice, apply the paste to the stain, let dry, pour on more lemon juice, and rub. Rinse clean with water.

- **McCormick Alum** and **McCormick Cream of Tartar.** To clean a stain from porcelain, mix equal parts McCormick Alum and McCormick Cream of Tartar, wet the stain, sprinkle the powder on the stain, let sit for several hours, scrub with a sponge, and rinse clean.

- **Morton Salt.** To clean a discolored bathtub or sink, sprinkle Morton Salt in the bathtub or sink, scrub with a damp sponge, and rinse.

- **20 Mule Team Borax.** To clean a porcelain bathtub or sink, make a paste from 20 Mule Team Borax and water, apply to the tub with a damp sponge, and rub well. Rinse clean.

RUST

- **Kool-Aid.** To clean rust from sinks or bathroom fixtures, make a paste from lemon Kool-Aid and water, apply the paste to the rust stain, let sit for one hour, brush, and rinse. The citric acid in the Kool-Aid solubilizes the iron oxide.

- **ReaLemon** and **Morton Salt.** To clean rust from fixtures, rub the spot with ReaLemon lemon juice and Morton Salt. Rinse clean and polish. The citric acid in the lemon juice dissolves the rust, and the abrasive salt scrubs it away.

- **Tang.** To clean rust from sink or bathroom fixtures, make a paste from Tang powdered drink mix and water, apply the paste to the rust stain, let sit for one hour, brush, and rinse. The citric acid in the Tang dissolves the rust.

SHOWER CURTAINS

- **Arm & Hammer Baking Soda.** To clean a plastic or vinyl shower curtain, fill the washing machine with water, add one-half cup Arm & Hammer Baking Soda and one-half cup of your regular detergent, place the shower curtain in the machine along with several towels, and wash on a gentle setting. When the rinse cycle finishes, immediately hang up the shower curtain in the shower to avoid wrinkles.

- **Clorox Bleach.** To clean mold and mildew off a plastic or vinyl shower curtain, place the shower curtain in your washing machine along with several towels, add one-and-a-half cups Clorox Bleach and your regular detergent, and wash on a gentle setting with warm water. When the rinse cycle finishes, immediately hang up the shower curtain back in the shower to avoid wrinkles.

- **Heinz White Vinegar.** To clean soap scum (or mold and mildew) off a plastic or vinyl shower curtain, place the shower curtain in your washing machine along with several towels, add one-and-a-half cups Heinz White Vinegar and your regular detergent, and wash on a gentle setting with warm water. When the rinse cycle finishes, immediately hang up the shower curtain back in the shower to avoid wrinkles.

- **Morton Salt** and **20 Mule Team Borax.** To hinder the growth of mildew on a shower curtain, fill the bathtub with warm water and add one-half cup Morton Salt and one-half cup 20 Mule Team Borax. Lay the shower curtain in the tub and let it soak for one hour. Without rinsing the shower curtain, hang it up and let dry.

- **Mr. Clean Magic Eraser.** To clean mold and mildew from a vinyl shower curtain, gently rub the stains with a damp Mr. Clean Magic Eraser.

- **Parsons' Ammonia.** To clean soap scum from a plastic shower curtain, take down the curtain, lay it in the bathtub, mix two cups Parsons' Ammonia and one gallon warm water in a bucket, and wash the curtain with the solution. Rinse clean and hang to dry.

- **20 Mule Team Borax.** To clean a shower curtain, place the shower curtain in your washing machine with several towels, add one-half cup 20 Mule Team Borax, and launder with warm water.

- **20 Mule Team Borax** and **ReaLemon.** To kill stubborn mold and mildew from a shower curtain, mix equal parts 20 Mule Team Borax and

ReaLemon lemon juice in bowl, lay the shower curtain in the bathtub, and use a sponge to scrub the mixture on the shower curtain. Rinse clean.

- **Vaseline Petroleum Jelly.** To help the shower curtain glide smoothly across the curtain rod and prevent rust, rub a thin coat of Vaseline Petroleum Jelly on the curtain rod.

SHOWER DOOR TRACKS

- **Heinz White Vinegar** and **Silly Putty.** To clean shower door tracks, plug the drain holes in the track with small balls of Silly Putty and fill the track with Heinz White Vinegar. Let sit for thirty minutes, remove the Silly Putty, and rinse the track with water.

- **Vaseline Petroleum Jelly.** To make shower doors glide smoothly and prevent rust, rub a thin coat of Vaseline Petroleum Jelly on the inside of the tracks.

SHOWER DOORS

- **Con-Tact Paper.** To freshen up dull looking shower doors, cut decals from Con-Tact Paper and adhere to the doors.

- **Heinz White Vinegar.** To clean shower doors, mix equal parts Heinz White Vinegar and water in a trigger-spray bottle, spray the solution on the glass doors, and wipe clean.

- **Johnson's Baby Oil.** To shine glass shower doors, dampen a soft, clean cloth with a few drops of Johnson's Baby Oil and polish the glass doors. The mineral oil gives the glass a glistening shine and simultaneously prevents soap scum and mineral buildup.

- **Old English Lemon Oil.** To clean soap scum from glass shower doors, apply Old English Lemon Oil with a soft, clean cloth.

- **Spray 'n Wash.** To clean soap scum off glass shower doors, spritz the shower doors with Spray 'n Wash stain remover, let sit for five minutes, and rinse clean with a damp, soft cloth.

- **Turtle Wax.** To prevent soap scum and mineral deposits from sticking to glass shower doors, apply a coat of Turtle Wax to the glass and buff.

SHOWERHEADS

- **Heinz White Vinegar** and **Forster Toothpicks.** To clean mineral deposits from a showerhead, remove the showerhead, place it in a pot containing equal parts Heinz White Vinegar and water, and bring to a boil for five minutes. If you cannot remove the showerhead from the shower, fill a Ziploc Storage Bag with Heinz White Vinegar, hold the open bag under the showerhead and raise it so the showerhead fits inside the bag bathed in vinegar, and secure the bag in place with a rubber band. Let sit overnight. The acetic acid in the vinegar dissolves the mineral deposits in the showerhead. Use a Forster Toothpick to poke out any remaining mineral deposits.

SHOWERS

- **Turtle Wax.** To make cleaning the shower walls easier, apply a coat of Turtle Wax to the tiles (but not the floor) of the shower and buff. The car wax prevents water, soap scum, and mineral deposits from adhering to the tile walls.

SOAP SCUM

- **Mr. Clean Magic Eraser.** To clean soap scum from a bathtub or shower, gently rub the stains with a damp Mr. Clean Magic Eraser, wash the item thoroughly with soapy water, rinse clean, and dry.

- **Old English Lemon Oil.** To clean soap scum from glass shower doors, apply Old English Lemon Oil with a soft, clean cloth.

- **S.O.S Steel Wool Soap Pads** and **Heinz White Vinegar.** Gently scrub the soap scum with a dry S.O.S Steel Wool Soap Pad (no water). Warm one cup Heinz White Vinegar in the microwave, pour it into a clean trigger-spray bottle, and spray the warm acetic acid (that's what vinegar is) on the shower, bathtub, or hot tub. Let sit for fifteen minutes, and then dampen an abrasive sponge with more vinegar and scrub the tub. Rinse thoroughly with water.

- **Spray 'n Wash.** To clean soap scum off glass shower doors, spritz the shower doors with Spray 'n Wash, let sit for five minutes, and rinse clean with a damp, soft cloth.

TILE

- **Arm & Hammer Baking Soda** and **20 Mule Team Borax.** Mix two cups Arm & Hammer Baking Soda, one cup 20 Mule Team Borax, and one cup hot water to make a thick paste. Apply the paste to the tile and grout and scrub with a brush. Rinse well.

- **Bon Ami.** To clean tile and grout, sprinkle Bon Ami on the grout and scrub with a wet sponge.

- **Parsons' Ammonia, Heinz White Vinegar,** and **Arm & Hammer Super Washing Soda.** Mix one cup Parsons' Ammonia, one cup Heinz White Vinegar, and one-half cup Arm & Hammer Super Washing Soda in a bucket of warm water, scrub the tile with the solution, and rinse well.

- **ReaLemon, Dawn Dishwashing Liquid, Arm & Hammer Baking Soda,** and **20 Mule Team Borax.** For a great homemade cleanser for tiles, countertops, and walls, mix two tablespoons ReaLemon lemon juice, one-half teaspoon Dawn Dishwashing Liquid, one tablespoon Arm & Hammer Baking Soda, and one teaspoon 20 Mule Team Borax, and two cups water in a sixteen-ounce trigger-spray bottle. Shake well.

TOILET BRUSHES

- **Clorox Bleach.** To make a holder for a toilet brush, cut out one side of a clean, empty Clorox Bleach jug.

Keep It Clean

HOW TO CLEAN TILE AND GROUT

■ Before cleaning tile, sweep or vacuum the floors.

■ To keep ceramic tile bright and shiny, clean the tile routinely with an all-purpose, non oil-based household cleanser that will not damage the grout. Cleansers containing acids can damage the grout and etch into the glazed surface of the tile. Cleansers containing ammonia can discolor the grout. For unglazed tile, use a concentrated tile cleaner with a neutral pH.

■ Use a cotton mop, cloth, sponge, or nonmetallic brush to scrub the entire area with the cleanser, and then rinse with clean water.

■ Make sure the grout is sealed. The grout should have been sealed with grout sealer after installation to prevent moisture from penetrating the grout, causing stains or discoloration. Unfortunately, however, grout sealer wears off, so you may need to reseal the grout once a year. You can buy grout sealer at a hardware store, and you only need to seal the grout, not the tiles.

■ To clean soap scum and other buildup from grout, clean the grout routinely with a concentrated household cleanser. It's much easier to scrub the grout regularly than to confront a heavy-duty buildup.

■ If scrubbing does not return the grout to its original color, use grout stain—an epoxy-based product specifically formulated to penetrate into the grout and seal the surface with a permanent color. First, clean the grout with a professional strength tile and grout cleaner, and then apply the grout stain according to the directions. Grout stain doubles as grout sealer, allowing you to do two jobs at once.

■ If you don't have a silicone grout sealer, you can seal the grout with three coats of lemon oil.

TOILETS

- **Arm & Hammer Baking Soda.** Pour one-half cup Arm & Hammer Baking Soda in the toilet bowl, brush, and flush.

- **Coca-Cola.** Pour a can of Coca-Cola in the toilet, let sit for one hour, and then brush and flush.

- **Country Time Lemonade.** To clean a toilet bowl, pour in two tablespoons Country Time Lemonade powdered drink mix. Let it stand for one hour. Brush and flush. The citric acid removes stains from porcelain and vitreous china.

- **Efferdent.** Drop two Efferdent denture cleansing tablets into the toilet, close the lid, and let it sit overnight. In the morning, brush and flush.

- **Gatorade.** Pour two cups Gatorade into the toilet bowl, let sit for one hour, and then brush and flush clean. The citric acid in Gatorade removes stains from vitreous china.

- **Heinz White Vinegar.** To clean hard-water stains from a toilet bowl, shut off the water to the toilet tank and flush until you empty all the water from the toilet bowl. Place a hand towel or washcloth in the bowl to cover the hard-water stains, and then saturate the cloth with Heinz White Vinegar. Let sit overnight and wipe any remaining residue clean with an abrasive sponge. Repeat if necessary. The acetic acid in the vinegar dissolves hard-water stains.

- **Kool-Aid.** To clean stains and rust from a toilet bowl, empty a packet of Lemon Kool-Aid into the toilet, close the lid, and let it sit overnight. In the morning, brush and flush. The citric acid in the Kool-Aid cleans the toilet bowl, oxidizing the rust. Soldiers in the military frequently use "bug juice" (generic Kool-Aid) to clean toilets and tank parts.

- **McCormick Cream of Tartar.** Sprinkle two to three tablespoons McCormick Cream of Tartar on the stains in the toilet, brush, and flush.

- **Mr. Clean Magic Eraser.** To remove a mineral ring from a toilet bowl, gently rub the stains with a damp Mr. Clean Magic Eraser.

- **ReaLemon** and **20 Mule Team Borax.** To clean stains from a toilet, make a paste from ReaLemon lemon juice and 20 Mule Team Borax, apply the paste to the stains, and let sit for fifteen minutes. Brush and flush.

- **Tang.** To clean stains and rust from a toilet bowl, dissolve three table-spoons Tang powdered drink mix in the toilet, close the lid, and let it sit overnight. In the morning, brush and flush. The citric acid in the Tang cleans the toilet bowl, oxidizing the rust.

- **Turtle Wax.** To prevent condensation from forming on the outside of the toilet tank, shut off the water to the toilet, flush until you empty all the water from the toilet tank, and apply a coat of Turtle Wax to the inside of the tank.

- **20 Mule Team Borax.** Pour one cup 20 Mule Team Borax into the toilet bowl, let sit overnight, and in the morning, simply flush the toilet.

- **20 Mule Team Borax** and **Heinz White Vinegar.** To clean stains from a toilet bowl, shut off the water to the toilet tank and flush until you empty all the water from the toilet bowl. Pour one cup Heinz White Vinegar over the stains, and then sprinkle one cup 20 Mule Team Borax over the vinegar. Let it sit for two hours, and then brush and flush.

WINDOWS

- **Con-Tact Paper.** To make your shiny clean bathroom windows private, cover your bathroom window with frosted Con-Tact Paper for bright light and privacy.

Camping, Picnics, and the Beach

AIR MATTRESSES

- **Krazy Glue.** To fix a leak in an air mattress without having to apply unsightly patches, apply Krazy Glue to seal the hole or leaky valve stems.

BATHING

- **Huggies Baby Wipes** and **Ziploc Storage Bags.** Can't get a hot shower in the wilderness? Pack Huggies Baby Wipes in a Ziploc Storage Bag in your backpack to give yourself a quick sponge bath when you're feeling filthy. You can also use the soiled wipes as emergency toilet paper.

BEER CAN CADDIES

- **Pam Cooking Spray.** To remove beer can caddies with ease, spray Pam Cooking Spray inside the caddy, wipe out any excess spray, then insert the can. After finishing the beer, the can slips out of the caddy easily and effortlessly.

CHANGING ROOM

- **Hula Hoop.** To make a portable changing room, attach an opaque shower curtain to a Hula Hoop using standard shower curtain rings, and then hang the Hula Hoop from a tree branch or have someone hold it in place while you change.

COOLERS

- **Clorox Bleach.** To clean a cooler, mix three-quarters cup Clorox Bleach and one gallon hot water, wash the cooler with the solution, rinse clean, and let dry with the cooler open.

- **McCormick Pure Vanilla Extract.** To deodorize a cooler, wash out the cooler with Clorox Bleach (see above tip), and then saturate a cloth with McCormick Pure Vanilla Extract and wipe down the insides.

- **Mr. Clean Magic Eraser.** To clean grease and grime off plastic coolers, gently rub the stains with a damp Mr. Clean Magic Eraser, wash the item thoroughly with soapy water, rinse clean, and dry.

FISHING

- **Pam Cooking Spray.** To lubricate a fishing reel, use Pam Cooking Spray as you would use silicone spray to make casting easier and quicker.

- **Sno Bol.** To clean corrosion off fishing rods, carefully wet the affected areas with Sno Bol Toilet Bowl Cleaner, let sit for five minutes, and rinse thoroughly. Dry well.

- **Ziploc Storage Bags.** Coil up fishing jigs and place each one in its own Ziploc Storage Bag before putting them in your tackle box. This prevents them from getting tangled up and making a mess out of your tackle box.

Ground Cloths

- **Glad Trash Bags.** To make a ground cloth and keep your sleeping bag clean and dry, place your sleeping bag on top of several Glad Trash Bags.

Hats

- **Alberto VO5 Hair Spray.** To rejuvenate the lifeless straws in a straw hat, give the hat a coat of Alberto VO5 Hair Spray to shine it up.

- **Frisbee.** After washing a beret with your regular wash load, insert a Frisbee into the beret so it dries to the proper size without any wrinkles.

- **Morton Salt** and **Aunt Jemima Corn Meal.** To clean a felt hat, pour one-half cup Morton Salt and one-half cup Aunt Jemima Corn Meal into a jar, secure the lid, and shake well. Brush the hat, rub the mixture into the felt with your fingers, and brush clean. Repeat if necessary.

- **Stayfree Maxi Pads.** To prevent perspiration stains on the inside of a hat's headband, stick a self-adhesive Stayfree Maxi Pads inside the hat along the headband where your forehead rests. When the maxi pad gets full of sweat, replace it with a fresh one.

- **Wonder Bread.** To clean a felt hat, rub a slice of Wonder Bread over the hat and brush away the crumbs. The bread works like an eraser, absorbing soil, grease, and grime.

Hiking Boots

- **Arm & Hammer Baking Soda.** To help your feet feel fresh and deodorize smelly shoes, sprinkle some Arm & Hammer Baking Soda inside your hiking boots before wearing them on a hike.

Packing

- **Maxwell House Coffee.** To keep toilet paper waterproof while camping and prevent a soggy mess, carry a roll of toilet paper inside an empty Maxwell House Coffee can.

- **Pringles.** To pack paper cups for a picnic and prevent them from getting soiled, fit five-ounce Dixie Cups inside a clean, empty Pringles can and seal the lid shut.

- **Scotch Transparent Tape.** To prevent salt and pepper from spilling out of the shakers and making a mess when traveling with a picnic basket, put a piece of Scotch Transparent Tape over the holes in the top of each shaker. Make sure to fold back one end of each piece of tape for easy removal at your picnic site.

- **Ziploc Storage Bags.** Organize utensils, food, clothes, maps, medications, and first aid supplies in Ziploc Storage Bags.

PICNIC TABLECLOTHS

- **Conair 1875 Watt Hair Dryer.** To remove ugly wrinkles from plastic tablecloths, blow with a Conair 1875 Watt Hair Dryer set on hot until the plastic softens.

- **Scotch Packaging Tape.** To prevent the wind from blowing away picnic tablecloths and making a mess, tape the corners to the table with Scotch Packaging Tape.

- **Velcro.** Adhere strips of Velcro on the four corners of the tablecloth and the table to keep it from blowing off the table.

POTS AND PANS

- **Ivory Soap.** To prevent campfire soot from sticking to the bottom of pots and pans, rub a bar of Ivory Soap across the bottoms of pots and pans before putting them over an open fire. The thin coat of soap makes washing the pots and pans a snap.

- **Murphy Oil Soap.** To prevent campfire soot from sticking to pots and pans, coat the outside of pots and pans with Murphy Oil Soap before using the cookware over an outdoor fire. The soap enables you to wash black soot from the fire right off.

- **Palmolive.** Before cooking over an open fire, coat the bottom of your pots and pans with Palmolive Dishwashing Liquid. The black soot that forms on the bottom of the pots and pans wipes right off.

- **Reynolds Wrap.** A crumpled-up piece of Reynolds Wrap aluminum foil makes an excellent pot scrubber.

COMING CLEAN
WITH MURPHY OIL SOAP

In 1890, Jeremiah T. Murphy, the son of Irish immigrants, founded the Phoenix Oil Company in Newburgh, Ohio, to manufacture oils for valves, cylinders, dynamos, machines, and harnesses. In 1905, when a German immigrant showed Murphy a sample of a vegetable oil soap, Murphy bought the recipe and made the first Murphy Oil Soap—a paste packed in large barrels that his customers would scoop out. By 1910, Murphy made his soap paste available in one- and five-pound cans, sold in hardware and department stores—only in the Great Lakes region. Murphy Oil Soap later evolved into the liquid soap known today. In 1968, the Phoenix Oil Company became the Murphy-Phoenix Company. In 1976, the company began expanding, selling Murphy Oil Soap in Syracuse, New York, and expanding to a new region each year, until the company achieved national distribution in 1986. In 1991, the Colgate-Palmolive Company acquired the Murphy Oil Soap line.

Strange Facts

- In 1966, Phoenix Oil built a plant in Madison, Ohio, to manufacture concrete-curing compounds used in road construction.

- Murphy Oil Soap is the chemical most commonly used to clean elephants.

- In a television commercial, ghosts use Murphy Oil Soap to clean a haunted house. A voice-over says, "If Murphy Oil Soap is not afraid to take on this house, it certainly won't be intimidated by yours."

Propane Lanterns

- **Heinz White Vinegar.** To prolong and brighten the light emitted from propane lanterns, soak new wicks for several hours in Heinz White Vinegar and let them dry before inserting. Propane lanterns will burn longer and brighter on the same amount of fuel.

Raincoats

- **Glad Trash Bags.** To improvise a raincoat and keep yourself clean and dry during a rainstorm, cut slits in a Glad Trash Bag for head and arms.

Sand

- **Johnson's Baby Powder.** To clean wet sand off beach toys or skins, sprinkle Johnson's Baby Powder on the toys or skin. The baby powder absorbs moisture, and the sand virtually falls off by itself.

Shower

- **Glad Trash Bags.** To make a solar-powered camping shower to clean yourself, fill a Glad Trash Bag with water, tie it to a solid tree branch, and let the sun heat the water. After you lather up with soap, poke a small hole in the bag to rinse off.

- **Playtex Living Gloves.** To make a camping shower, fill a Playtex Living Glove with water and hang it from a tree. Gently poke four or five holes in it. Instant shower.

Sinks

- **Clorox Bleach.** To make a camping sink to clean your hands, poke a small hole in the side of a clean, empty Clorox Bleach bottle (near the bottom) and then plug the hole with a golf tee. Fill the bottle with water, and then pull out the plug to wash your hands.

SLEEPING BAGS

- **Arm & Hammer Baking Soda.** To prevent your sleeping bag from acquiring musty odors while packed away, air it out well, sprinkle some Arm & Hammer Baking Soda inside the bag, and roll it up. Baking soda absorbs moisture and neutralizes odors. Before using the sleeping bag next time, simply shake it well to empty out the baking soda.

- **Bounce.** Before rolling up a sleeping bag for storage, place a sheet of Bounce inside the bag. When you unroll the bag next time, it will smell springtime fresh.

SOAP

- **L'eggs Sheer Energy Panty Hose.** To hang soap from the water spigot and keep it clean when camping, cut off a leg from a used pair of L'eggs Sheer Energy Panty Hose, place a bar of soap inside the foot, tie a knot to secure the bar of soap, then tie the other end of the panty hose to the water spigot or a nearby branch.

SOLAR-POWERED WATER HEATER

- **Clorox Bleach** and **Coca-Cola.** To heat water, save empty Clorox Bleach jugs and two-liter Coca-Cola bottles. Paint the clean, empty jugs and bottles black with tempera paint and fill them with water. Set them in the sun in the morning, and by late afternoon, the water will be hot enough to use for washing dishes or bathing.

TAR

- **Colgate Regular Flavor Toothpaste.** To clean tar from skin, rub a dollop of Colgate Regular Flavor Toothpaste into the tar, and then rinse clean with water.

- **Miracle Whip.** Remove tar from skin by spreading a teaspoon of Miracle Whip on the tar. Let sit for two minutes, rub, and wipe off.
- **Wish-Bone Thousand Island Dressing.** To clean tar from skin, rub a dollop of Wish-Bone Thousand Island Dressing on the tar and wipe clean with a cloth.

TENTS

- **Oral-B Dental Floss.** When hiking or camping, Oral-B Dental Floss makes a durable, strong thread for tough repairs on a tent.

THERMOS BOTTLES

- **Arm & Hammer Baking Soda.** To freshen a Thermos bottle, fill the bottle with warm water, add two tablespoons Arm & Hammer Baking Soda, shake well, and let sit for ten minutes. Rinse well. (For more ways to clean a Thermos bottle, see page 225.)

UMBRELLAS

- **Oral-B Dental Floss.** If one of the fabric tacks breaks free from one of the ribs of an umbrella, sew it back together using Oral-B Dental Floss as a durable thread.
- **Scotch-Brite Heavy Duty Scrub Sponge** To soak up excess water from inside an umbrella stand, place a Scotch-Brite Heavy Duty Scrub Sponge at the bottom of the umbrella stand.
- **Scotchgard Fabric Protector.** To better waterproof an umbrella, spray the fabric with a protective coat of Scotchgard Fabric Protector.
- **Vaseline Petroleum Jelly.** To prevent the hinges on a new umbrella

from rusting, rub a dab of Vaseline Petroleum Jelly on each hinge, which also helps the umbrella glide open and closed more freely.

WATERPROOFING

- **Glad Trash Bags.** To waterproof a backpack and prevent a soggy mess inside, cover the backpack with a Glad Trash Bag and cut small slits in the bag for the straps of the backpack.
- **Scotchgard Fabric Protector.** To waterproof tents, backpacks, and sleeping bags, spray your gear with Scotchgard Fabric Protector.

WINDBREAKER

- **Glad Trash Bags.** To improvise a windbreaker, cut holes in a Glad Trash Bag for your head and arms and wear it under your coat.

ZIPPERS

- **ChapStick.** To make a stubborn zipper glide with greater ease and keep the teeth from rusting, coat the teeth with some ChapStick lip balm. The wax lubricates the teeth and helps the zipper zip smoothly. (For more ways to lubricate a zipper, see page 280.)
- **Vaseline Petroleum Jelly.** To prevent metal zippers on camping gear from rusting, give the teeth a coat of Vaseline Petroleum Jelly.
- **Velcro.** If the zipper on your tent door or sleeping bag breaks, replace it with strips of Velcro.

Carpets and Rugs

ALCOHOLIC BEVERAGE STAINS

- **Arm & Hammer Baking Soda.** Blot up as much of the alcoholic beverage as possible. Make a paste by mixing equal parts Arm & Hammer Baking Soda and water. Apply the paste to the stain, let dry, and brush clean.

- **Canada Dry Club Soda.** To clean an alcoholic beverage stain from carpeting, blot up as much liquid as possible, pour Canada Dry Club Soda on the stain, and blot with towels. Repeat until the color from the spill disappears. The carbonation in the club soda lifts the stain from the carpet.

- **Parsons' Ammonia.** After blotting up as much liquid as possible, mix five teaspoons Parsons' Ammonia and one cup water, use a sponge to apply the solution to the stain, rinse with cold water, and blot well. (Do not use ammonia on woolen carpeting or rugs.)

BLEACHED SPOTS

- **McCormick Food Coloring.** To hide a bleached area of carpeting, mix a shade to match with McCormick Food Coloring and sponge it on the carpet fibers. Let dry well.

- **Rit Dye** and **Heinz White Vinegar.** Dye the bleached area to match with the appropriate color Rit Dye. Let dry, mix equal parts Heinz White Vinegar and water, sponge the solution onto the dyed area, and let dry. The vinegar sets the dye.

- **Sharpie Fine Point Permanent Marker.** To cover up a bleached area of carpeting, touch up the spot with a Sharpie Fine Point Permanent Marker in a matching color.

BLOODSTAINS

- **Adolph's Original Meat Tenderizer.** To clean a bloodstain from carpet, cover the stain with a paste made from Adolph's Original Meat Tenderizer and cool water. Wait twenty minutes and sponge off with cool water. The enzymes in the meat tenderizer break up the proteins in the blood. Blot well.

- **Ivory Dishwashing Liquid.** To clean a bloodstain from carpet, rinse quickly with cool water. Follow with a mix of one-quarter teaspoon Ivory Dishwashing Liquid with one cup cool water. Blot and dry quickly.

- **Kingsford's Corn Starch.** Make a paste from Kingsford's Corn Starch and water, cover the bloodstain with the paste, rub gently, let dry, and vacuum. Repeat if necessary.

BURNS

- **Dawn Dishwashing Liquid** and **20 Mule Team Borax.** To clean a burn in carpeting, saturate a soft, clean cloth with water, add a few drops of Dawn Dishwashing Liquid, rub the affected area, and let sit for five minutes. Mix one tablespoon 20 Mule Team Borax and one cup water, sponge the solution into the burn, rinse clean, and let dry.

- **Elmer's Glue-All.** If the burn mark still shows after attempting to clean the area with the above tip, use a pair of scissors to cut away the burned carpet fibers. Then cut some carpet fibers from an inconspicuous spot (from under a bed or the corner of a closet), and glue them into place with Elmer's Glue-All.

CANDLE WAX

- **Bounty Paper Towels.** To remove candle wax from carpet, place a sheet of Bounty Paper Towels over the wax and press gently with a warm iron. The heat from the iron melts the wax, and the quicker-picker-upper absorbs it. If the dyes in wax won't come out, find a trained carpet professional to cut the fibers and replace the area with a new carpet insert.

CARPET CLEANING

- **Aunt Jemima Corn Meal.** To rejuvenate carpeting, sprinkle Aunt Jemima Corn Meal through a small mesh strainer, scrub with a brush, let sit two hours, and vacuum.

- **Heinz White Vinegar.** To clean carpeting, mix one cup Heinz White Vinegar and three cups hot water, dampen a clean cloth with the solution, wring out the excess liquid, and rub the carpet thoroughly. Let dry.

- **Johnson's Baby Shampoo.** Use a capful of Johnson's Baby Shampoo in your carpet shampooer to clean carpet, simultaneously scenting your home with baby freshness.

- **Morton Salt** and **Heinz White Vinegar.** Mix one part Morton Salt to two parts Heinz White Vinegar, apply the solution to the carpet with a sponge, let dry, and vacuum.

- **Murphy Oil Soap.** In a bowl, whip one-quarter cup Murphy Oil Soap and three tablespoons water with a whisk until you make a large head of foam. Rub the foam into stains on the carpet, rinse well, and blot.

Keep It Clean
HOW TO VACUUM CARPET

■ The most effective way to keep your carpet clean is by vacuuming regularly. Consistent vacuuming keeps particles out of the indoor air you breath and also prevents loose soil on the carpet surface from being ground into the carpet pile, preserving the cushiness of your carpet. In fact, daily vacuuming can remove more than 80 percent of dry soil from carpet.

■ Vacuum daily in high-traffic or pet areas, vacuum twice weekly in medium-traffic areas, and vacuum weekly in light-traffic areas, using attachments at carpet edges.

■ Before vacuuming, dust blinds, windowsills, and furniture surfaces to avoid having to vacuum again after dusting.

■ Push the vacuum cleaner forward slowly and then pull the vacuum cleaner backward slowly, making overlapping strokes, moving slightly to the left or right every four strokes.

■ Use the long, thin crevice tool to vacuum dust buildup from corners and crevices.

■ Remove and replace (or empty) vacuum bags when they are half to two-thirds full.

COFFEE OR TEA STAINS

● **Canada Dry Club Soda.** To clean coffee or tea stains from carpeting, blot up as much liquid as possible, pour Canada Dry Club Soda on the stain, and blot with towels. Repeat until the color from the spill disappears. The carbonation in the club soda lifts the stain from the carpet.

- **Heinz White Vinegar** and **Dawn Dishwashing Liquid.** Mix one cup Heinz White Vinegar with three drops Dawn Dishwashing Liquid, apply the mixture with a sponge to the coffee or tea stain, blot well, rinse, and blot again.

CRAYON

- **Bounty Paper Towels.** To remove crayon wax from carpet, place a sheet of Bounty Paper Towels over the wax stain and press gently with a warm iron. The heat from the iron melts the wax, and the quicker-picker-upper absorbs it.
- **Conair 1875 Watt Hair Dryer.** If a crayon has melted into the carpet, aim a Conair 1875 Watt Hair Dryer at the crayon and blow just enough warm air to soften the wax and free it from the carpet.

DIRT STAINS

- **Gillette Foamy.** To clean dirt stains from carpet, spray a dab of Gillette Foamy shaving cream on the spot, rub into the spot with your fingers, and blot clean with damp, clean cloth.
- **Tide.** To clean dirt stains from carpeting, whip one teaspoon liquid Tide and two cups water with a whisk in a bowl to make a head of foam. Apply the resulting foam to the dirt stain, brush the foam into the stain, and blot well.

DISINFECTING

- **Aunt Jemima Corn Meal, 20 Mule Team Borax,** and **Arm & Hammer Baking Soda** To disinfect areas of the carpeting, mix one cup Aunt Jemima Corn Meal, one cup 20 Mule Team Borax, and one-half cup Arm & Hammer Baking Soda. Sprinkle the mixture over the problem areas; rub with a soft, clean cloth; and let sit overnight. In the morning, vacuum clean.

FRUIT STAINS

- **Ivory Dishwashing Liquid.** Blot the stain with a clean, white cloth to absorb as much of the stain as possible. Follow with a mix of one-quarter teaspoon Ivory Dishwashing Liquid and one cup cool water. Blot, repeat, and rinse with clear water on a clean, white towel or a white paper towel. Dry.

- **Morton Salt.** To clean a fruit stain from carpeting, dampen the spot with a little water, pour a mountain of Morton Salt to cover the stain, rub the salt into the stain, and let sit for ten minutes. Brush and vacuum. Repeat if necessary. Salt absorbs liquids.

GLUE

- **Heinz White Vinegar.** To clean glue out of carpet, saturate the stain with Heinz White Vinegar and blot with a clean, dry cloth.

GREASE OR OIL STAINS

- **Arm & Hammer Baking Soda.** To clean a grease or oil stain from carpeting, cover the stain with Arm & Hammer Baking Soda, rub it in, and let dry. Brush and vacuum clean. The baking soda absorbs the grease and oil.

- **Kingsford's Corn Starch.** To clean a grease stain from carpet, cover the stain with Kingsford's Corn Starch, let sit for fifteen minutes, and vacuum clean.

GUM

- **Conair 1875 Watt Hair Dryer.** To clean gum from carpet, aim a Conair 1875 Watt Hair Dryer at the gum and blow warm air on the gum to soften it up. Use a fork or comb to scrape the gum from the carpet.

- **Skippy Peanut Butter.** Rub a dollop of Skippy Peanut Butter into the gum, let sit for five minutes to give the oils in the peanut butter time to soften the gum, and work the gum out of the carpet with a comb, fork, or clean, old toothbrush. Then use one of the tips listed under Grease or Oil Stains (opposite) to clean the peanut butter from the carpet.

- **Spray 'n Wash.** Saturate the gum with Spray 'n Wash stain remover to soften it and use a fork or comb to free the gum from the carpeting.

- **Star Olive Oil** and **Dawn Dishwashing Liquid.** Saturate the gum with Star Olive Oil to soften it, and work the gum out of the carpet with a fork or clean, old toothbrush. Use a few drops of Dawn Dishwashing Liquid on a damp sponge to wash the olive oil out of the carpet. Rinse and blot well.

- **Ziploc Storage Bags, Vaseline Petroleum Jelly,** and **Dawn Dishwashing Liquid.** Fill a Ziploc Storage Bag with ice and set it on top of the gum stain, allowing the gum to freeze. Scrape off as much of the frozen gum as possible, and then coat the gum left in the carpet with Vaseline Petroleum Jelly. The petroleum jelly dissolves the gum, enabling you to scrape it out of the carpet. Use a few drops of Dawn Dishwashing Liquid on a damp sponge to wash the petroleum jelly out of the carpet. Rinse and blot well.

Hair Dye Stains

- **Alberto VO5 Hair Spray.** To clean dried hair dye from carpet, blot up as much of the hair dye as possible, saturate the stain with Alberto VO5 Hair Spray, let sit for five minutes, and rinse clean. (Test the hair spray on an inconspicuous spot first to make sure the acetone does not affect the color of the carpet).

- **Ivory Dishwashing Liquid.** Blot the hair dye stain with a clean white cloth to absorb as much of the stain as possible. Follow with a mix of one-quarter teaspoon Ivory Dishwashing Liquid and one cup cool water. Blot, repeat, and rinse with clear water on a clean, white towel or a white paper towel. Dry. Professional cleaning may be required.

- **Johnson's Baby Shampoo.** To clean water-soluble hair dye from carpet, blot up as much of the hair dye as possible, wet the stain with water and rub in a few drops of Johnson's Baby Shampoo. Blot, rinse, and blot again. Repeat if necessary.

- **Sea Breeze.** To clean dried hair dye from carpet, saturate the stain with Sea Breeze Astringent and let sit for five minutes. Blot, rinse, and blot dry. (Test Sea Breeze on an inconspicuous spot to make sure the astringent doesn't affect the color of the carpet.)

Ink Stains

- **Alberto VO5 Hair Spray.** To remove ink spots from carpet, spray Alberto VO5 Hair Spray on the affected area and blot with a paper towel or cotton swab until the stain comes up. The acetone in Alberto VO5 Hair Spray removes indelible marker and ballpoint pen marks.

- **Kingsford's Corn Starch.** Mix Kingsford's Corn Starch with enough milk to make a paste. Apply the paste on the ink stain, let it dry, and then brush it off. The milk dissolves the ink, and the cornstarch absorbs it.

- **Purell Instant Hand Sanitizer.** Saturate an ink stain on carpet with Purell Instant Hand Sanitizer and blot with a paper towel or soft cloth. Repeat as many times as necessary until the ink stain vanishes.

Ketchup Stains

- **Ivory Dishwashing Liquid.** Blot the ketchup stain with a clean, white cloth to absorb as much of the stain as possible. Follow with a mix of one-quarter teaspoon Ivory Dishwashing Liquid and one cup cool water. Blot, repeat, and rinse with clear water on a clean, white towel or a white paper towel. Dry.

Mildew

- **Listerine.** To kill mildew in carpeting, mix two teaspoons Listerine antiseptic mouthwash and two cups water in a sixteen-ounce trigger-spray bottle and spray the solution on the affected area. Let dry.

- **Parsons' Ammonia.** To kill mildew in carpeting, mix five teaspoons Parsons' Ammonia and one cup water, use a sponge to apply the solution to the affected area, blot, rinse with cold water, blot again, and let dry. (Do not use ammonia on woolen carpeting or rugs.)

Mud

- **Arm & Hammer Baking Soda** and **Gillette Foamy.** Cover wet mud with a mountain of Arm & Hammer Baking Soda and let dry overnight. In the morning, vacuum the baking soda and dried dirt from the carpet. Then work a dollop of Gillette Foamy shaving cream into the spot, rinse with water, and blot well.
- **Morton Salt.** To absorb fresh stains from carpet, cover the stain with a mountain of Morton Salt, let sit for ten minutes, brush clean, and vacuum.

Nail Polish

- **Cutex Non-Acetone Nail Polish Remover** and **Gillette Foamy.** To clean spilled nail polish from carpeting, blot up as much of the nail polish as possible using rags, tissues, or paper towels. Use an eyedropper to apply a few drops of Cutex Non-Acetone Nail Polish Remover to an inconspicuous spot on the carpet and blot well to make sure the nail polish remover does not lighten the color. If you're satisfied with the test spot, apply a few drops of the nail polish remover to the stain, blotting immediately. Repeat until you remove as much nail polish as possible. Then work a dollop of Gillette Foamy shaving cream into the spot, rinse with water, and blot well.
- **Spray 'n Wash.** To clean nail polish from carpet, spray Spray 'n Wash stain remover on the wet nail polish stain, let sit for three minutes, and then blot with a wet cloth. Repeat as many times as necessary.

Odors

- **Arm & Hammer Baking Soda.** To absorb odors from carpeting, sprinkle a generous amount of Arm & Hammer Baking Soda over the carpet or rug. Let sit overnight. In the morning, vacuum clean.

- **20 Mule Team Borax.** If the carpet smells musty, sprinkle some 20 Mule Team Borax on the carpet, let sit for one hour, and vacuum clean.

PAINT, LATEX

- **Ivory Dishwashing Liquid.** Rinse the stain with a mix of one-quarter teaspoon Ivory Dishwashing Liquid and one cup cool water. Blot, repeat, and dry.

RUBBER CEMENT

- **Vaseline Petroleum Jelly** and **Dawn Dishwashing Liquid.** Coat the rubber cement in the carpet with Vaseline Petroleum Jelly. The petroleum jelly dissolves the adhesive, allowing you to rub the rubber cement out of the carpet. Use a few drops of Dawn Dishwashing Liquid on a damp sponge to wash the petroleum jelly out of the carpet. Blot well.

SHAMPOOING

- **Tide and Parsons' Ammonia.** Mix one-half cup Tide powder, one teaspoon Parsons' Ammonia, and one quart warm water in a bucket. Whip with a whisk to work up a tall froth. Using a sponge, rub the froth only into the carpet. Whip the liquid to create more forth when needed. Let the carpet dry and vacuum.

- **Ziploc Storage Bags.** To protect the legs of furniture while shampooing the carpet, place each leg inside a Ziploc Storage Bag and seal the bag as tightly as possible with a rubber band or tape.

Sheepskin

- **Arm & Hammer Baking Soda, 20 Mule Team Borax,** and **ReaLemon.** To machine wash a sheepskin rug, add one cup Arm & Hammer Baking Soda, one cup 20 Mule Team Borax, one cup ReaLemon lemon juice to the wash cycle. Hang the rug over a chair to dry, and then brush the fleece.

- **Aunt Jemima Corn Meal.** To give a sheepskin rug a dry shampoo, rub Aunt Jemima Corn Meal into the rug, shake it out, repeat if necessary, and vacuum clean.

- **Murphy Oil Soap** and **Pantene Classic Care Conditioner.** To wash a sheepskin rug by hand, mix one tablespoon Murphy Oil Soap and one gallon water, wash the sheepskin in the solution, and add one teaspoon Pantene Classic Care Conditioner to each gallon of rinse water. Hang the rug over a chair to dry, and then brush the fleece.

- **20 Mule Team Borax** and **ReaLemon.** To clean a sheepskin rug, mix one cup 20 Mule Team Borax, one cup ReaLemon lemon juice, and one gallon water. Fill a trigger-spray bottle with the solution and spray the fleece. Let sit for two hours, and then rinse clean with a hose. Hang the rug over a chair to dry, and then brush the fleece.

- **Woolite.** Wash a sheepskin rug in the washing machine with cold water and Woolite. Hang the rug over a chair to dry, and then brush the fleece.

Soot

- **Morton Salt** and **Gillette Foamy.** Cover a soot stain on carpet with a mountain of Morton Salt and let sit for more than two hours, allowing the salt enough time to absorb the soot. Vacuum well, work a dollop of Gillette Foamy shaving cream into the spot, rinse with water, and blot well.

Static Electricity

- **Downy Fabric Softener.** Mix three tablespoons Downy Fabric Softener and two cups water in a sixteen-ounce trigger-spray bottle. Spray the

Keep It Clean

HOW TO CLEAN CARPET STAINS

- Act quickly. The longer you wait, the more likely the stain will become permanent.

- Blot the spill. Use a clean, dry, white absorbent cloth or white paper towel to absorb as much liquid as quickly as possible. (Do not use a colored cloth or printed paper towels; the colors may bleed into the carpet.) To prevent the stain from spreading, start blotting from the outer edge of the spot and work your way toward the center. Blot up as much liquid as possible, leaving the affected area only slightly damp.

- Do not scrub or use a brush. (Otherwise you risk fraying the carpet.)

- Treat the stain with a carpet-cleaning product labeled with the Carpet and Rug Institute (CRI) Seal of Approval.

- Test any spot cleaner on an inconspicuous spot to make sure the cleaner doesn't discolor the carpet or damage the fibers. Apply several drops of the cleaner to the testing area, hold a white cloth on the wet area for ten seconds, and then examine the carpet and cloth to see if any color has transferred to the cloth or if the color of the carpet has changed.

- When using a carpet cleaning product, apply a small amount of the product to a white cloth and blot the cleaner into the carpet gently, starting from the outer edges of the stain and working your way into the center. Repeat several times if necessary. Keep using the cleaning solution as long as the stain continues to transfer to the cloth.

- After you've removed the stain completely, rinse the affected area thoroughly with cold water and blot with a dry cloth until all of the solution has been absorbed. Otherwise, the soap in the cleaning solution acts like glue, causing the spot to attract soil again quickly.

- To dry the spot, lay a one-half inch thick layer of white paper towels to the affected area and place several heavy books on top of it to press the paper towels against the carpet. Change paper towels if necessary.

solution on the carpet until moderately damp and let dry. The antistatic elements in the fabric softener reduce static electricity in the carpet.

STUBBORN MYSTERY STAINS

- **Arm & Hammer Baking Soda, Morton Salt,** and **Heinz White Vinegar.** Make a paste by mixing equal parts Arm & Hammer Baking Soda and Morton Salt, a few drops Heinz White Vinegar, and water. Apply the paste to the stain, let dry, and brush clean.

- **Canada Dry Club Soda.** To clean beverage stains (coffee, tea, Kool-Aid, red wine, and soda) from carpeting, blot up as much liquid as possible, pour Canada Dry Club Soda on the stain, and blot with towels. Repeat until the color from the spill disappears. The carbonation in the club soda lifts the stain from the carpet.

- **Gillette Foamy.** To clean red stains from carpet (ketchup, spaghetti sauce, red wine), spray a small dab of Gillette Foamy shaving cream on the spot, rub into the spot with your fingers, and blot clean with damp, clean cloth.

- **Heinz White Vinegar** and **Kingsford's Corn Starch.** Mix equal parts Heinz White Vinegar and Kingsford's Corn Starch, work the paste into the stain with a soft, clean cloth, let sit for two days, and vacuum clean. The vinegar dissolves the stain; the cornstarch absorbs it.

- **Hydrogen Peroxide.** If you've tried the other tips listed here to clean a stain from carpet and you're still left with a stain, dab the spot with Hydrogen Peroxide, then dab with cold water on a clean cloth, repeat if necessary, and let dry. (Be sure to test the Hydrogen Peroxide on a inconspicuous spot first to make sure it doesn't affect the color of the carpet.)

- **Ivory Dishwashing Liquid.** Blot the stain with a clean white cloth to absorb as much as the stain as possible. Follow with a mix of one-quarter teaspoon Ivory Dishwashing Liquid and one cup cool water. Blot, repeat, and rinse with clear water on a clean, white towel or a white paper towel. Dry.

- **Kingsford's Corn Starch.** To clean a wet stain from carpet, cover the stain with Kingsford's Corn Starch, let sit for fifteen minutes, and vacuum clean. Repeat if necessary.

- **Morton Salt.** To absorb fresh stains from carpet, cover the stain with a mountain of Morton Salt, let sit for ten minutes, brush clean, and vacuum.

- **Murphy Oil Soap** and **Heinz White Vinegar.** Mix one teaspoon Murphy Oil Soap, one-quarter cup Heinz White Vinegar, and one-half cup water. Sponge the solution onto the stain, rinse well, and blot.

- **Smirnoff Vodka.** Saturate a sponge with Smirnoff Vodka, rub the stain, rinse with water, and blot well.

- **Spray 'n Wash.** Spray Spray 'n Wash stain remover on the stain, let sit for five minutes, and then wipe clean with a clean, wet cloth. The fragrance in Spray 'n Wash also freshens the carpet, and the stain remover prepares the stained area for the next time you have the carpet steam cleaned.

- **Windex.** To clean a mystery stain from a carpet or rug, spray with Windex, blot well, rinse with water, and blot dry.

- **Wine Away**. To clean red wine, grape juice, Kool-Aid, coffee, and tea stains from carpet, apply Wine Away Red Wine Stain Remover, wait until the stain disappears, and blot with a wet cloth.

TAR

- **Glycerin, Bounty Paper Towels,** and **Gillette Foamy.** To clean tar from carpet, apply Glycerin to the spot, let sit for one hour, and blot with Bounty Paper Towels. Repeat as many times as necessary. Then work a dollop of Gillette Foamy shaving cream into the spot, rinse with water, and blot well.

URINE

- **Arm & Hammer Baking Soda.** To deodorize blotted-up urine stains in carpet, cover the stain with a mountain of Arm & Hammer Baking Soda.

Let sit for forty-eight hours, giving the baking soda enough time to neutralize the odor, then brush up the baking soda and vacuum the spot. (For more ways to clean urine stains from carpet, see page 341.)

Vacuum Cleaners

- **Bounce.** Putting a sheet of Bounce in the bag of your vacuum cleaner before vacuuming helps eliminate the musty smell in the house.

- **Forster Clothespins.** To prevent a retractable vacuum cleaner cord from springing back into the machine, clip a Forster Clothespin to the electrical cord at the length you desire.

Keep It Clean
DOES YOUR VACUUM CLEANER CLEAN?

- If your vacuum cleaner doesn't have sufficient suction, consult the instruction manual to determine the likely spots in the hoses and attachments that may be clogged with dirt or hair.

- Remove tangled hair from the bristles of the bottom roller brushes and have the brushes replaced when they are worn out.

- Replace or clean the filter.

- Replace the belt (or have a vacuum repair shop replace the belt for you). A worn-out belt is stretched out and doesn't provide enough traction to rotate the brushes.

- Empty containers or replace bags when half or two-thirds full.

- Examine the vacuum cleaner for any rough edges or bent metal that can snag carpet.

- **Johnson's Cotton Balls.** Saturate a Johnson's Cotton Ball with perfume or cologne, and place it in the bag of your vacuum cleaner before cleaning to fragrance the air.

Vomit

- **Arm & Hammer Baking Soda.** To clean vomit from carpet, scrape up all the chunks and blot up as much of the excess liquid as possible, and then cover the stain with a mountain of Arm & Hammer Baking Soda. Let sit overnight, giving the baking soda enough time to absorb the liquid, dry, and deodorize the stench, and then brush up the baking soda and vacuum the spot.

- **Canada Dry Club Soda** After scraping up as much of the vomit as possible, pour Canada Dry Club Soda on the stain and blot with towels. Repeat until the color from the stain disappears. The carbonation in the club soda lifts the stain from the carpet.

- **Parsons' Ammonia.** After cleaning up as much vomit as possible, mix five teaspoons Parsons' Ammonia and one cup water, use a sponge to apply the solution to the stain, blot, rinse with cold water, and blot again. (Do not use ammonia on woolen carpeting or rugs.)

- **20 Mule Team Borax.** Clean up as much of the vomit as possible, dissolve one tablespoon 20 Mule Team Borax in two cups water, apply the solution to the stain with a sponge, and blot clean.

Wine Stains

- **Arm & Hammer Baking Soda.** After blotting up as much of the wine as possible, pour a mountain of Arm & Hammer Baking Soda over the remaining stain, let sit until the wine is absorbed, and vacuum clean.

- **Canada Dry Club Soda.** To clean wine stains from carpeting, blot up as much liquid as possible, pour Canada Dry Club Soda on the stain, and blot with towels. Repeat until the color from the spill disappears. The carbonation in the club soda lifts the stain from the carpet.

- **Gillette Foamy.** To clean red wine stains from carpet, blot up as much wine as possible, spray a small dab of Gillette Foamy shaving cream on the spot, rub into the spot with your fingers, and blot clean with damp, clean cloth.

- **Hydrogen Peroxide.** If you've tried the other tips listed here to clean a wine stain from carpet and you're still left with a stain, dab the spot with Hydrogen Peroxide, then dab with cold water on a clean cloth, repeat if necessary, and let dry. (Be sure to test the Hydrogen Peroxide on an inconspicuous spot first to make sure it doesn't affect the color of the carpet.)

- **Ivory Dishwashing Liquid.** Rinse quickly with cool water. Follow with a mix of one-quarter teaspoon Ivory Dishwashing Liquid and one cup cool water. Blot, repeat, and dry.

- **McCormick Cream of Tartar.** Blot up as much wine as possible, make a paste of McCormick Cream of Tartar and water, apply to the remaining stain, let sit for thirty minutes, blot up with a wet cloth, and follow with the Gillette Foamy tip above.

- **Morton Salt.** To absorb a fresh wine stain from carpet, cover the stain with a mountain of Morton Salt, let sit for ten minutes, brush clean, and vacuum. Repeat if necessary.

Driveways, Patios, and Garage Floors

CONCRETE FLOORS

- **Arm & Hammer Super Washing Soda** and **Murphy Oil Soap.** To scrub a concrete floor clean, mix one-quarter cup Arm & Hammer Super Washing Soda, two tablespoons Murphy Oil Soap, and two gallons warm water in a bucket. Scrub the floor with the solution and rinse clean.

- **Bon Ami**. To clean built-up dirt and grime from a garage floor, wet the surface, sprinkle with Bon Ami, and scrub with a broom or scrub brush. Rinse well with water.

- **Simple Green.** To clean cat spray, cat urine, dog urine, or skunk spray from cement or concrete, open all windows and doors to the room (if indoors), and set up fans to ventilate. In a bucket, mix one cup Simple

Green All-Purpose Cleaner to ten cups hot water and scrub the cement or concrete surfaces down with the solution. After scrubbing, mop away as much moisture as possible. Run the fans with the windows and doors open until everything dries.

GREASE SPLATTERS

- **Morton Salt** and **Dawn Dishwashing Liquid.** To clean grease splatters from concrete patios or wood decks, immediately pour a mountain of Morton Salt over the splatter. Let sit for ten minutes and sweep up. Repeat if necessary. Scrub the remaining grease stain with a few drops of Dawn Dishwashing Liquid and rinse clean.

MOLD

- **Clorox Bleach.** To eliminate mold from a concrete floor, mix three cups Clorox Bleach and one gallon water and mop the solution onto the moldy concrete. Let sit for twenty-four hours, rinse with water, and sweep with a broom. (Do not spill any of the bleach solution on grass.)

OIL STAINS

- **Cascade.** To clean old grease or oil stains from a concrete floor, make a paste from Cascade powder and water, scrub the paste into the spot, and let sit overnight. In the morning, add more water, scrub, and rinse clean.

- **Coca-Cola.** Pour enough Coca-Cola over the stain to saturate it, let sit for thirty minutes, and then rinse clean with a garden hose. Repeat several times if necessary.

- **Dawn Dishwashing Liquid.** Cover the grease or oil stain with a large puddle of Dawn Dishwashing Liquid, spreading out the detergent with a broom if necessary. Let sit for twelve hours and spray clean with a garden hose.

- **Easy-Off Oven Cleaner.** To clean difficult stains from a concrete floor, spray the stain with Easy-Off Oven Cleaner (making sure the area is well ventilated), let sit for fifteen minutes, scrub with a brush, and rinse clean with a garden hose. Repeat if necessary.

- **Jonny Cat Litter.** To absorb oil stains from a concrete garage floor or driveway, pour Jonny Cat Litter on the spot, grind the cat box filler into the spot with the heel of your shoe or a block of wood, and let it sit overnight. In the morning, sweep up the cat box filler, which will have absorbed all the oil. Repeat if necessary.

- **Kingsford's Corn Starch.** To clean up a fresh oil spill, cover the stain with Kingsford's Corn Starch, let sit until the cornstarch absorbs all the oil, and then sweep clean.

- **Parsons' Ammonia.** To remove oil and grease from driveways and cement, add one-half to one cup Parsons' Ammonia to one gallon warm water and apply to the surface. Brush or scrub, and then hose clean.

- **Spray 'n Wash** and **Dawn Dishwashing Liquid.** To clean old grease or oil stains from a concrete floor, spray the spot with Spray 'n Wash stain remover, let sit for ten minutes, pour a few drops of Dawn Dishwashing Liquid on the spot, and scrub with a brush. Rinse clean.

- **USA Today.** Place several sheets of *USA Today* over the oil stain, saturate the newspapers with water, and let dry. As the newsprint dries, it will absorb the oil.

Rust

- **Kool-Aid** and **Glad Trash Bags.** To clean rust from a concrete floor or patio, wet the stain, sprinkle with lemon-flavored Kool-Aid, cover the stain with a Glad Trash Bag, and let sit for fifteen minutes. Remove the plastic trash bag, scrub with a brush, and rinse clean.

- **ReaLemon** and **Morton Salt.** To clean rust stains from concrete caused by metal patio furniture, saturate the stains with ReaLemon lemon

THE HEADS-UP
ON BLUE BONNET

In 1927, Blue Bonnet, a small, independent margarine vendor, began selling Blue Bonnet oleomargarine, named after the bluebonnet flower, which was named after its resemblance to a woman's sunbonnet. In 1943, Standard Brands purchased Blue Bonnet and turned the margarine into a national brand with the slogan "Everything's Better With Blue Bonnet On It!" Unfortunately, restrictive laws in much of the United States and Canada protected dairy producers from competing with cheaper vegetable-oil-based spreads, subjecting margarine to excessive taxes, or prohibiting margarine from being colored yellow like butter. The Margarine Act of 1950 freed markets, and Blue Bonnet introduced the quarter-pound stick of margarine, which quickly became the standard format for margarine and butter in the United States. In 1981, Standard Brands merged with Nabisco, and in 1998, Nabisco sold Blue Bonnet to ConAgra.

Strange Facts

- In 1869, Emperor Louis Napoleon III of France offered a prize to anyone who developed a satisfactory substitute for butter. In 1870, French chemist Hippolyte Mège-Mouriez used margaric acid (a fatty acid component isolated in 1813 by Michael Chevreul and named after the pearly drops that reminded him of the Greek word *margarites*) to create a butter substitute that he named oleomargarine, which became known as margarine.

- In 1886, New York and New Jersey outlawed the manufacture and sale of yellow-colored margarine. By 1902, thirty-two states banned colored margarine.

- During World War II, many Americans switched from butter to margarine.

- In 1967, Wisconsin became the last state to repeal restrictions on margarine.

- In the United States, people use twice as much margarine as butter.

- The Blue Bonnet girl depicted on packages of Blue Bonnet Margarine is named Blue Bonnet Sue.

juice, cover with Morton Salt, and let dry in the sun. Then scrub clean and rinse well.

- **Zud Heavy Duty Cleanser.** To remove rust stains from concrete, make a paste from Zud Heavy Duty Cleanser and water and scrub the paste into the rust spots. Let sit for thirty minutes, scrub with hot water, and rinse clean.

Snow

- **Blue Bonnet Margarine.** To prevent snow from sticking to a shovel, coat the shovel with Blue Bonnet Margarine.

- **Land O Lakes Butter.** Before shoveling your walkway, sidewalk, or driveway, coat the shovel with Land O Lakes Butter so snow slides off the shovel immediately.

- **Pam Cooking Spray.** To simplify snow shoveling, spray a light coat of Pam Cooking Spray on your snow shovel before starting. The cooking oil helps snow slide right off the shovel.

- **SC Johnson Paste Wax.** To prevent your snow shovel from rusting and to prevent the snow from sticking to it, give your snow shovel a coat of SC Johnson Paste Wax.

Sweeping

- **Aunt Jemima Corn Meal.** To prevent dust clouds while sweeping the floor, toss a handful of Aunt Jemima Corn Meal on the floor before sweeping. The dust sticks to the corn meal, enabling you to sweep up dirt without difficulty.

- **Maxwell House Coffee.** Before sweeping the floor in the garage or workshop, sprinkle used Maxwell House Coffee grounds on the floor as a sweeping compound. Dirt and dust stick to the coffee grounds, making sweeping less of a chore.

Dryers

ChapStick, Crayon, and Lipstick

- **Bar Keepers Friend.** If crayons or a tube of lipstick or ChapStick go through the dryer, leaving melted wax all over the inside of the dryer, sprinkle Bar Keepers Friend on a damp sponge, rub the wax marks, and wipe clean with damp rag.

- **Bon Ami.** Sprinkle some Bon Ami onto the drum and rub with a wet rag. Then wipe clean with a clean wet rag.

- **Colgate Regular Flavor Toothpaste.** Squeeze a dollop of Colgate Regular Flavor Toothpaste on a sponge, a Teflon scrubber, a stiff nail brush, or a clean, used toothbrush and scrub the spots. Toothpaste is a mild abrasive. Wipe clean with a damp rag.

- **Comet.** Sprinkle some Comet cleanser onto a damp sponge and scrub the wax marks, wipe clean with a wet rag, and then run a few wet towels through the dryer.

- **ConAir 1875 Watt Hair Dryer.** Heat the crayon marks with a ConAir 1875 Watt Hair Dryer and when the wax melts, wipe it off the wall of the drum with a paper towel.

- **Mr. Clean Magic Eraser.** Dampen a Mr. Clean Magic Eraser and gently rub the wax marks.

FABRIC SOFTENER

- **Arm & Hammer Baking Soda.** Instead of using fabric softener sheets in the dryer to soften clothes, add one-quarter cup Arm & Hammer Baking Soda to the wash cycle. (For more substitutes for fabric softener, see page 243.)

- **Downy Fabric Softener.** To make your own fabric softener dryer sheet, fill a trigger-spray bottle with one part Downy Fabric Softener and two parts water, shake well, mist a clean, old washcloth with the solution, and toss the wet washcloth in the dryer with the clothes. Mist the washcloth for additional loads. Always shake the mixture well before using and label the spray bottle to avoid any potential mishaps.

GUM

- **Bounce.** To remove chewing gum from the inside of a dryer, run the empty dryer for a few minutes to warm up the gum, then dampen a clean, used sheet of Bounce, and use it to wipe off the gum.

- **Downy Fabric Softener.** Pour a few drops of Downy Fabric Softener on a scouring pad sponge and rub the gum. Wipe clean with a paper towel.

- **Huggies Baby Wipes.** Simply wipe gum from the inside of the dryer with a Huggies Baby Wipe.

- **Mr. Clean Magic Eraser.** Dampen a Mr. Clean Magic Eraser and gently rub the gum from the dryer drum.

- **Tide.** Pour a few drops of Tide liquid detergent on the scouring side of a sponge and gently scrub the gum, and then wipe clean with a damp cloth.

INK

- **Bounce.** Dampen a clean, used sheet of Bounce with warm water and use it to wipe off the ink stains.

- **Clorox Bleach**. In a bucket, mix two cups Clorox Bleach and one gallon water. Saturate a clean, old bath towel in the mixture, wring out the excess liquid, toss the wet towel in the dryer, and turn the machine on the Fluff setting (so the towel tumbles inside the dryer without any heat). Repeat for as many cycles as necessary. Then dry the inside of the drum with a clean, soft cloth.

- **Clorox Clean-Up.** Spray Clorox Clean-Up in the dryer, toss in a few towels or rags, and run the dryer for fifteen minutes. The tumbling action lets the towels do the scrubbing work for you.

- **Mr. Clean Magic Eraser** and **Cutex Non-Acetone Nail Polish Remover.** Make sure the room is well ventilated (open the windows and place a fan in the window if necessary), dampen a Mr. Clean Magic Eraser

● ●

Keep It Clean
HOW TO CLEAN STAINS FROM INSIDE A DRYER

- Garments containing unstable dyes, such as denim blue jeans or brightly colored cotton items, may discolor the inside of the dryer drum with blue or gray stains. You can avoid this problem by turning these garments inside out before tossing them into the dryer.

- To clean the dryer drum, make a paste with powdered laundry detergent and warm water. With a soft cloth, rub the paste on the stains until they come out. Wipe clean with a damp cloth. To dry the inside of the drum, tumble a load of towels or clean clothes.

● ●

with Cutex Non-Acetone Nail Polish Remover and gently rub the ink from the dryer drum. Then wash the nail polish residue out of the drum with soapy water and dry with a soft, clean cloth.

- **Tide.** Pour a few drops of Tide liquid detergent on the scouring side of a sponge and gently scrub the ink, and then wipe clean with a damp cloth.

LINT

- **Bounce.** Use a clean, used sheet of Bounce to clean off the lint filter in the dryer. The lint will cling to the Bounce sheet.

- **Heinz White Vinegar.** To prevent lint in the dryer, add one-quarter cup Heinz White Vinegar in the final rinse of the washing machine.

- **L'eggs Sheer Energy Panty Hose.** When drying clothes covered with lint, toss a clean, used pair of L'eggs Sheer Energy Panty Hose into the dryer along with the linty clothes. The nylon works like a magnet, attracting all the lint.

- **ReaLemon.** To prevent lint in the dryer, add one-quarter cup ReaLemon lemon juice in the final rinse cycle of the washing machine.

MOVING

- **Pam Cooking Spray.** To move a dryer on a vinyl, linoleum, or tile floor so you can clean behind it, spray the floor in front of the dryer with a small amount of Pam Cooking Spray so it glides easily.

SCUFFMARKS

- **Mr. Clean Magic Eraser.** To clean scuffmarks on the inside of a dryer drum, rub the marks with a damp Mr. Clean Magic Eraser.

STATIC CLING

- **Heinz White Vinegar.** To prevent static cling in the dryer, add one-quarter cup Heinz White Vinegar in the final rinse of the washing machine.

- **Reynolds Wrap.** To reduce static cling in your dryer, crumple up a ball of Reynolds Wrap aluminum foil and place it in the dryer with the clothes as they tumble dry.

TAR

- **Miracle Whip.** To clean tar from the dryer drum, rub Miracle Whip on the tar, let sit for fifteen minutes, and wipe clean with a soft cloth. Repeat if necessary.

- **Pam Cooking Spray.** Spray Pam Cooking Spray on tar stuck to the inside of the dryer drum, let sit for fifteen minutes, and wipe clean with a soft cloth.

TISSUE

- **L'eggs Sheer Energy Panty Hose.** If you accidentally ran a tissue through the washing machine and now all the clothes are covered with small pieces of tissue paper, toss a clean, used pair of L'eggs Sheer Energy Panty Hose into the dryer along with the tissue-covered clothes. The nylon works like a magnet, attracting all the tissue pieces.

Dusting

Acrylic Furniture

- **Bounce.** Wipe acrylic furniture with a clean, used sheet of Bounce. The antistatic elements in Bounce help eliminate the static electricity that attracts dust.

Air Freshening

- **Glade Air Freshener.** To dust and deodorize your home simultaneously, spray your dust rag with Glade Air Freshener.

Artificial Flowers

- **Morton Salt.** To clean dust from silk or polyester flowers, place the artificial flowers in a larger paper grocery store bag, add one-quarter cup

Morton Salt, fold the top of the bag closed, and shake the bag vigorously. Open the bag and shake any remaining salt off the flowers.

- **Pledge.** To clean dust off polyester flowers, saturate a sponge with Pledge furniture polish and wipe the flower petals and leaves.

- **Windex.** To clean dust off polyester flowers, spray the flower petals and leaves with Windex and wipe with a soft, clean cloth.

BLINDS

- **Bounce.** Wipe the dust from blinds with a clean, used sheet of Bounce. The antistatic elements in Bounce prevent the dust from resettling as quickly. (For more ways to clean dust from blinds, see page 80.)

CARVINGS

- **Oral-B Toothbrush.** To clean the carvings on furniture, spray an Oral-B Toothbrush with your regular furniture polish and brush out the dust.

CEILING FANS

- **Pledge.** To make dusting wood ceiling fan blades easier, give the blades a coat of Pledge furniture polish and buff with a soft, clean cloth.

COBWEBS

- **L'eggs Sheer Energy Panty Hose** and **Wilson Tennis Balls.** To get rid of cobwebs, cut off one leg from a pair of clean, old L'eggs Sheer Energy Panty Hose, insert a Wilson Tennis Ball into the foot, and toss the tennis ball with a nylon tail at the cobweb.

- ***USA Today.*** To eliminate cobwebs, roll up a section of *USA Today* lengthwise and secure with rubber bands. Using scissors, cut fringes two inches into one end, then use the rolled-up newspaper as a duster.

CRYSTAL CHANDELIERS

- **Mrs. Stewart's Liquid Bluing.** A few drops of Mrs. Stewart's Liquid Bluing in the rinse water makes fine crystal sparkle. The bluing purportedly repels dust particles so the crystal stays clean longer.

DASHBOARDS

- **Bounce.** Shine the dashboard of a car with a clean, used sheet of Bounce. The antistatic elements in Bounce will help repel dust from the dashboard and prevent it from settling.

DRAWERS

- **L'eggs Sheer Energy Panty Hose.** To dust drawers, cut off a piece of clean, old pair of L'eggs Sheer Energy Panty Hose, cover the nozzle of your vacuum cleaner attachment with the piece of nylon, hold in place with rubber bands, and vacuum the drawers. This way, you can vacuum dust and debris from the inside of the drawers without accidentally sucking up any small items.

DUST REPELLENT

- **Downy Fabric Softener.** To prevent dust from settling on blinds, refrigerators, and glass-top tables, mix one-half cup Downy Fabric Softener and two cups water in a trigger-spray bottle. Spray the solution on a soft cloth and wipe down the blinds, refrigerator, or glass-top table. Dry with a soft, clean cloth. The antistatic elements in the fabric softener help repel dust.

DUSTBUSTERS

- **Oral-B Toothbrush.** To clean the filter on a Dustbuster and make it last longer, scrub gently with a clean, old Oral-B Toothbrush.

Framed Artwork

- **Bounce.** To collect dust and prevent more dust from settling, polish the glass over paintings and pictures with a clean, used sheet of Bounce.

Glass Tabletops

- **Downy Fabric Softener.** To prevent dust from settling on glass tabletops, mix one-half cup Downy Fabric Softener and two cups water in a trigger-spray bottle. Spray the solution on a soft cloth and wipe the glass tabletop. Dry with a soft, clean cloth. The antistatic elements in the fabric softener help repel dust.

Hard-to-Reach Spots

- **L'eggs Sheer Energy Panty Hose.** To dust hard-to-reach areas, cut off a leg from a pair of clean, old L'eggs Sheer Energy Panty Hose and insert a yardstick into the nylon leg. Slide the nylon-covered yardstick under the refrigerator and through other narrow passages to collect the dust for you.

Houseplants

- **Miracle Whip** and **Bounty Paper Towels.** Using a sheet of Bounty Paper Towels, rub Miracle Whip on houseplant leaves to make them shine and to prevent dust from settling on them. (For more ways to shine leaves on a houseplant, see page 157.)

Knickknacks

- **Conair 1875 Watt Hair Dryer.** To dust knickknacks with ease, blow cool air from a Conair 1875 Watt Hair Dryer at the items to waft away the dust.

Lampshades

- **Bounce.** To prevent a paper lampshade from attracting excessive dust, rub the shade with a clean, used sheet of Bounce. The antistatic elements in the fabric softener sheet remove static electricity, which attracts dust in the first place.

Needlework

- **Johnson's Baby Shampoo.** To clean excessive dirt and grime from needlework, wash in a sink full of water mixed with one teaspoon Johnson's Baby Shampoo. Rinse and let air dry.

Radiators

- **Conair 1875 Watt Hair Dryer.** To dust off a radiator, dampen a towel, wring it out well, and hang it behind the radiator. Aim a Conair 1875 Watt Hair Dryer at the radiator and turn it on cool to blow all the dust into the damp towel.

Shutters

- **Bounce.** To clean plantation shutters, open up the shutters and wipe the louvers from the back side with a clean, used sheet of Bounce. The antistatic elements in the dryer sheet help collect the dust, and the residue will help prevent dust from adhering to the shutters.

Sweeping

- **Aunt Jemima Corn Meal.** To prevent dust clouds while sweeping the floor, toss a handful of Aunt Jemima Corn Meal on the floor before sweeping. The dust sticks to the corn meal, enabling you to sweep up dirt without difficulty.

- **Maxwell House Coffee.** Before sweeping the floor in the garage or workshop, sprinkle used Maxwell House Coffee grounds on the floor as a sweeping compound. Dirt and dust stick to the coffee grounds, making sweeping less of a chore.

Television Screens

- **Bounce.** Wipe a glass television screen and the cabinet with a clean, used sheet of Bounce. The antistatic elements in Bounce help prevent dust from settling on the screen.

- **Downy Fabric Softener.** To prevent dust from settling on a glass television screen, mix two ounces Downy Fabric Softener and one cup water; dampen a soft, clean cloth in the solution; and wipe the screen clean. Buff dry.

Electronic Equipment

CALCULATORS AND CAMERAS

- **Huggies Baby Wipes.** To clean a calculator, wipe the device with a Huggies Baby Wipe.

- **Revlon Red Nail Enamel.** To remind yourself to turn off your calculator or camera flash attachment, paint the off button with Revlon Red Nail Enamel.

CELL PHONES

- **Huggies Baby Wipes.** To clean grime from a cell phone, wipe the device with a Huggies Baby Wipe.

- **Mr. Clean Magic Eraser.** To clean smudge marks from cell phones, cut a half-inch square of the Mr. Clean Magic Eraser, soak it in water, squeeze out the excess liquid, and gently rub the white foam on the dirty surface of the cell phone.

COMPACT DISCS

- **Arm & Hammer Baking Soda.** To clean compact discs, mix two tablespoons Arm & Hammer Baking Soda and two cups water in a sixteen-ounce trigger-spray bottle. Spray the solution on the compact disk and use a soft, clean cloth to wipe outward from the center hole to the outer edge.

- **Colgate Regular Flavor Toothpaste.** To clean scuffmarks from a compact disk and prevent it from skipping, rub a dab of Colgate Regular Flavor Toothpaste on the disk with a clean, soft cloth. Rinse clean with water and dry thoroughly.

- **Con-Tact Paper.** When it comes to organizing homemade videotapes, DVDs, or CDs, decorating home videos, DVDs, or CDs with unique labels made from Con-Tact Paper makes them easy to find.

- **Mr. Coffee Filters.** To clean a compact disc or DVD, wipe and blot dry with a Mr. Coffee Filter, which is lint-free.

COMPUTERS

- **Huggies Baby Wipes.** To clean grime from a computer keyboard, wipe the keyboard with a Huggies Baby Wipe.

- **Mr. Clean Magic Eraser.** To clean grime from the textured plastic parts of a computer monitor, keyboard, and mouse, gently rub the stains with a damp Mr. Clean Magic Eraser.

- **Q-tips Cotton Swabs.** To clean a computer keyboard or the rollers inside a computer mouse, dampen one end of a Q-tips Cotton Swab with water and rub it between the keys or along the small rollers inside a computer mouse.

iPods

- **Mr. Clean Magic Eraser.** To clean smudge marks from an iPod, cut a half-inch square of a Mr. Clean Magic Eraser, soak it in water, squeeze out the excess liquid, and gently rub the white foam on the dirty surface of the iPod.

Telephones

- **Listerine.** Sanitize a telephone receiver by dampening a clean, soft cloth with Listerine antiseptic mouthwash and wiping the receiver.

Televisions

- **Bounce.** Wipe a glass television screen and the cabinet with a clean, used sheet of Bounce. The antistatic elements in Bounce help prevent dust from settling on the screen.
- **Downy Fabric Softener.** To prevent dust from settling on a glass television screen, mix two ounces Downy Fabric Softener and one cup water; dampen a soft, clean cloth in the solution; and wipe the screen clean. Buff dry.
- **Murphy Oil Soap.** To clean a television's plastic casing, pour a few drops of Murphy Oil Soap on a wet, soft, clean cloth and rub the plastic. Buff dry with another soft, clean cloth.

Video Games

- **Bounce.** To clean a handheld video game console (such as a Nintendo Game Boy or PlayStation), wipe the unit with a clean, used sheet of Bounce. The antistatic elements in Bounce help eliminate static electricity from the device.

Fireplaces, Radiators, and Woodstoves

CLEANING

- **Arm & Hammer Super Washing Soda.** Dissolve three-quarters cup Arm & Hammer Super Washing Soda in two gallons hot water, use a scrub brush to apply the solution to the stone walls of a fireplace, and rinse clean.

- **Heinz White Vinegar.** To clean soot from tiles around a fireplace, brush on full-strength Heinz White Vinegar, scrub well, dip a clean cloth in a bucket of water, and rinse and wipe the tiles clean.

GLASS DOORS

- **Easy-Off Oven Cleaner.** To clean the inside of glass fireplace doors, spray the cool doors with Easy-Off Oven Cleaner (making sure the room is well ventilated), let sit for one minute, and (wearing protective rubber gloves) wipe clean. Wash, rinse, and dry.

- **Heinz White Vinegar** and **Parsons' Ammonia.** To clean glass doors on a fireplace, mix one-half cup Heinz White Vinegar, one tablespoon Parsons' Ammonia, and one gallon water in a bucket. Rinse the glass with the solution.

POLISHING

- **Crisco All-Vegetable Shortening.** To polish a woodstove, rub a light coat of Crisco All-Vegetable Shortening on the woodstove and buff with a soft, clean cloth.
- **Pam Cooking Spray.** To polish a woodstove, spray a light coat of Pam Cooking Spray on the woodstove and buff with a soft, clean cloth.
- **Wesson Oil.** To polish a woodstove, rub a light coat of Wesson Oil on the woodstove and buff with a soft, clean cloth.

RADIATORS

- **Conair 1875 Watt Hair Dryer.** To dust off a radiator, dampen a towel, wring it out well, and hang it behind the radiator. Aim a Conair 1875 Watt Hair Dryer at the radiator and turn it on cool to blow all the dust into the damp towel.

SOOT

- **Arm & Hammer Super Washing Soda.** Mix one-half cup Arm & Hammer Super Washing Soda and two gallons hot water in a bucket and scrub the solution into the affected areas. Rinse well.
- **Sanford Art Gum Eraser.** To clean soot from the stonework in front of a fireplace, rub the soot with a Sanford Art Gum Eraser.

HARD TIMES WITH EASY-OFF

In 1932, Herbert McCool worked part time fixing electric stoves and cleaning ovens for an appliance store in Regina, Canada. He began to experiment with different chemicals to create an oven cleaner to make his job easier, ultimately developing a way to make caustic soda stick to the walls of an oven. Delighted with the results and eager to make extra money during the Depression, McCool decided to sell his oven cleaner door to door. He named the product "Easy-Off," referring to the ease with which grease comes off the inside of an oven when you use it. His five-year-old daughter, Shirley, designed the label for Easy-Off, and his wife, Doris, cooked and bottled the oven cleaner in the basement of their home.

When McCool died in 1946, Doris moved to Montreal and continued making Easy-Off, distributed through major stores. In 1954, Doris sold the American rights for Easy-Off to American Home Products.

Today, Reckitt Benckiser owns Easy-Off.

Strange Fact

- In 1987, Professor James Beck, chairman of the art history department at Columbia University, told the *New York Times* that art restorers at the Vatican were removing the final coat of sizing that Michelangelo painted over the fresco on the ceiling of the Sistine Chapel "with a product that works like the oven cleaner Easy-Off."

- **Simple Green.** To clean soot from the firebox, use a broom and dustpan to sweep the ash from the interior of the fireplace. With a wire brush, scrub the creosote deposits from the firebox walls and floor and sweep it away. Spray the firebox walls and floor with clean water (to fill the pores in the brick and stone), apply a solution of one part Simple Green All-Purpose Cleaner to ten parts water, and scrub it into brick or stone hearth and firebox walls and floor. Wipe away the soapy water with a sponge and let dry.

Floors

BROOMS AND MOPS

- **Bubble Wrap** and **Scotch Packaging Tape.** If you have difficulty holding a broom or mop, cut a strip of Bubble Wrap, wrap it around the handle of the broom or mop, and secure in place with a piece of Scotch Packaging Tape, creating a more convenient grip.

- **L'eggs Sheer Energy Panty Hose.** To keep a corn broom tightly bound, cut a four-inch band from one of the legs of a clean, old pair of L'eggs Sheer Energy Panty Hose and slip it like a giant rubber band around the broom bristles about four inches from the end.

- **Morton Salt.** To prolong the life of a broom (made from sorghum, not plastic), dissolve one-half cup Morton Salt in a bucket of hot water and dip the bristles in the solution. The salt water toughens up the bristles so they last longer.

- **Playtex Living Gloves.** To prevent the end of a broom or mop handle from scratching or marking walls, cut off a finger from a clean, used pair of Playtex Living Gloves and slip the finger over the end of the broom or mop handle.

- **Ziploc Freezer Bags.** To shake out a dry mop indoors without making a huge mess, place a Ziploc Freezer Bag over the mop head, seal the bag shut on the mop stick, and shake vigorously. The dust will shake off into the bag, which you can then discard.

CANDLE WAX

- **Bounty Paper Towels.** To remove candle wax from a wooden floor, place a sheet of Bounty Paper Towels over the wax stain and press gently with a warm iron. The heat from the iron melts the wax, and the quicker-picker-upper absorbs it.

- **Conair 1875 Watt Hair Dryer** and **Bounty Paper Towels.** To clean candle wax from a wood floor, heat the wax with a Conair 1875 Watt Hair Dryer and then wipe clean with Bounty Paper Towels.

- **Hidden Valley Original Ranch Dressing.** To remove candle wax from a wood floor, rub a dollop of Hidden Valley Original Ranch Dressing into the wax.

- **Nivea Creme.** To remove candle wax from a wooden floor, rub a dollop of Nivea Creme on the wax.

CERAMIC TILE

- **Arm & Hammer Super Washing Soda.** In a bucket, mix one-quarter cup Arm & Hammer Super Washing Soda and two gallons water. Mop the floor with the solution as usual.

- **Bon Ami.** To clean grout and tile, sprinkle Bon Ami on the grout and scrub with a wet sponge.

- **Canada Dry Club Soda.** Mop the floor with Canada Dry Club Soda and buff dry with a soft, clean cloth. The effervescent action of the club soda cleans the floor.

- **Murphy Oil Soap** and **Heinz White Vinegar.** Pour one ounce Murphy Oil Soap and one-half cup Heinz White Vinegar in a bucket, and then add two gallons warm water. Mix well. Using the solution, mop the floor as usual.

- **Parsons' Ammonia** and **20 Mule Team Borax.** To clean tile, mix two tablespoons Parsons' Ammonia, one tablespoon 20 Mule Team Borax, and one gallon warm water in a bucket. Use a rag mop to clean the floor with the solution.

- **20 Mule Team Borax.** To disinfect a tile floor, pour one-half cup 20 Mule Team Borax in a bucket, add two gallons warm water, mix well, and mop as usual.

Gum

- **Conair 1875 Watt Hair Dryer** and **MasterCard.** To remove a piece of chewing gum from a sealed wood floor or ceramic tile, aim a Conair 1875 Watt Hair Dryer set on warm at the chewing gum to warm it up and scrape the gum off the floor with an old MasterCard.

- **Skippy Peanut Butter.** Rub a dollop of Skippy Peanut Butter into the gum, let sit for five minutes, then scrape clean. The oils in the peanut butter dissolve the gum.

- **Vaseline Petroleum Jelly.** Rub a dab of Vaseline Petroleum Jelly into the gum, which will then rub off in little balls.

Knee Pads

- **Bubble Wrap** and **Scotch Packaging Tape.** Make knee pads for scrubbing the floor by simply rolling up two foot-long sheets of Bubble

Wrap. Use Scotch Packaging Tape to adhere the air-cushioning material to the front of each knee.

- **L'eggs Sheer Energy Panty Hose.** Cut off the legs from a pair of clean, used L'eggs Sheer Energy Panty Hose; stuff them with foam rubber, old sponges, rags, crumpled-up newspaper, or Bubble Wrap; and tie the ends to create handy kneeling pads.

- **Scotch-Brite Heavy Duty Scrub Sponge.** Sew pockets onto the knees of an old pair of pants and slip Scotch-Brite Heavy Duty Scrub Sponges inside to make excellent knee pads.

- **Stayfree Maxi Pads.** Peel the adhesive strips from the backs of two Stayfree Maxi Pads and stick the pads to your knees.

KOOL-AID STAINS

- **Heinz White Vinegar** and **Hydrogen Peroxide.** To clean a Kool-Aid stain from a vinyl floor, apply equal parts Heinz White Vinegar and water, let sit for five minutes, wipe clean, and apply Hydrogen Peroxide. Rinse clean with water.

SCRATCHES

- **Crayola Crayons.** To fill an unsightly scratch in a wood floor, rub a matching Crayola Crayon into the scratch, warm the wax with a blow dryer, and buff with a rag.

- **Kiwi Shoe Polish.** To touch up a scratch in a wood floor, stain the scratched wood with Kiwi Shoe Polish in a matching color and buff.

SCUFFMARKS

- **Arm & Hammer Baking Soda.** To clean scuffmarks from floors, sprinkle Arm & Hammer Baking Soda on a damp sponge and rub the spots.

- **Bon Ami.** To clean scuffmarks from floors, sprinkle Bon Ami on a damp cloth or sponge and gently rub the spots clean.

- **Colgate Regular Flavor Toothpaste.** To clean scuffmarks from vinyl, linoleum, or tile floors, squeeze a dab of Colgate Regular Flavor Toothpaste on a damp, clean, soft cloth, and rub. Clean with a clean, wet cloth.

- **Johnson's Baby Oil.** To remove a scuffmark from the floor, pour a drop of Johnson's Baby Oil on the mark and rub with a soft, clean cloth. Wash the spot with soapy water, rinse, and dry.

- **Mr. Clean Magic Eraser.** To clean scuffmarks from floors, gently rub the scuffmarks with a damp Mr. Clean Magic Eraser.

- **Sanford Art Gum Eraser.** Clean scuffmarks off vinyl, linoleum, or ceramic tile floors by rubbing the marks with a Sanford Art Gum Eraser.

- **Vaseline Petroleum Jelly.** Wipe scuffmarks from the floor by covering the spots with a dab of Vaseline Petroleum Jelly and then rubbing with a soft, clean cloth. Wash the spots with soapy water, rinse, and dry.

- **Wilson Tennis Balls.** Rub the scuffmarks with a Wilson Tennis Ball, which erases them like magic. If you don't want to get down on your hands and knees, carefully cut an X in the tennis ball, unscrew the broomstick from a broom, and insert one end of the broomstick into the X. Then use the tennis ball on the end of the broom stick like a giant pencil eraser on the scuffmarks.

SOAP RESIDUE

- **Heinz White Vinegar** and **Old English Lemon Oil.** To clean soap residue and simultaneously brighten a dull hardwood floor, mix one-half cup Heinz White Vinegar, two tablespoons Old English Lemon Oil, and one gallon warm water in a bucket. Mop the floor with the solution and let dry.

SWEEPING

- **Aunt Jemima Corn Meal.** To prevent dust clouds while sweeping the floor, toss a handful of Aunt Jemima Corn Meal on the floor before sweeping. The dust sticks to the corn meal, enabling you to sweep up dirt without difficulty.

TAR

- **Blue Bonnet Margarine.** To clean tar from a vinyl floor, scrape off as much tar as possible without damaging the floor and rub Blue Bonnet Margarine into the remaining tar stain. Scrape gently and wipe clean with a soft, dry cloth.

VINYL AND LINOLEUM FLOORS

- **Arm & Hammer Super Washing Soda.** To mop an unwaxed floor, mix one-quarter cup Arm & Hammer Super Washing Soda and two gallons water in a bucket. Mop the floor with the solution as usual. (Do not use this mixture on a waxed floor.)
- **Canada Dry Club Soda.** Mop the floor with Canada Dry Club Soda and buff dry with a soft, clean cloth.
- **Downy Fabric Softener.** To give a waxed floor a healthy shine, mix one cup Downy Fabric Softener and one gallon hot water in a bucket and mop the floor with the solution.
- **Heinz White Vinegar.** Mop vinyl floors with one-half cup Heinz White Vinegar mixed in one gallon warm water.

- **Kingsford's Corn Starch** and **Murphy Oil Soap.** Mix one cup Kingsford's Corn Starch, one teaspoon Murphy Oil Soap, and one cup water in a bowl to make a paste. Using a sponge, shine a linoleum floor with the paste. Rinse well and buff dry.

Keep It Clean
THE LOW-DOWN ON WOOD FLOORS

- To maintain a wood floor, simply sweep the floor with a soft bristle broom and vacuum dust and dirt from beveled edges with a soft floor attachment. Clean the floors from time to time with a professional wood-floor cleaning product.

- Do not clean wood floors with products made for vinyl or tile floors.

- Placing throw rugs inside and outside doorways helps avoid tracking in grit, dirt, and other debris that might scratch the wood floors.

- Never wet-mop a wood floor. Standing water can dull the finish, damage the wood, and leave a discoloring residue.

- Wipe up spills immediately with a soft, clean cloth.

- Do not over-wax a wood floor. If the floor seems dull, buff the floor to shine the wax coating.

- To avoid wax buildup on light traffic areas and under furniture, wax these spots every other time you wax the floor.

- To prevent table and chair legs from scratching wood floors, adhere felt pads under each leg.

- Avoid walking on wood floors with cleats, sports shoes, or high heels, which can easily dent the floor.

- **Murphy Oil Soap.** Wash linoleum floors with a mop dampened in a soapy solution made from one teaspoon Murphy Oil Soap and a bucket of warm water. Rinse well, mop up excess water, and let air dry. For an even better shine, see previous tip.

- Never slide heavy wood furniture across a wood floor. Lift it up, carry it across the floor, and place it down gently.

- To protect wood flooring in the kitchen, place an area rug in front of the kitchen sink.

- To prevent heat from shrinking the planks in your wood floor during the winter months, use a humidifier to fill the air with moisture and minimize wood movement and shrinkage.

- To maintain polyurethane or other surface finish on a wood floor, simply dust-mop, sweep, or vacuum the floor regularly.

- Never wax a surface-finished floor. When cleaning no longer restores the shine on a polyurethane or other surface finish on a wood floor, recoat the floor with the surface finish.

- To maintain a wax or penetrating-stain finish, dustmop or vacuum regularly and use a buffer to revive the shine. If buffing no longer restores shine, you may need to rewax with a cleaner and liquid wax specifically for wood floors. A properly maintained wood floor usually requires waxing once or twice a year.

- To clean a discolored or soiled wax finish, use a combination non-water-based liquid cleaner/wax made specifically for wood flooring. Spread the product with a cloth and rub gently to remove grime and old wax. Wipe the floor clean, let it dry for twenty minutes, and then buff thoroughly.

- Rub scuff marks from wood floors with an art-gum eraser. Fill dents with clear nail polish.

- **Murphy Oil Soap** and **Heinz White Vinegar.** Pour one ounce Murphy Oil Soap and one-half cup Heinz White Vinegar in a bucket, and then add two gallons warm water. Mix well. Using the solution, mop the floor as usual.

- **ReaLemon.** After washing linoleum floors, mix three tablespoons ReaLemon lemon juice and one quart water and rinse the floor with the lemony solution to give it a glossy finish.

- **20 Mule Team Borax.** To clean and disinfect the floor, dissolve one tablespoon 20 Mule Team Borax in one gallon warm water in a bucket. Dampen a mop with the solution, wash the floor, and let dry.

WATER SPOTS

- **Colgate Regular Flavor Toothpaste.** To remove white water spots from a penetrating-sealed wood floor, squeeze a dab of Colgate Regular Flavor Toothpaste on a damp, clean, soft cloth and rub the spot until the white mark disappears.

- **Hidden Valley Original Ranch Dressing.** To remove white water spots from a penetrating-sealed wood floor, wipe on Hidden Valley Original Ranch Dressing, let stand for an hour, and wipe off.

- **Kraft Mayo.** To eliminate a white water spot from a penetrating-sealed wood floor, rub Kraft Mayo into the mark and let sit overnight. In the morning, wipe clean.

- **Vaseline Petroleum Jelly.** To eradicate a white water spot from a penetrating-sealed wood floor, rub Vaseline Petroleum Jelly into the spot, let it sit for twenty-four hours, and wipe clean.

WAX

- **Arm & Hammer Super Washing Soda** and **Heinz White Vinegar.** To remove wax from a floor, mix Arm & Hammer Super Washing Soda and water, cover the floor with a thick coat of the solution, let dry, and scrub clean. Rinse clean with one-quarter cup Heinz White Vinegar mixed in a bucket of water.

- **Bounty Paper Towels.** To remove excess wax buildup from floors, place a sheet of Bounty Paper Towels over the wax buildup and press gently with a warm iron. The heat from the iron melts the wax, and the quicker-picker-upper absorbs it.

WOOD FLOORS

- **Johnson's Baby Powder.** To eliminate squeaks in floorboards, sprinkle Johnson's Baby Powder into the cracks between the floorboards.
- **Kiwi Brown Shoe Polish.** To rejuvenate worn areas of a hardwood floor, mix Kiwi Brown Shoe Polish with your regular floor wax.
- **Lipton Tea Bags.** Brew two Lipton Tea Bags in one quart boiling water and let cool to room temperature. Dampen a soft, clean cloth in the tea, wring out well, and wipe the wood floor, barely dampening it and keeping the cloth clean. Buff dry with a soft cloth.
- **Reynolds Cut-Rite Wax Paper.** To shine up a dull spot on a wood floor with a finished surface, rub the spot with a sheet of Reynolds Cut-Rite Wax Paper.

YELLOWING

- **Parsons' Ammonia** and **Spic and Span.** To clean yellowing wax from a vinyl floor, mix one cup Parsons' Ammonia, one-quarter cup Spic and Span, and one-half gallon water in a bucket. Apply the solution to a three-foot-square area, let sit for five minutes, and rinse clean. Repeat to finish the entire floor.

Flowers

ARTIFICIAL FLOWERS

- **Morton Salt.** To clean dust from silk or polyester flowers, place the artificial flowers in a large, paper, grocery store bag, add one-quarter cup Morton Salt, fold the top of the bag closed, and shake the bag vigorously. Open the bag and shake any remaining salt off the flowers.
- **Pledge.** To clean dust off polyester flowers, saturate a sponge with Pledge furniture polish and wipe the flower petals and leaves.
- **Windex.** To clean dust off polyester flowers, spray the flower petals and leaves with Windex and wipe with a soft, clean cloth.

FLOWER POTS

- **Mr. Coffee Filters.** Before planting flowers in a pot, cover the drainage hole by inserting a stack of three Mr. Coffee Filters in the bottom of the pot, and then cover the coffee filters with a one-inch thick layer of pebbles. The coffee filter will prevent dirt from leaking out of the pot.

PROLONGING

- **Alberto VO5 Hair Spray.** Just before cut flowers are about to wilt, make the flowers last longer by spraying the flowers with a fine mist of Alberto VO5 Hair Spray.

- **Ivory Dishwashing Liquid.** To revive wilted flowers in a vase, add one teaspoon Ivory Dishwashing Liquid to the water.

- **Listerine.** To prolong the life of freshly cut flowers, add three-quarters teaspoon Listerine antiseptic mouthwash for each cup of water in the vase. The antiseptic kills any bacteria in the water.

- **ReaLemon, Domino Sugar,** and **Clorox Bleach.** To prolong the life of freshly cut flowers, mix two tablespoons ReaLemon lemon juice, one tablespoon Domino Sugar, one-half teaspoon Clorox Bleach, and one quart water, pour the solution into a vase, and add the flowers.

- **Sprite.** To prolong the life of fresh flowers in a vase, pour a can of Sprite into the vase and fill the rest with water.

STEMS

- **Glad Flexible Straws.** To lengthen stems of flowers that you accidentally cut too short, insert the end of the stem into a Glad Flexible Straw.

- **Scotch Transparent Tape.** To keep flowers standing upright in a vase, tape pieces of Scotch Transparent Tape in a crisscross over the mouth the of the vase and insert the flower stems through openings.

VASES

- **Cascade.** To clean the filth from the inside of a vase, fill the vase with water, add one teaspoon Cascade Gel, shake well, and let sit overnight. In the morning, rinse clean.

- **Efferdent.** To clean the gunk from the inside of a flower vase, fill the vase with warm water and drop in two Efferdent denture cleansing tablets. Let sit overnight, wash, and rinse clean.

- **Heinz White Vinegar.** To clean mineral deposits from glass vases, fill the sink with equal parts Heinz White Vinegar and water and soak the vases in the solution. Rinse clean.

- **Lipton Tea Bags.** To clean stains from the inside of a vase, brew three Lipton Tea Bags into a strong pot of tea, let cool, pour inside the vase, and let sit overnight. In the morning, rinse clean. The tannic acid in the tea cleans the gunk off the vase.

- **Morton Salt.** Pour one-quarter cup Morton Salt into the empty vase, fill the vase with ice cubes, and swirl the vase so that the ice cubes whirl around inside it, scrubbing the stains with the abrasive salt.

- **Nestea Iced Tea Mix.** To clean dirt and grime from inside a vase, fill the vase with water, add three table-spoons Nestea Iced Tea Mix, shake well, and let sit overnight. In the morning, rinse clean. The tannic acid in the tea dissolves the grunge in the vase.

- **Parsons' Ammonia.** To clean a vase, fill it with hot water, add one teaspoon Parsons' Ammonia, let sit for fifteen minutes, and rinse well. The ammonia loosens the grime.

- **Uncle Ben's Original Converted Brand Rice** and **Heinz White Vinegar.** To clean out a dirty vase, pour in one-half cup Uncle Ben's Original Converted Brand Rice and one-half cup Heinz White Vinegar. Put the palm of your hand flat against the neck of the vase and shake vigorously, allowing the rice to scrape against the inside walls of the vase. Wash and rinse clean.

Food

BREAD BAGS

- **Forster Clothespins.** To seal an open bread bag, use a Forster Clothespin to clip the bag closed.

BROWN SUGAR

- **Wonder Bread.** To revive a box of hardened brown sugar, empty the brown sugar into a plastic container, place a slice or two of Wonder Bread on top of the sugar, seal the lid on the container, and let sit for two or three weeks. The bread absorbs the excess moisture from the brown sugar.

BROWNIES

- **Mr. Coffee Filters.** To separate brownies and prevent a sticky mess, place Mr. Coffee Filters between layers of brownies when serving on a plate to keep the layers from sticking to each other.

CABBAGE AND CAULIFLOWER ODORS

- **Heinz White Vinegar.** To eliminate the odor created by cooking cabbage or cauliflower, set a glass half-filled with Heinz White Vinegar on the kitchen counter.

- **Wonder Bread.** To prevent cooked cabbage or cauliflower from exuding a foul odor, place a slice of stale Wonder Bread on top of the cabbage or cauliflower to absorb the odor, and when finished cooking, discard the soggy bread.

CAKES

- **Domino Sugar.** To prevent Bundt cakes from sticking to the pan and making a mess to clean, after greasing the pan with shortening, sprinkle the shortening with Domino Sugar. After baking, let the cake cool for ten minutes and remove it from the pan.

- **Oral-B Dental Floss.** To cut clean slices of cake and avoid mussing up a knife, hold a strand of Oral-B Dental Floss as if you were going to floss your teeth and cut through the cake.

- **Pam Cooking Spray.** To prevent Saran Wrap from sticking to a cake, spray the underside of the plastic wrap with a thin coat of Pam Cooking Spray before covering the cake.

- **Reynolds Cut-Rite Wax Paper.** To avoid greasing a cake pan, place each pan on a sheet of Reynolds Cut-Rite Wax Paper, trace around the bottom of the pan, cut out the wax paper circle, and place it in the pan. After baking and cooling, loosen the sides of the cake with a knife. Invert the cake onto a cooling rack, remove the pan, and peel off the wax paper for a smooth surface that's ready to frost.

- **Ziploc Storage Bags.** To pipe icing on a cake, fill a pint-size Ziploc Storage Bag with icing, twist the bag to force icing to one corner, seal, and use scissors to snip a small bit off the corner. Squeeze out icing to make polka dots or squiggles or write names. Use a separate bag for each color.

- **Ziploc Storage Bags.** To mix cake batter and avoid dirtying a bowl, fill a gallon-size Ziploc Storage Bag with cake batter ingredients, and then squeeze the bag to mix.

Celery

- **Reynolds Wrap.** To prolong the shelf life of celery for weeks and prevent a slimy mess in your refrigerator vegetable drawer, wrap the celery in Reynolds Wrap aluminum foil when storing it in the refrigerator.

Cheese

- **Heinz White Vinegar** and **Bounty Paper Towels.** To prolong the shelf life of cheese and prevent a moldy mess, saturate a sheet of Bounty Paper Towels with Heinz White Vinegar, wring it out, and place the towel and cheese together in an airtight container.

- **Oral-B Dental Floss.** To cut cheese into neat slices without mussing up a knife, hold a strand of Oral-B Dental Floss as if you were going to floss your teeth and cut through the cheese.

Chocolate

- **Ziploc Storage Bag.** To decorate cookies and cakes with melted chocolate without making a mess, fill a Ziploc Storage Bag with chocolate chips, seal the bag shut, and place it in a pot of boiling water to melt the chocolate. Snip one corner, and you have the perfect decorating tool.

Cookies

- **Oral-B Dental Floss.** To lift cookies from a cookie sheet without making a mess, slide a strand of Oral-B Dental Floss between fresh baked cookies and the cookie sheet.

- **Reynolds Cut-Rite Waxed Paper** and **Scotch Transparent Tape.** To make your own cookie dough roll, place your homemade cookie dough on a sheet of Reynolds Cut-Rite Waxed Paper, roll up the paper, seal the ends with Scotch Transparent Tape, and freeze or refrigerate.

- **Ziploc Storage Bags** and **Wonder Bread.** To soften cookies that have lost their moistness, place the cookies in a Ziploc Storage Bag along with a slice of Wonder Bread, seal the bag, and let sit overnight. In the morning, the cookies will be moist again.

Corn

- **Bounty Paper Towels.** To remove the silk from an ear of corn neatly, shuck the ear of corn, and then wipe it in a single stroke from top to bottom with a dampened sheet of Bounty Paper Towels.
- **L'eggs Sheer Energy Panty Hose.** To quickly remove the silk from an ear of corn, rub the ear with a balled-up pair of clean, old L'eggs Sheer Energy Panty Hose.
- **Reynolds Cut-Rite Wax Paper.** To cook corn in a microwave oven and avoid having to wash a pot, wrap the ear of corn in a sheet of Reynolds Cut-Rite Wax Paper, twist the ends, and microwave for two minutes.

Corn Syrup

- **Pam Cooking Spray.** When a recipe calls for corn syrup, spray your utensils and measuring cups with Pam Cooking Spray to make cleanup trouble-free.

Cupcakes

- **Pam Cooking Spray.** To prevent paper liners from sticking to cupcakes, spray the inside of the liners with Pam Cooking Spray before filling them with cupcake batter.

Deviled Eggs

- **Ziploc Storage Bags.** To fill deviled eggs without making a mess, put the ingredients for deviled eggs in a Ziploc Storage Bag, cut a corner off the bag, and fill the eggs.

DOUGH

- **Kingsford's Corn Starch.** To prevent pastry dough from sticking to the cutting board and rolling pin, sprinkle the cutting board and rolling pin with tasteless Kingsford's Corn Starch before rolling out the dough.

- **Oral-B Dental Floss.** To cut cookie or bun roll dough into neat slices and avoid making a mess with a knife, slide a strand of Oral-B Dental Floss under the roll, cross the two ends over the top of the roll, and pull.

- **Pam Cooking Spray.** To prevent pastry dough from sticking to the cutting board and rolling pin, spray the surface with a light coat of Pam Cooking Spray.

Keep It Clean
AVOIDING A STICKY MESS

To prevent food from sticking to a stainless-steel pan, follow these simple proper cooking techniques:

- Let foods come to room temperature before cooking. Tossing eggs directly from the refrigerator into a heated pan causes them to stick. Instead, let the chilled food sit at room temperature for ten to fifteen minutes before placing them in a heated pan.

- Preheat the pan gradually. Don't be tempted to preheat the pan on high temperatures to speed things along. Instead, preheat the pan on low to medium temperature setting.

- Add oil or butter. Add a small amount of oil, butter, or margarine to the pan, and heat it for one minute before adding food.

- Never use aerosol cooking sprays. They leave a gummy residue that is difficult to remove and causes food to stick to the pan.

EGGS

- **Crayola Crayons.** To differentiate hard-boiled eggs from raw eggs in the refrigerator and avoid making a messy mistake, mark the hard-boiled eggs with a Crayola Crayon.

- **McCormick Food Coloring.** To tell the difference between hard-boiled eggs and raw eggs in the refrigerator, add a few drops of McCormick Food Coloring (blue, red, or green) to the water when boiling the eggs to tint them.

- **Morton Salt.** If you accidentally drop an egg on the kitchen floor, cover the spill with Morton Salt. The salt absorbs the egg, allowing you to pick up the mess with a sheet of paper towel.

- **Wesson Oil.** To shell hard-boiled eggs neatly and easily, add two tablespoons Wesson Oil in the water when boiling.

FISH

- **Colgate Regular Flavor Toothpaste.** To clean the smell of fish from your hands, squeeze a dollop of Colgate Regular Flavor Toothpaste into the palm of your hand, rub your hands together under running water, and rinse clean.

- **Colman's Mustard Powder.** To deodorize any cookware or countertop that smells like fish, mix two tablespoons Colman's Mustard Powder and one-half cup water, wash the affected item or area in the solution, and then rinse clean and dry.

- **Heinz White Vinegar.** To deodorize fish, soak the fish in a mixture of equal parts Heinz White Vinegar and water for a few minutes. This gets rid of the fishy odor—without affecting the fish flavor.

- **Listerine.** To clean the smell of fish from your hands, rub one teaspoon Listerine antiseptic mouthwash between your hands, and then wash with soap and water. The antiseptic kills the fish odor.

- **Maxwell House Coffee.** To deodorize your hands from smelling from fish, fill your palm with Maxwell House Coffee grounds (used or unused), add water if using fresh grounds, rub your hands together for one minute, then rinse with running water.

- **ReaLemon.** Rubbing your hands with ReaLemon lemon juice removes the smell of fish. Simply pour a little lemon juice into the palm of your hand and rub your hands together.

- **Skippy Peanut Butter.** To avoid the foul odor when frying fish, put a teaspoon of Skippy Peanut Butter in the pan while you're frying the fish.

FLOUR

- **McCormick Bay Leaves.** To keep insects out of your flour canister, place a McCormick Bay Leaf in the flour. The smell of bay leaves repulses insects.

- **Wrigley's Doublemint Gum.** To keep weevils out of flour, place a stick of Wrigley's Doublemint Gum in your flour canister. Weevils, repulsed by mint, stay out of the flour, and the gum does not flavor the flour.

- **Ziploc Storage Bags.** To avoid having to clean your flour sifter after every use, keep the flour sifter in a Ziploc Storage Bag.

FROZEN FOOD

- **Forster Clothespins.** To seal open bags of frozen food and prevent the contents from spilling all over your freezer, use a Forster Clothespin to clip bags of frozen vegetables closed.

FRUIT AND VEGETABLES

- **Arm & Hammer Baking Soda.** To clean pesticides and insects from fruits and vegetables, wet the fruits and vegetables, sprinkle them with a little Arm & Hammer Baking Soda, and then rinse well.

- **Bounty Paper Towels.** To keep vegetables and fruit fresh in the refrigerator and prevent a soggy mess, line the bottom of the fruit and vegetable bin in your refrigerator with Bounty Paper Towels to absorb the excess moisture.

- **Clorox Bleach.** To clean pesticides and insects from fruits and vegetables, add one-half cup Clorox Bleach in a sink filled with enough water to cover the fruit and vegetables. Let soak for ten minutes, and then rinse clean. The chlorine bleach kills lingering bugs.

- **Heinz White Vinegar.** To wash sprays and chemicals from store-bought vegetables, fill your kitchen sink with cold water and add three-quarters cup Heinz White Vinegar. Soak the fruits and vegetables in the water for ten minutes and wipe them with a clean sponge to loosen any residue. Rinse clean with cold water.

GARLIC

- **Colgate Regular Flavor Toothpaste.** To clean the smell of garlic from your hands, squeeze a dollop of Colgate Regular Flavor Toothpaste into the palm of your hand, rub your hands together under running water, and rinse clean.

- **Forster Toothpicks.** To make a garlic clove easy to handle and avoid getting the smell of garlic on your hands, stick a Forster Toothpick into a clove of garlic before tossing it into a marinade, so you can remove it easily.

- **L'eggs Sheer Energy Panty Hose.** To store garlic cloves, fill the foot of a pair of L'eggs Sheer Energy Panty Hose and hang it high to keep the contents dry.

GINGER

- **Smirnoff Vodka.** To preserve diced, fresh ginger in your refrigerator, peel and chop fresh ginger, put in a jar, and top off with Smirnoff Vodka. The ginger will last up to one year in the refrigerator.

Gloves

- **Ziploc Storage Bags** and **Pam Cooking Spray.** To improvise plastic gloves when spreading sticky foods, put each hand inside its own Ziploc Storage Bag, coat the outside of the bag with Pam Cooking Spray, and spread the messy ingredients.

Honey

- **Pam Cooking Spray.** Before working with honey, spray your utensils and measuring cups with Pam Cooking Spray to make cleaning up the mess afterward much simpler.

Ice Cream Cones

- **Jet-Puffed Marshmallows.** To prevent ice cream cone drips, stuff a Jet-Puffed Marshmallow in the bottom of a sugar cone before adding the scoops of ice cream.
- **Skippy Peanut Butter.** To stop a leak from an ice cream cone, put a teaspoon of Skippy Peanut Butter in the bottom of the cone before adding the ice cream. You not only stop the leaks, but you get a treat at the bottom of the cone.

Jars

- **Playtex Living Gloves.** To unscrew the stubborn lid from a jar, put on a pair of Playtex Living Gloves to improve your grip.

Ketchup

- **Glad Flexible Straws.** To unclog a freshly opened ketchup bottle without making a mess, insert a Glad Flexible Straw all the way into the bottle to add air and start the ketchup flowing.

LEFTOVERS

- **Post-it Notes.** To prevent leftovers from going bad, put Post-it Notes on containers of leftovers in your refrigerator to remind you to eat them by a certain day.

- **Ziploc Storage Bags.** To organize your refrigerator, keep leftovers for single servings in Ziploc Storage Bags for quick meals.

LETTUCE

- **Bounty Paper Towels** and **Ziploc Storage Bags.** To prolong the life of lettuce heads, wrap the lettuce heads in sheets of Bounty Paper Towels, seal in a gallon size Ziploc Storage Bag, and store in the refrigerator. The paper towels absorb excess moisture.

MEASURING

- **Reynolds Cut-Rite Wax Paper.** To avoid getting powder all over your kitchen and to minimize the amount of wasted ingredients when measuring flour, sugar, baking mix, or other dry ingredients, crease a sheet of Reynolds Cut-Rite Wax Paper down the middle, open it up, and place it on the kitchen countertop. Spoon the ingredient into a dry measuring cup and level off with a knife or spatula, letting the excess fall on the wax paper. Pick up the wax paper and pour the excess back in its original canister.

MEATS

- **Heinz White Vinegar.** To kill bacteria in meats, marinate the meat in Heinz White Vinegar, which simultaneously tenderizes the meat. Use one-quarter cup vinegar for a two- to three-pound roast, marinate overnight, and then cook without draining or rinsing the meat. Add herbs to the vinegar when marinating as desired.

- **Saran Wrap.** To avoid making a mess when tenderizing meat with a meat hammer, cover the meat with a piece of Saran Wrap before pounding. The plastic wrap prevents the juice from splattering everywhere.
- **Ziploc Storage Bags.** Use Ziploc Storage Bags to marinate food. The bags allow the marinade to really cover the food, and you only have to turn over the bag (rather than stirring the marinade in a bowl).

MILK

- **Forster Clothespins.** To prevent milk from absorbing odors in the refrigerator, clip the milk carton shut with a Forster Clothespin.

MOLASSES

- **Pam Cooking Spray.** Before working with molasses, spray your utensils and measuring cups with Pam Cooking Spray to make cleaning up the mess afterward much simpler.

NUTS

- **Ziploc Storage Bags.** To chop walnuts, almonds, and pecans without making a huge mess, place the nuts in a Ziploc Storage Bag, roll up the bag to let the excess air escape, seal the bag, and hit it with a meat hammer or a rolling pin.

OIL

- **Mr. Coffee Filters.** To recycle frying oil, line a sieve with a Mr. Coffee Filter to strain oil after deep-fat frying.

ONIONS

- **Colgate Regular Flavor Toothpaste.** To clean the smell of onions from your hands, squeeze a dollop of Colgate Regular Flavor Toothpaste into the palm of your hand, rub your hands together under running water, and rinse clean.

- **L'eggs Sheer Energy Panty Hose.** To store onions, use a pair of scissors to cut off one of the legs from a pair of clean, used L'eggs Sheer Energy Panty Hose, drop an onion into the foot of the leg, tie a knot above the onion, and continue adding onions and tying knots between them. Hang the onion-filled panty hose leg from a hook on the back of a door. When you need an onion, simply cut one off from the bottom.

- **Maxwell House Coffee.** To deodorize your hands from smelling from onions, fill your palm with Maxwell House Coffee grounds (used or unused), add water if using fresh grounds, rub your hands together for one minute, and then rinse with running water.

- **Morton Salt.** To clean the smell of onion from hands, wet your hands, rub a teaspoon of Morton Salt between them, and then wash with soap and water.

- **ReaLemon.** Rubbing your hands with ReaLemon lemon juice removes the smell of onions. Simply pour a little lemon juice into the palm of your hand and rub your hands together.

- **Reynolds Wrap.** To prolong the life of green onions and prevent a mess, wrap each green onion in Reynolds Wrap aluminum foil.

PASTA

- **Pam Cooking Spray.** To prevent pasta from bubbling over in a pot of boiling water, making a starchy mess all over your stove, spray the inside of the pot with Pam Cooking Spray before filling it with water.

PIE

- **Glad Flexible Straws.** To bake a pie without having it boil over, cut a Glad Flexible Straw into three-inch lengths and insert vertically into the piecrust, leaving one end exposed. Bake the pie as directed. The straws allow the steam to escape, preventing the pie from boiling over and making a huge mess.

Plastic Containers

- **Pam Cooking Spray.** To prevent tomato sauce stains on plastic containers, spray the insides of the containers with Pam Cooking Spray before filling the container with any food containing tomatoes. The thin coat of oil prevents the sauce from staining the plastic.
- **USA Today.** To deodorize a plastic food container, stuff the container with crumpled pages from *USA Today*, replace the lid securely, and let sit overnight. Then wash with soapy water.

Potato Chip and Pretzel Bags

- **Forster Clothespins.** To seal open bags of potato chips or pretzels and keep the contents from spilling all over your pantry, use a Forster Clothespin to clip the bags closed.
- **Scotch Packaging Tape.** Seal an open potato chip bag with Scotch Packaging Tape, which adheres and re-adheres.

Potatoes

- **Morton Salt.** To make peeling potatoes a snap and far less messy, dissolve one-half cup Morton Salt in one gallon water and soak the potatoes in the salt water for thirty minutes before peeling.

Recipe Cards

- **Alberto VO5 Hair Spray.** To laminate recipe cards, spray the cards with Alberto VO5 Hair Spray to give them a protective gloss.
- **Forster Clothespins.** To keep a recipe card accessible, clip the recipe card you're using to a cabinet door with a Forster Clothespin to keep it at

eye level and clean. You can also glue or screw the clothespin to a nearby surface to make a permanent holder.

- **Scotch Packaging Tape.** To laminate recipe cards, cover the card with several strips of Scotch Packaging Tape.

- **Scotch Transparent Tape.** To save recipes clipped from magazines or newspapers, simply use Scotch Transparent Tape to attach the clipped recipes to index cards.

SALAD

- **Ziploc Storage Bags.** To toss a salad without making a mess, simply put all of your ingredients in a one-gallon Ziploc Storage Bag, add the dressing, and seal the bag. Shake the bag until the salad is tossed and coated with dressing. Wash the bag with soapy water to reuse it.

SALAD MIX

- **Bounty Paper Towels.** To prevent a mess and prolong the life of salad mix, place a sheet of Bounty Paper Towels in an open bag of salad mix. The paper towel absorbs excess moisture, preventing the lettuce from turning brown as quickly as possible.

SALT

- **Uncle Ben's Original Converted Brand Rice.** To prevent moisture from clumping up salt, add a few grains of uncooked Uncle Ben's Original Converted Brand Rice to the salt shaker to absorb excess moisture.

SAUSAGES

- **Maxwell House Coffee.** To remove the grease from cooked sausage without the messy hassle of blotting the sausages on sheets of paper towel, when the sausage is almost cooked in the pan, mix instant Maxwell House

Coffee in hot water until it dissolves, then add it to the pan. The coffee absorbs all the grease and adds a nice flavor to the sausage.

SHOPPING

- **Forster Clothespins.** To make shopping with coupons easier and more organized, bring a Forster Clothespin to the supermarket when you go shopping and clip it to the shopping cart. When you find an item in the grocery store that you have coupon for, clip the coupon in the Forster clothespin. This way, when you get to the check-out counter, you'll have all your coupons ready.

- **Post-it Notes.** Keep a running grocery list on a Post-it Note stuck to your refrigerator door.

STORAGE

- **Pringles** and **Con-Tact Paper.** To store bread crumbs, flours, sugar, pasta, or biscuits in an airtight container, cover empty Pringles cans with Con-Tact Paper and label.

STRAWBERRIES

- **Glad Flexible Straw.** To remove stems from strawberries without cutting off the entire top and making an unnecessary mess, push one end of a Glad Flexible Straw through the middle bottom of the strawberry. The entire stem will poke through the top in one piece.

- **Mr. Coffee Filters.** To keep unwashed strawberries fresh in the refrigerator and prevent a mess, place the strawberries in a container, place a folded Mr. Coffee Filter on top of the strawberries, secure the lid in place, and store upside-down in the refrigerator. The coffee filter absorbs excess moisture.

SUGAR

- **Gatorade.** A clean, empty, one-gallon Gatorade bottle makes an excellent container for storing sugar.
- **Nabisco Original Premium Saltine Crackers.** To prevent sugar from caking up, put a couple of Nabisco Original Premium Saltine Crackers in the sugar canister. The crackers absorb excess moisture.

TACOS

- **Mr. Coffee Filters.** Mr. Coffee Filters make great holders for messy foods and, when folded in half, fit a taco perfectly.

TEA

- **Forster Clothespins.** To neatly make a pot of tea, clip the strings of several tea bags together with a Forster Clothespin, place the tea bags in the tea pot, and let the clothespin hang over the lip of the pot.

TURKEY

- **Oral-B Dental Floss.** To truss a turkey neatly and efficiently, use durable Oral-B Dental Floss.

WAFFLES

- **Pam Cooking Spray.** To prevent waffles from sticking to a waffle iron, spray Pam Cooking Spray on the grids.

WEIGHING

- **Mr. Coffee Filters.** To weigh chopped foods without making a mess, place the chopped ingredients in a Mr. Coffee Filter on a kitchen scale.

Furniture

ACRYLIC

- **Bounce.** Wipe acrylic furniture with a clean, used sheet of Bounce. The antistatic elements in Bounce help eliminate the static electricity that attracts dust.

BLACK LACQUER

- **Lipton Tea Bags.** To clean black lacquer furniture, brew a strong pot of Lipton Tea, let it cool, dampen a clean, soft cloth in the tea, and rub it on the item. Buff dry with another clean, soft cloth.

- **Turtle Wax.** Polish black lacquer furniture with Turtle Wax, making sure you buff well to remove the excess wax.

Brass

- **Old English Lemon Oil.** To clean a brass headboard, dust and then rub with a soft, clean cloth dampened with Old English Lemon Oil.

Burn Marks

- **Colgate Regular Flavor Toothpaste.** To clean minor burn marks from wood furniture, rub the spot with Colgate Regular Flavor Toothpaste, and then wipe clean with a soft, clean cloth.

Candle Wax

- **Conair 1875 Watt Hair Dryer** and **Bounty Paper Towels.** To clean candle wax from wood furniture, heat the wax with a Conair 1875 Watt Hair Dryer, and then wipe clean with Bounty Paper Towels.

- **Hidden Valley Original Ranch Dressing.** To remove candle wax from wood or Formica furniture, rub a dollop of Hidden Valley Original Ranch Dressing onto the wax.

- **Nivea Creme.** To remove candle wax from furniture, rub a dollop of Nivea Creme on the wax.

Cane

- **Morton Salt** and **Dawn Dishwashing Liquid.** To make droopy cane seats taut again, mix one-quarter cup Morton Salt, one teaspoon Dawn Dishwashing Liquid, and one gallon warm water in a bucket. Using a sponge, wipe down both sides of the cane seats with the salty, soapy solution. Rinse clean with a wet cloth and let dry in the sun.

- **ReaLemon** and **Morton Salt.** To clean cane furniture, mix one-quarter cup ReaLemon lemon juice, one-quarter cup Morton Salt, and one gallon warm water in a bucket. Using a brush, scrub the cane with the solution, let sit for fifteen minutes, and rinse clean.

CARVINGS

- **Oral-B Toothbrush.** To clean the carvings on furniture, spray an Oral-B Toothbrush with your regular furniture polish and brush out the dust from the crevices.

- **Q-tips Cotton Swabs.** To clean nooks and crannies in carved furniture, use a Q-tips Cotton Swab dipped in your favorite furniture polish

CLEANING

- **Dawn Dishwashing Liquid.** To clean grease and grime from dirty wood furniture, mix four drops Dawn Dishwashing Liquid in four cups warm water, dampen a soft, clean cloth in the soapy solution, wring it out well, and wipe down the furniture. Rinse thoroughly and buff dry with a soft, clean cloth.

- **Kingsford's Corn Starch.** To clean dirty wood furniture, dissolve two teaspoons Kingsford's Corn Starch in one cup warm water in a sixteen-ounce trigger-spray bottle. Spray the solution on the wood, let dry, and wipe clean.

- **Murphy Oil Soap** and **Heinz White Vinegar.** To clean grease and dirt from furniture, mix one-half teaspoon Murphy Oil Soap, one-quarter cup Heinz White Vinegar, and one-quarter cup warm water. Saturate a sponge in the solution and scrub the furniture, rinse clean with water, and polish as usual.

DISINFECTING

- **20 Mule Team Borax** and **Murphy Oil Soap.** To disinfect germs from wood furniture, mix one teaspoon 20 Mule Team Borax, one-quarter teaspoon Murphy Oil Soap, and one cup hot water in a sixteen-ounce trigger-spray bottle. Spray on wood furniture, rinse, and dry with a soft, clean cloth.

DRAWERS

- **Ivory Soap.** To make drawers slide open and closed easily, run a bar of Ivory Soap along the runners to lubricate them.

- **Pam Cooking Spray.** Spray the metal or wood runners with Pam Cooking Spray to lubricate the drawers so they glide smoothly.

- **WD-40.** To lubricate drawers, spray the metal runners with WD-40 to give them a light coat.

FABRIC UPHOLSTERY

- **Adolph's Original Meat Tenderizer.** To clean a bloodstain from upholstery, cover the stain with a paste made from Adolph's Original Meat Tenderizer and cool water. Wait twenty minutes and sponge off with cool water. Blot dry. The enzymes in the meat tenderizer break up the proteins in the blood.

- **Bounty Paper Towels.** To remove candle wax from upholstery, place a sheet of Bounty Paper Towels over the wax stain and press gently with a warm iron. The heat from the iron melts the wax, and the quicker-picker-upper absorbs it.

- **Dawn Dishwashing Liquid.** To clean stains from upholstery, use a whisk to whip one-half teaspoon Dawn Dishwashing Liquid in a quart of water in a bowl to create as much foam as possible. With a sponge, rub only the resulting suds into the upholstery. Rinse well, blot, repeat if necessary, and let dry.

- **Kingsford's Corn Starch.** To clean bloodstains from upholstery, make a paste from Kingsford's Corn Starch and water, cover the stain with the paste, and let dry. Brush clean. Repeat if necessary.

- **Morton Salt.** To clean grease stains from upholstery, immediately cover the stain with Morton Salt, let sit for ten minutes, and then brush clean. Salt absorbs grease.

- **Scotchgard Fabric Protector.** To prevent upholstery from stains, spray the upholstery with a coat of Scotchgard Fabric Protector, which causes liquids to bead up on the surface rather than being absorbed.

GLASS TABLETOPS

- **Downy Fabric Softener.** To prevent dust from settling on glass tabletops, mix one-half cup Downy Fabric Softener and two cups water in a trigger-spray bottle. Spray the solution on a soft cloth and wipe the glass tabletop. Dry with a soft, clean cloth. The antistatic elements in the fabric softener help repel dust.

- **Heinz White Vinegar.** To make homemade glass tabletop cleaner, mix equal parts Heinz White Vinegar and water in a trigger-spray bottle.

- **Kingsford's Corn Starch.** To clean a glass tabletop, dissolve one cup Kingsford's Corn Starch in one gallon warm water. Dampen a sponge with the solution, wipe the glass tabletop, and buff dry with a soft, clean lint-free cloth.

- **ReaLemon.** To clean a glass tabletop, saturate a soft, clean rag with ReaLemon lemon juice and rub it on the glass tabletop.

GRAYING WOOD

- **Heinz White Vinegar.** To revitalize wood furniture that has developed a gray film, mix one tablespoon Heinz White Vinegar and one cup water; dampen a soft, clean cloth with the solution; and lightly rub the solution into the wood.

GUM

- **Bounty Paper Towels.** To remove chewing gum from wood furniture, place a sheet of Bounty Paper Towels over the gum and press the paper towel with a warm iron. The heat from the iron melts the gum, and the paper towel allows you to pull it off the furniture gently.

Leather Upholstery

- **Dove White Beauty Bar.** Rub a Dove White Beauty Bar across a mildly damp, soft cloth and rub the cloth on the leather. Wipe dry with a fresh damp cloth and buff with a dry towel. After the leather dries, treat it with a leather conditioner. (For more ways to clean leather furniture, see page 282.)

- **Mr. Clean Magic Eraser.** To clean leather upholstery, saturate a Mr. Clean Magic Eraser with water, squeeze out the excess water, and gently rub the leather.

- **Murphy Oil Soap.** To clean leather upholstery, use a whisk to whip one-quarter cup Murphy Oil Soap and three tablespoons water in a bowl to create as much foam as possible. With a sponge, rub only the resulting foam into the upholstery. Rinse well, blot, and let dry. (For more ways to clean leather, see page 282.)

Mattresses

- **Arm & Hammer Baking Soda.** To freshen a musty mattress, sprinkle Arm & Hammer Baking Soda between the mattress and the box spring and leave it in place. The baking soda absorbs moisture and neutralizes musty odors.

- **Bounce.** To rejuvenate a musty mattress, place a sheet of Bounce under the mattress cover.

- **Canada Dry Club Soda** and **Arm & Hammer Baking Soda.** To clean urine from a mattress, blot up as much liquid as possible, pour Canada Dry Club Soda over the stained area, and immediately blot. Let the spot dry completely, then cover with Arm & Hammer Baking Soda, let sit for one hour, then vacuum up. The baking soda will deodorize the smell of urine.

- **Heinz White Vinegar.** To clean urine from a mattress, blot up the urine, flush several times with lukewarm water, and then apply a mixture

Keep It Clean
GOING TO THE MATTRESSES

■ You need a new mattress if your mattress is more than eight years old, you wake up feeling more tired than when you went to sleep, you feel coils or bumps in the mattress, your mattress looks worn and uneven, or you hear creaks and groans in the mattress.

■ When buying a new mattress, make sure you buy a new box spring as well.

■ Rotating a mattress regularly helps restore its comfort. Otherwise, body indentations, formed when the layers of upholstery padding conform to a person's individual body contours, misshape the mattress.

■ To keep a mattress clean, cover the mattress with a protective mattress pad.

■ To clean a mattress, simply vacuum the mattress with an appropriate vacuum cleaner attachment.

■ To clean a stain on the mattress, use mild soap with cold water and apply lightly. Never saturate a mattress with any liquid and never use cleaning fluid on a mattress. The chemicals could damage the foams inside the mattress and the upholstery.

of equal parts Heinz White Vinegar and cool water. Blot up, rinse, and let dry. The vinegar will deodorize the smell of the urine.

● **Jonny Cat Litter.** To deodorize a musty old mattress, sprinkle a layer of Jonny Cat Litter on top of the mattress, let sit undisturbed for one week, and brush clean. The cat box filler will absorb excess moisture and smells from the mattress.

- **Listerine.** To deodorize the smell of urine from a mattress, apply Listerine antiseptic mouthwash to the affected area and let the antiseptic dry.

- **Massengill Disposable Douche.** To get rid of the smell of urine in a mattress, apply Massengill Disposable Douche to the spot and let dry.

- **Odorzout.** To eliminate odors emanating from a dry urine stain on a mattress, sprinkle Odorzout over the affected area to absorb the odor.

- **Pampers.** Place a Pampers disposable diaper over the stain, sit several heavy books on top of the diaper to keep it pressed flat against the stain, and let sit for one hour. The diaper, filled with superabsorbent polymer flakes, will soak up most of the urine.

- **Spot Shot.** To clean a urine or other liquid stain from a mattress, absorb as much liquid as possible with paper towels, stand the mattress on its side against a wall, and spray the stain with Spot Shot Instant Carpet Stain Remover. (Stand the mattress against the wall to prevent the Spot Shot from being absorbed into the mattress.)

- **20 Mule Team Borax.** To neutralize urine odors in mattresses and mattress covers, dampen the spot with water, rub in 20 Mule Team Borax, let dry, then vacuum or brush clean.

ODORS

- **Bounce.** To deodorize musty odors from old furniture, place a sheet of Bounce in the drawers and cabinets.

- **Dial Soap.** To freshen the air in drawers, place wrapped bars of Dial Soap in dresser drawers.

- **Downy Fabric Softener.** To freshen musty old furniture, dampen a soft, clean cloth with Downy Fabric Softener and rub it on the inside of the shelves, cabinets, and drawers.

- **L'eggs Sheer Energy Panty Hose** and **Jonny Cat Litter.** To deodorize furniture drawers, cut off one foot from a pair of clean, old L'eggs Sheer Energy Panty Hose, fill it with Jonny Cat Litter, tie a knot in the open end, and place the sachet in the drawer. The cat box filler absorbs moistness and foul odors.

- **Wonder Bread** and **Heinz White Vinegar.** To deodorize a musty wooden trunk, dresser, or chest, place a slice of Wonder Bread in a bowl, saturate the bread slice with Heinz White Vinegar, and place the bowl and bread inside the closed trunk, on a  shelf in the closed chest, or in a closed drawer of the dresser. Let sit for twenty-four hours. Repeat if necessary.

PAPER

- **Wesson Oil.** To remove a piece of paper stuck on wood furniture, saturate the paper with Wesson Oil, let sit for five minutes, and peel off.

PET HAIR

- **Bounce.** To remove pet hair from furniture, simply wipe the affected area with a clean, used sheet of Bounce, which works like a magnet, attracting all the hairs.

- **Playtex Living Gloves.** To remove pet hair from furniture, put on a pair of Playtex Living Gloves, fill a bucket halfway with water, dip the gloves in the water, wipe the area affected by the pet hair, and dip the gloves in the water again. The wet rubber attracts the pet hair, and the water in the bucket rinses it off.

- **Scotch Packaging Tape.** Wrap Scotch Packaging Tape around your hand with the sticky-side out and pat the furniture with the tape. The pet hairs will stick to the tape.

Pianos

- **Colgate Regular Flavor Toothpaste.** To clean ivory or plastic piano keys, squeeze a dollop of Colgate Regular Flavor Toothpaste on a damp, soft, clean cloth. Rub the keys and wipe clean.

- **Nestlé Carnation NonFat Dry Milk.** To clean ivory piano keys, make a paste from Nestlé Carnation NonFat Dry Milk and water. Rub the paste on the white keys with a soft, clean cloth, and rinse with a damp, soft, clean cloth.

- **ReaLemon** and **Morton Salt.** To clean ivory piano keys, make a paste from ReaLemon lemon juice and Morton Salt and, using a soft, clean cloth, rub the paste into the keys and wipe clean.

Polish Removing

- **Heinz White Vinegar.** To remove furniture polish, mix equal parts Heinz White Vinegar and water. Dampen a soft, clean cloth with the solution and wipe the polish off the furniture. Buff dry with a soft, clean cloth. The vinear deodorizes the furniture.

- **Kingsford's Corn Starch.** To clean excess furniture polish from wood furniture, sprinkle a little Kingsford's Corn Starch on the furniture and buff with a soft, clean cloth. The corn starch absorbs the superfluous polish, evening out the shine.

- **Q-tips Cotton Swabs.** To clean the nooks and crannies in furniture, use a Q-tips Cotton Swab dipped in your favorite furniture polish.

Polishing

- **Nivea Creme.** To polish wood surfaces, put a dollop of Nivea Creme onto a soft cloth and polish the natural wood.

- **Old English Lemon Oil.** To polish wood furniture, put a few drops of Old English Lemon Oil on a soft, clean cloth and rub the wood gently.

- **Star Olive Oil** and **Heinz White Vinegar.** Mix one cup Star Olive Oil and one-quarter cup Heinz White Vinegar in a trigger-spray bottle. Shake well before each use. Spray on a clean, soft cloth, wipe it into wood furniture, and wipe it off with another soft, clean cloth.

- **Star Olive Oil** and **ReaLemon.** To make an excellent furniture polish, mix two cups Star Olive Oil and one-half cup ReaLemon lemon juice in a sixteen-ounce trigger-spray bottle. Shake well before using. Spray on a clean, soft cloth, wipe it into wood furniture, and wipe it off with another soft, clean cloth.

RESTORING

- **Vaseline Petroleum Jelly.** To rejuvenate dry wood, dab Vaseline Petroleum Jelly on a soft, clean cloth and rub it into the furniture.

SCRATCHES

- **Crayola Crayons.** To fill an unsightly scratch in wood furniture, rub a matching Crayola Crayon into the scratch, warm the wax with a blow dryer, and buff with a rag.

- **Kiwi Shoe Polish.** To cover up a scratch in wood furniture, stain the bare wood with the appropriate color of Kiwi Shoe Polish.

- **Wesson Oil.** To eliminate a scratch or blemish on varnished furniture, pour a few drops of Wesson Oil on a soft, clean cloth and rub the affected spot.

SLIPCOVERS

- **Dawn Dishwashing Liquid.** To clean grease stains from the headrest and arms of slipcovers, rub a few drops of Dawn Dishwashing Liquid into the stains. Launder with cool water and your regular detergent. Dry according to the label instructions.

- **Fels-Naptha Soap.** To clean greasy soiling from slipcovers, lather up a bar of Fels-Naptha Soap and rub the lather into the stains on the arms and headrest. Launder with cool water and your regular detergent. Dry according to the label instructions.

- **Scotchgard Fabric Protector.** To protect clean slipcovers from stains, hang the slipcovers outdoors and mist them with a light coat of Scotchgard Fabric Protector. Scotchgard Fabric Protector prevents spills and stains from soaking into the fabric, so you can blot them up or wipe them off easily.

STICKERS

- **Conair 1875 Watt Hair Dryer.** To remove a sticker from wood furniture, use a Conair 1875 Watt Hair Dryer aimed at the sticker to melt the adhesive backing and peel up the sticker.

- **Johnson's Baby Oil.** To remove a sticker from wood furniture, dampen a cotton ball with Johnson's Baby Oil and rub the sticker until you can pry it loose. Buff with a soft, clean cloth. The mineral oil dissolves the adhesive.

- **Mr. Clean Magic Eraser.** To remove the adhesive residue from price-tag stickers, simply rub the remaining adhesive goo with a damp Mr. Clean Magic Eraser.

- **Wesson Oil.** To remove a sticker from wood furniture, dampen a cotton ball with Wesson Oil and rub the sticker until you can pry it loose. Buff with a soft, clean cloth. The vegetable oil dissolves the adhesive.

STRIPPING

- **Lipton Tea Bags.** To remove old furniture polish and grime from wood furniture, brew two Lipton Tea Bags in one quart boiling water and let cool to room temperature. Dampen a soft, clean cloth in the tea, wring out well, and wipe the furniture, barely dampening it and keeping the cloth clean. Buff dry with a second clean, soft cloth. Apply a new coat of polish if desired.

Vinyl or Plastic Upholstery

- **Arm & Hammer Baking Soda.** To eliminate the smell of vinyl or plastic, make a paste from Arm & Hammer Baking Soda and water, sponge the paste onto the vinyl or plastic upholstery, and scrub. Rinse clean and dry.

- **Balmex.** To clean ink from vinyl upholstery, apply Balmex, wait five minutes, and wipe clean.

- **Heinz White Vinegar** and **Murphy Oil Soap.** To clean vinyl or plastic upholstery, mix one-quarter cup Heinz White Vinegar, one-quarter teaspoon Murphy Oil Soap, and one-quarter cup water in a bowl. Saturate a sponge with the solution and scrub the vinyl or plastic. Rinse and dry.

- **Mr. Clean Magic Eraser.** To clean magic marker, permanent ink, and ballpoint ink from vinyl or plastic, gently rub the stains with a damp Mr. Clean Magic Eraser.

- **Murphy Oil Soap** and **Arm & Hammer Baking Soda.** To clean vinyl or plastic upholstery, mix one teaspoon Murphy Oil Soap, one-quarter cup Arm & Hammer Baking Soda, and one-quarter cup water in a bowl. Using a sponge, wash the vinyl or plastic with the solution, rinse well, and dry with a soft, clean cloth.

- **Nivea Creme.** To clean ink from vinyl upholstery, apply Nivea Creme and wipe clean.

Water Rings

- **Blue Bonnet Margarine.** To remove a white ring from wood furniture, rub Blue Bonnet Margarine into the ring and let sit overnight. In the morning, wipe clean.

- **Colgate Regular Flavor Toothpaste.** To remove a white ring from wood furniture, squeeze a dab of Colgate Regular Flavor Toothpaste on a damp, clean, soft cloth and rub the ring until the white mark disappears like magic.

- **Hidden Valley Original Ranch Dressing.** To remove white rings and spots from wood furniture, wipe on Hidden Valley Original Ranch Dressing, let stand for an hour, and wipe off.

- **Kraft Mayo.** To eliminate a water mark from wood furniture, rub Kraft Mayo into the mark and let sit overnight. In the morning, wipe clean with a soft cloth and buff.

- **Land O Lakes Butter.** To remove a water ring from wood furniture, rub Land O Lakes Butter into the mark and let sit overnight. In the morning, wipe clean.

- **Vaseline Petroleum Jelly.** To eradicate a white ring from wood furniture, rub Vaseline Petroleum Jelly into the ring, let it sit for twenty-four hours, and wipe clean.

- **Wesson Oil** and **Morton Salt.** Make a paste from Wesson Oil and Morton Salt, apply the paste to the water ring, let sit for fifteen minutes, and wipe clean.

WICKER AND RATTAN

- **Morton Salt.** Dissolve one-quarter cup Morton Salt in one gallon warm water. Use a firm brush to scrub the wicker or rattan furniture with the solution. Salt stops wicker and rattan from turning yellow.

Grooming and Beauty

BAD BREATH

- **Arm & Hammer Baking Soda.** Dissolve two teaspoons Arm & Hammer Baking Soda in a glass of warm water and use the solution as a mouthwash. The sodium bicarbonate solution raises the acid level in your mouth, inhibiting bacteria from producing smelly sulfur compounds.

- **Country Time Lemonade.** Put one teaspoon Country Time Lemonade powdered drink mix in your mouth, swish around, and swallow. The citric acid stimulates saliva production, hinders the odor-producing enzymes in your mouth, and makes your breath lemon fresh.

- **Hydrogen Peroxide.** Mix equal parts Hydrogen Peroxide (three percent solution) and water, rinse your mouth with the solution for thirty seconds, and spit out. The Hydrogen Peroxide kills the bacteria that generate odors in your mouth.

- **Lipton Tea Bags.** According to scientists at the College of Dentistry at the University of Illinois in Chicago, compounds in tea, known as polyphenols, can halt the growth of sulphur-producing bacteria in the mouth and inhibit the enzyme that catalyses the formation of smelly hydrogen sulphide. To fight bad breath, drink a cup of tea brewed with a Lipton Tea Bag, or let the tea cool and use it as a mouthwash.

- **McCormick Pure Peppermint Extract.** Mix one tablespoon McCormick Pure Peppermint Extract in one cup water, and gargle with the mixture to leave your breath minty fresh.

BATHING

- **Arm & Hammer Baking Soda.** Give yourself soft, smooth-feeling skin and a relaxing bath by dissolving one-half cup Arm & Hammer Baking Soda in a bathtub filled with warm water.

- **Heinz Apple Cider Vinegar.** Adding one cup Heinz Apple Cider Vinegar—which contains iron, phosphorous, potassium, magnesium, and sodium—to bath water softens skin and helps restore its natural acid balance. Soak for roughly twenty minutes.

- **Nestlé Carnation NonFat Dry Milk.** For a luxurious milk bath worthy of Cleopatra, add a handful of Nestlé Carnation NonFat Dry Milk powder to warm running bath water. The lactic acid in the milk softens the skin, and the proteins in the milk leave the skin feeling silky smooth. Add a second handful if desired.

CHAPPED LIPS

- **Balmex.** Apply a dab of Balmex, the diaper rash ointment that contains aloe and zinc oxide, to your lips to keep them moisturized and nourished, providing a barrier against wetness.

- **Crisco All-Vegetable Shortening.** Moisturize chapped lips with a dab of Crisco All-Vegetable Shortening.

- **Lipton Tea Bag.** Dampen a Lipton Tea Bag with warm water, and press it over clean lips for five minutes. The tannic acid retains moisture and keeps lips smooth and taut.

- **SueBee Honey.** Mix one tablespoon SueBee Honey and one teaspoon water and melt the mixture in a microwave oven for approximately twenty seconds. Let cool, and then apply to chapped lips.

CLEANSING

- **Arm & Hammer Baking Soda.** Make a paste from Arm & Hammer Baking Soda and water, smooth over your face, wait ten minutes, and rinse thoroughly with warm water.

- **Dannon Strawberry Yogurt.** Mix the yogurt well, apply the mixture to your face, wait ten minutes, and then wash clean with warm water. The alpha-hydroxy acid in the strawberries and the lactic acid in the yogurt help exfoliate the dead skin cells, leaving your face smooth and soft.

- **Heinz Apple Cider Vinegar.** Use a cotton ball to dab Heinz Apple Cider Vinegar on your face, avoiding your eyes, wait ten minutes, and then wash clean with warm water. The malic acid in the vinegar helps exfoliate the dead skin cells, leaving your face smooth and soft.

- **McCormick Cream of Tartar.** Mix McCormick Cream of Tartar with enough water to make a thick paste. Apply the mixture to your face, wait ten minutes, and then wash clean with warm water. The tartaric acid in the cream of tartar helps exfoliate the dead skin cells, leaving your face smooth and soft.

- **Nestlé Carnation NonFat Dry Milk.** If you have oily skin, mix one-quarter cup Nestlé Carnation NonFat Dry Milk with enough water to make a thick paste. Apply the milky paste to your face, let sit for ten minutes, and then wash off. The lactic acid in the milk helps exfoliate the dead skin cells, leaving your face smooth and soft. You can also use this solution to remove makeup.

CONDITIONER

- **Blue Bonnet Margarine.** To condition hair, massage Blue Bonnet Margarine into dry hair, cover hair with a shower cap for thirty minutes, and then shampoo and rinse thoroughly.

- **Cool Whip.** To condition your hair, apply one-half cup Cool Whip to dry hair once a week as a conditioner. Leave on for thirty minutes, and then rinse a few times before shampooing thoroughly.

- **Dannon Yogurt.** In a bowl, mix five tablespoons Dannon Plain Yogurt and one egg yolk with a whisk to create a creamy paste. Set aside while you shampoo your hair and dry with a towel. Massage the conditioning mixture into your hair, cover with a plastic shower cap (or wrap your head in Saran Wrap—above the eyes, nose, and mouth), wrap in a warm towel, and wait fifteen minutes. Rinse your hair clean with warm water, followed by a final rinse of cold water. The lecithin in egg yolk helps enrich dry hair, adding volume and body.

- **Kraft Mayo.** Massage Kraft Mayo into dry hair, let sit for thirty minutes, and then rinse several times before shampooing thoroughly. The oil and eggs in the mayonnaise revitalize dry hair and give it a lustrous shine.

CONTACT LENSES

- **Con-Tact Paper.** To identify contact lenses quickly, add a colorful dot of Con-Tact Paper to your contract lens holder to easily determine the left and right lenses.

Curling Irons

- **Cutex Nail Polish Remover.** To clean a curling iron, saturate a cotton ball with Cutex Nail Polish Remover and rub the cool, unplugged curling iron. Rinse clean and dry.

- **Easy-Off Oven Cleaner.** To clean a curling iron encrusted with mousse, gel, or other hair products, unplug the curling iron, let it cool completely, spray with Easy-Off Oven Cleaner, let sit for five minutes, and then wipe clean.

- **Johnson's Baby Shampoo.** To clean hairspray buildup from a curling iron, use a damp, soft, clean cloth to rub a few drops of Johnson's Baby Shampoo on the cool, unplugged curling iron. Rinse clean and dry.

- **Purell Instant Hand Sanitizer.** Clean residue from a curling iron by coating the cool, unplugged appliance with Purell Instant Hand Sanitizer. Wait two minutes, and then wipe clean. The ethyl alcohol in Purell dissolves the grunge.

- **Scrubbing Bubbles.** To clean a curling iron, spray Scrubbing Bubbles on the cool, unplugged curling iron, let sit for a few minutes, wipe clean with a paper towel dampened with water, and then dry with a second paper towel.

Dandruff

- **Fruit of the Earth Aloe Vera Gel.** Rub Fruit of the Earth Aloe Vera Gel into your scalp, let set five minutes, and then shampoo and rinse. Aloe moistures the scalp, putting an end to the flaking instantly.

- **Listerine.** After shampooing your hair, rinse with Listerine. Thymol, one of the active ingredients in Listerine, is a mild antiseptic that helps reduce dandruff.

- **Phillips' Milk of Magnesia.** To relieve dandruff, before shampooing your hair, apply a capful of Phillips' Milk of Magnesia to your hair and massage into the scalp, let sit for five minutes, and then rinse clean. The milk of magnesia moisturizes the scalp.

- **Purell Instant Hand Sanitizer.** To prevent dandruff, rub Purell Instant Hand Sanitizer into your scalp, wait five minutes, and then rinse clean. The ethyl alcohol in Purell kills the bacteria responsible for your dry scalp.

DENTURES AND RETAINERS

- **Arm & Hammer Baking Soda.** To clean dentures, wet a toothbrush, dip it into a box of Arm & Hammer Baking Soda to coat the brush with powder, and scrub the dentures. The abrasive baking soda will clean away stains while simultaneously deodorizing the false teeth.

- **Heinz White Vinegar.** Soak dentures overnight in Heinz White Vinegar, and then brush away tartar with a toothbrush. The vinegar kills bacteria and softens any plaque buildup for easy cleaning.

- **L'eggs Sheer Energy Panty Hose.** Cut a small piece of nylon from a used, clean pair of L'eggs Sheer Energy Panty Hose and use it to polish dentures. The nylon is a mild abrasive.

DEODORANT

- **Old Spice Aftershave Lotion.** To prevent body odor, use a cotton ball to apply Old Spice Aftershave Lotion to your underarms. The spicy mixture acts as a deodorant.

- **Phillips' Milk of Magnesia.** Use a cotton ball to apply Phillips' Milk of Magnesia to your underarms. The milky liquid acts as a deodorant.

- **Purell Instant Hand Sanitizer.** To deodorize body odor, rub a dollop of Purell Instant Hand Sanitizer into your underarms. Purell kills the existing bacteria and prevents new bacteria from populating your armpits, where they die, decompose, and emit foul smells.

Feet

- **Listerine.** To deodorize smelly feet, soak your feet in Listerine for ten minutes to let the antiseptic solution kill any odor-causing bacteria. Rinse clean and pat dry.

- **Nestea Iced Tea Mix** and **Kingsford's Corn Starch.** To deodorize smelly feet, mix Nestea Iced Tea Mix according to the directions in two quarts of warm water, soak your feet in the mixture for twenty to thirty minutes, and then pat dry and apply Kingsford's Corn Starch. Repeat twice a day to bring odor under control, and then continue twice a week to keep odor at bay. The tannin in the tea dries the feet.

Hair Buildup

- **Arm & Hammer Baking Soda.** Washing your hair once a week with a tablespoon of Arm & Hammer Baking Soda mixed with your regular shampoo removes conditioner and styling gel buildup from your hair. Rinse thoroughly, and then condition and style as usual. (For more ways to shampoo hair, see page 144.)

- **Bon Ami.** To cleanse styling gel and hair spray buildup from hair, dissolve one tablespoon Bon Ami in two cups water, pour the solution through your hair (being certain not to get any in your eyes), and let set for three minutes. Shampoo and condition as usual.

Hair Dye

- **Colgate Regular Flavor Toothpaste.** To remove hair dye from skin, apply a dollop of Colgate Regular Flavor Toothpaste on a damp cloth and rub the stained skin gently in a circular motion. Repeat if necessary.

- **Fantastik.** If you dye your hair too dark, spray Fantastik in your discolored mane (avoiding your eyes), work it in well, and then rinse. Repeat for several days, if necessary.

- **Tide.** To prevent hair dye from coloring your hair a brassy red color, wash your hair with Tide before coloring it. Doing so removes any excess hair product from your hair that might chemically interact with the coloring to produce undesired results.

- **Vaseline Petroleum Jelly.** To avoid dying your skin with hair coloring, rub a thin coat of Vaseline Petroleum Jelly along your hairline before coloring your hair.

HAIRBRUSHES AND COMBS

- **Heinz White Vinegar.** To clean grease and grime from a hairbrush, mix equal parts Heinz White Vinegar and water and soak the hairbrush in the solution overnight. In the morning, wipe clean with a soft, clean rag.

- **Parsons' Ammonia.** To clean hairbrushes and combs, add three tablespoons Parsons' Ammonia to one quart warm water, soak the hairbrushes and combs in the solution for thirty minutes, rinse clean with water, and let dry.

- **Spray 'n Wash.** When you're about to wash a load of laundry, spray dirty combs and hairbrushes with Spray 'n Wash stain remover and wash them along with the clothes. Make sure you remove the combs and brushes before transferring the load of wet clothes to the dryer.

- **20 Mule Team Borax** and **Dawn Dishwashing Liquid.** Mix one tablespoon 20 Mule Team Borax, one tablespoon Dawn Dishwashing Liquid, and one cup water and soak dirty hairbrushes and combs in the solution. Rinse well and let dry.

Makeup

- **Cool Whip.** To remove makeup, wet your face with lukewarm water, spread a handful of Cool Whip on your face, rinse clean with lukewarm water, and blot dry.

- **Huggies Baby Wipes.** To remove lipstick, blush, rouge, eyeliner, eye shadow, or oil-based clown makeup from your face, swab with a Huggies Baby Wipe.

- **Miracle Whip.** Remove makeup by applying a generous coat of Miracle Whip to your face, waiting two minutes, and then rinsing clean. Miracle Whip also exfoliates and moisturizes the skin.

- **Nestlé Coffee-mate Original.** To remove makeup, apply Nestlé Coffee-mate Original liquid to your face with a cotton ball, wipe clean, and rinse. (If using the powder, simply mix with enough water to make a milky solution.)

- **Noxzema Original Deep Cleansing Cream**. To wash makeup off your face, rub a dab of Noxzema Original Deep Cleansing Cream over your face, and then wash clean with water. Noxzema also moisturizes your skin and leaves it feeling fresh and tingly.

- **Stayfree Maxi Pads.** In a pinch, a Stayfree Maxi Pad makes an excellent makeup sponge for applying or removing makeup.

Moisturizer

- **ChapStick.** Rubbing ChapStick into dry skin anywhere on your body (face, hands, elbows, knees, feet) seals in moisture and helps heal chapping, dry skin.

- **Cool Whip.** Applying Cool Whip as a skin cream moisturizes the skin. The coconut and palm kernel oils in Cool Whip moisturize, soothe, and reinvigorate the skin.

- **Crisco All-Vegetable Shortening.** After taking a shower, moisturize your entire body with Crisco All-Vegetable Shortening.

- **Wesson Canola Oil.** A few drops of this fragrant emollient, rubbed into your body, moisturizes skin.

NAIL POLISH

- **Alberto VO5 Conditioning Hairdressing.** Apply a dab of Alberto VO5 Conditioning Hairdressing to painted fingernails and buff with a cotton ball to rejuvenate the shine of the nail polish. The proteins in Alberto VO5 Conditioning Hairdressing also strengthen the nails, preventing chips and breaks.

- **Alberto VO5 Hair Spray.** If you don't have any nail polish remover, in a pinch you can remove nail polish by spraying your nails with Alberto VO5 Hair Spray. The acetone in the hair spray dissolves nail polish. Then rinse clean with soap and water.

- **Efferdent.** To whiten yellowed fingernails, dissolve two Efferdent denture cleansing tablets in a bowl of water, and then soak your fingernails in the denture cleansing solution for five minutes.

- **Heinz White Vinegar.** Remove nail polish stains by soaking your fingernails in Heinz White Vinegar for ten minutes.

- **Hydrogen Peroxide.** Whiten yellow fingernails by rubbing a cotton ball dampened with Hydrogen Peroxide over your fingernails.

- **Morton Salt** and **ReaLime**. Whiten yellowing fingernails by mixing one teaspoon Morton Salt and two teaspoons ReaLime lime juice in a bowl of warm water. Soak your fingernails for ten minutes.

- **Vaseline Petroleum Jelly.** Prevent the cap from getting sealed shut on a nail polish bottle by rubbing a thin coat of Vaseline Petroleum Jelly around the threads on the rim of the bottle.

Razors and Shaving

- **Arm & Hammer Clean Shower.** Spraying your safety razor blades with Arm & Hammer Clean Shower after each use cleans and triples the life of the razor.

- **Blue Bonnet Margarine.** If you run out of shaving cream, slather Blue Bonnet Margarine on wet skin for a silky smooth shave.

- **Cool Whip.** Apply Cool Whip to wet skin as a substitute for shaving cream. The dessert topping simultaneously moisturizes the skin.

- **Heinz White Vinegar.** After shaving, apply Heinz White Vinegar as an aftershave lotion. The vinegar evaporates within an hour, and the odor dissipates quickly.

- **Johnson's Baby Powder.** Before shaving your legs with an electric razor, dust your legs lightly with Johnson's Baby Powder to lubricate the skin and prevent friction burns.

- **Murphy Oil Soap.** Fill a sink with water, add two squirts of Murphy Oil Soap, slather on your legs with the soapy water, and shave. The natural oils in the soap moisturize the skin for a close shave.

- **Skippy Peanut Butter.** While on a camping trip, former U.S. Senator Barry Goldwater discovered that he could shave with peanut butter. Just slather Skippy Peanut Butter on your legs and shave away. The oils in the peanut butter lubricate the skin for a smooth shave. Just be sure you use the creamy, not the chunky.

- **Star Olive Oil.** After shaving your bikini line, apply Star Olive Oil to the area to prevent ingrown hairs.

- **Vaseline Petroleum Jelly.** When you finish shaving, dip your safety-razor blade in Vaseline Petroleum Jelly to prevent the blade from rusting, extending the life of your razor.

- **WD-40.** To prolong the life of your safety razor blades, spray them with WD-40, a water-displacement formula that prevents the blades from rusting.

SHAMPOO

- **Arm & Hammer Baking Soda.** Washing your hair once a week with a tablespoon of Arm & Hammer Baking Soda mixed with your regular shampoo removes conditioner and styling gel buildup from your hair. Rinse thoroughly, and then condition and style as usual.

- **Bayer Aspirin.** Unless you are allergic to aspirin, drop two Bayer Aspirin tablets into your regular shampoo to absorb excess product from the shampoo, enabling the shampoo to clean your hair more effectively.

- **Budweiser.** Open a can of Budweiser beer and let it sit at room temperature until it goes flat. Shampoo oily hair with the king of beer and rinse thoroughly. Beer absorbs the oils from your hair, but shampooing your hair too often with beer may dry out your scalp, causing dandruff.

- **Dawn Dishwashing Liquid.** Use a few drops of Dawn Dishwashing Liquid as shampoo to cut through grease and grime in hair. The detergent in Dawn thoroughly cleanses hair, stripping styling gel and hair spray buildup from hair.

- **Mott's Apple Juice** and **Heinz White Vinegar.** For oily hair, mix one cup Mott's Apple Juice and one tablespoon Heinz White Vinegar, and, after shampooing your hair, pour the mixture through your hair, comb thoroughly, wait fifteen minutes, and then shampoo lightly and rinse clean. The pectin in the apple juice, enhanced by the vinegar, absorbs excess oil.

TEETH

- **Arm & Hammer Baking Soda.** To whiten teeth, dip a wet toothbrush into Arm & Hammer Baking Soda to coat the bristles with a thick layer of powder and brush your teeth, concentrating along the gum line.

The sodium bicarbonate lowers the pH level in your mouth (neutralizing odor-producing bacteria) and deodorizes your mouth, and the abrasive granules gently polish your teeth.

TONERS

- **Heinz White Vinegar.** Mix equal parts Heinz White Vinegar and water and apply the toning solution to your face with a cotton ball. Let dry.

- **McCormick Pure Mint Extract** and **McCormick Alum.** For dry skin, mix two drops McCormick Pure Mint Extract and one-half teaspoon McCormick Alum in one cup distilled water. Apply to the face with a cotton ball and let dry.

- **ReaLemon.** Lemon juice, a natural astringent, removes any residue and refreshes your face. Add one teaspoon ReaLemon lemon juice to one cup cold water, saturate a cotton ball with the solution, and apply to your face. Let dry and do not rinse. Lemon juice shrinks the pores.

WHITE HAIR

- **Mrs. Stewart's Liquid Bluing.** To whiten white hair, add a couple of drops of Mrs. Stewart's Liquid Bluing to the rinse water when washing gray or white hair. The bluing eliminates yellowing and gives hair a lush whiteness that products made especially for that purpose cannot achieve. Mrs. Stewart's Liquid Bluing is perfectly safe, and a few drops cost less than a penny.

Hand Cleaners

Fish

- **Colgate Regular Flavor Toothpaste.** To clean the smell of fish from your hands, squeeze a dollop of Colgate Regular Flavor Toothpaste into your palm and rub your hands together under running water.

- **Listerine.** To clean the smell of fish from your hands, rub a teaspoon of Listerine mouth wash between your hands, and then wash with soap and water. The antiseptic kills the fish odor.

- **Maxwell House Coffee.** To deodorize your hands from smelling from fish, fill your palm with Maxwell House Coffee grounds (used or unused), add water if using fresh grounds, rub your hands together for one minute, then rinse with running water.

- **ReaLemon.** Rubbing your hands with ReaLemon lemon juice removes the smell of fish. Simply pour a little lemon juice into the palm of your hand and rub your hands together.

GARLIC

- **Arm & Hammer Baking Soda.** To remove garlic smells from your hands, wash with a small handful of Arm & Hammer Baking Soda.

- **Campbell's Tomato Juice.** Washing your hands with Campbell's Tomato Juice eradicates garlic odors.

- **Colgate Regular Flavor Toothpaste.** Squeeze a dollop of Colgate Regular Flavor Toothpaste into your palm and wash hands under running water to deodorize the stench of garlic from your hands and leave them smelling minty fresh.

- **Heinz White Vinegar.** To get rid of the smell of garlic on your hands, pour Heinz White Vinegar over your hands, rub them together well, and then rinse with soap and water.

- **Listerine.** To clean the smell of garlic from your hands, rub a teaspoon of Listerine mouth wash between your hands, and then wash with soap and water. The antiseptic kills the garlic odor.

- **Maxwell House Coffee.** To clean the smell of garlic from your hands, rub a handful of used Maxwell House Coffee grounds between your hands, and then rinse clean.

- **ReaLemon.** Washing your hands with ReaLemon lemon juice eliminates the smell of garlic.

- **Skippy Peanut Butter.** Use a dollop of Skippy Peanut Butter to remove garlic smells from your hands.

GREASE AND GRIME

- **Arm & Hammer Baking Soda.** Clean dirt, grime, and oil from hands by sprinkling Arm & Hammer Baking Soda onto wet hands with liquid soap. Rub vigorously, rinse, and dry.

- **Blue Bonnet Margarine.** Need an emergency hand cleaner? Open the refrigerator and grab the Blue Bonnet Margarine. It works great, and you'll smell like popcorn.

- **Crisco All-Vegetable Shortening.** Clean grease and grime from your hands by rubbing in Crisco All-Vegetable Shortening. Then wash with soap and water.

- **Domino Sugar.** To clean grease from skin, sprinkle Domino Sugar on your hands, and then lather with soap and water. The sugar acts like an abrasive, scrubbing grease from your skin.

- **Gillette Foamy.** Rubbing a dollop of Gillette Foamy shaving cream between your hands dissolves grime without water.

- **Huggies Baby Wipes.** Keep a box of Huggies Baby Wipes nearby to wash grease and grime from your hands.

- **Johnson's Baby Oil.** Before washing greasy hands, massage Johnson's Baby Oil into your skin. Then wash with soap and water. The mineral oil dissolves grease.

- **Miracle Whip.** Clean dirt, grease, and grime from your hands with a dollop of Miracle Whip. Rub the salad dressing—first introduced at the 1933 Chicago World's Fair—between your hands, let set for five minutes, and then rinse clean with soap and water.

- **Morton Salt.** Sprinkle Morton Salt on your soapy hands to help dissolve grease. Salt breaks down many greases, and the abrasive grit helps scrub skin clean.

- **Noxzema Original Deep Cleansing Cream.** To clean grease and grime from skin, rub a dab of Noxzema Original Deep Cleansing Cream—originally sold as "Dr. Bunting's Sunburn Remedy—into the skin and wash clean with soap and water.

- **Pam Cooking Spray.** If your hands get sticky and greasy, clean them with Pam Cooking Spray, dispensed from a convenient aerosol can.

- **Play-Doh.** Clean grease and grime from hands. Squeezing Play-Doh between your hands cleans grease, grime, and dirt from the skin.

- **ReaLemon.** To clean stains and food smells from hands, rub with ReaLemon lemon juice.

- **Wesson Oil** and **Ivory Dishwashing Liquid.** Place a dollop of Wesson Oil in your palm, rub thoroughly all over your hands, and then use the same amount of Ivory Dishwashing Liquid and rinse with water.

INK

- **Balmex.** To clean ink from hands, apply Balmex and wipe clean.
- **Nivea Creme.** To clean ink from hands, apply Nivea Creme, rub in, and wipe clean.

ONION

- **Listerine.** To clean the smell of onion from your hands, rub a teaspoon of Listerine mouth wash between your hands, and then wash with soap and water. The antiseptic kills the onion odor.
- **Speed Stick.** To deodorize the smell of onions from hands, rub a Speed Stick deodorant over your fingers and hands, let sit for five minutes, and then wash clean with soapy water.

PAINT

- **Nivea Creme.** To clean oil-based paint from hands, use Nivea Creme, which removes paint and stain from hands more gently than turpentine.

SAP

- **Nestlé Carnation NonFat Dry Milk.** To clean sap from pine trees off hands, wash your hands with one tablespoon of Nestlé Carnation Non-Fat Dry Milk and water.
- **Vaseline Petroleum Jelly.** To clean sap or pitch from hands, rub a few dabs of Vaseline Petroleum Jelly between your hands. Then wash clean with soapy water.

Holidays and Parties

Birthdays

- **Mr. Coffee Filters.** To make neat party favors, place candy in the middle of a Mr. Coffee Filter and tie the sides together with a ribbon.

- **Oral-B Dental Floss.** Oral-B Dental Floss cuts cake into neat slices.

Christmas

- **Alberto VO5 Hair Spray.** Spraying a wreath with Alberto VO5 Hair Spray rejuvenates the wreath, making it look new again.

- **Alberto VO5 Hair Spray.** To prevent angel hair decorating a nativity set from drifting freely and making a mess, spray the angel hair with Alberto VO5 Hair Spray to hold it in place. (Be sure to keep the angel hair away from open flames.)

- **Aunt Jemima Original Syrup.** To prolong the life of a Christmas tree and prevent the needles from dropping everywhere, cut an extra inch off the bottom of the tree, stand the tree in a bucket of cold water to which one cup Aunt Jemima Original Syrup has been added, and let the tree soak for two or three days before decorating.

- **Bounce.** Wrap each Christmas ornament in a clean, used sheet of Bounce. When you unwrap the ornaments next year, use the Bounce sheet to wipe the ornament before you hang it on the tree, allowing the antistatic elements to repel dust from the ornament.

- **Bounce.** To keep cats from knocking the ornaments off the Christmas tree at night or whenever you leave the house during the day, surround the tree with Bounce sheets. You can put the Bounce sheets down at night and pick them up every morning. The oleander fragrance repels cats.

- **Cascade.** To clean a homemade lace Christmas wreath, place it in the dishwasher with some Cascade. When the cycle completes, the wreath will be as white and clean as the day it was made.

- **Con-Tact Paper.** To decorate windows with snow, cut snowflakes from white Con-Tact Paper.

- **Epsom Salt.** To frost a window, mix Epsom Salt with stale beer until the beer can hold no more. Then, apply the mixture to the glass with a sponge. When it dries, the window will be frosted.

- **Forster Clothespins.** Use Forster Clothespins to clip strings of Christmas lights to your house and trees in your yard.

- **Glad Trash Bags.** Store an artificial Christmas tree inside a large Glad Trash Bag, and store a Christmas wreath in its own Glad Trash Bag.

- **Maxwell House Coffee.** Store each string of Christmas lights wound in a loop inside its own clean, empty Maxwell House Coffee can.

- **McCormick Cinnamon Sticks** and **L'eggs Sheer Energy Panty Hose.** Cut off the foot of a clean, used pair of L'eggs Sheer Energy Panty Hose, fill it with a few McCormick Cinnamon Sticks, and tie a knot in the open end. Place the sachet in the storage box with your Christmas decorations so when you open the box next year, it will smell crisp and fresh.

- **Mr. Coffee Filters.** To make paper snowflakes, fold a Mr. Coffee Filter many times and cut tiny holes. When opened, it will look like a snowflake.

- **Pam Cooking Spray.** Before decorating windows with artificial snow, spray the glass lightly with Pam Cooking Spray to make cleaning effortless.

- **Pampers.** To prolong the life of a Christmas tree and prevent the needles from dropping, saturate a Pampers disposable diaper with water, cut open the diaper with a pair of scissors, and place the superabsorbent polymer flakes from the core of the diaper into a one-gallon bowl. Pour two cups water over the diaper crystals, let sit for five minutes. Add two more cups water, let sit for five minutes, and repeat until the polymer flakes swell to the brim of the bowl. Pour the water-filled crystals in a Christmas tree stand with the tree already in place. The tree soaks up water from the crystals, and since the water will not evaporate as quickly, you don't have to add water as frequently.

- **WD-40.** Spray windows with WD-40 before spraying with artificial snow so the decorative spray will wipe off easier.

- **Wesson Oil** and **Bounty Paper Towels.** To clean the sap from a Christmas tree from the tree stand or your hands, rub with Wesson Oil and wipe with Bounty Paper Towels.

- **Ziploc Storage Bags.** Roll up each individual strand of Christmas lights and store in its own Ziploc Storage Bag. The next year, you can easily test each individually packed strand of lights.

- **Ziploc Storage Bags.** To store Christmas ornaments, place each ornament in its own Ziploc Storage Bag, blow air into the bag, and seal tight. The air provides cushioning to protect the ornament.

HALLOWEEN

- **Miracle Whip.** To remove Halloween makeup, generously coat the face with Miracle Whip, let sit for two minutes, and then wash off.

Hanukkah

- **Conair 1875 Watt Hair Dryer.** To clean candle wax from a menorah, aim a Conair 1875 Watt Hair Dryer set on hot at the wax so it melts off.
- **Pam Cooking Spray.** Before setting up Hanukah candles, spray a light coat of Pam Cooking Spray on the menorah. This way, melted wax will glide off easily.

Holiday Lanterns

- **Maxwell House Coffee.** To make decorative holiday lanterns, spray paint clean, empty Maxwell House Coffee cans with appropriate colors for the holiday, punch holes in the side of the can (a heart design on a red can for Valentines Day, for instance), fill the can halfway with sand, and place a lit candle inside to make attractive sidewalk decorations.

Thanksgiving

- **Oral-B Dental Floss.** To truss a turkey, use durable and sturdy Oral-B Dental Floss.

Weddings

- **Hartz Parakeet Seed.** Instead of throwing rice, which is difficult to clean up and dangerous for birds, give your guests packets of Hartz Parakeet Seed instead. When the wedding is over and the guests have all gone home, the birds and squirrels will clean up the birdseed.

Wrapping Paper

- **L'eggs Sheer Energy Panty Hose.** To store wrapping paper, cut off a leg from a pair of clean, old L'eggs Sheer Energy Panty Hose and slip it over a roll of wrapping paper.

Houseplants

Aphids and Other Insects

- **Arm & Hammer Baking Soda.** To kill aphids on houseplants, mix two teaspoons Arm & Hammer Baking Soda and two cups water in a trigger-spray bottle and mist the plants with the solution once or twice a week.

- **Heinz White Vinegar** and **Q-tips Cotton Swabs.** To remove mealy bugs from houseplants, dab the bugs with a Q-tips Cotton Swab dipped in a mixture of equal parts Heinz White Vinegar and water.

- **Ivory Dishwashing Liquid.** To repel insects (such as aphids, whiteflies, and spider mites) from houseplants, put a drop of Ivory Dishwashing Liquid in a spray bottle, fill the rest of the bottle with water, shake well, and mist the leaves and soil of your houseplants.

- **Murphy Oil Soap.** To kill whiteflies on houseplants, mix equal parts Murphy Oil Soap and water in a clean, empty spray bottle and mist the infected plants.

- **Nestlé Carnation NonFat Dry Milk.** To kill aphids on houseplants, mix one-half cup Nestlé Carnation NonFat Dry Milk with two cups water in a sixteen-ounce trigger-spray bottle and mist the infected plants with the solution. The aphids get stuck in the milky residue as it dries on the plant leaves.

FERNS

- **Parsons' Ammonia.** To fertilize ferns, water the plant with a mixture of two tablespoons Parsons' Ammonia and one quart water to enrich the nitrogen content of the soil.

FERTILIZER

- **Jell-O.** To give houseplants additional nitrogen, mix an envelope of powdered Jell-O into one cup of boiling water, stir until the gelatin powder dissolves, mix with three cups cold water, and then apply around the base of the plant.

- **Lipton Tea Bags.** Put Lipton Tea Bags (new or used) on the soil around houseplants and cover the tea bags with mulch. Every time you water the plants, the nutrients from the decomposing tea leaves work their way into the soil, enriching it for the plants.

- **Maxwell House Coffee.** Add used Maxwell House Coffee grounds to your houseplants to fertilize the soil. The smell of the coffee also repels cats from digging up the soil.

- **Nestea Iced Tea Mix.** Mix up a quart of unsweetened Nestea Iced Tea Mix according to the directions (without adding sugar or ice) and fertilize houseplants with the solution. Or simply sprinkle the powdered mix directly on the soil. As the tea decomposes, the nutrients work their way into the soil.

FLOWER POTS AND PLANTERS

- **Bounce.** To prevent the soil from leaking out of a planter, line the bottom of the planter with a clean, used sheet of Bounce. The dryer sheet allows drainage—without breaking apart from the water.

- **Huggies Pull-Ups.** If your planter is leaking water, set the pot inside a pair of Huggies Pull-Ups, creating an absorbent diaper for the plant. Place the pot inside a second, larger pot to conceal the Huggies Pull-Up.

- **L'eggs Sheer Energy Panty Hose.** To prevent the soil from leaking from the bottom of a planter, placea used pair of L'eggs Sheer Energy Panty Hose in the bottom of the pot, allowing water to drain.

- **Mr. Coffee Filters.** Before planting flowers in a pot, cover the drainage hole by inserting a stack of three Mr. Coffee Filters in the bottom of the pot, and then cover the coffee filters with a one-inch thick layer of pebbles. The coffee filter will prevent dirt from leaking out of the pot.

- **Reynolds Wrap.** Wrapping Reynolds Wrap aluminum foil around the base of houseplant containers keeps humidity high and prevents the soil from drying out as quickly.

LIGHT

- **Reynolds Wrap.** Increase the natural light for houseplants during the winter months by wrapping a sturdy piece of cardboard with Reynolds Wrap aluminum foil. Position the homemade mirror behind the plant, facing the window. The foil will reflect the sunlight, causing the plant to grow more evenly.

Rejuvenating

- **Castor Oil.** Rejuvenate a houseplant ailing from a nutrient deficiency by dribbling one tablespoon Castor Oil into the soil and then watering well.

- **Heinz Apple Cider Vinegar.** To revive undernourished plants, mix one tablespoon Heinz Apple Cider Vinegar in one gallon water in a watering can and water potted plants with the solution. The vinegar neutralizes the pH of the water, making vital nutrients in the water more available to the plants.

- **Saran Wrap.** To revitalize a wilting houseplant, water the plant thoroughly and then loosely wrap Saran Wrap around the leaves and the base of the plant, creating a miniature greenhouse. Remove the plastic wrap after a few days.

Shining

- **Blue Bonnet Margarine.** To clean plant leaves, use a soft, clean cloth to wipe Blue Bonnet Margarine on the leaves.

- **Cool Whip.** Using a soft cloth, wipe Cool Whip on the leaves to give them an incredible shine. Cool Whip contains both coconut oil and palm-kernel oil.

- **Kraft Mayo** and **Bounty Paper Towels.** Using a sheet of Bounty Paper Towels, rub Kraft Mayo on houseplant leaves to make them shine and to prevent dust from settling on them.

- **Land O Lakes Butter.** Using a soft, clean cloth, wipe Land O Lakes Butter on the leaves.

Keep It Clean
GETTING IN HOT WATER

- Overwatering kills more houseplants than any other single cause. The leaves of an overwatered plant will wilt, turn yellow, and fall off. The base of the stem may also rot, which is a symptom of root damage.

- Underwatering a houseplant causes far less damage than overwatering. Revive a plant wilted from dryness by misting the leaves lightly, watering the soil, and placing the plant in direct sunlight.

- Watering plants at night encourages foliage diseases. Watering plants in the early morning prevents moisture from evaporating rapidly (as during the midday sun) and enables the plants to dry by nightfall.

- Watering plants, trees, and lawns for thirty minutes twice a week is better than watering plants, trees, and lawns for ten minutes every day. The more deeply a plant is watered, the deeper the water penetrates the soil, encouraging roots to grow deeper and ultimately requiring less water. (Young plants, however, have shallow roots and should be watered lightly and frequently.)

- **Nestlé Carnation NonFat Dry Milk.** Mix three ounces Nestlé Carnation NonFat Dry Milk with two cups water and, using a soft cloth, wipe the milky solution on houseplant leaves to give them a fine gloss.

- **Nestlé Coffee-mate Original.** To give the large leaves of houseplants a nice shine, mix equal parts Nestlé Coffee-mate Original liquid and water and wipe the leaves with the milky solution. (If using the powder, simply mix with enough water to make a milky solution.)

Watering

- **Canada Dry Club Soda.** When a bottle of Canada Dry Club Soda goes flat, use it to water your houseplants.

- **Lipton Tea Bags.** Invigorate houseplants and ferns by watering once a week with a weak, tepid brewed Lipton Tea. The tea attracts acid-producing bacteria and fills the soil with nutrients.

- **Maxwell House Coffee.** If you've made too much Maxwell House Coffee, don't throw out the excess. Instead, let it cool and use it to water your houseplants. The coffee is filled with nutrients.

- **Nestea Iced Tea Mix.** To give your houseplants an acidic treat, mix up a glass of Nestea Iced Tea according to the directions (without adding any sugar or lemon) and water your houseplants with the tea.

- **Pampers.** Saturate a Pampers disposable diaper with water and using a pair of scissors, carefully cut open the diaper and mix the superabsorbent polymer flakes with the potting soil. The polymer flakes absorb three hundred times their weight in water, keeping the soil moist for your houseplant. The gelatinous polymer also stores nutrients, slowly feeding the plants.

Winterizing

- **Bubble Wrap** and **Scotch Packaging Tape.** To protect plastic, wood, and fiberglass planters left outside during the winter months, wrap the planters with Bubble Wrap and secure in place with Scotch Packaging Tape. The extra insulation helps protect both the plant and the planter. Or before planting, cut a piece of Bubble Wrap to fit around the inside of a terra-cotta pot before filing with soil to insulate plant roots and prevent constant freezing and thawing. (Do not line the bottom of the planter to allow for drainage.)

Insects and Pests

ANTS

- **Crayola Chalk.** Draw a thick line of Crayola Chalk around window frames, doors, and other entry points. Ants will not cross a chalk line.

- **Dawn Dishwashing Liquid.** To kill ants, mix one-quarter teaspoon Dawn Dishwashing Liquid and two cups water in a sixteen-ounce trigger-spray bottle. Spray the soapy solution on the ants. They die instantly. The soap dissolves their exoskeletons.

- **Heinz White Vinegar.** To repel ants from the countertop, cabinets, and pantry, wipe down the countertop and cabinet doors with Heinz White Vinegar on a sponge.

- **McCormick Ground (Cayenne) Red Pepper.** To prevent ants from entering your house or getting into kitchen cabinets, sprinkle McCormick Ground (Cayenne) Red Pepper in the crevices at entry points. Red pepper repels ants.

- **McCormick Ground Sage.** Sprinkle McCormick Ground Sage in the crevices and entry points wherever ants are giving your trouble. Ants dislike sage.

- **Minute Rice.** Sprinkle uncooked Minute Rice over an anthill or wherever ants are a problem. The ants take the rice back to their nest for the colony to devour. When the ants eat it, the rice swells in their stomachs, killing the whole nest—without any pesticides.

- **ReaLemon.** To discourage ants from entering your house, squirt some ReaLemon lemon juice on window sills and along the threshold of doors.

- **Simple Green.** To kill ants, mix one teaspoon Simple Green All-Purpose Cleaner with two cups water in a sixteen-ounce trigger-spray bottle. Shake well and spray the insects. The soap penetrates their exoskeletons almost instantly, killing the pests.

- **20 Mule Team Borax** and **Domino Confectioners Sugar.** To kill ants, mix equal parts 20 Mule Team Borax and Domino Confectioners Sugar and sprinkle in crevices where ants enter. (Unless you have pets or small children because borax can be toxic if consumed by pets or children.) Attracted by the sugar, ants carry the mixture back to their nest and feed it to the colony, killing all the inhabitants.

APHIDS

- **Arm & Hammer Baking Soda.** To kill aphids on houseplants or rose bushes, mix two teaspoons Arm & Hammer Baking Soda and two cups water in a trigger-spray bottle and mist the plants with the solution once a week.

- **Ivory Dishwashing Liquid.** To kill aphids on houseplants, mix one-quarter teaspoon Ivory Dishwashing Liquid and two cups water in a sixteen-ounce trigger-spray bottle. Spray the soapy solution on the plant leaves and let dry. The soap dissolves the exoskeletons of the insects.

- **Nestlé Carnation NonFat Dry Milk.** To kill aphids on houseplants, mix Nestlé Carnation NonFat Dry Milk with water according to the instructions on the box, fill a trigger-spray bottle with the solution, and mist the infected plants with the solution. The aphids get stuck in the milky residue as it dries on the plant leaves.

- **Vaseline Petroleum Jelly** and **Post-it Notes.** To eliminate aphids on a houseplant, coat a yellow Post-it Note with Vaseline Petroleum Jelly and stick it near the infected plant. Aphids are attracted to the color yellow and get stuck in the petroleum jelly.

BIRDS

- **Slinky.** Birds nesting under your awnings and making a mess? Stretch out a Slinky and wrap it into a tangled ball, and then wedge it into the crevice where birds nest. Or stretch a Slinky across the spot.

CATS AND DOGS

- **Arm & Hammer Baking Soda.** To prevent neighborhood dogs from urinating on your lawn and causing yellow burn spots, dissolve one cup Arm & Hammer Baking Soda in one gallon water in a watering can and saturate the urine spots every three days. The baking soda deodorizes the area, preventing the offending dog from recognizing the spot, and simultaneously neutralizes the acidity of the urine, enabling the grass to regain its color.

- **Heinz White Vinegar.** To repel stray cats, fill a trigger-spray bottle with Heinz White Vinegar and spray around the border of the garden and the birdbath. The smell of vinegar repulses cats and neutralizes the smell of cat urine used to mark their territory.

- **Maxwell House Coffee.** Fertilizing houseplants and plants around your garden with used Maxwell House Coffee grounds repels cats and prevents them from digging up the soil.

- **McCormick Black Pepper.** Keep neighborhood dogs and cats out of your garbage cans by sprinkling McCormick Black Pepper around the trash bins. Both these animals have a keen sense of smell. They catch a whiff of the pepper and take off for someone else's garbage cans.

- **McCormick Ground (Cayenne) Red Pepper.** To keep neighborhood cats out of your flower or vegetable garden, sprinkle McCormick Ground (Cayenne) Red Pepper on the soil. Cats have a keen sense of smell, and one whiff of cayenne pepper sends them elsewhere. When it rains, be sure to re-pepper the garden.
- **Pine-Sol.** To keep dogs away from garbage cans, spray the cans with Pine-Sol. Pine oil repels dogs.

COCKROACHES

- **Arm & Hammer Baking Soda** and **Domino Sugar.** Mix together equal parts Arm & Hammer Baking Soda and Domino Sugar, sprinkle the powdered mixture on saucers or small containers, and place them around the house. Lured by the sugar, the cockroaches eat the baking soda, and unable to digest it, they implode.
- **Domino Sugar** and **20 Mule Team Borax.** To kill cockroaches, mix equal parts Domino Sugar and 20 Mule Team Borax and sprinkle the mixture in cracks and crevices where cockroaches are invading your home. Attracted by the sugar, the roaches ingest the borax, which kills them.
- **McCormick Bay Leaves.** To keep cockroaches out of kitchen cabinets and drawers, place a McCormick Bay Leaf on each shelf and in each drawer. The smell of bay leaves repulses cockroaches.
- **Simple Green.** To kill cockroaches, mix one teaspoon Simple Green All-Purpose Cleaner with two cups water in a sixteen-ounce trigger-spray bottle. Shake well and spray the insects. The soap penetrates their exoskeletons almost instantly, killing the pests.

CRICKETS

- **Scotch Packaging Tape.** To catch crickets, place a long strip of Scotch Packaging Tape adhesive-side up along the floor, wall, doorframe, or wherever crickets roam. The crickets get stuck on the tape, which you can discard and replace until crickets take up residence elsewhere.

- **20 Mule Team Borax.** If you do not have any pets or children living in your home, sprinkle 20 Mule Team Borax in cracks, crevices, or wherever crickets are giving you a problem. (Borax can be toxic if consumed by pets or children.)

DEER

- **Dial Soap** and **L'eggs Sheer Energy Panty Hose.** Cut off the leg from a pair of clean, old L'eggs Sheer Energy Panty Hose, slip a bar of Dial Soap into the foot, and hang it from a fruit tree, fence post, or around crops to prevent deer from eating plants. The deer are repelled by the smell of deodorant soap.

- **Slinky.** To prevent deer from destroying your garden, drape a few metal Slinkys around the perimeter of the garden by simply stretching them across two fence posts or draping them over tree branches. That trademark "Slinkity" sound and the shiny reflection of the metal frightens away deer. You can also hang Slinky Juniors from sturdy trees and bushes, which simultaneously adds a unique decorative touch that is sure to make you the envy of all your neighbors.

EARWIGS

- **Epsom Salt.** Sprinkling Epsom Salt along window sills, door thresholds, and baseboards repels earwigs.

- **McCormick Bay Leaves.** To scare earwigs away, crush up several McCormick Bay Leaves and sprinkle them along baseboards, window sills, and door thresholds.

FLEAS

- **20 Mule Team Borax.** If you do not have any pets or children living in your home, sprinkle 20 Mule Team Borax on the floors, carpet, and upholstery, let sit for forty-eight hours, and vacuum. (Borax can be toxic if consumed by pets or children.)

Flies

- **Grandma's Molasses.** To trap flies, pour some Grandma's Molasses in a saucer and set it out wherever flies are giving you a problem. The flies, attracted to the sticky sweet molasses, get stuck in it.
- **Simple Green.** Mix one teaspoon Simple Green All-Purpose Cleaner with two cups water in a sixteen-ounce trigger-spray bottle. Shake well and spray insects. They die instantly.

Fruit Flies

- **Alberto VO5 Hair Spray.** Spray a pesky fly with a quick burst of Alberto VO5 Hair Spray, which immediately solidifies and immobilizes the insect.
- **Budweiser.** To kill fruit flies, pour a little Budweiser beer in a coffee mug, set it wherever fruit flies are giving you trouble, and cover the top of the mug with a funnel. The fruit flies, attracted to the beer, climb inside the trap, and unable to escape, drown in the beer. To kill any confused fruit flies flying around in the mug, pour boiling water over them.
- **Heinz Apple Cider Vinegar.** To kill fruit flies, fill a coffee mug with Heinz Apple Cider Vinegar, set it on the kitchen counter or wherever fruit flies are congregating, and put a funnel on top of the mug. The fruit flies, attracted to the apple cider vinegar, fly in and unable to get out, drown in the vinegar.

Gnats

- **Heinz Apple Cider Vinegar.** Fill a bowl with Heinz Apple Cider Vinegar and place it wherever gnats are swarming. Attracted by the sweet vinegar, the fungus gnats fly to the rim of the bowl, climb inside, and drown in the acidic solution.
- **L'eggs Sheer Energy Panty Hose.** If swarming gnats are pestering you, pull the waist of a pair of clean, used L'eggs Sheer Energy Panty Hose over your head and down to your neck to make a see-through facemask. The

synthetic fibers keep gnats out of your eyes, ears, nose and mouth—although your neighbors may think you're getting ready to rob a bank, in which case, you may have some explaining to do if the police show up at your door.

- **McCormick Pure Vanilla Extract.** To repel gnats, rub a few dabs of McCormick Pure Vanilla Extract on your skin.
- **Vicks VapoRub.** Apply Vicks VapoRub to your skin to repel gnats. The scent of eucalyptus repels the feisty pests.

GOPHERS AND MOLES

- **McCormick Ground (Cayenne) Red Pepper.** To get moles and gophers to tunnel elsewhere, fill the holes with McCormick Ground (Cayenne) Red Pepper.
- **Playtex Living Gloves.** To capture gophers or moles more effectively, wear Playtex Living Gloves when baiting a trap for gophers or moles—to avoid leaving a human scent on the trap or bait.

INSECTS

- **McCormick Alum.** Dissolve two tablespoons McCormick Alum in three quarts boiling water. Let cool and paint baseboards and cracks with the solution. Alum kills insects.

MEALWORMS

- **Wrigley's Doublemint Gum.** To keep mealworms from invading your kitchen pantry, place a few sticks of wrapped Wrigley's Doublemint Gum on the shelves. Mealworms are repelled by mint.

MICE AND RATS

- **Bounce.** Repel mice and rats by placing sheets of Bounce in cracks and crevices. The oleander fragrance in Bounce repels rodents.

INSIDE PLAYTEX LIVING GLOVES

In 1932, Russian immigrant Abraham Nathaniel Spanel founded the International Latex Corporation in Rochester, New York, and began selling a latex beach and shower cap, baby pants, and a makeup cape—all under the Playtex name. In 1940, the company introduced the first Playtex Living Girdle, making Playtex a household name. In 1954, using the latex technology developed for the manufacture of girdles, the International Latex Corporation began to market Playtex Living Gloves. In 1960, Playtex introduced its first infant feeding product.

Strange Facts

- Playtex is a hybrid of the words *perforated* and *latex,* with playful overtones.

- The word *glove* originates from the Anglo-Saxon word *glof,* meaning "palm of the hand."

- Playtex Products, Inc. and Playtex Apparel, Inc., are two distinctly separate, completely unaffiliated companies. Both companies are licensed to use the trademark name Playtex. Playtex Products (a publicly-held company) makes personal care products while Playtex Apparel (a subsidiary of Sara Lee) makes lingerie.

- The International Latex Corporation developed the spacesuits for the Apollo Lunar Space Suit, including the space suits worn by Neil Armstrong and Buzz Aldrin when they walked on the moon.

- **McCormick Pure Peppermint Extract.** Saturate cotton balls with McCormick Pure Peppermint Extract and place them at the entry points, along baseboards, or wherever mice are giving you trouble. Peppermint repels mice and simultaneously freshens the air in your home.

- **Skippy Peanut Butter.** Bait a mouse or rat trap with Skippy Peanut Butter. Mice and rats have an uncanny ability to get cheese out of a trap without setting it off, but peanut butter sticks to the trap.

Mosquitoes

- **Bounce.** To repel mosquitoes while you're working in the garden, tie a sheet of Bounce through a belt loop or the plastic flap in the back of a baseball cap. Oleander, the fragrance in Bounce, repels insects. If one sheet of Bounce doesn't work for you, fill your other belt loops with sheets of Bounce, turning yourself into a interesting fashion statement.

- **Lemon Joy.** To kill swarming mosquitoes, mix two or three drops of Lemon Joy in a bowl of water and place the bowl on the patio. Mosquitoes will converge on it, get stuck in the soapy solution, and die.

- **Pam Cooking Spray.** Mosquito eggs, larvae, and pupae incubate in still water. Eliminating pools of still water helps reduce the proliferation of mosquitoes. If you can't drain pools of still water from holes in large tree trunks, spray the water surface with a fine coat of Pam Cooking Spray so the vegetable oil can smother any developing mosquito larvae.

- **Vicks VapoRub.** Apply Vicks VapoRub to your skin to repel mosquitoes. Mosquitoes hate the scent of eucalyptus.

- **Wesson Oil.** To prevent mosquitoes from breeding in a rain barrel, add a teaspoon of Wesson Oil to the water. The oil forms a thin film on the water surface, suffocating mosquito larvae.

Moths

- **McCormick Whole Cloves** and **L'eggs Sheer Energy Panty Hose.** Use McCormick Whole Cloves as an alternative to mothballs. Cut off the foot of a clean, used pair of L'eggs Sheer Energy Panty Hose, fill it with cloves, and hang it as a sachet in your closet. Cloves repel moths and smell much nicer than mothballs.

- **USA Today.** Store woolens with crumpled-up pages of *USA Today.* Newsprint repels moths.

PIGEONS

- **Vaseline Petroleum Jelly.** To discourage pigeons from landing on your balcony railing, coat the top rail with Vaseline Petroleum Jelly. The pigeons detest the way petroleum jelly feels on their toes and find a more comfortable place to land.

RABBITS

- **McCormick Black Pepper.** To keep rabbits away from flower beds and vegetable gardens, sprinkle McCormick Black Pepper in your garden around and over beans plants, carrots, lettuce, peas, ornamentals, strawberries, and the bark of apple trees. Rabbits have  a keen sense of smell and are repelled by the scent of pepper. When it rains, be sure to re-pepper the garden.

- **Tabasco Pepper Sauce, McCormick Garlic Powder,** and **Ivory Dishwashing Liquid.** Mix two tablespoons Tabasco Pepper Sauce, two tablespoons McCormick Garlic Powder, three drops Ivory Dishwashing Liquid, and two cups water in a sixteen-ounce trigger-spray bottle, and then apply to beans plants, carrots, lettuce, peas, ornamentals, strawberries, and the bark of apple trees to repel rabbits. (Be sure to wash all vegetables thoroughly before preparing or eating—unless, of course, you enjoy spicy vegetables.)

RACCOONS AND SQUIRRELS

- **McCormick Black Pepper.** To keep squirrels and raccoons away from flower beds and vegetable gardens, sprinkle McCormick Black Pepper in your garden. These animals have a keen sense of smell and are repelled by the scent of pepper. When it rains, be sure to re-pepper the garden.

- **Murphy Oil Soap** and **McCormick Ground (Cayenne) Red Pepper.** To repel squirrels, mix one teaspoon Murphy Oil Soap, one teaspoon McCormick Ground (Cayenne) Red Pepper, and two cups water in a sixteen-ounce trigger-spray bottle. Spray this harmless solution on plants, around garbage cans, or along a fence to keep squirrels at bay.

- **Parsons' Ammonia.** To keep dogs, cats, raccoons, and squirrels away from your garbage cans, fill a spray bottle with Parsons' Ammonia and lightly mist the garbage bags and pails with the pungent liquid.

REPELLENT

- **Heinz White Vinegar.** Instead of applying insecticides to your skin, use a cotton ball to apply Heinz White Vinegar. The pungent smell fades away once the vinegar dries, and insects are repelled by the taste.

- **Lipton Chamomile Tea.** Brew a strong cup of Lipton Chamomile Tea, let cool to room temperature, and apply the tea to your skin. Chamomile repels most insects.

SKUNKS

- **Bounce.** Repel skunks by hanging fresh sheets of Bounce from your fence posts, shrubs, or trees. The fragrance (oleander, a natural repellent) keeps skunks away. Misting the Bounce sheets with water every so often revives the scent.

- **Parsons' Ammonia.** Repel skunks by soaking old sponges in a mixture of one part Parsons' Ammonia and one part water and place the sponges where the animals tend to congregate.

- **Simple Green.** To clean skunk spray (or cat spray, cat urine, or dog urine) from cement or concrete, open all windows and doors to the room (if indoors) and set up fans to ventilate. In a bucket, mix one cup Simple Green All-Purpose Cleaner to ten cups hot water and scrub the cement or concrete surfaces down with the solution. After scrubbing, mop away as much moisture as possible. Run the fans with the windows and doors open until everything dries.

- **Tabasco Pepper Sauce, McCormick Chili Powder,** and **Ivory Dishwashing Liquid.** Mix three teaspoons Tabasco Pepper Sauce, one teaspoon McCormick Chili Powder, one-half teaspoon Ivory Dishwashing Liquid, and two cups water in a sixteen-ounce trigger-spray bottle. Spray the solution liberally around the perimeter of the yard to repel skunks.

SLUGS AND SNAILS

- **Budweiser.** Fill saucers with Budweiser beer and place them around the garden. Slugs and snails love beer, get drunk, and drown.

- **Coca-Cola.** Fill jar lids with flat Coca-Cola and set in the garden. Slugs and snails, attracted by sweet soda, will slither into the jar lids and be killed by the acids in the Coke.

- **Heinz White Vinegar.** Mix equal parts Heinz White Vinegar and water in a trigger-spray bottle, patrol your garden at night, and spray the solution directly on slugs on plants. The gastropods die almost immediately. Spraying the soil at the base of the plant will prompt slugs to surface and die. Do not make the solution stronger than equal parts vinegar and water, or you'll risk damaging plant foliage.

- **Morton Salt.** Sprinkle Morton Salt lightly around your garden or on the sidewalk close to the grass. When slugs attempt to crawl through the salt, the sodium chloride kills them by reverse osmosis—dehydrating them.

SPIDERS

- **Ivory Dishwashing Liquid.** To kill a spider, mix one-quarter teaspoon Ivory Dishwashing Liquid and two cups water in a sixteen-ounce trigger-spray bottle. Spray the soapy solution on the spider. The soap dissolves the exoskeleton of the arachnid.

WASPS

- **Alberto VO5 Hair Spray.** Spray the wasp with a quick burst of Alberto VO5 Hair Spray, which immediately solidifies and immobilizes the insect, giving it the ultimate bee hive hairdo.

- **Chicken of the Sea Tuna** and **Comet.** Open a can of Chicken of the Sea Tuna, sprinkle with powdered Comet cleanser, and set outside wherever wasps cluster. Attracted to the tuna, the wasps ingest the Comet cleanser, which kills them.

- **Domino Sugar** and **ReaLemon.** To kill wasps, drill several one-half-inch holes in the plastic lid of a clean, empty jar. Mix five tablespoons Domino Sugar, three tablespoons ReaLemon lemon juice, and two cups water in the jar and place it where wasps gather. The wasps, attracted to the sugar solution, will fly into the jar and drown in the highly acidic lemonade.

- **Simple Green.** To kill wasps, mix one teaspoon Simple Green All-Purpose Cleaner with two cups water in a sixteen-ounce trigger-spray bottle. Shake well and spray the insects. The soap penetrates their exoskeleton almost instantly, killing the pests.

WHITEFLIES

- **Murphy Oil Soap.** To kill whiteflies on houseplants, mix equal parts Murphy Oil Soap and water in a spray bottle and mist the infected plants. The whiteflies die on contact.

- **Vaseline Petroleum Jelly** and **Post-it Notes.** To eliminate whiteflies on a houseplant, coat a yellow Post-it Note with Vaseline Petroleum Jelly and stick it near the infected plant. Whiteflies are attracted to the color yellow and get stuck in the petroleum jelly.

Ironing

Cleaning

- **Arm & Hammer Baking Soda.** To clean the gunked-up residue from the soleplate of an iron, make a paste from Arm & Hammer Baking Soda and water and use a sponge to rub the paste onto the soleplate of the cool, unplugged iron. Rinse and dry.

- **Colgate Regular Flavor Toothpaste.** To clean residue from the silver soleplate on an iron, squeeze a dollop of Colgate Regular Flavor Toothpaste on a damp, soft cloth and rub the bottom of the cool, unplugged iron. Rinse well.

- **Easy-Off Oven Cleaner, Reynolds Cut-Rite Wax Paper,** and **Q-tips Cotton Swabs.** To clean a silver soleplate encrusted with burnt fabric or other gunk, cover the plastic body of the iron with a protective layer of Reynolds Cut-Rite Wax Paper, and, in a well-ventilated area, spray Easy-Off Oven Cleaner on the bottom of the cool, unplugged iron. Let sit for ten minutes, rinse thoroughly with water, and clean out the steam holes with damp Q-tips Cotton Swabs. Before ironing any clothes, set the iron on warm with the steam setting on, and iron an old towel to make sure you've cleaned all the oven cleaner off the soleplate.

- **Forster Toothpicks.** Use Forster Toothpicks to clean the steam holes on the bottom of a cool, unplugged iron.

- **Heinz White Vinegar.** To clean the steam vents on an iron, fill the water receptacle with a mixture of equal parts Heinz White Vinegar and water. Set the iron on a steam setting, let it steam for five minutes, and then unplug the iron and let it cool. Empty the excess vinegar solution from the iron, fill the receptacle with water, and, with the iron set on a steam setting, iron a clean, old towel.

- **Morton Salt.** To clean the silver soleplate on an iron, sprinkle Morton Salt over a paper grocery bag, warm the iron on a non-steam setting, and iron the paper bag. The abrasive salt cleans the gunk from the bottom of the iron.

- **Mr. Clean Magic Eraser.** Scrub the bottom of a cool, unplugged iron with a damp Mr. Clean Magic Eraser to remove the burned-on gunk.

- **Purell Instant Hand Sanitizer.** To clean gunk from the bottom of an iron, squeeze a dollop of Purell Instant Hand Sanitizer on the bottom of the cool, unplugged iron and rub with a slightly dampened soft, clean cloth. Rinse and dry.

- **Reynolds Cut-Rite Wax Paper.** To clean the soleplate of an iron, heat the iron without steam and run it back and forth over a sheet of Reynolds Cut-Rite Wax Paper.

● **Shout.** To clean the soleplate of an iron with a nonstick finish (such as Teflon), spray Shout stain remover on a damp, soft cloth and wipe the bottom of the cool, unplugged iron. Before ironing any clothes, set the iron on warm with the steam setting on and iron an old towel to make sure you've cleaned all of the Shout off the soleplate.

Keep It Clean
CARING FOR YOUR IRON

■ Be sure to empty the water tank of your iron after each use. Water left in the tank may discolor clothing and the soleplate. Simply unplug the iron and hold it upside down over a sink.

■ Let the iron cool completely before wrapping the cord loosely around it.

■ Store the iron in an upright heel-rest position, not laying flat on its soleplate. Otherwise, dust can settle in the opening of the water reservoir, causing blockage, and prevent the iron from steaming.

■ Never iron over zippers, pins, metal rivets, or snaps, because these may scratch the soleplate.

■ To clean gunk and grime from a soleplate with a nonstick finish, unplug the iron, let it cool, and wipe the soleplate with a sudsy cloth. Do not clean it with any abrasive cleaners or metal scouring pads.

■ To clean starch buildup and other residue from a silver soleplate, unplug the iron, let it cool, and clean the soleplate with a damp cloth or sponge dipped in a paste made of baking soda and water. Do not clean it with any abrasive cleaners or metal scouring pads.

■ Before ironing clothes, preheat the iron for five minutes to let the thermostat stabilize.

■ Be sure to set the iron on the proper setting for the type of fabric you're ironing.

- **S.O.S Steel Wool Soap Pads.** To clean the bottom of a cool, unplugged iron without a nonstick finish, scrub the bottom with a damp S.O.S Steel Wool Soap Pad, rinse clean, and dry.

- **Spray 'n Wash.** To clean the soleplate of an iron with a nonstick finish (such as Teflon), spritz Spray 'n Wash stain remover on a damp, soft cloth and wipe the bottom of the cool, unplugged iron. Before ironing any clothes, set the iron on warm with the steam setting on and iron an old towel to make sure you've cleaned all of the stain remover off the soleplate.

HEMLINES

- **Heinz White Vinegar.** To vanquish a hem line on a wool skirt, mix one-half cup Heinz White Vinegar and one cup warm water in a bowl; saturate a soft, clean cloth in the solution; and wring it out. Lay the damp cloth over the hemline on the skirt and press it with a warm iron.

IRONING BOARDS

- **Faultless Spray Starch.** Keep your ironing board clean for a longer time by spraying the ironing board cover with Faultless Spray Starch and then ironing it.

- **Reynolds Wrap.** Cover the ironing board with Reynolds Wrap aluminum foil with the shiny side up, and then put the ironing cover over it. The foil reflects the heat back up as you iron, heating the back side of the fabric you're ironing, conserving energy and speeding up your ironing.

PERMANENT PRESS

- **Heinz White Vinegar.** To tame creases in permanent-press garments, mix one-half cup Heinz White Vinegar and one cup warm water in a bowl; saturate a soft, clean cloth in the solution; and wring it out. Lay the damp cloth over the crease and press it with a warm iron.

PLEATS

- **Forster Clothespins.** To hold pleats in place while ironing, use Forster Clothespins to clip the fabric together.

SCORCH MARKS

- **Hydrogen Peroxide.** To remove light scorch marks, mix two ounces Hydrogen Peroxide and six ounces water; dampen a soft, clean cloth in the solution; place the dampened cloth over the scorch mark; and press with an iron on a medium to hot setting. (Test this method first on an inconspicuous spot to make sure the Hydrogen Peroxide doesn't harm the color of the fabric.)

- **ReaLemon.** Saturate a light scorch mark on white clothes with ReaLemon lemon juice and lay the garment in the sun to bleach the mark away. Reapply more lemon juice if necessary.

STARCH

- **Kingsford's Corn Starch.** Dissolve two tablespoons Kingsford's Corn Starch in one cup water in a sixteen-ounce trigger-spray bottle. Shake well and use like ordinary spray starch.

- **Lipton Tea Bags.** Brew a strong cup of Lipton Black Tea and let cool. Pour the black tea in a spray bottle and use like ordinary spray starch on dark clothes only.

STEAMING

- **Dickinson's Witch Hazel.** To make clothes smell sweet, add one teaspoon Dickinson's Witch Hazel to the water in the steam iron.

Jewelry

Costume Jewelry

- **Colgate Regular Flavor Toothpaste.** Squeeze a dollop of Colgate Regular Flavor Toothpaste on a clean, old toothbrush and scrub the costume jewelry. Rinse well and dry.

- **Efferdent.** To clean costume jewelry, fill your bathroom sink with hot water, drop in two Efferdent denture cleansing tablets, add your costume jewelry, and let sit for thirty minutes. Rinse clean and dry.

- **Revlon Clear Nail Enamel.** To make costume jewelry last longer, paint a light protective coat of Revlon Clear Nail Enamel on the item.

Diamonds

- **Parsons' Ammonia.** Mix equal parts Parsons' Ammonia and warm water and drop the diamond jewelry in the solution for ten minutes. Rub gently with an old, soft, clean toothbrush. Let air dry.

GOLD

- **Mr. Clean Magic Eraser.** To polish gold jewelry, gently rub the stains with a damp Mr. Clean Magic Eraser, wash the item thoroughly with soapy water, rinse clean, and dry.

- **Parsons' Ammonia.** Soak gold jewelry in equal parts Parsons' Ammonia and lukewarm water for ten minutes, rub with a soft brush, and let dry without rinsing.

- **Simple Green.** Place gold jewelry in a drinking glass, fill with Simple Green All-Purpose Cleaner (from the trigger-spray bottle), swirl the jewelry a few times, and let stand for one hour. Rinse thoroughly with water and dry well.

PEARLS

- **Star Olive Oil.** To shine pearls, pour a few drops of Star Olive Oil on a soft, clean cloth and rub each individual pearl with the cloth. The pearls will glimmer like new.

SILVER

- **Arm & Hammer Baking Soda** and **ReaLemon.** To clean tarnish from silver jewelry, make a paste from Arm & Hammer Baking Soda and ReaLemon lemon juice and brush the paste onto the jewelry with a clean, old toothbrush. Let dry, and then brush and rinse clean. Polish the jewelry with a clean, soft cloth.

- **Colgate Regular Flavor Toothpaste.** To clean tarnish from silver, squeeze a dollop of Colgate Regular Flavor Toothpaste on a soft, clean cloth and rub the item. Rinse and dry.

- **Mr. Clean Magic Eraser.** To polish silver, gently rub the silver with a damp Mr. Clean Magic Eraser, wash the item thoroughly with soapy water, rinse clean, and dry.

Keep It Clean

TAKING CARE OF THE FAMILY JEWELS

- To prevent diamonds from scratching other jewelry, wrap individual pieces of jewelry in tissue or cloth and store them in separate compartments in a jewelry box or in their original boxes or bags.
- Do not put on your jewelry until after you have applied makeup, perfume, and hair spray.
- Avoid touching gemstones and pearls. Oil from your skin builds up on the jewels, dulling their appearance.
- Take off your jewelry when doing housework or manual labor. Cleaning solvents can harm pearls and other gemstones.

- **SC Johnson Paste Wax.** After polishing collectors' silver spoons, give them two or three coats of SC Johnson Paste Wax to protect them from tarnish.
- **Wesson Oil.** After cleaning silver, polish the item with a few drops of Wesson Oil on a soft, clean cloth.

STORING

- **Glad Flexible Straw.** To prevent fine gold and silver chains from getting tangled and knotted in your jewelry box, cut a Glad Flexible Straw to a little less than half the length of the chain, thread the chain through the straw, and fasten the clasp.
- **Kleenex Tissues.** Wrap delicate jewelry in one or more Kleenex Tissues for safekeeping in your jewelry box or in your luggage while traveling.

Kitchens

ALUMINUM COOKWARE

- **Arm & Hammer Baking Soda, Heinz White Vinegar, McCormick Cream of Tartar,** and **Tide.** To clean aluminum cookware, mix one-quarter cup Arm & Hammer Baking Soda, one-quarter cup Heinz White Vinegar, one-quarter cup McCormick Cream of Tartar, and two tablespoons Tide powder. Use a sponge to rub the paste into the aluminum cookware and scour with a nylon scrubber. Rinse clean.

APPLIANCES

- **Arm & Hammer Baking Soda, Clorox Bleach,** and **20 Mule Team Borax.** To prevent white appliances from yellowing, mix one-half cup Arm & Hammer Baking Soda, one-half cup Clorox Bleach, two tablespoons 20 Mule Team Borax, and two quarts water in a bucket. Using a rag or a sponge, wash white appliances with the solution, rinse clean, and dry with a soft, white cloth. (Do not get this solution on anything that might be dyed by bleach.)

- **Canada Dry Club Soda.** Dampen a sponge with Canada Dry Club Soda (even if it has gone flat) and wipe down white appliances to keep them clean and shiny.

- **McCormick Cream of Tartar** and **Heinz White Vinegar.** Mix two teaspoons McCormick Cream of Tartar and enough Heinz White Vinegar to make a paste and rub the paste on the appliance with a soft, clean cloth. Rinse clean with warm water and dry with another soft, clean cloth.

- **Mr. Clean Magic Eraser.** To clean grease and grime from the tiny nooks and crannies of appliances, gently rub the stains with a damp Mr. Clean Magic Eraser.

- **ReaLemon** and **McCormick Alum.** To clean mineral stains from appliances, mix three tablespoons ReaLemon lemon juice, one teaspoon McCormick Alum, and two cups hot water in a sixteen-ounce trigger-spray bottle. Spray the solution on the mineral stains on appliances, let sit for ten minutes, and then rinse clean and dry.

- **20 Mule Team Borax** and **Heinz White Vinegar.** Mix one teaspoon 20 Mule Team Borax, three tablespoons Heinz White Vinegar, and two cups hot water in a sixteen-ounce trigger-spray bottle. Spray the solution on appliances and wipe clean with a soft, clean cloth.

BLENDERS

- **Dawn Dishwashing Liquid.** To clean the inside of blender easily, pour three drops Dawn Dishwashing Liquid inside the blender, fill halfway with warm water, and blend for three minutes. Rinse clean.

BROILER PANS

- **Parsons' Ammonia, Bounty Paper Towels,** and **Glad Trash Bags.** To clean a broiler pan, place the pan inside a Glad Trash Bag, place several Bounty Paper Towels in the pan, saturate the paper towels with Parsons' Ammonia, and seal the bag shut. Let the bag sit overnight outside or in a well-ventilated garage. In the morning, open the bag carefully to avoid breathing the ammonia fumes, remove the broiler pan, leaving the paper towels in the bag, and discard the bag. Wash the pan with soapy water, rinse clean, and dry.

- **Wonder Bread.** Before using the oven broiler, remove the top tray with the holes, place a slice of Wonder Bread in the bottom of the pan, and replace the top tray. When you broil meat, the slice of bread will absorb the resulting grease.

BUTCHER BLOCK

- **Arm & Hammer Baking Soda.** To deodorize and clean butcher block, sprinkle Arm & Hammer Baking Soda on the block, scrub with a damp sponge, and rinse clean.

- **Clorox Bleach.** To clean stains from butcher block, mix two table-spoons Clorox Bleach and two cups warm water and use a sponge to scrub the wood with the solution. Rinse clean and dry with a soft, clean cloth.

- **Heinz White Vinegar.** To clean butcher block, mix equal parts Heinz White Vinegar and water and wash with the solution.

- **Johnson's Baby Oil.** To give butcher block a protective coating, rub Johnson's Baby Oil into the wood with a fine, dry steel wool pad. Let soak for twenty-four hours and repeat. Blot up the excess oil.

- **ReaLemon.** To clean stains from butcher block, saturate the stains with ReaLemon lemon juice and rub clean with a damp sponge. Rinse well and dry with soft, clean cloth.

CABINETS

- **Mr. Clean Magic Eraser.** To clean fingerprints, grease, and grime from kitchen cabinet doors, gently rub the stains with a damp Mr. Clean Magic Eraser.

- **Turtle Wax.** To protect wooden cabinets from grease stains, rub on a thin coat of Turtle Wax, let dry, and buff.

Can Openers

- **Arm & Hammer Baking Soda.** To clean the cutting wheel and lid holder on an electric can opener, wet a clean, old toothbrush with water, dip the bristles into an open box of Arm & Hammer Baking Soda, and scrub the pieces. Rinse well.

- **Reynolds Cut-Rite Wax Paper.** To make an electric or manual can opener glide more easily when opening cans, place a sheet of Reynolds Cut-Rite Wax Paper over the top of an unopened can, hold it securely in place, and run the can through the opener. The wax will lubricate the can opener.

- **Wesson Oil.** Lubricate a hand-held or electric can opener with a few drops of Wesson Oil. Let sit for five minutes, and then wipe off the excess oil with a paper towel or soft cloth.

Casserole Dishes

- **Arm & Hammer Baking Soda.** To clean burned-on food from a casserole dish, fill the casserole dish with warm water, dissolve one tablespoon Arm & Hammer Baking Soda in the water, and let soak overnight. In the morning, wash clean.

- **Bon Ami.** Mildly abrasive Bon Ami cuts grease and cleans baked-on food from glass baking dishes much faster than dishwashing liquid, simultaneously preventing unsightly soap scum buildup.

- **Bounce.** To clean burned-on food from a casserole dish, fill the casserole dish with hot water, lay a fresh sheet of Bounce in the water, and let sit overnight. In the morning, the burned-on food will wipe right out.

- **Cascade.** Fill the casserole dish with water, add one teaspoon Cascade Gel, and let sit overnight. In the morning, rinse clean.

- **Efferdent.** To clean baked-on food from the inside of a casserole dish, fill the dish with water, drop in two or three Efferdent denture cleansing tablets, and let sit overnight. In the morning, wipe clean with a sponge and rinse.

- **Mr. Clean Magic Eraser.** To clean baked-on stains from casserole dishes, gently rub the stains with a damp Mr. Clean Magic Eraser, wash the item thoroughly with soapy water, rinse clean, and dry.

CAST-IRON PANS

- **Crisco All-Vegetable Shortening** and **Bounty Paper Towels.** To re-season a cast-iron pan, use a sheet of Bounty Paper Towels to run a dab of Crisco All-Vegetable Shortening on the inside and outside of the pan after each use. Wipe off the excess.

- **Easy-Off Oven Cleaner.** To clean the outside of a cast-iron pan, spray it with Easy-Off Oven Cleaner in a well-ventilated area. Let sit for ten minutes, and then rinse clean. Wash the outside only with soapy water, rinse, and dry. Re-season. (See Crisco All-Vegetable Shortening above.)

- **Heinz White Vinegar.** To clean the inside of a cast-iron pan, fill the pan with warm water, add two or three tablespoons Heinz White Vinegar, and boil. Re-season. (See Crisco All-Vegetable Shortening above.)

- **McCormick Alum** and **Heinz White Vinegar.** Mix three tablespoons McCormick Alum and enough Heinz White Vinegar to make a thick paste. Rub the paste on the cast-iron pan using an abrasive scouring pad. Rinse clean and dry.

- **Morton Salt.** To clean the inside of a cast-iron pan, sprinkle Morton Salt inside the pan and wipe clean.

- **Mr. Coffee Filter.** To store cast-iron pans, place a Mr. Coffee Filter inside the pan. The coffee filter absorbs moisture, preventing rust.

- **Pam Cooking Spray.** To clean rust spots from a cast-iron pan, spray Pam Cooking Spray on the spots and rub vigorously with a soft, clean cloth. Wipe off the excess oil.

Keep It Clean
IRON-CLAD RULES FOR CAST-IRON COOKWARE

- Seasoning cast-iron cookware prevents rust and creates a natural, permanent nonstick cooking surface. Cast iron can be seasoned and re-seasoned. Over time and use, cast-iron cookware develops a shiny, black surface—the sign of a well-seasoned skillet.

- To season a cast-iron utensil, wash the utensil in hot, soapy water. Rinse and dry completely. Apply a thin, even coat of Crisco All-Vegetable Shortening to the inside and outside of the utensil (including the lid) with a soft cloth or paper towel. Preheat the oven to 350 degrees. Place the utensil upside down on the top shelf of the oven. Place a sheet of Reynolds Wrap aluminum foil on a baking sheet and place the baking sheet on the bottom shelf of the oven to catch any drippings. Bake for one hour, and then turn off the oven and let the utensil remain in the oven until cool.

- Clean cast-iron cookware immediately after use. Wear Playtex Living Gloves and use only boiling water and a nylon scrub brush. Do not use any soap, unless you intend to re-season the cookware. Dry thoroughly, spray lightly with Pam Cooking Spray, wipe with a paper towel, and store properly.

- Do not clean cast-iron cookware in a dishwasher.

- Store cast-iron cookware in a cool, dry place with the lids off to allow air circulation.

- If rust appears on cast iron, clean with steel wool or sandpaper, and re-season.

- Never store food in cast-iron cookware.

- To remove heavy food or grease buildup, scour with an S.O.S Steel Wool Soap Pad, rinse clean, and re-season.

- Re-season cast-iron cookware after cooking acidic foods, such as beans or tomatoes.

- **Reynolds Cut-Rite Wax Paper.** To prevent rust from forming on cast-iron pan between uses, rub a sheet of Reynolds Cut-Rite Wax Paper over the pan after washing. Then store with a sheet of Reynolds Cut-Rite Wax Paper in the pan.

- **S.O.S Steel Wool Soap Pads.** To clean a cast-iron pan, scrub with a wet S.O.S Steel Wool Soap Pad, rinse, and wipe. Re-season. (See Wesson Oil below.)

- **Wesson Oil.** To re-season a cast-iron pan, saturate a paper towel with Wesson Oil and rub the inside of the pan after each use. Wipe off the excess oil.

CHINA

- **Arm & Hammer Baking Soda.** To clean tea stains from china, sprinkle Arm & Hammer Baking Soda on a damp sponge and rub gently.

- **Bon Ami.** When a metal utensil or object scrapes across china, it leaves a gray mark. Sprinkle Bon Ami on a damp cloth or sponge and gently rub the gray mark.

- **Clorox Bleach.** To clean coffee or tea stains from china, mix three-quarters cup Clorox Bleach and one gallon warm water in your sink and soak the china in the solution for five minutes. Rinse well and rub with a soft sponge.

- **Colgate Regular Flavor Toothpaste.** To clean black or gray marks from china caused by cutlery, squeeze a dab of Colgate Regular Flavor Toothpaste on a soft, clean cloth and gently rub the spots.

- **Kleenex Tissues.** To protect china, separate your good dishes by putting a Kleenex Tissue between each dish.

- **Morton Salt.** To clean tea stains from china, sprinkle Morton Salt on a damp sponge and rub gently.

- **Mr. Coffee Filters.** To prevent scratches when stacking china in the cabinet, place a Mr. Coffee Filter between each plate or saucer.

- **Nestlé Carnation NonFat Dry Milk.** To cover up thin cracks in china, mix one and one-third cups Nestlé Carnation NonFat Dry Milk with three and three-quarters cups warm water and soak the china in the solution for thirty minutes.

CHROME BURNER RINGS AND GUARDS

- **Parsons' Ammonia, Bounty Paper Towels,** and **Glad Trash Bags.** To clean burned-on grease and gunk from chrome burner rings and guards, wrap each item in a sheet or two of Bounty Paper Towels, place the items inside a Glad Trash Bag, saturate the paper towels with Parsons' Ammonia, and seal the bag shut. Let the bag sit overnight outside or in a well-ventilated garage. In the morning, open the bag carefully to avoid breathing the ammonia fumes, remove the burner rings and guards, leaving the paper towels in the bag, and discard the bag. Wash the items with soapy water, rinse clean, and dry.

CLEANSER CANS

- **Revlon Clear Nail Enamel.** Prevent the metal rims on the bottom of cleanser cans from leaving rust stains by giving the metal rim a protective coat of Revlon Clear Nail Enamel.
- **Scotch Packaging Tape.** To prevent the metal rims on the bottom of cleanser cans from leaving rust stains, wrap Scotch Packaging Tape around the bottom of the cans, covering the metal rims.

COFFEE AND TEA CUPS

- **Arm & Hammer Baking Soda.** To clean coffee or tea stains from mugs or cups, sprinkle Arm & Hammer Baking Soda on a damp sponge, rub off the stains, and rinse clean.
- **Colgate Regular Flavor Toothpaste.** To clean tea stains from porcelain tea cups, squeeze a dollop of Colgate Regular Flavor Toothpaste on a damp cloth, rub the stains, rinse, and dry.

- **Efferdent.** To clean coffee or tea stains from inside a mug or cup, fill the mug or cup with water, drop in one Efferdent denture cleansing tablet, and let sit overnight. In the morning, rinse clean.

- **McCormick Cream of Tartar.** To clean coffee or tea stains from cups, sprinkle McCormick Cream of Tartar inside the cup and wipe with a clean, damp sponge. Rinse and dry.

- **Mr. Clean Magic Eraser.** To clean stubborn coffee or tea stains from inside a mug, gently rub the stains with a damp Mr. Clean Magic Eraser, wash the item thoroughly with soapy water, and rinse clean.

COFFEE FILTERS

- **Bounty Paper Towels.** Run out of coffee filters? Cut a sheet of Bounty Paper Towels to fit in the coffee basket. Put in fresh ground coffee and proceed as usual.

- **Cool Whip.** To keep coffee filters folded, store them in a clean, empty Cool Whip canister so they maintain their shape.

COFFEEMAKERS

- **Arm & Hammer Baking Soda** and **ReaLemon.** To clean a glass coffee pot, pour equal parts Arm & Hammer Baking Soda and ReaLemon lemon juice into the pot and scrub with a sponge. (For more ways to clean glass coffeepots, see page 190.)

- **Calgon Water Softener.** To clean the mineral buildup from the heating element inside your coffeemaker, fill the water tank on the coffeemaker with water, add two tablespoons Calgon Water Softener, and run the machine through its regular cycle. Rinse thoroughly.

- **Clorox Bleach** or **Heinz White Vinegar.** To clean the basket that holds the coffee filter, if the coffeemaker is white, remove the basket, fill the kitchen sink with soapy water, add one-quarter cup Clorox Bleach if the basket is white (use one-quarter cup Heinz White Vinegar if the basket is a dark color) and soak the basket in the solution for thirty minutes. Rinse clean.

- **Heinz White Vinegar.** To clean mineral buildup on the heating element inside your coffeemaker, fill the water tank on the coffeemaker to the halfway mark with Heinz White Vinegar, place a coffee filter in the basket, put the coffee pot in place, and run the machine through its cycle. Turn off the machine, fill the water tank to the halfway mark with vinegar a second time, let sit for thirty minutes, and then run the vinegar through the machine. The acetic acid in the vinegar dissolves the mineral buildup. Run fresh water through the machine twice to get rid of any vinegar residue, and then wash the coffee pot with soapy water and rinse clean.

- **Tang.** To clean mineral deposits from the heating element inside a coffeemaker, fill the coffee pot with water, dissolve two tablespoons Tang powdered drink mix in the water, and pour the orange drink into the water tank. Place a coffee filter in the basket, put the coffee pot in place, and run the machine through its cycle. The citric acid in the Tang dissolves the mineral buildup. Run fresh water through the machine twice to get rid of any Tang residue, and then wash the coffee pot with soapy water and rinse clean.

COFFEEPOTS

- **Arm & Hammer Baking Soda** and **ReaLemon.** To clean a glass coffeepot, pour equal parts Arm & Hammer Baking Soda and ReaLemon lemon juice into the pot and scrub with a sponge.

- **Coca-Cola.** To clean stains from inside a glass coffeepot, fill the coffeepot with Coca-Cola, let sit for one hour, and rinse clean.

- **Efferdent.** Fill a glass coffeepot with water, drop in two Efferdent denture cleansing tablets, let sit for thirty minutes, and rinse clean.

- **McCormick Cream of Tartar** and **Heinz White Vinegar.** To clean stains from a glass coffeepot, mix two teaspoons McCormick Cream of Tartar and enough Heinz White Vinegar to make a paste and rub the paste on the coffeepot with a damp sponge. Rinse clean with warm water and dry with a soft, clean cloth.

- **Morton Salt.** Pour one-half cup Morton Salt into the empty coffeepot, fill with ice cubes, and swirl the coffeepot so that the ice cubes whirl around inside it, scrubbing the stains with the abrasive salt.

- **ReaLemon** and **Morton Salt.** To clean a glass coffeepot, pour equal parts ReaLemon lemon juice and Morton Salt into the pot and scrub with a sponge. Rinse clean.

- **Uncle Ben's Original Converted Brand Rice** and **Heinz White Vinegar.** To clean out a dirty coffee pot, pour in one half cup Uncle Ben's Original Converted Brand Rice and one half cup Heinz White Vinegar. Swirl the coffeepot vigorously, allowing the rice to scrape against the inside walls of the glass. Wash and rinse clean.

COOKTOPS

- **Arm & Hammer Baking Soda.** To clean a glass or smooth ceramic cooktop, let the cooktop cool, make a paste from Arm & Hammer Baking Soda and water, and apply the paste using a soft cloth. Rinse well and dry with a clean kitchen towel.

- **Bon Ami.** To clean stains and burned-food from a glass or smooth ceramic cooktop, let the cooktop cool and sprinkle Bon Ami on a clean, soft, damp rag and wipe gently. Follow with the Dawn Dishwashing Liquid tip on page 192.

- **Canada Dry Club Soda.** Once you have cleaned a glass or smooth ceramic cooktop with any of the tips listed here, rinse the cooktop with Canada Dry Club Soda (carbonated or flat). The effervescence of the club soda gives the cooktop a beautiful shine.

- **Colgate Regular Flavor Toothpaste.** To clean stains and burned-food from a glass or smooth ceramic cooktop, let the cooktop cool and squeeze a dollop of Colgate Regular Flavor Toothpaste on a clean, soft, damp rag and wipe gently. Rinse well and dry with a clean kitchen towel. Follow with the Dawn Dishwashing Liquid tip on page 192.

- **Dawn Dishwashing Liquid.** To clean a glass or smooth ceramic cooktop, let the cooktop cool and wipe it clean with a soft cloth dampened with soapy water made with a few drops of Dawn Dishwashing Liquid. Rinse well and dry with a clean kitchen towel.

COPPER

- **Alberto VO5 Hair Spray.** To protect the shine on ornamental copper, give the item a light coat of Alberto VO5 Hair Spray after polishing it.

- **Heinz White Vinegar** and **Morton Salt.** To clean copper bottoms of pots, mix equal parts Heinz White Vinegar and Morton Salt in a bowl, dampen a sponge with the solution, and gently rub the copper. Wash, rinse, and dry.

- **ReaLemon** and **Morton Salt.** To clean copper bottoms of pots, mix equal parts ReaLemon lemon juice and Morton Salt in a bowl, dampen a sponge with the solution, and gently rub the copper. Wash, rinse, and dry.

COUNTERTOPS

- **Arm & Hammer Baking Soda.** To clean coffee, tea, or other stubborn stains from a countertop, mix a paste from Arm & Hammer Baking Soda and water, cover the stains with the paste, let sit for fifteen minutes, and rinse clean.

- **Balmex.** To clean grease and dirt from a Formica countertop, squeeze Balmex onto a soft cloth and rub the Formica surface.

- **Bon Ami.** To clean countertops, sprinkle Bon Ami on the area to be cleaned and rub with a very wet cloth and wipe dry to a gleaming finish.

- **Canada Dry Club Soda.** To clean counters, wipe down the surface with Canada Dry Club Soda. Rinse with warm water and dry.

- **Heinz White Vinegar** and **Parsons' Ammonia.** Mix one-half tablespoon Heinz White Vinegar, one-half tablespoon Parsons' Ammonia, and two cups warm water in a sixteen-ounce trigger-spray bottle. Spray the solution on the countertop (except marble) and wipe with a soft, clean cloth. Rinse with water and dry.

- **McCormick Cream of Tartar** and **ReaLemon.** To clean stains or rust from a countertop (including Formica), make a paste from McCormick Cream of Tartar and ReaLemon lemon juice, rub the paste into the stain, let sit for ten minutes, rinse clean, and dry.

- **Nivea Creme.** To clean grease and dirt from a Formica countertop, place a dollop of Nivea Creme on a soft, clean cloth and rub.

- **ReaLemon.** To clean stains off a Formica countertop, rub the spots with ReaLemon lemon juice.

- **ReaLemon, Dawn Dishwashing Liquid, Arm & Hammer Baking Soda,** and **20 Mule Team Borax.** For a great homemade cleanser for countertops, mix two tablespoons ReaLemon lemon juice, one-half teaspoon Dawn Dishwashing Liquid, one tablespoon Arm & Hammer Baking Soda, one teaspoon 20 Mule Team Borax, and two cups water in a sixteen-ounce trigger-spray bottle. Shake well.

- **Spray 'n Wash.** To clean stubborn stains off a countertop, give the trouble spot a spritz of Spray 'n Wash stain remover, let sit for thirty minutes, and then rub with an abrasive sponge. Wash with soapy water, rinse, and dry.

- **Turtle Wax.** To protect plastic laminate countertops from getting scratched or stained, give the countertop a coat of Turtle Wax and buff well.

- **Windex.** Spray a light mist of Windex on the countertop and wipe clean with a soft, clean cloth.

CROCKPOTS

- **Murphy Oil Soap.** To clean baked-on food from the inside of a CrockPot, fill the CrockPot with water, add one tablespoon Murphy Oil Soap, and heat the CrockPot on high for one hour. Carefully rinse clean and dry.

CRYSTAL

- **Heinz White Vinegar.** When washing crystal in the sink, fill the sink with water, add a few drops of your regular dishwashing liquid, and add one cup Heinz White Vinegar to help cut through grease.

- **Mrs. Stewart's Liquid Bluing.** A few drops of Mrs. Stewart's Liquid Bluing in the rinse water makes fine crystal sparkle. The bluing purportedly repels dust particles so the crystal stays clean longer.

CUTTING BOARDS

- **Arm & Hammer Baking Soda.** To eliminate odors from a cutting board, sprinkle Arm & Hammer Baking Soda on the board, scrub with a damp sponge, and rinse well.

- **Clorox Bleach.** To disinfect a cutting board, mix two teaspoons Clorox Bleach and two cups water in a clean trigger-spray bottle. Spray the solution on the cutting board, let sit for ten minutes, and rinse clean with hot water.

- **Colman's Mustard Powder.** To deodorize a cutting board, wet the cutting board with water, sprinkle with Colman's Mustard Powder, and rub with a damp sponge. Then rinse clean and dry.

- **Morton Salt** and **Clorox Bleach.** To clean a wooden cutting board, cover the cutting board with Morton Salt. Mix two teaspoons Clorox Bleach and one cup water and saturate the salt with the solution. Scrub with a brush, rinse with hot water, and dry with a soft, clean cloth.

- **ReaLemon.** To bleach a discolored cutting board, apply ReaLemon lemon juice and let sit overnight. In the morning, wash with soapy water and rinse clean.

DISHES

- **Bon Ami.** To remove stubborn stains from dishes, cups, flatware, and utensils, apply Bon Ami with a damp sponge or cloth, rub off the stains, and wash as usual.

- **Heinz White Vinegar.** When washing dishes in the sink, fill the sink with water, add a few drops of your regular dishwashing liquid, and add three tablespoons Heinz White Vinegar to help cut through grease and put an end to spotting.

- **Johnson's Baby Shampoo.** If you run out of dishwashing soap, wash your dishes in the kitchen sink with Johnson's Baby Shampoo.

- **20 Mule Team Borax.** To prevent spotting on dishes and glassware when washing dishes by hand, add one teaspoon 20 Mule Team Borax to the rinse water.

DISHWASHERS

- **Arm & Hammer Baking Soda.** To deodorize a smelly dishwasher, fill a bowl with Arm & Hammer Baking Soda, place it inside the empty dishwasher, shut the door, and let it sit undisturbed for twenty-four hours.

- **Canada Dry Club Soda.** To clean a stainless steel dishwasher, fill a trigger-spray bottle with Canada Dry Club Soda, spray the dishwasher, and wipe clean with a soft cloth. (For more ways to clean stainless-steel dishwashers, see page 219.)

- **Kool-Aid.** To clean soap scum from the tubes of a dishwasher and rust from the interior, empty a packet of Kool-Aid (lemon leaves a nice scent) in the soap receptacle and run through the regular cycle without any dishes inside. The citric acid in the Kool-Aid does the trick.

- **Tang.** To clean rust or yellow stains from inside a dishwasher, fill the soap receptacle dish with Tang powdered drink mix and run the dishwasher through its regular cycle without any dishes or detergent. The citric acid in the Tang cleans the rust from inside the machine. Repeat if necessary.

- **20 Mule Team Borax.** To deodorize a smelly dishwasher, sprinkle 20 Mule Team Borax on the inside bottom of the dishwasher and let sit overnight. In the morning, use a damp sponge to wipe the borax around the inside of the dishwasher. Let the next load of dishes rinse the borax clean.

- **20 Mule Team Borax** and **Arm & Hammer Baking Soda.** To prevent water spots from forming on dishes or glassware, add one-half teaspoon 20 Mule Team Borax and one-quarter teaspoon Arm & Hammer Baking Soda to the dishwasher detergent in the receptacle dish before running the dishwasher.

- **WD-40.** To clean the exterior of a stainless steel dishwasher, spray WD-40 on a soft, clean cloth and rub the outside of the machine.

DRAIN BOARDS

- **Heinz White Vinegar.** To clean mineral stains from a rubber drain board, place the drain board in the sink (making sure the drain board is level) and pour one cup Heinz White Vinegar over it. Let sit overnight. In the morning, wipe clean with a sponge and rinse with water.

EGGBEATERS

- **Pam Cooking Spray.** To make cleaning eggbeaters a snap, spray the beaters with Pam Cooking Spray before beating the eggs, so they wash off easier.

ELECTRIC FRYING PANS

- **Arm & Hammer Baking Soda.** To clean burned-on grease from an electric frying pan, cover the grease with Arm & Hammer Baking Soda, let sit for fifteen minutes, and then scrub with a damp sponge. Rinse clean with warm water.

Enamel Pots and Broiling Pans

- **Arm & Hammer Baking Soda.** To clean baked-on food from an enamel pot, fill the pot with water, add three tablespoons Arm & Hammer Baking Soda, boil for fifteen minutes, and let cool. Scrub with an abrasive sponge, rinse, and dry.

- **Calgon Water Softener.** To clean baked-on food and grease from an enamel broiling pan, cover the bottom of the pan with powdered Calgon Water Softener, cover with a wet hand towel, and let sit overnight. In the morning, rinse and dry the pan.

Flatware

- **Bon Ami.** To remove stubborn stains from flatware and utensils, apply Bon Ami with a damp sponge or cloth, rub off the stains, and then wash clean as usual.

- **Canada Dry Club Soda.** To give dull stainless steel flatware an instant shine, place the flatware in a pan and cover it with Canada Dry Club Soda. Let sit until the carbonation bubbles stop.

Food Grinders

- **Cheerios.** To clean a food grinder quickly, run one-half cup Cheerios through the grinder to push out any tidbits of food.

Food Processors

- **Uncle Ben's Original Converted Brand Rice.** To eliminate spicy food odors from a food processor bowl, fill the bowl with Uncle Ben's Original Converted Brand Rice and pulverize it. The rice takes up the pungent stench.

- **Wonder Bread.** To remove food odors from a food processor bowl, grind several slices of Wonder Bread. The bread absorbs the odors.

FORMICA

- **Arm & Hammer Baking Soda.** In a bowl, mix one-quarter cup Arm & Hammer Baking Soda with enough water to make a thick paste. Use a sponge to apply the paste to Formica countertops or cabinets, scrub, and rinse clean.

- **Balmex.** To clean grease and dirt from a Formica countertop, squeeze Balmex onto a soft cloth and rub the Formica surface.

- **Canada Dry Club Soda.** To clean Formica countertops or cabinets, saturate a sponge with Canada Dry Club Soda and wipe the surfaces. Rinse clean.

- **Morton Salt.** To clean Formica, mix one-half cup Morton Salt in a bowl with enough water to make a thick paste. Using a damp sponge, rub the salty paste on the Formica countertop or cabinets and rinse clean.

- **Murphy Oil Soap, Heinz White Vinegar,** and **Star Olive Oil.** Mix one teaspoon Murphy Oil Soap, six tablespoons Heinz White Vinegar, one teaspoon Star Olive Oil, and one cup warm water in a sixteen-ounce trigger-spray bottle. Shake well, spray the Formica countertop and cabinets, and scrub with a sponge. Rinse clean.

- **Windex.** To clean ink stains from frozen food packages on a Formica countertop, spray Windex on the affected area and wipe clean.

FREEZERS

- **Arm & Hammer Baking Soda.** To deodorize the freezer, place an open box of Arm & Hammer Baking Soda in the back of the compartment. Be sure to change the box once a month.

- **Campbell's Tomato Juice.** To eliminate the smell of spoiled meat from your freezer, use a sponge to scrub the walls, ceiling, and floor of the freezer compartment with Campbell's Tomato Juice. Wash with soapy water, rinse clean and dry well.

- **Conair 1875 Watt Hair Dryer.** To defrost a freezer, you can speed up the process, if you wish, by blowing hot air from a Conair 1875 Watt Hair Dryer at the ice, being careful not to get the blow dryer wet.

- **Glycerin.** To make cleaning the inside of a freezer easier, dampen a clean, soft cloth with Glycerin and wipe the inside of the freezer to give it a light coat. Glycerin prevents food spills from sticking.

- **Maxwell House Coffee.** To eliminate the smell of spoiled meat from your freezer, empty the freezer, place a pan filled with Maxwell House Coffee grounds inside, shut the door, and let sit for several days. The coffee grounds absorb the foul odor.

- **Pam Cooking Spray.** After defrosting a freezer and drying it thoroughly, spray a light coat of spray Pam Cooking Spray on the inside walls, ceiling, and floor of the freezer to make future defrosting trouble-free.

- **20 Mule Team Borax.** To clean out a defrosted freezer, dissolve one-quarter cup 20 Mule Team Borax in one gallon warm water and wash out the freezer with the solution. Rinse clean and dry.

- **USA Today.** To deodorize a smelly freezer, empty the freezer, fill it with crumpled-up pages of *USA Today,* shut the door, and let sit undisturbed for several days. The newsprint absorbs the stench.

GARBAGE DISPOSERS

- **Arm & Hammer Baking Soda.** To keep a garbage disposer smelling crisp and clean, dissolve one cup Arm & Hammer Baking Soda in a sink filled halfway with warm water and drain the sink with the disposal running.

- **Bon Ami.** To clean a garbage disposer, plug the drain, fill the sink halfway with hot soapy water made with Bon Ami, and then unplug the drain and flood the running disposal.

- **Heinz White Vinegar.** To deodorize your garbage disposer, pour one cup Heinz White Vinegar into the drain, let sit for five minutes, and then

Keep It Clean

TRASHY TALK ABOUT GARBAGE DISPOSERS

- Use only cold water when using a garbage disposer. Why? Cold water hardens greasy matter, making it easier to grind up and preventing grease from adhering to the insides of the pipes. Of course, when not using the garbage disposer, it's perfectly fine to run hot water through the disposer.

- If a pungent odor starts wafting up from your garbage disposer, that's generally a sure sign that grease or food particles have accumulated in the grinding chamber and baffle, attracting odor-causing bacteria. That means you haven't been running the water long enough after using the disposer to allow the food particles to wash through. To avoid this problem in the first place, simply let the water run for an additional fifteen seconds to make sure all the ground-up food particles have washed through the grinding chamber and baffle.

- Never use chemical or solvent drain compounds (such as Drano or Liquid-Plumr) in the garbage disposer. These can damage the disposer.

- To deodorize a garbage disposer, turn off the disposer and disconnect the power supply. Holding a scouring pad, reach through sink opening and slowly and carefully scrub the underside of the splash baffle and the inside upper lip of grind chamber.

- To clean a disposer, place a stopper in the sink opening and fill the sink halfway with warm water. Dissolve one-quarter cup Arm & Hammer Baking Soda in the sink water. Turn on the disposer and simultaneously remove the stopper from the sink, allowing the baking soda and water to drain through the disposer, washing away loose food particles.

- The folks at Maytag suggest that you use a disposer cleaner regularly to eliminate odor-causing bacteria. Maytag recommends Disposer Care, a non-corrosive, biodegradable foaming additive.

flush the drain clean by running the cold water for two minutes. Or mix equal parts Heinz White Vinegar and water in a pitcher and fill your ice cube trays with the solution. Freeze the ice cube trays and run the vinegar ice cubes through the garbage disposer. Be sure to label the ice cube trays so no one accidentally uses the vinegar cubes.

- **20 Mule Team Borax.** To disinfect a garbage disposer, pour one-quarter cup 20 Mule Team Borax into the drain every two weeks.

GARBAGE PAILS

- **Bounty Paper Towels.** To absorb moisture from the bottom of a kitchen garbage pail and prevent mold and mildew odors, place a sheet of Bounty Paper Towels on the bottom of the trash pail.
- **Jonny Cat Litter.** To absorb moisture from the bottom of a kitchen garbage pail and prevent odors, pour a one-inch layer of Jonny Cat Litter on the bottom of the trash pail.

GLASS

- **Wonder Bread.** To lift tiny pieces of broken glass from the kitchen floor, pat the small glass shards with a slide of Wonder Bread.

GLASS STOVETOP

- **Easy-Off Oven Cleaner.** To clean a melted plastic bag off a glass stovetop, make sure the room is well ventilated and spray the plastic with Easy-Off Oven Cleaner. Let sit for fifteen minutes, and then, wearing protective gloves, carefully scrape off the plastic with a single-edge razor blade. Wash with soapy water, rinse clean, and dry.
- **MasterCard.** Use an old MasterCard as a scraper to remove baked-on food from a glass stovetop without scratching the surface.
- **Reynolds Cut-Rite Wax Paper.** To clean a melted plastic bag off a glass stovetop, cover the melted plastic with a sheet of Reynolds Cut-Rite

Wax Paper and press the wax paper gently with a warm iron. When the plastic softens from the heat of the iron, use a single-edge razor blade to carefully scrape off the plastic.

GLASSWARE

- **Clorox Bleach** and **Heinz White Vinegar.** To clean a milky film from glassware, place only the glassware in your dishwasher. Set a bowl filled with one cup Clorox Bleach on the bottom rack of the dishwasher and run the dishwasher through the wash cycle without any dishwasher detergent and stopping before the dry cycle begins. Open the dishwasher and fill the bowl with one cup Heinz White Vinegar and run the dishwasher through the complete cycle without adding any dishwashing detergent. This method simultaneously cleans the interior of the dishwasher.

- **Efferdent.** To clean a glass stained by mineral deposits, fill the glass with water, drop in one Efferdent denture cleansing tablet, and let sit overnight. In the morning, rinse clean.

- **Heinz White Vinegar.** To clean mineral deposits from glassware, fill the sink with equal parts Heinz White Vinegar and water and soak the glasses in the solution. Rinse clean. Or fill a glass bowl with two cups Heinz White Vinegar, set the bowl upright in the bottom rack of your dishwasher, and run the glasses through a two-cycle wash.

GRATERS

- **Oral-B Toothbrush.** To clean a grater with ease, scrub with a clean, old Oral-B Toothbrush.

- **Pam Cooking Spray.** To make cleaning a grater simple, spray the grater with Pam Cooking Spray before using it. The food grates easier, and cleanup is effortless.

- **Ziploc Freezer Bags.** To make grating food neater, hold the grater inside a Ziploc Freezer Bag as you grate the food item inside the bag.

Kitchen Magnets

- **L'eggs Sheer Energy Panty Hose.** To clean kitchen magnets, cut off one leg from a pair of clean, old L'eggs Sheer Energy Panty Hose, place the kitchen magnets in the leg, knot the open end, and run it through the dishwasher in the silverware rack or tied to one of the racks.

Measuring Spoons

- **Revlon Red Nail Enamel.** To make the raised markings on your measuring spoons easy to read, carefully paint the raised marking with Revlon Red Nail Enamel.

Meat Grinders

- **Nabisco Original Premium Saltine Crackers.** Grind several Nabisco Original Premium Saltine Crackers through your meat grinder to absorb dampness and flush out any odds and ends.
- **Wonder Bread.** To clean meat scraps and moisture from a meat grinder, run a few slices of Wonder Bread through the grinder.

Microwave Ovens

- **Arm & Hammer Baking Soda.** Make a paste from Arm & Hammer Baking Soda and water and use a sponge to wipe the paste inside and around the door of the microwave oven. Rinse clean.
- **Bon Ami.** To remove stubborn stains on the interior of a microwave oven, sprinkle Bon Ami on a damp sponge, scrub, and rinse clean.
- **Bounty Paper Towels.** To clean the inside of a microwave oven, saturate a sheet of Bounty Paper Towels with water, place the paper towel in the microwave oven, and heat on high for four minutes. Let the paper towel cool and use it to wipe down the inside walls of the microwave oven.

Keep It Clean

HOT IDEAS FOR MICROWAVE OVENS

■ If you are not sure whether a dish or utensil is microwave-safe, fill a cup with water and place it inside your microwave oven, next to the dish you wish to test. Turn on the heat in the microwave oven for one minute at high power. After one minute, the water should be warm, and the dish you are testing should be cool. If the dish is warm, then it is absorbing microwave energy and is not acceptable for use in a microwave oven.

■ To stop food from splattering on the walls and ceiling of the microwave oven when cooking, cover the food with a microwave-safe lid, waxed paper, plastic wrap, or paper toweling during cooking to prevent spattering. Do not use paper or other flammable materials to cover the food if you are using a heating element or browning dish to brown the food.

■ Clean up spatters and spills when they happen. Use a damp cloth and mild soap. Do not use harsh detergents or abrasives. Continuing to use the microwave oven after food has been spattered inside the oven can cause the oven to work less efficiently and causes that food to bake into the floor, walls, or ceiling of the oven.

● **Cutex Non-Acetone Nail Polish Remover.** To clean yellowish brown stains from the interior of a microwave oven, unplug the appliance, saturate a cotton ball with Cutex Non–Acetone Nail Polish Remover, and rub the stain. Wash clean with soapy water, rinse thoroughly, and dry. Repeat if necessary.

● **Dawn Dishwashing Liquid** and **Mr. Coffee Filter.** Clean the door of a microwave oven with a few drops of Dawn Dishwashing Liquid on a Mr. Coffee Filter saturated with water.

- To help loosen baked-on food particles or liquids, heat two cups water (add the juice of one lemon if you desire to keep the oven fresh) in a four-cup measuring glass at high power for five minutes or until boiling. Let stand in the oven for one to two minutes. The resulting steam helps loosen baked on food or liquids.

- Remove the glass tray when cleaning. To prevent the glass tray from breaking, handle it carefully and do not put the glass tray in water immediately after cooking. Wash the tray carefully in warm, sudsy water or in the dishwasher.

- Clean the outside surface of the oven and the door window with mild soap and a damp, soft cloth. Dry with a soft cloth. To prevent damage to the operating parts of the oven, don't let water seep into the openings.

- To deodorize the interior of a microwave oven, unplug the microwave oven to avoid the possibility of electrical shock. Wash the interior with baking soda or a nonabrasive detergent and let it dry. If the odor persists, mix six tablespoons baking soda and one cup water (or mix one cup lemon juice and one cup water), place the solution in a microwave- safe dish of appropriate size, and heat for two to three minutes on high power.

- Leave the door to the microwave oven open for two to three hours (when the microwave is not in use) to let the microwave air out. Pungent odors such as fish or burned popcorn may take several days to dissipate.

- **Heinz White Vinegar.** To deodorize a smelly microwave oven, pour one cup Heinz White Vinegar in a bowl and cook it in the microwave oven for five minutes, allowing the vinegar to boil. The steam from the vinegar wafts through the fan mechanism, neutralizing the smells in the microwave oven.

- **Maxwell House Coffee.** To deodorize a microwave oven, put two tablespoons Maxwell House Coffee grounds in a small bowl, place the bowl inside the unplugged microwave oven, shut the door, and let sit overnight.

The coffee grounds absorb smells as potent as burnt popcorn. Or mix two tablespoons Maxwell House Coffee in a mug filled halfway with water and cook for two minutes on the high setting.

- **McCormick Pure Vanilla Extract.** Is burned popcorn smelling up the inside of your microwave oven? Pour one tablespoon McCormick Pure Vanilla Extract in a coffee mug and cook it in the microwave for thirty seconds or more. Leave the microwave door shut overnight. In the morning, remove the coffee mug and use a damp sponge to wipe down the inside of the microwave oven.

- **Mr. Coffee Filters.** To prevent splatters in the microwave oven, cover bowls or dishes when cooking with Mr. Coffee Filters, which make excellent covers.

- **Purell Instant Hand Sanitizer.** To clean the exterior of a microwave oven, pour a dollop of Purell Instant Hand Sanitizer on a soft, clean cloth and rub in on the microwave oven.

- **ReaLemon.** To deodorize a microwave oven, pour two tablespoons ReaLemon lemon juice in a coffee mug, fill the rest of the mug with water, and cook it in the microwave for one minute on the high setting. The steam from the lemony water will infuse the inside of the microwave, neutralizing odors.

- **Simple Green.** To clean yellowish brown stains from the interior of a microwave oven, mix equal parts Simple Green All-Purpose Cleaner and water. With a sponge or spray bottle, apply the solution to the inside of the microwave oven and let soak for three minutes. Scrub with a nylon brush or nonabrasive scrubbing pad. Rinse thoroughly with a clean sponge and water.

MIXERS

- **Pam Cooking Spray.** To prevent an electric mixer from making a mess, spray the beaters with Pam Cooking Spray before mixing batter. The oil helps keep the batter in the bowl.

- **Reynolds Cut-Rite Wax Paper.** To avoid making a mess when whipping food with an electric beater, cut two small holes in the middle of a sheet of Reynolds Cut-Rite Wax Paper, slip the stem of the beaters through the holes, and attach to the machine. Lower the beaters into the mixing bowl, keeping the wax paper over the bowl, and turn on the machine. The wax paper catches the splatters.

- **Reynolds Wrap.** To avoid splatters all over the kitchen counter when using a mixer, cover the mixing bowl with a sheet of Reynolds Wrap and punch holes in the aluminum foil to insert the beaters.

NONSTICK COOKWARE

- **Easy-Off Oven Cleaner.** To clean the bottom (not the inside) of a nonstick pan, spray the bottom only with Easy-Off Oven Cleaner in a well-ventilated area, let sit for ten minutes, and wash clean with soapy water. Rinse, dry, and season the pan with Wesson Oil (See below).

- **Heinz White Vinegar** and **Arm & Hammer Baking Soda.** To clean stains from nonstick cookware, mix one-half cup Heinz White Vinegar, two tablespoons Arm & Hammer Baking Soda, and one cup water and boil the solution in the cookware for fifteen minutes. Wash, rinse, and dry. Then season the pan with Wesson Oil (See below).

- **ReaLemon.** To clean white mineral stains from nonstick cookware, saturate a soft, clean cloth with ReaLemon lemon juice and rub the stains. Wash, rinse, and dry. Then season the pan with Wesson Oil (See below).

- **Wesson Oil.** To season nonstick cookware, pour a few drops of Wesson Oil into the pan; rub the oil into the surface with a soft, dry cloth; and wipe up the excess.

ODORS

- **Heinz White Vinegar.** To eliminate the smell of fried fish and other fried foods from the kitchen, set a glass half-filled with Heinz White Vinegar on the kitchen counter.

- **McCormick Ground Cinnamon.** To mask the smell of burned food, sprinkle some McCormick Ground Cinnamon in a saucepan and warm it up on the stove.

- **ReaLemon.** To eliminate the smell of burned foods from the kitchen, boil one tablespoon of ReaLemon lemon juice in a saucepan for three minutes.

Oven Racks

- **Cascade.** To clean the oven racks, place an old towel on the floor of the bathtub, fill the tub with enough hot water to cover the racks, add one-half cup Cascade Gel, and let sit for one hour. Wipe the racks clean with a sponge and rinse.

- **Easy-Off Oven Cleaner.** In the morning, take the oven racks outside, spray them with Easy-Off Oven Cleaner, and let sit in the sun. In the afternoon, rinse the oven racks clean with the garden hose.

- **Parsons' Ammonia, Bounty Paper Towels,** and **Glad Trash Bags.** To clean oven racks, unroll Bounty Paper Towels around the rack to wrap it in a paper towel, place the rack inside a Glad Trash Bag, saturate the paper towels with Parsons' Ammonia, and seal the bag shut. Let the bag sit overnight outside or in a well-ventilated garage. In the morning, open the bag carefully to avoid breathing the ammonia fumes, remove the rack, leaving the paper towels in the bag, and discard the bag. Wash the rack with soapy water, rinse clean, and dry.

- **Simple Green.** To clean the oven racks, soak for one hour in a sink filled with a mixture of one-half cup Simple Green All-Purpose Cleaner and four cups water. Then rinse clean and dry.

Ovens

- **Arm & Hammer Baking Soda.** To clean baked-on food from the inside of an oven or to clean grease from the inside of an oven window, make a paste from Arm & Hammer Baking Soda and water, apply the paste to the spot with a damp sponge, and scrub. Rinse clean.

- **Canada Dry Club Soda.** To clean the outside of a stainless steel oven, fill a trigger-spray bottle with Canada Dry Club Soda, spray the oven, and wipe clean with a soft cloth. (For more ways to clean a stainless-steel oven, see page 219.)

- **Dixie Cups.** To protect the light bulb in the oven while you're using strong cleansers, cover the light bulb with a Dixie Cup. The translucent cup allows light to shine so you can see what you're cleaning. (Be sure to remove the paper cup before using the oven.)

- **Fantastik.** Preheat the oven to 150 degrees Fahrenheit, turn off, spray the interior walls, ceiling, and floor with Fantastik, and let sit for fifteen minutes to cool. Wipe with a soft, clean cloth.

- **Morton Salt.** If something bubbles over in the oven and starts smoking, open the oven and pour a mountain of salt to cover the spill on the oven floor. The salt stops the smoke so you can continue cooking. The next day, after the oven and the spill have cooled, use a spatula to lift out the congealed spill.

- **Mr. Clean Magic Eraser.** To clean baked-on food from the inside of an oven, scrub the trouble spots with a damp Mr. Clean Magic Eraser.

- **Parsons' Ammonia, Heinz White Vinegar,** and **Arm & Hammer Baking Soda.** To clean an oven, preheat the oven to 200 degrees for fifteen minutes, and then turn off the oven, keeping the oven door closed. Place a saucer filled with Parsons' Ammonia on the top shelf of the oven and place a glass bowl filled with two cups of boiling water on the bottom shelf. Close the oven door and let sit overnight. In the morning, remove the saucer and bowl and discard the contents. Mix one cup Heinz White Vinegar, one-half cup Arm & Hammer Baking Soda, and two teaspoons Parsons' Ammonia and use a sponge to apply the paste to the oven walls, let sit for fifteen minutes, and then rinse clean with a damp cloth.

- **Simple Green.** In a bucket, mix equal parts Simple Green All-Purpose Cleaner and warm water. With a sponge or spray bottle, apply the solution to the inside of the oven and let soak for three minutes. Scrub with a nylon brush or nonabrasive scrubbing pad. Rinse thoroughly with a clean sponge and water.

PEWTER

- **Crayola Chalk, Ziploc Storage Bags,** and **Smirnoff Vodka.** Place the twelve sticks from a box of white Crayola Chalk (or one stick of Crayola Sidewalk Chalk) in a Ziploc Storage Bag, roll up the bag to minimize the amount of air inside it, seal the bag shut, and use a hammer to pound the bag until the chalk becomes a fine powder. Empty the chalk powder into a bowl and add enough Smirnoff Vodka to make a thick paste. Apply the paste to the pewter by rubbing with a soft, clean cloth or a clean, old toothbrush. Let dry, rinse clean with hot water, and buff dry with a soft, clean cloth.

- **Star Olive Oil.** To clean pewter, dip an extra fine steel wool pad (available at the hardware store) in Star Olive Oil and rub. Rinse clean and buff with a soft, clean cloth.

PLASTIC CONTAINERS

- **Arm & Hammer Baking Soda.** Are your Tupperware and Rubbermaid containers stained red from tomato sauce? Use Arm & Hammer Baking Soda as you would any cleansing powder to scrub the stains from the containers.

- **Colman's Mustard Powder.** To deodorize plastic containers, fill the container with warm water, dissolve one-quarter teaspoon Colman's Mustard Powder, and let sit for one hour. Wash with soapy water, rinse clean, and dry.

- **Mr. Clean Magic Eraser.** To clean tomato sauce stains inside plastic food containers, gently rub the stains with a damp Mr. Clean Magic Eraser, wash the item thoroughly with soapy water, and rinse clean.

- **ReaLemon.** To bleach stains from plastic containers, apply ReaLemon lemon juice to the stains and place the open containers in the sun to dry.

Keep It Clean
GETTING DRASTIC WITH PLASTIC

- To remove a label or price sticker from a plastic container, rub a few drops of Wesson Oil or Star Olive Oil into the label to soften it and loosen the adhesive. Lift off the label and wipe away any remaining adhesive. To clean off any adhesive residue, place a liberal amount of Johnson's Baby Powder on the spot, let stand for thirty minutes, and rub it off.

- Do not reheat or store foods high in tomato content in a plastic container. Tomato sauce may stain the plastic permanently.

- Do not clean plastic containers with abrasive cleaning pads or cleansers. These scuff the plastic surfaces, allowing stains to penetrate deeper into the plastic.

- To remove stains from plastic containers, soak the stained plastic pieces in a solution of one tablespoon Clorox Bleach per cup of warm water for thirty minutes. Or cover the stain with liquid Palmolive Automatic Dishwasher detergent, let stand for thirty minutes, and rinse thoroughly.

- To deodorize plastic containers, wash them with Arm & Hammer Baking Soda sprinkled on a clean, damp sponge. Or dissolve one-half cup Arm & Hammer Baking Soda in a sink full of water and soak the plastic containers in the solution.

- *USA Today.* To eliminate odors from plastic containers, crumple up a page from *USA Today* into a ball, place it inside the container, and seal shut. The newspaper absorbs the odors overnight.

Playtex Living Gloves

- **Johnson & Johnson Cotton Balls.** To extend the life of Playtex Living Gloves, stuff a Johnson & Johnson Cotton Ball into each fingertip of the gloves to prevent your fingernails from tearing through them.

- **Johnson's Baby Powder.** Wearing rubber gloves while washing the dishes can irritate skin. Sprinkle Johnson's Baby Powder inside the gloves to reduce friction against the skin and to help the gloves slip on and off easily.

- **Kingsford's Corn Starch.** Sprinkling Kingsford's Corn Starch inside a pair of rubber gloves absorbs moisture, enabling your hands to slip inside almost effortlessly.

Porcelain

- **Efferdent.** To clean porcelain items, fill the kitchen sink with warm water, drop in two Efferdent denture cleansing tablets, and let the porcelain items soak in the mixture for ten minutes. Wash with soapy water, rinse clean, and dry.

Pots and Pans

- **Arm & Hammer Baking Soda.** To clean a scorched pan, fill the cookware with warm water, stir in four tablespoons Arm & Hammer Baking Soda, and boil until the scorch marks bubble to the surface.

- **Arm & Hammer Super Washing Soda** and **Murphy Oil Soap.** To clean baked-on food from pots and pans, dissolve two tablespoons Arm & Hammer Super Washing Soda and three drops Murphy Oil Soap in a sink filled with hot water. Soak the pots or pans in the solution for two hours. Wash as usual.

- **Bon Ami.** To clean burned-on food from pots and pans, soak dirty pots and pans for thirty minutes, wipe with a sponge sprinkled with Bon Ami to remove any caked-on food, and then wash as usual.

- **Bounce.** To clean burned-on food from a pan, fill the pan with hot water, lay a fresh sheet of Bounce into the water, and let sit overnight. In the morning, the burned-on food will wipe right out.

- **Clorox Bleach** and **Clabber Girl Baking Powder.** To clean stains from nonstick pots and pans, mix one-half cup Clorox Bleach, two tablespoons Clabber Girl Baking Powder, and one cup water. Pour the solution into the pot or pan and boil for ten minutes without letting it bubble over the top. Wash clean with soapy water and dry well.

- **Heinz White Vinegar.** To clean a burned pan, fill the pan with boiling water, add three tablespoons Heinz White Vinegar, and let sit overnight. In the morning, wipe clean with a sponge and rinse.

- **Morton Salt.** To clean burned-on food from the bottom of an enamel pot, cover the bottom of the pot with two inches of water, add five tablespoons Morton Salt, and let sit overnight. In the morning, boil the solution. Wash, rinse, and dry.

- **Mr. Clean Magic Eraser.** To clean baked-on stains from pots and pans, gently rub the stains with a damp Mr. Clean Magic Eraser, wash the item thoroughly with soapy water, rinse clean, and dry. Do not use the Mr. Clean Magic Eraser on nonstick coatings on pots and pans.

- **Play-Doh.** To clean baked-on food from a frying pan, rub a ball of Play-Doh in the cool pan to remove the baked-on food, and then wash the pan thoroughly with dishwashing soap and water. The combination of flour and salt in the Play-Doh cleans the pan.

Keep It Clean

HOW TO CLEAN COOKWARE

Stainless Steel Cookware

- The best way to prevent staining or buildup from food or grease is to clean your cookware thoroughly after each use.

- To prevent water spotting, rinse your stainless steel cookware in warm water after washing and towel dry thoroughly.

- If a spotted, white film appears on the cookware when it dries, you have hard water and you're seeing the minerals. Rub the white spots with a sponge or brush damped with ReaLemon lemon juice or Heinz White Vinegar. (The acids wash off the minerals.) Wash, rinse, and towel dry.

- To remove stubborn stains or discoloration, rub Bon Ami or Barkeepers Friend on the stains with a nonabrasive pad, cloth, or sponge. (Never scrub with steel wool or harsh abrasive cleaners; they may scratch the stainless steel.)

- You can also clean stainless steel cookware in an automatic dishwasher using a mild dishwashing detergent.

Nonstick Pans

- Wash nonstick pans thoroughly after each use with a mild dishwashing detergent, warm water, and a soft nylon brush—to remove food and grease particles that may burn when the pan is reheated.

- Never use steel wool or any abrasive cleansers on nonstick cookware.

- To remove burned-on food particles from the nonstick surface, mix three parts water and one part Heinz White Vinegar in the pan, bring the solution to boil on medium heat for five to ten minutes, remove from the heat, and let stand until cool. Wash with the pan with warm, soapy water and a soft nylon brush, rinse clean, and dry.

- **Simple Green.** To clean baked-on food from pots, pans, and Dutch ovens, rinse the cookware to remove any loose food or drippings. Mix one-half cup Simple Green All-Purpose Cleaner and five cups water and pour the solution into the cookware. Let it sit overnight. In the morning, wipe clean with a sponge, wash it clean with soapy water, and rinse well.

Range Hoods

- **Balmex.** To clean grease from a range hood, squeeze Balmex onto a soft cloth and rub the grease stains.

- **Bon Ami.** To clean a range hood, sprinkle Bon Ami on a wet sponge, rub, rinse, and wipe dry with a soft, clean cloth.

- **Cascade.** Pour a few drops of Cascade Gel on a wet sponge, rub the grease stains on the range hood, rinse, and dry with soft, clean cloth.

- **Cascade.** To clean grease and grime from the filter in the range hood, place the filter in the dishwasher along with your dishes and Cascade Gel and run through the regular cycle. Repeat if necessary.

- **Nivea Creme.** To clean grease and dirt from an oven range hood, place a dollop of Nivea Creme on a soft, clean cloth and rub the stains.

- **Spray 'n Wash.** To clean grease from a range hood, spray Spray 'n Wash stain remover on the grease stains, let it set for a few minutes, and then wipe with a soft, clean cloth.

Refrigerator Drip Trays

- **Arm & Hammer Baking Soda.** To clean the refrigerator drip tray, remove the tray from underneath the refrigerator and scrub it with Arm & Hammer Baking Soda and water. Rinse, dry well, and return it to its original place.

- **20 Mule Team Borax.** To kill the mold that grows in the refrigerator drip tray, once a month pull out the tray from underneath the refrigerator, fill it with water, add one tablespoon 20 Mule Team Borax, and scrub. Rinse well. Dry with a soft, clean cloth, and put the drip tray back in place.

REFRIGERATORS

- **Arm & Hammer Baking Soda.** To keep the inside of the refrigerator smelling sweet, place an open box of Arm & Hammer Baking Soda on the back of a middle shelf.

- **Arm & Hammer Baking Soda.** To clean the gasket (the white rubber trim around the inside of the refrigerator door), sprinkle Arm & Hammer Baking Soda on a damp sponge and wipe the rubber gasket. Rinse clean and dry.

- **Bon Ami.** Remove stubborn stains and spills from the exterior and interior of a refrigerator by using Bon Ami sprinkled on a wet sponge. Also wipe down the door gasket, which can be a source of odor.

- **Canada Dry Club Soda.** To clean a stainless steel refrigerator, fill a trigger-spray bottle with Canada Dry Club Soda, spray the refrigerator, and wipe clean with a soft cloth. (For more ways to clean a stainless-steel refrigerator, see page 219.)

- **Glycerin.** To make cleaning the inside of the refrigerator easier, dampen a clean, soft cloth with Glycerin and wipe the inside of the refrigerator, including the shelves and bins to give them a light coat. Glycerin prevents food spills from sticking.

- **Heinz White Vinegar.** To clean the inside of the refrigerator and prevent mildew and odors, wipe the interior with a sponge or rag dampened with Heinz White Vinegar.

- **Johnson's Baby Oil.** To prevent the gasket (the white rubber trim around the inside of the refrigerator door) from drying up and cracking, give it a light coat of Johnson's Baby Oil.

- **Jonny Cat Litter.** To deodorize a refrigerator, fill a bowl with Jonny Cat Litter and set it on a shelf. The cat box litter absorbs odors.

- **L'eggs Sheer Energy Panty Hose** and **Maxwell House Coffee.** To deodorize a smelly refrigerator, cut off one foot from a clean, used pair of L'eggs Sheer Energy Panty Hose, fill it with Maxwell House Coffee grounds, tie a knot in the open end, and place the sachet on a shelf in the refrigerator. If you're leaving the house to go on vacation, also unplug the refrigerator and leave the door open.

- **McCormick Pure Lemon Extract.** To freshen the air in a refrigerator, dampen a cotton ball with a few drops of McCormick Pure Lemon Extract and place it on a saucer in the refrigerator.

- **McCormick Pure Orange Extract.** Looking for another way to freshen the air in a refrigerator? Dampen a cotton ball with a few drops of McCormick Pure Orange Extract and place it on a saucer on a shelf in the refrigerator.

- **McCormick Pure Vanilla Extract.** Put a few drops of McCormick Pure Vanilla Extract on a cotton ball and place it on a saucer in the refrigerator to freshen the air.

- **Murphy Oil Soap.** To clean a stainless steel refrigerator, pour a few drops of Murphy Oil Soap on a wet, soft, clean cloth and rub the exterior of the refrigerator. Buff dry with another soft, clean cloth.

- **Pam Cooking Spray.** To move a heavy refrigerator on a vinyl, linoleum, or tile floor so you can clean behind it, spray the floor in front of the refrigerator with a small amount of Pam Cooking Spray so it glides easily.

- **Turtle Wax.** To make cleaning the exterior of the refrigerator easier, give the outside a coat of Turtle Wax and buff well.

- **USA Today.** To deodorize a smelly refrigerator, empty the refrigerator, fill it with crumpled-up pages of *USA Today,* shut the door, and let it sit undisturbed for several days. The newsprint absorbs the stench.

- **Vaseline Petroleum Jelly.** After cleaning the exterior of a stainless steel refrigerator, rub a thin coat of Vaseline Petroleum Jelly over the stainless steel and buff with a soft, clean cloth to give the refrigerator a brilliant shine.

- **WD-40.** To clean a stainless steel refrigerator, wipe the exterior clean with a wet soft cloth, and then spray a little WD-40 on the stainless steel exterior and buff with a soft, clean cloth.

- **Windex.** To shine the chrome trim on a refrigerator, give a soft, clean cloth a spritz of Windex and wipe the chrome clean.

- **Wonder Bread.** To deodorize refrigerator odors, place a few slices of Wonder Bread on the back of a middle shelf in the refrigerator. The white bread absorbs odors.

SERVING SPOONS

- **Pam Cooking Spray.** To prevent food from sticking to a serving spoon, spray Pam Cooking Spray on the serving spoon before dishing out sticky foods.

SHELVES

- **Conair 1875 Watt Hair Dryer.** To remove Con-Tact Paper from pantry shelves, aim a Conair 1875 Watt Hair Dryer set on high to melt the adhesive backing and peel up the paper.

SILVERWARE

- **Arm & Hammer Baking Soda.** To clean silverware, sprinkle Arm & Hammer Baking Soda on a damp sponge and rub the silverware.

- **Arm & Hammer Baking Soda** and **Reynolds Wrap.** To clean tarnished silverware easily and efficiently, place a sheet of Reynolds Wrap aluminum foil on the bottom of the inside of a large pan, fill the pan with a two-inch layer of water, and dissolve two tablespoons Arm & Hammer Baking Soda in the water. Lay the tarnished silverware on the submerged sheet of aluminum foil, and heat the water to 150 degrees Fahrenheit (never allowing the water to boil). The chemical reaction removes the tarnish from the silverware and adheres it to the aluminum foil.

- **Calgon Water Softener, Morton Salt,** and **Reynolds Wrap.** To clean silverware with little effort, plug the drain in your kitchen sink, add enough hot water to fill the sink with two inches of water, dissolve one tablespoon Calgon Water Softener and one tablespoon Morton Salt in the water, and place a sheet of Reynolds Wrap aluminum foil in the bottom of the sink. Place the tarnished silverware on the sheet of aluminum foil, let sit for one minute, and wipe clean with a soft cloth.

- **Colgate Regular Flavor Toothpaste.** Squeeze a dollop of Colgate Regular Flavor Toothpaste on a soft, clean cloth and rub the silverware. The mild abrasives in the toothpaste clean the silver. Rinse clean and dry.

- **Mr. Clean Magic Eraser.** To polish silverware, gently rub the silverware with a damp Mr. Clean Magic Eraser, wash the item thoroughly with soapy water, rinse clean, and dry.

- **Nestlé Carnation NonFat Dry Milk** and **Heinz White Vinegar.** To clean tarnish from silver, mix one-half cup Nestlé Carnation NonFat Dry Milk, two cups water, and two cups Heinz White Vinegar. Place the silverware in a pan, and pour in the milky solution to cover the items. Let soak overnight. In the morning, wash the silverware with soapy water, rinse, and polish dry.

- **ReaLemon.** Soak the silverware in ReaLemon lemon juice. Rinse clean with hot water and buff dry.

- **Star Olive Oil.** To give the above tip using Colgate Regular Flavor Toothpaste a boost, put a few drops of Star Olive Oil on the cloth before adding the dollop of toothpaste.

STAINLESS STEEL APPLIANCES

- **Canada Dry Club Soda.** To clean the exterior of a stainless steel refrigerator, dishwasher, or oven, fill a trigger-spray bottle with Canada Dry Club Soda, spray the outside of the appliance, and wipe clean with a soft cloth.

- **Johnson's Baby Oil** and **Bounty Paper Towels.** To clean the outside of a stainless steel refrigerator, dishwasher, or oven, polish the stainless steel with a drop of Johnson's Baby Oil, and then buff dry with a sheet of Bounty Paper Towels.

- **McCormick Cream of Tartar** and **Heinz White Vinegar.** Mix two teaspoons McCormick Cream of Tartar and enough Heinz White Vinegar to make a paste. Rub the paste on the stainless steel appliance with a soft, clean cloth. Rinse clean with warm water and dry with another soft, clean cloth.

- **Murphy Oil Soap.** To clean a stainless steel appliance, pour a few drops of Murphy Oil Soap on a wet, soft, clean cloth and rub the exterior of the appliance. Buff dry with another soft, clean cloth.

- **Star Olive Oil** and **Bounty Paper Towels.** To clean the outside of a stainless steel refrigerator, dishwasher, or oven, polish the stainless steel with a drop of Star Olive Oil and then buff dry with a sheet of Bounty Paper Towels.

- **Vaseline Petroleum Jelly.** After cleaning the exterior of a stainless steel appliance, rub a thin coat of Vaseline Petroleum Jelly over the stainless steel and buff thoroughly with a soft, clean cloth to give the appliance a brilliant shine.

- **WD-40.** To clean a stainless steel appliance, wipe the exterior clean with a wet, soft cloth, and then spray a little WD-40 on the stainless steel exterior and buff with a soft, clean cloth.

- **Windex.** To give a stainless steel appliance a nice shine, spray Windex on a soft, clean cloth and wipe the stainless steel clean.

STAINLESS STEEL FLATWARE

- **Bon Ami.** To remove stubborn stains from stainless steel flatware, apply Bon Ami with a damp sponge or cloth, rub off the stains, and wash as usual in soapy water.

- **Clorox Bleach** and **Calgon Water Softener.** To clean stainless steel flatware, mix one-quarter cup Clorox Bleach, one-quarter cup Calgon Water Softener, and one gallon hot water and soak the cutlery in the solution for thirty minutes. Wash as usual, rinse clean, and dry.

- **Colgate Regular Flavor Toothpaste.** To clean stubborn stains from stainless steel flatware, squeeze a dab of Colgate Regular Flavor Toothpaste on a soft, clean cloth and rub the stains. Wash as usual, rinse clean, and dry.

- **Morton Salt.** To clean egg stains from stainless steel flatware, sprinkle Morton Salt on a damp sponge and rub.

- **ReaLemon** and **Morton Salt.** Mix together enough ReaLemon lemon juice and Morton Salt to make a gritty paste; use a soft, clean cloth to rub the paste on stainless steel cutlery; rinse clean with warm water; and polish dry with another soft, clean cloth.

- **20 Mule Team Borax.** Make a paste from 20 Mule Team Borax and water; use a soft, clean cloth to rub the paste on stainless steel flatware; rinse clean with warm water; and polish dry with another soft, clean cloth.

STAINLESS STEEL SINKS

- **Arm & Hammer Baking Soda.** To clean a stainless steel sink, sprinkle Arm & Hammer Baking Soda on a damp sponge and rub the stainless steel. Rinse well and dry with a clean, soft cloth.

- **Bon Ami.** To clean a stainless steel kitchen sink, sprinkle Bon Ami in the sink, rub with a wet sponge, and rinse.

- **Canada Dry Club Soda.** Saturate a soft, clean cloth with Canada Dry Club Soda (carbonated or flat), wipe down the stainless steel sink, and then dry well.

- **Colgate Regular Flavor Toothpaste.** To clean stubborn stains from a stainless steel sink, squeeze a dab of Colgate Regular Flavor Toothpaste on a soft, clean cloth and rub the stains. Rinse clean and dry.

- **Easy-Off Oven Cleaner.** To clean stubborn stains from a stainless steel sink, spray with Easy-Off Oven Cleaner (making sure the room is well ventilated), let sit for ten minutes, and rinse clean.

- **Gold Medal Flour.** To polish a stainless steel sink, dry the sink with a soft, clean cloth, sprinkle one tablespoon Gold Medal Flour in the sink, and rub with a dry, soft, clean cloth. Rinse clean with water and dry well.

- **Heinz White Vinegar.** To remove rust marks or water spots from a stainless steel sink, wipe down the sink with a soft, clean cloth saturated with Heinz White Vinegar. Rinse clean with water and dry with a soft, clean cloth.

- **Johnson's Baby Oil** and **Bounty Paper Towels.** To shine a stainless steel sink, rub a few drops of Johnson's Baby Oil into the sink and buff with Bounty Paper Towels.

- **McCormick Cream of Tartar** and **Hydrogen Peroxide.** To clean stains from a stainless steel sink, make a paste from McCormick Cream of Tartar and Hydrogen Peroxide. Apply the paste to the stains, let dry, and then wipe clean with a soft, wet cloth.

- **Morton Salt.** To clean grease and soap scum from a stainless steel sink, sprinkle Morton Salt in the sink and scrub with a damp sponge.

- **20 Mule Team Borax.** Sprinkle 20 Mule Team Borax in the sink, rub with a damp sponge, and rinse clean with warm water.

- **Zippo Lighter Fluid.** To clean rust from stainless steel, dampen a clean cloth with Zippo Lighter Fluid and rub the rust away. Wash with soapy water, rinse, and dry.

STEEL WOOL PADS

- **Arm & Hammer Baking Soda.** To prevent a steel wool pad from rusting, dissolve three tablespoons Arm & Hammer Baking Soda in a bowl of water and store the steel wool pad in the solution.

- **Dawn Dishwashing Liquid.** To prevent steel wool pads from leaving rust marks on your sink or kitchen counter, cut a clean, empty Dawn Dishwashing Liquid bottle three inches from the bottom to make a handy plastic container.

- **Ziploc Freezer Bags.** To prevent a steel wool pad from rusting, place the steel wool pad in a Ziploc Freezer Bag and store it in the freezer after each use. To defrost, simply run the pad under hot water.

STOVE KNOBS

- **Cascade.** To clean the knobs on a stove, pull off the knobs (making sure the stove remains off), mix one-quarter cup Cascade Gel and one gallon water, and let the  knobs soak in the solution for one hour. Scrub with a clean, old toothbrush, if necessary. Rinse and dry.

STOVES

- **Arm & Hammer Baking Soda.** To clean grease splatters from the wall behind the stove, make a paste from Arm & Hammer Baking Soda and water, apply the paste to the wall, let stand for one hour, and rinse clean.

- **Bon Ami.** To clean a stovetop, sprinkle Bon Ami on the area to be cleaned, rub with a wet sponge, rinse clean, and wipe dry to attain a gleaming finish.

- **Cascade.** To clean the drip pans of a stove, mix one-quarter cup Cascade Gel and one gallon water and let the pans soak in the solution for one hour. Rinse and dry.

- **Con-Tact Paper.** To prevent stains on the wallpaper behind your stove, clean the wallpaper thoroughly, let dry, and then paper over it with clear, washable Con-Tact Paper.

- **Easy-Off Oven Cleaner** and **Glad Trash Bags.** To clean grease and burned-on food from drip pans, place the drip pans in a Glad Trash Bag, spray the pans with Easy-Off Oven Cleaner, seal the bag closed, and let it sit outside overnight. The next morning, remove the drip pans from the bag (being careful not to breath any fumes), hose them down thoroughly, and carefully dispose of the bag.

- **Nestlé Carnation NonFat Dry Milk, Clorox Bleach,** and **Bounty Paper Towels.** To clean grease stains from behind a stovetop, mix one teaspoon Nestlé Carnation NonFat Dry Milk, one-quarter cup Clorox Bleach, and one-quarter cup water in a glass bowl. Saturate a sheet or two of Bounty Paper Towels with the solution and drape the wet paper towel so it sticks to the wall, covering the grease stains. Let soak for one minute, remove, and rinse clean. Repeat if necessary.

- **Spray 'n Wash.** To clean baked-on grease from a stovetop, spray Spray 'n Wash stain remover on baked-on grease on the stovetop, let it set for a few minutes, and then wipe clean.

STRAINERS

- **L'eggs Sheer Energy Panty Hose.** As a substitute for a food strainer, cut off one of the legs from a clean pair of L'eggs Sheer Energy Panty Hose, stretch the opening across the mouth of a pot or bowl, and pour the food into the leg. Lift up the panty hose leg and squeeze the food through the nylon mesh into the pot or bowl.

TEA KETTLES

- **Heinz White Vinegar.** To clean lime deposits from inside an electric or regular tea kettle, fill the tea kettle with equal parts Heinz White Vinegar and water, let sit over night, and rinse thoroughly in the morning. The acetic acid in the vinegar dissolves the lime deposits.

- **McCormick Cream of Tartar.** For a quick way to clean lime deposits from inside a tea kettle, fill the kettle with water, mix in one teaspoon McCormick Cream of Tartar, and bring the mixture to a boil. Rinse clean.

TEAPOTS

- **Efferdent.** To clean tea stains from the inside of teapot, fill the teapot with warm water, drop in two Efferdent denture cleansing tablets, let sit for two hours, and rinse clean.
- **Mr. Clean Magic Eraser.** To clean tea stains from a teapot, gently rub the stains with a damp Mr. Clean Magic Eraser, wash the teapot thoroughly with soapy water, rinse clean, and dry.

THERMOS BOTTLES

- **Arm & Hammer Baking Soda.** To freshen a Thermos bottle, fill the bottle with warm water, add two tablespoons Arm & Hammer Baking Soda, shake well, and let sit for ten minutes. Rinse well.
- **Cascade.** Pour one teaspoon Cascade Gel into the Thermos bottle, add boiling water, screw the lid on the bottle tightly, shake well, and let sit for one hour. Rinse thoroughly.
- **Uncle Ben's Original Converted Brand Rice** and **Heinz White Vinegar.** To clean out a Thermos bottle, pour in one half cup Uncle Ben's Original Converted Brand Rice and one half cup Heinz White Vinegar. Screw the lid on the bottle and shake vigorously, allowing the rice to scrape against the inside walls of the Thermos. Wash and rinse clean.

TOASTERS

- **Arm & Hammer Baking Soda.** To clean a chrome or white plastic toaster, sprinkle Arm & Hammer Baking Soda on a damp rag and scrub the unplugged toaster. Rinse clean.

- **Cutex Nail Polish Remover.** To remove melted pieces of a plastic bread bag from the outside of a toaster, unplug the toaster and use a cotton ball to apply Cutex Nail Polish Remover to the plastic. The acetone in the nail polish remover works as a solvent on the plastic. Rinse clean.

- **Gold Medal Flour.** To clean an unplugged chrome toaster, sprinkle Gold Medal Flour on a damp sponge, scrub, rinse clean, and dry.

- **Heinz White Vinegar.** Saturate a sponge with Heinz White Vinegar and polish the chrome on an unplugged toaster.

- **Murphy Oil Soap.** To clean a chrome toaster, mix one teaspoon Murphy Oil Soap and two cups water in a sixteen-ounce trigger-spray bottle. Spray the chrome on the unplugged toaster with the solution and wipe with a soft, clean cloth. Rinse and dry.

- **ReaLemon.** Saturate a soft, clean cloth with ReaLemon lemon juice and wipe the unplugged chrome toaster clean.

- **Windex.** Spray the chrome on an unplugged toaster with Windex and rub with a soft, clean cloth.

Woks

- **Morton Salt.** To prevent oil splatters when cooking with a wok, add one-half teaspoon Morton Salt to the oil before cooking and leave out one-half teaspoon salt from the recipe.

- **Wesson Oil.** To season a steel wok after cleaning it with soapy water, saturate a paper towel with Wesson Oil and rub the inside of the wok, giving it an even coat of oil.

Wooden Salad Bowls

- **Wesson Oil** and **Bounty Paper Towels.** To preserve wooden salad bowls, saturate a sheet of Bounty Paper Towels with Wesson Oil and wipe down the bowl. The oil moisturizes the wood, preventing it from drying and cracking.

Lampshades and Lighting

Ceiling Fans

- **Pledge.** To make dusting ceiling fans easier, give the wooden blades a coat of Pledge furniture polish and buff with a soft, clean cloth.
- **Turtle Wax.** To make washing the blades of a ceiling fan easier, apply Turtle Wax to both sides of the blade and buff.

Crystal Chandeliers

- **Heinz White Vinegar.** Place a kitchen table under the chandelier and cover the table with a plastic tablecloth and a few layers of newspaper. Fill a drinking glass with two ounces Heinz White Vinegar and three-quarters of the way full with warm water. Hold the glass under an individual crystal prism, raise the glass until the crystal prism is submerged in the liquid, and lower the glass again. Repeat with each crystal prism. Let drip dry.

- **Mrs. Stewart's Liquid Bluing.** A few drops of Mrs. Stewart's Liquid Bluing in the rinse water makes a crystal chandelier sparkle. The bluing purportedly repels dust particles so the crystal stays clean longer.

FABRIC LAMPSHADES

- **Dawn Dishwashing Liquid.** If no glue was used to make the lampshade, add a few drops of Dawn Dishwashing Liquid to the running water as you fill the bathtub with cool water. Gently twirl the lampshade in the soapy water. Remove the shade, empty the water from the tub, and rinse the shade with cool water. Twirl the shade to shake off the excess water and let dry (but never in the sun).

PAPER LAMPSHADES

- **Bounce.** To prevent a paper lampshade from attracting excessive dust, rub the shade with a clean, used sheet of Bounce. The antistatic elements in the fabric softener sheet remove static electricity, which attracts dust in the first place.

- **Mr. Clean Magic Eraser** and **Conair 1875 Watt Hair Dryer.** Dampen a Mr. Clean Magic Erase with warm water, wring it out well, and gently wipe the lamp shade using even pressure on the sponge. Dry the lampshade with a Conair 1875 Watt Hair Dryer to prevent any moisture from creating yellow edges.

- **Play-Doh.** To clean dirt and grime from a lampshade, roll a ball of white Play-Doh over the shade. The modeling dough gently lifts grease and grime.

PARCHMENT LAMPSHADES

- **Mr. Clean Magic Eraser.** Dampen a Mr. Clean Magic Eraser with warm water, wring it out well, and gently wipe the lamp shade using even pressure on the sponge.

TAKING A SHINE TO WINDEX

In 1910, Cincinnati-based Philip W. Drackett began distributing bulk industrial chemicals formulated and packaged for use in institutional settings. In 1923, Drackett and his son, Harry Rogers Drackett, invented Drano chemical drain cleaner, and the company began expanding into consumer products. In 1933, Harry invented Windex window cleaner (originally packaged in cans because the solvent was flammable). After World War II and the invention of modern surfactants, the company reformulated Windex as a nonflammable cleanser, packaging the product in a glass bottle with a plastic sprayer.

In 1965, Bristol-Myers—the company founded in 1887 by William McLaren Bristol and John Ripley Myers—acquired the Drackett Company. The Professional Products Division, established in 1968, catered to commercial and institutional users, reformulating and repackaging its well-known retail brands for commercial use.

In 1992, S.C. Johnson & Son, Inc. of Racine, Wisconsin, bought the Drackett Company, absorbing the company's retail divisions but leaving the Professional Division intact as a stand-alone operating unit, based in Cincinnati, Ohio.

Strange Facts

- Windex is a combination of the word *window* and the suffix *-ex*, short for *express*, denoting the power to clean windows quickly.

- In the hit 2002 comedy movie *My Big Fat Greek Wedding*, the immigrant father of the bride, played by Michael Constantine (who starred as principal Seymour Kaufman on *Room 222*), proudly embraces American culture by obsessively using Windex as a cure-all for every problem he encounters—psoriasis, poison ivy, baldness, warts, and acne.

- The Drackett Company patented the shape of the Windex bottle.

- S.C. Johnson & Son, better known as Johnson Wax because of its popular floor wax products, is one of the largest makers of consumer chemical specialty products in the world.

- Windex shares the –ex suffix with such other popular brand-name products as Balmex, Blistex, Cutex, Desenex, Kleenex, Kotex, Playtex, Purex, Pyrex, Rolex, Tilex, and Timex.

- **Play-Doh.** To clean dirt and grime from a lampshade made from parchment, roll a ball of white Play-Doh over the shade. The modeling dough gently lifts grease and grime.
- **Wonder Bread.** Remove the crust from a slice of Wonder Bread and rub the bread (just like a sponge) over the lampshade. The dirt and grime falls off with the breadcrumbs.

PLASTIC LAMPSHADES

- **Dawn Dishwashing Liquid** and **Pledge.** Fill the kitchen sink with warm water and add a few drops of Dawn Dishwashing Liquid. Use a sponge to wash plastic lampshades in the soapy solution. Dry thoroughly. Spray some Pledge furniture polish on a soft, clean cloth and shine the lampshade, restoring the luster to the plastic.

Laundry

ACID STAINS

- **Arm & Hammer Baking Soda.** Rinse the acid stain immediately with cold running water, make a paste of Arm & Hammer Baking Soda and water, apply the paste over the affected area of the garment, let sit for one hour, and then rinse thoroughly with cold water.

- **Parsons' Ammonia.** Rinse the acid stain immediately with cold running water, place the garment on a pad of paper towels, dampen the stain with full-strength Parsons' Ammonia (unless the fabric is silk or wool, in which case use a mixture of equal parts ammonia and cold water), and then rinse thoroughly with cold water. The pH in the ammonia neutralizes the acid.

ADHESIVE TAPE

- **Johnson's Baby Oil** and **Dawn Dishwashing Liquid.** To remove the adhesive glue from tape or bandages from fabric, saturate the spot with Johnson's Baby Oil, let sit for ten minutes, work in a few drops of Dawn Dishwashing Liquid, and rinse well. Launder as usual.

- **Pam Cooking Spray** and **Dawn Dishwashing Liquid.** To remove adhesive tape from fabric, spray the spot with Pam Cooking Spray, let sit for ten minutes, work in a few drops of Dawn Dishwashing Liquid, and rinse well. Launder as usual.

- **Wesson Oil** and **Dawn Dishwashing Liquid.** To remove adhesive tape from fabric, saturate the spot with Wesson Oil, let sit for ten minutes, work in a few drops of Dawn Dishwashing Liquid, rinse well, and launder.

Baby Formula Stains

- **Adolph's Original Meat Tenderizer.** Cover the baby formula stain with a paste made from Adolph's Original Meat Tenderizer and cool water. Wait twenty minutes and sponge off with cool water. The enzymes in the meat tenderizer break up the proteins in the baby formula.

- **Arm & Hammer Baking Soda.** To clean a fresh formula stain, sprinkle some Arm & Hammer Baking Soda on a wet cloth and dab the stain.

- **Cascade.** To clean a stubborn formula stain from white clothes, wet the stain with water and rub in a few drops of Cascade Gel. Let sit overnight and launder as usual.

- **Clorox 2.** To clean a baby formula stain from colored clothes, rinse the stain with water, apply Clorox 2 (a non-chlorine bleach) directly to the stain, and rub in gently. Let sit for five minutes and launder as usual.

- **ReaLemon.** Saturate baby formula stains on white clothes with ReaLemon lemon juice and set the garment in the sun to bleach the stain away. Apply more lemon juice to the stain before laundering as usual.

Barbeque Sauce Stains

- **Cascade.** To clean barbeque sauce stains from clothes, saturate the stain with water, rub a few drops of Cascade Gel into the stain, let sit for thirty minutes, and launder as usual.

- **Heinz White Vinegar** and **Wine Away.** To clean barbeque sauce stains from clothes, immediately rinse the stain from both sides of the fabric with cool water, saturate the affected area with Heinz White Vinegar, let sit for five minutes, and then rinse clean with cool water. Apply Wine Away Red Wine Stain Remover, wait until the stain disappears, and blot with a wet cloth.

BASEBALL CAPS

- **Johnson's Baby Shampoo.** In a bucket, dissolve one capful Johnson's Baby Shampoo in one gallon cool water, submerge the cap in the soapy solution, and using a nylon brush, gently scrub the baseball cap. Rinse clean and let dry.

- **Resolve Carpet Cleaner.** To clean a baseball cap, spray Resolve Carpet Cleaner on the cap, rub with a damp cloth, and let dry.

BATHING SUITS

- **Downy Fabric Softener.** To prolong the life of a bathing suit, after a swim in a chlorinated pool, mix one teaspoon Downy Fabric Softener in a bucket of cold water, soak the bathing suit in the solution for fifteen minutes, and then rinse clean in cold water.

BEER STAINS

- **Heinz White Vinegar** and **Dawn Dishwashing Liquid.** Mix equal parts Heinz White Vinegar and Dawn Dishwashing Liquid, sponge the solution on the beer stain, and then rinse the garment in warm water.

BERRY STAINS

- **Canada Dry Club Soda.** Rinse the berry stain with Canada Dry Club Soda and launder as usual.

- **Glycerin.** Rub Glycerin into the berry stain and launder as usual.

- **Heinz White Vinegar.** Soak the stain in Heinz White Vinegar and launder as usual.

- **Nestlé Carnation NonFat Dry Milk.** To remove a berry stain from washable fabrics, mix three ounces Nestlé Carnation NonFat Dry Milk and one cup water and soak the stain in the milky solution. The enzymes dissolve the stain.

- **Wine Away.** To clean blueberry, cranberry, raspberry, or strawberry stains, spray Wine Away Red Wine Stain Remover on the stain, and then launder immediately using your regular detergent.

BLACK COTTONS OR LINGERIE

- **Lipton Tea Bags.** To blacken faded cotton clothes or lingerie, add two cups strongly brewed Lipton Tea to the final rinse water during the washing machine cycle.

- **Maxwell House Coffee.** To revive faded black cotton clothes or black lingerie, add two cups strongly brewed Maxwell House Coffee to the final rinse water in the washing machine.

- **Mrs. Stewart's Liquid Bluing.** To blacken faded black jeans, cotton clothes, or lingerie, wash the jeans in the washing machine with your regular detergent. Mix one teaspoon Mrs. Stewart's Liquid Bluing into an empty, gallon plastic container, fill with cold water, and shake well. Pour the solution into the machine during the rinse cycle.

BLEACH ALTERNATIVES

- **Arm & Hammer Super Washing Soda.** Dislike using bleach? Add one-quarter cup Arm & Hammer Super Washing Soda to the wash cycle as an alternative to bleach.

- **Cascade.** Mix two tablespoons to one-half cup Cascade (powder or gel) in a bucket of hot water and soak white clothes in the solution for thirty minutes or longer. Empty the entire bucket into the washing machine, add your regular detergent as usual, and launder.

- **Heinz White Vinegar** and **ReaLemon.** Instead of using bleach, mix one-quarter cup Heinz White Vinegar, one-quarter cup ReaLemon lemon juice, and one gallon warm water in a bucket and soak clothes in the solution for fifteen minutes. Then launder as usual.

- **Hydrogen Peroxide.** Mix one cup Hydrogen Peroxide and two quarts cold water, soak the white garment (including wool) in the solution overnight, and then launder according to the directions for that fabric.

- **McCormick Cream of Tartar** and **ReaLemon.** Mix enough McCormick Cream of Tartar with ReaLemon lemon juice to make a paste, apply it to food stains on white clothes, let sit for thirty minutes, and then launder as usual. Together, cream of tartar and lemon juice work like an all-natural bleach.

- **ReaLemon.** Mix one-half cup ReaLemon lemon juice and one gallon hot water in a bucket. Soak white cotton or polyester garments in the lemony water for thirty minutes or longer. (Do not use lemon juice for bleaching silk.) Launder as usual.

BLOODSTAINS

- **Adolph's Original Meat Tenderizer.** Cover the bloodstain with a paste made from Adolph's Original Meat Tenderizer and cool water. Wait thirty minutes and sponge off with cool water. The enzymes in the meat tenderizer break up the proteins in the blood. Launder in cool water with your regular detergent.

- **Canada Dry Club Soda.** Saturate a fresh bloodstain on washable fabric with Canada Dry Club Soda, let sit for fifteen minutes, and launder in cool water with your regular detergent.

- **Clorox 2.** Apply Clorox 2 (a non-chlorine bleach) directly to the stain, rub in gently, let sit for five minutes, and launder as usual.

- **Coca-Cola.** Saturate the bloodstain with Coca-Cola, let sit five minutes, and then launder as usual. Coke removes blood from clothing—even dried blood that has gone through the washing machine and dryer.

- **Gillette Foamy.** Spray a dab of Gillette Foamy shaving cream on the fresh bloodstain, rub with a sponge, and rinse clean.

- **Hydrogen Peroxide.** Saturate the bloodstain on washable fabric with Hydrogen Peroxide as soon as possible, let sit for five minutes, and then launder as usual.

- **Kingsford's Corn Starch.** To quickly clean a fresh bloodstain, cover the spot with Kingsford's Corn Starch, let sit for ten minutes, then run cool, soapy water through the back side of the fabric. Apply a stain remover to the spot and launder as usual. The cornstarch absorbs the blood from the fabric.

- **Morton Salt.** To clean a fresh bloodstain from washable fabric, dissolve one-half cup Morton Salt in a bucket of warm water and immediately soak the garment in the solution overnight. Launder in cool water with your regular detergent.

- **Parsons' Ammonia** and **Dawn Dishwashing Liquid.** To dissolve bloodstains from clothes, mix equal parts Parsons' Ammonia, Dawn Dishwashing Liquid, and water and apply the mixture to the spot. Let sit for five minutes, and then rinse thoroughly with water. (Do not use ammonia on acrylic, silk, spandex, or wool.)

- **Spot Shot.** Saturate the stain with Spot Shot Instant Carpet Stain Remover, let sit for one minute, and launder as usual. (Do not use on dry-clean-only fabrics, non-colorfast garments, or silk.)

BOOSTERS

- **Arm & Hammer Super Washing Soda.** To boost the strength of your laundry detergent, add one-half cup Arm & Hammer Super Washing Soda to your laundry.

- **20 Mule Team Borax.** Boost the strength of your laundry detergent by adding one-half cup 20 Mule Team Borax to your wash load with your regular detergent. Borax brightens and deodorizes clothes, and it helps remove stains.

BRIGHTENERS

- **Heinz White Vinegar.** To brighten, soften, and deodorize clothes, add one-half cup Heinz White Vinegar to the final rinse cycle. The smell of vinegar will dissipate once you dry the clothes.
- **McCormick Cream of Tartar.** Dissolve two teaspoons McCormick Cream of Tartar in one gallon hot water and soak the garments in the solution overnight. Launder as usual.

BUTTER OR MARGARINE STAINS

- **Arm & Hammer Super Washing Soda.** Scrape off as much of the butter or margarine as possible, make a paste of Arm & Hammer Super Washing Soda and water, rub the paste into the stain, and rinse clean.
- **Dawn Dishwashing Liquid.** After scraping off as much of the butter or margarine, rub a few drops of Dawn Dishwashing Liquid into the stain on the washable fabric and launder as usual. Dawn cuts through grease.
- **WD-40** and **Dawn Dishwashing Liquid.** To clean a dried butter or margarine stain from a washable fabric, spray the spot with WD-40 to resuscitate the grease, rub a few drops of Dawn Dishwashing Liquid into the stain, and launder in the hottest water possible.

BUTTONS

- **Oral-B Dental Floss.** For buttons that get a lot of rough treatment, sew them in place with a strand of Oral-B Dental Floss to make those buttons more durable.
- **Revlon Clear Nail Enamel.** To prevent buttons from falling off shirts, jackets, or pants, give the threads in the center of the button a protective coat of Revlon Clear Nail Enamel.

CANDLE WAX

- **Bounty Paper Towels.** Place a sheet of Bounty Paper Towels over the wax stain and press gently with a warm iron. The heat from the iron melts the wax, and the quicker-picker-upper absorbs it.

CANDY STAINS

- **Dawn Dishwashing Liquid** and **Heinz White Vinegar.** To clean candy from clothes, mix one tablespoon Dawn Dishwashing Liquid, one tablespoon Heinz White Vinegar, and four cups warm water. Soak the garment in the solution for thirty minutes, rinse clean with warm water, apply stain remover to the spot, and launder as usual.

CHOCOLATE STAINS

- **Canada Dry Club Soda.** To pre-treat chocolate stains on dry-clean-only fabrics, keep the stain wet with Canada Dry Club Soda until you take the garment to a dry cleaner.

- **Clorox 2.** After scraping off as much of the chocolate as possible, soak the stained washable fabric in a mixture of one tablespoon Clorox 2 (a non-chlorine bleach) and one gallon warm water for thirty minutes. Apply your regular detergent to the stain, rub in well, and then flush clean under cold running sink water. Launder as usual.

- **Hydrogen Peroxide.** Rub Hydrogen Peroxide into the chocolate stain, blot, and launder as usual.

- **Hydrogen Peroxide** and **Parsons' Ammonia.** To clean a chocolate stain from a washable fabric, mix one-half cup Hydrogen Peroxide and one teaspoon Parsons' Ammonia. Test a drop of the solution on an inconspicuous area of the garment for colorfastness. Soak the stain in the solution for ten minutes and rinse clean under cold running sink water. Repeat if necessary. Launder as usual.

- **Parsons' Ammonia.** Scrape off as much chocolate as possible. To clean off the remaining stain, mix one tablespoon Parsons' Ammonia and two cups cold water. With a soft cloth, dab the solution onto the stain, working from the outer edge of the stain to the center. Rinse and launder as usual.

- **Purell Instant Hand Sanitizer.** After scraping off as much of the chocolate as possible, saturate the remaining stain with Purell Instant Hand Sanitizer, and then flush clean under cold running sink water. Launder as usual.

- **20 Mule Team Borax.** To clean off a chocolate stain, make a paste from 20 Mule Team Borax and water, rub the paste onto the stain, let sit for ten minutes, and rinse clean.

- **Wesson Oil** and **Dawn Dishwashing Liquid.** Rub a few drops of Wesson Oil into the chocolate stain, and then add a few drops of Dawn Dishwashing Liquid and rinse the oil stain clean. Launder as usual.

COFFEE AND TEA STAINS

- **Alberto VO5 Hair Spray** and **Ivory Soap.** To clean a coffee or tea stain from washable clothes, spray the wet stain with Alberto VO5 Hair Spray, rub a wet bar of Ivory Soap into the stain, and rinse clean in cold water. Launder as usual.

- **Canada Dry Club Soda.** Saturate the stain with Canada Dry Club Soda and rinse clean. Launder as usual.

- **Efferdent.** To clean a coffee or tea stain from white fabric, dissolve two Efferdent denture cleansing tablets in one-half cup warm water and dampen the stain with the solution. Let sit for one hour and launder as usual.

- **Heinz White Vinegar.** Soak the stain in Heinz White Vinegar for fifteen minutes, and then launder as usual.

- **Morton Salt.** In a pinch, dampen a napkin with water, sprinkle ample Morton Salt on the wet napkin, and blot the coffee or tea stain. Keep the stain wet until you can launder as usual.

- **ReaLemon.** To clean tea stains from white fabric, saturate the tea stain with ReaLemon lemon juice and hang the garment in the sun.

- **20 Mule Team Borax.** To clean coffee or tea stains from washable fabrics, drape the garment over the kitchen sink, sprinkle 20 Mule Team Borax to cover the coffee or tea stain, and pour a tea kettle of boiling water around the stain, working toward the center. Repeat if necessary, let soak for thirty minutes, and launder as usual.

COLOR BLEEDS

- **Carbona Color Run Remover.** If colors from one garment run and damage the color of another garment, use Carbona Color Run Remover according to the directions on the box for a single garment or a full wash load. (Do not use Carbona Color Run Remover on denim, khaki, synthetic materials, or silk; Carbona may also damage buttons and zippers.)

- **Clorox Bleach.** If color from one garment bleeds to a bleachable garment in the wash, immediately rewash the affected garment with one cup Clorox Bleach in the regular cycle of the washing machine.

COLORFASTNESS

- **Epsom Salt.** To prevent colors from running and retain color brightness in clothes, add one-half cup Epsom Salt to the wash water the first time you wash the garments. Soak the garments for fifteen minutes, and then launder as usual.

- **Heinz White Vinegar.** To set the bright colors in cotton clothes, mix one-half cup Heinz White Vinegar in a bucket of water and soak the garments in the mixture overnight. Launder as usual. The vinegar water binds the dye into the cotton fabrics.

- **Morton Salt.** To set the bright colors in cotton clothes, dissolve one-half cup Morton Salt in a bucket of water and soak the garments in the salt solution for twenty-four hours. Launder as usual. The salt water binds the dye into the cotton fabrics.

- **Parsons' Ammonia.** To stop colors from running, add one teaspoon Parsons' Ammonia to the wash water in the machine when laundering the garment for the first time.

CRAYON STAINS

- **Bounty Paper Towels** and **Dawn Dishwashing Liquid.** To remove crayon from a garment made from washable fabric, place the stained garment on top of a sheet of Bounty Paper Towels, cover the stain with a second sheet of paper towel, and press the top sheet gently with a warm iron. The heat from the iron melts the crayon wax, and the quicker-picker-upper absorbs it. If any pigment from the crayon remains in the garment, rub a few drops of Dawn Dishwashing Liquid into the stain and launder as usual.

- **Spray 'n Wash, Ivory Soap,** and **Arm & Hammer Baking Soda.** To clean crayon from clothes, remove as much of the wax as possible, apply Spray 'n Wash stain remover to the stain and launder with one-half cup Ivory Soap flakes (grate a bar of Ivory Soap through a cheese grater) and one cup Arm & Hammer Baking Soda.

- **WD-40** and **Dawn Dishwashing Liquid. Spray** WD-40 on a crayon stain (both sides of the fabric), let sit for ten minutes, rub in a few drops of Dawn Dishwashing Liquid, and launder as usual in the hottest water possible for that fabric. (Do not use WD-40 on silk.)

CURRY STAINS

- **Glycerin.** To clean curry stains from washable fabrics, mix three table-spoons Glycerin (available in drug stores) and four tablespoons warm water, rub the mixture into the stain, let sit for one hour, and launder in warm water with your regular detergent.

- **Parsons' Ammonia.** Mix one tablespoon Parsons' Ammonia and two cups water, soak the curry-stained garment in the solution for fifteen minutes, and launder as usual.

- **20 Mule Team Borax.** Dissolve one tablespoon 20 Mule Team Borax in two cups water, apply the solution onto the stain by dabbing gently with a sponge, let sit for five minutes, and rinse well under cold water. Launder as usual.

DETERGENT

- **Simple Green.** To clean and freshen laundry, once the washer has filled with water, add one-quarter cup Simple Green All-Purpose Cleaner to the water in a full wash load.

EGG STAINS

- **Adolph's Original Meat Tenderizer.** To clean egg from washable fabrics, scrape off as much of the egg as possible and cover the remaining stain with a paste made from Adolph's Original Meat Tenderizer and cool water. Work the paste into the stain well, let sit for three hours, keeping the spot wet, and rinse clean. Repeat until the stain vanishes, and then launder as usual.

- **Clorox 2.** To clean egg from washable fabrics, scrape off as much of the egg as possible and soak the garment overnight in Clorox 2 (a non-chlorine bleach). Rub a few drops of your regular detergent into the stain and launder as usual. Make sure the stain is gone before drying the garment, which will make the stain permanent.

FABRIC SOFTENER STAINS

- **Dawn Dishwashing Liquid.** To clean blue spots from liquid fabric softener from clothes, wet the garment, rub a few drops of Dawn Dishwashing Liquid into the spot, and launder as usual.

- **Heinz White Vinegar.** To get rid of blue spots on clothes, soak the spotted item in Heinz White Vinegar for twenty minutes and then launder as usual.

- **Ivory Soap.** To clean spots on clothes from fabric softener dryer sheets, rub the stain with a wet bar of Ivory Soap and launder as usual.
- **Johnson's Baby Shampoo.** To clean blue spots from liquid fabric softener from clothes, wet the garment, rub a few drops of Johnson's Baby Shampoo into the spot, and launder as usual.

FABRIC SOFTENERS

- **Arm & Hammer Baking Soda.** To soften clothes, add one-quarter cup Arm & Hammer Baking Soda to the wash cycle.
- **Downy Fabric Softener.** To make your own fabric softener dryer sheet, fill a trigger-spray bottle with one part Downy Fabric Softener and two parts water; shake well; mist a clean, old washcloth with the solution; and toss the wet washcloth in the dryer with the clothes. Mist the washcloth for additional loads. Always shake the mixture well before using and label the spray bottle to avoid any potential mishaps.
- **Heinz White Vinegar.** Add one-quarter cup Heinz White Vinegar in the final rinse as a fabric softener. The side benefit? Vinegar simultaneously deodorizes the clothes.
- **Pantene Classic Care Conditioner.** In a pinch, use one-quarter cup Pantene Classic Care Conditioner in the final rinse as a substitute for fabric softener.
- **20 Mule Team Borax.** To soften clothes, add one-quarter cup 20 Mule Team Borax to the wash cycle.

FLEECE

- **Aunt Jemima Corn Meal.** To give a fleece-lined jacket a dry shampoo, rub Aunt Jemima Corn Meal into the fleece, let sit overnight, shake it out, and brush clean.
- **Johnson's Baby Powder.** To clean a fleece-lined jacket, dust the fleece with Johnson's Baby Powder and let sit overnight. The next morning,

Keep It Clean
HOW TO DO YOUR LAUNDRY

- Start by sorting your laundry by fabric type, color, and water temperature. Find instructions for proper fabric care on the label in each garment.

- You can sort clothes by using separate laundry baskets, bins, or rolling carts. Or you can sort them into piles on the laundry room floor.

- Sort all laundry into five main groups: whites (everything white), lights (pastels and striped whites), darks (blacks, blues, and browns), brights (reds, yellows, oranges), and delicates (lingerie and linens). Other groups might include baby clothes, hand washables, and dry clean only.

- Separate heavily soiled garments from lightly soiled garments.

- Avoid washing lint generators (towels, sweatshirts, and flannel) with lint magnets (corduroy, velvets, and permanent-press clothes).

- Check all clothes for stains and sort out those that require pre-treatment or soaking. Pre-treat the stained garments appropriately.

- Keep your wash loads reasonably sized. Don't stuff clothes into the washing machine. Fill the tub three-quarters of the way with clothes.

- Wash reds or new, colored garments separately the first few times—in case the colors bleed and stain other items. Add an old white handkerchief or sock with the reds or new items; if the handkerchief or sock comes out white, then the garments can be laundered without fear of bleeding.

- To test a garment for colorfastness, dampen it with water in an inconspicuous spot and blot with an old white cloth. If color transfers to the white, the item will bleed.

- Check all pockets and pant cuffs for items you don't wish to launder.

- Secure zippers, buttons, snaps, and buckles to prevent snagging.

- Unroll shirt cuffs and tie drawstrings.

- Place washable delicates in a mesh bag to prevent them from getting roughed up by tougher fabrics.

brush out the powder. The baby powder absorbs grease and grime and leaves the fleece smelling baby soft.

- **Woolite.** Wash a fleece jacket in the washing machine with cold water and Woolite. Hang the jacket over a chair to dry, and then brush the fleece.

FOOD DYE STAINS

- **Parsons' Ammonia** and **Morton Salt.** To clean food dye stains from washable fabrics, mix one tablespoon Parsons' Ammonia and one cup cool water, flush the stain with the solution, rub Morton Salt into the stain, and let sit for one hour. Brush off the salt, repeat if necessary, and launder as usual.
- **Wine Away.** To clean red, blue, or purple food dye from washable fabrics, spray Wine Away Red Wine Stain Remover on the stain, and then launder immediately, using your regular detergent.

FOOD STAINS

- **Efferdent.** To clean food stains from white linen table clothes, linen napkins, and cotton clothes, dissolve two Efferdent denture cleansing tablets in one cup warm water and pour the fizzy blue mixture on the spot or stain. Let sit for fifteen minutes, and then launder as usual.
- **McCormick Cream of Tartar** and **ReaLemon.** Mix enough McCormick Cream of Tartar with ReaLemon lemon juice to make a paste, apply it to food stains on white clothes, let sit for thirty minutes, and then launder as usual. Together, cream of tartar and lemon juice work like bleach.
- **Morton Salt.** The moment you spill food on clothes, wet the spot, cover the stain with Morton Salt, let sit for five minutes, and launder as usual.
- **Mr. Clean Magic Eraser.** Blot a food stain from clothes. Place a cloth underneath the article to absorb any water, dampen the Mr. Clean Magic Eraser, and gently blot the stain.
- **ReaLemon.** Saturate food stains on white clothes with ReaLemon lemon juice and set the garment in the sun to bleach the stain away. Apply more lemon juice to the stain before laundering as usual.

Furniture Polish Stains

- **WD-40** and **Dawn Dishwashing Liquid.** To clean oil-based furniture polish from washable fabrics, spray WD-40 on the stain, let sit for ten minutes, rub in a few drops of Dawn Dishwashing Liquid, and rinse well under the hottest sink water possible for that fabric. Apply your regular stain remover to the spot and launder as usual. (Do not use WD-40 on silk.)

Gloves

- **Alberto VO5 Conditioning Hairdressing.** Rub a few dabs of Alberto VO5 Conditioning Hairdressing into the leather and buff it dry with a paper towel or a soft, clean cloth.

- **Murphy Oil Soap.** To clean leather gloves, put the gloves on your hands and wash with a few drops of Murphy Oil Soap and water. Place the gloves flat on a countertop and let air dry.

Glue Stains

- **Cutex Regular Nail Polish Remover.** To remove model glue from washable fabrics, blot the stain with a cotton ball saturated with Cutex Regular Nail Polish Remover, and then launder as usual. (Be sure to test the nail polish remover on an inconspicuous spot first to make sure it doesn't affect the color of the garment.)

- **Heinz White Vinegar.** To clean plastic adhesives from washable fabrics, bring one cup Heinz White Vinegar to a boil and carefully soak the stain in the hot vinegar. Repeat if necessary.

- **Ivory Soap.** To clean most glues from washable fabrics, immediately wash the spot with Ivory Soap and water.

- **20 Mule Team Borax.** To remove glue from washable fabrics, work in a few drops of your regular liquid detergent, sprinkle 20 Mule Team Borax over the spot, rub briskly, and then rinse in the hottest water possible for that fabric.

- **Vaseline Petroleum Jelly** and **Dawn Dishwashing Liquid.** To clean rubber cement from washable fabrics, coat the stain with Vaseline Petroleum Jelly and rub gently. After brushing off the resulting balls of rubber cement, apply a few drops of Dawn Dishwashing Liquid to the spot to help dissolve the petroleum jelly and launder as usual.

GRASS STAINS

- **Clorox 2.** To clean grass stains from washable fabrics, apply Clorox 2 (a non-chlorine bleach) to the grass stain, rub in gently, let sit for thirty minutes, and launder as usual.

- **Colgate Regular Flavor Toothpaste.** Rub Colgate Regular Flavor Toothpaste into grass stains on washable fabrics. Scrub gently with a sponge or a clean, used toothbrush. Rinse well and launder as usual.

- **Domino Sugar.** To clean grass stains from clothes, dissolve one part Domino Sugar in two parts water, heat the mixture in the microwave oven for one minute, and then pour over the stains. Let sit for one hour, and then wash clean in your regular wash load.

- **Heinz White Vinegar** and **Dawn Dishwashing Liquid.** To get rid of grass stains, mix equal amounts Heinz White Vinegar, Dawn Dishwashing Liquid, and water and work the mixture into the stain. Let sit for five minutes, and then toss in your regular wash load.

- **Purell Instant Hand Sanitizer.** To clean grass stains from washable fabric, rub Purell Instant Hand Sanitizer into the stain, rub in a few drops of your regular liquid laundry detergent, and launder as usual.

- **Simple Green.** Wet the grass stain with water and spray on a solution of equal parts Simple Green All-Purpose Cleaner and water. Rub the fabric against itself gently, and then launder as usual.

- **Spot Shot.** Saturate the stain with Spot Shot Instant Carpet Stain Remover, let sit for one minute, and launder as usual. (Do not use on dry-clean-only fabrics, non-colorfast garments, or silk.)

GRAVY STAINS

- **Spot Shot.** To clean gravy stains from washable fabrics, soak the garment in cold water for three hours to dissolve the starch used to thicken the gravy, saturate the stain with Spot Shot Instant Carpet Stain Remover, and launder as usual. (Do not use on dry-clean-only fabrics, non-colorfast garments, or silk.)

GREASE AND OIL STAINS

- **Arm & Hammer Baking Soda.** To absorb as much grease or oil as possible from clothes before treating the stain with one of the other methods listed here, cover the stain with Arm & Hammer Baking Soda, rub in gently, let sit for thirty minutes, and brush clean.

- **Bon Ami.** To clean grease stains from clothes, wet the grease stain, sprinkle Bon Ami over the spot, rub in to form a paste, and let set overnight. In the morning, rinse clean with warm water.

- **Canada Dry Club Soda.** To wash grease stains from clothes, saturate the stain with Canada Dry Club Soda, let sit for five minutes, and blot. Launder as usual.

- **Coca-Cola.** To clean grease from clothes, pour a can of Coca-Cola in the washing machine with your regular detergent and launder as usual. The sugars and phosphoric acid in the Real Thing break down the grease stains.

- **Crisco All-Vegetable Shortening.** To clean a grease stain from clothes, rub Crisco All-Vegetable Shortening into the stain, let sit for fifteen minutes, and launder as usual.

- **Dawn Dishwashing Liquid.** Rub a few drops of Dawn Dishwashing Liquid into any greasy stain, let sit for a few minutes, and launder as usual. Dawn cuts through grease.

- **Hydrogen Peroxide.** To remove grease stains that have dried and turned yellow, soak the stain in a mixture of equal parts Hydrogen Peroxide and water. (Be sure to test an inconspicuous spot first to make certain the garment is colorfast.)

- **Johnson's Baby Powder.** To clean a grease stain from clothes, cover the stain with Johnson's Baby Powder, rub the powder into the stain, and brush clean. Launder as usual.

- **Johnson's Baby Shampoo.** To clean grease stains from delicates, rub a few drops of Johnson's Baby Shampoo into the stain, soak in warm water for ten minutes, and rinse clean.

- **Kingsford's Corn Starch.** To absorb as much grease or oil as possible from clothes before treating the stain with one of the other methods listed here, cover the stain with Kingsford's Corn Starch, rub in gently, let sit for thirty minutes, and brush clean. Corn starch is highly absorbent.

- **Purell Instant Hand Sanitizer.** Saturate a grease stain on clothing with Purell Instant Hand Sanitizer and launder as usual.

- **Spot Shot.** Saturate the stain with Spot Shot Instant Carpet Stain Remover, let sit for one minute, and launder as usual. (Do not use on dry-clean-only fabrics, non-colorfast garments, or silk.)

- **20 Mule Team Borax.** Cover the stain with 20 Mule Team Borax, rub in, and wipe off.

- **WD-40** and **Dawn Dishwashing Liquid.** Spray WD-40 on a tough grease stain, let sit for ten minutes, and then rub in a few drops of Dawn Dishwashing Liquid. Rinse clean with the hottest water possible for that fabric, apply your regular stain remover, and launder as usual. (Do not use WD-40 on silk.)

- **Wonder Bread.** To clean a grease stain from clothes, rub the stain with a slice of Wonder Bread, which absorbs the grease.

GUM

- **Heinz White Vinegar.** Saturate the affected area with Heinz White Vinegar and rub the vinegar onto the gum until it pries loose.

- **Skippy Peanut Butter.** Rub a dollop of Skippy Peanut Butter into the gum, let sit for five minutes, then scrape clean. The oils in the peanut butter dissolve the gum. Then use one of the tips listed under Grease and Oil Stains on page 248 to clean the peanut butter from the garment.

- **Star Olive Oil.** To clean gum from washable fabric, saturate the gum with Star Olive Oil, pry off as much as possible, and launder as usual.

- **Vaseline Petroleum Jelly.** Rub a dab of Vaseline Petroleum Jelly into the gum, which will then rub off in little balls. Then use one of the tips listed under Grease and Oil Stains on page 248 to remove the petroleum jelly from the garment.

- **Ziploc Freezer Bags, Heinz White Vinegar,** and **Dawn Dishwashing Liquid.** To remove chewing gum from clothes, insert the affected garment into a Ziploc Freezer Bag and place it in the freezer overnight. In the morning, scrape the gum off with the dull, straight edge of a butter knife. Mix equal parts Heinz White Vinegar and Dawn Dishwashing Liquid, rub the solution into the remaining stain, rinse well, and launder as usual.

HAIR DYE STAINS

- **Alberto VO5 Hair Spray.** To clean dried hair dye from washable fabric, saturate the stain with Alberto VO5 Hair Spray, let sit for five minutes, and rinse clean. (Test the hair spray on an inconspicuous spot first to confirm that the acetone does not alter the color of the fabric.)

- **Heinz White Vinegar.** To clean hair dye stains from washable fabrics, act immediately before the dye dries. Fill a sink with warm water, add two cups Heinz White Vinegar and two tablespoons of your regular detergent, and soak the garment or towel in the solution for three to four hours. Launder as usual.

- **Johnson's Baby Shampoo.** To clean water-soluble hair dye from washable fabric, wet the stain with water and rub in a few drops of Johnson's Baby Shampoo. Launder as usual.

- **Sea Breeze.** To clean dried hair dye from washable fabric, saturate the stain with Sea Breeze Astringent, let sit for five minutes, and rinse clean. (Test Sea Breeze on an inconspicuous spot to make sure it doesn't affect the color of the fabric.)

HARD WATER

- **Arm & Hammer Super Washing Soda.** If you have hard water, boost the strength of your laundry detergent by adding one-half cup Arm & Hammer Super Washing Soda to your wash load with your regular detergent. The sodium carbonate precipitates calcium carbonate.

- **20 Mule Team Borax.** If you have hard water, boost the strength of your laundry detergent by adding one-half cup 20 Mule Team Borax to your wash load with your regular detergent. Borax brightens and deodorizes clothes, and it helps remove stains.

ICE CREAM STAINS

- **Adolph's Original Meat Tenderizer.** After blotting up as much of the ice cream stain as possible, cover the spot with a paste made from Adolph's Original Meat Tenderizer and cool water. Wait thirty minutes and rinse clean with cold water. The enzymes in the meat tenderizer break up the proteins in the cream. If the stain remains, treat it with your regular stain remover and launder as usual.

- **Canada Dry Club Soda.** Dampen a paper towel with Canada Dry Club Soda, dab the ice cream stain with it, and then blot with a dry paper towel. The combination of the effervescence and sodium bicarbonate in the club soda seems to magically lift ice cream stains out of fabrics.

- **Parsons' Ammonia** and **Dawn Dishwashing Liquid.** To eliminate ice cream stains on clothes, mix equal parts Parsons' Ammonia, Dawn Dishwashing Liquid, and water and apply the mixture to the spot.

Let sit for five minutes and rinse thoroughly with water. (Do not use ammonia on acrylic, silk, spandex, or wool.)

INK STAINS

- **Alberto VO5 Hair Spray.** To remove ink spots from clothes, spray Alberto VO5 Hair Spray on the affected area and blot with a paper towel or cotton swab until the stain comes up. The acetone in Alberto VO5 Hair Spray removes indelible marker and ballpoint pen marks from fabric.

- **Colgate Regular Flavor Toothpaste.** Some types of ink can be removed from clothes by briskly rubbing a dab of Colgate Regular Flavor Toothpaste into the stain and rinsing clean with cold water.

- **Efferdent.** If you managed to get rid of most of the ink stain using one of the other methods listed here, but there's still some ink on the white fabric, dissolve two Efferdent denture cleansing tablets in one cup warm water and soak the affected area of the garment in the solution for ten minutes. Rinse clean.

- **Kingsford's Corn Starch.** Mix Kingsford's Corn Starch with enough milk to make a paste. Apply the paste to the ink stain, let it dry, and then brush it off. The milk dissolves the ink, and the corn starch absorbs it.

- **Nestlé Carnation NonFat Dry Milk.** To remove an ink stain from washable fabrics, mix three ounces Nestlé Carnation NonFat Dry Milk and one cup water and soak the ink stain in the milky solution. The enzymes dissolve the ink.

- **Old Spice Aftershave Lotion.** Saturate the ink stain with Old Spice Aftershave Lotion, and then blot with a paper towel. The alcohol in the aftershave dissolves the ink.

- **Purell Instant Hand Sanitizer.** Saturate an ink stain on clothing with Purell Instant Hand Sanitizer and blot with a paper towel or soft cloth. Repeat as many times as necessary until the ink stain vanishes.

- **ReaLemon** and **Morton Salt.** Mix equal parts ReaLemon lemon juice and Morton Salt and rub the stain with the mixture. Dry in the sun.

JAM STAINS

- **Clorox 2.** To clean jam stains from washable fabrics, apply Clorox 2 (a non-chlorine bleach) to the jam stain, rub in gently, let sit for thirty minutes, and launder as usual.
- **Heinz White Vinegar.** To clean jam stains from clothes, soak the spotted item in Heinz White Vinegar for twenty minutes and then launder as usual with your regular detergent.

JEANS

- **Morton Salt.** To soften a stiff pair of new blue jeans, dissolve one cup Morton Salt in a bucket of cold water and soak the jeans in the salty solution overnight. In the morning, launder as usual.
- **Mrs. Stewart's Liquid Bluing.** To re-blue denim jeans that have faded, wash the jeans in the washing machine with your regular detergent, mix one teaspoon Mrs. Stewart's Liquid Bluing into an empty, gallon plastic container; fill with cold water; shake well; and then pour into the machine during the rinse cycle.

JUICE STAINS

- **Clorox 2.** To clean juice stains from washable fabrics, apply Clorox 2 (a non-chlorine bleach) to the juice stain, rub in gently, let sit for thirty minutes, and launder as usual.
- **Heinz White Vinegar** and **Dawn Dishwashing Liquid.** To get rid of juice stains, mix equal amounts Heinz White Vinegar, Dawn Dishwashing Liquid, and water and work the mixture into the stain. Let sit for five minutes, and then toss in your regular wash load.

- **Morton Salt.** To clean fruit juice stains from clothes, sprinkle Morton Salt on the stain and rinse in cold water. Launder in warm water with your regular detergent.

- **ReaLemon.** To remove fruit-based stains from clothes, saturate the stain with ReaLemon lemon juice, let sit for thirty minutes, and launder as usual.

- **20 Mule Team Borax.** Immediately blot up as much liquid as possible, dissolve one teaspoon 20 Mule Team Borax in one cup warm water, sponge the solution on the stain, and launder as usual.

- **Wine Away.** To clean red or purple juice stains from washable fabrics, spray Wine Away Red Wine Stain Remover on the stain, and then launder immediately using your regular detergent.

KETCHUP STAINS

- **Heinz White Vinegar** and **Wine Away.** To clean ketchup stains from clothes, immediately rinse the stain from both sides of the fabric with cool water, saturate the affected area with Heinz White Vinegar, let sit for five minutes, then rinse clean with cool water. Apply Wine Away Red Wine Stain Remover to the remaining stain, wait until it disappears, and blot with a wet cloth.

KOOL-AID STAINS

- **Canada Dry Club Soda.** To clean Kool-Aid stains from clothes, immediately saturate the stain with Canada Dry Club Soda and rinse clean under cold running water from the sink.

- **Clorox Bleach, Tide,** and **Cascade.** To clean Kool-Aid stains from clothes, mix one-quarter cup Clorox Bleach, one-quarter cup Tide, one-quarter cup Cascade Gel, and one gallon hot water in a bucket. Soak the stained clothes in the solution for twenty minutes, rinse thoroughly, and launder as usual.

- **Wine Away.** If the Kool-Aid stain fails to wash out completely using Canada Dry Club Soda (page 254), spray Wine Away Red Wine Stain Remover on the stain, and then launder immediately using your regular detergent.

LACE

- **Arm & Hammer Baking Soda** and **Dawn Dishwashing Liquid.** To clean yellowing from lace, mix one-quarter cup Arm & Hammer Baking Soda and one-half teaspoon Dawn Dishwashing Liquid in a pot of hot water. Place the garment in the solution and boil on the stove for five minutes. Rinse clean and dry.

LAUNDROMATS

- **Glad Trash Bags.** Do you bring your laundry to a Laundromat? If so, avoid carrying along your bottles of detergent. Before leaving the house, sort your laundry into Glad Trash Bags and add the proper amount of powdered laundry detergent and powdered bleach into the bags. When you get to the Laundromat, empty the contents of each bag into its own washing machine.

LAUNDRY BAGS

- **Glad Trash Bags.** If you don't have a cloth laundry bag, use a Glad Trash Bag to tote your dirty laundry.

LINE DRYING

- **Heinz White Vinegar.** To prevent clothes from freezing to the clothesline in winter, wipe the line first with a cloth saturated with Heinz White Vinegar.

- **L'eggs Sheer Energy Panty Hose.** To prevent sweaters from getting points at the shoulders from hanging from clothespins on a clothes line, feed the legs of a clean, old pair of L'eggs Sheer Energy Panty Hose down the neck of the sweater and through the arms of the sweater. Clip the clothespins to the waist and feet of the panty hose.

- **Morton Salt.** To prevent clothes from freezing to the clothesline during the winter, add a handful of Morton Salt to the rinse cycle of the washing machine, lowering the freezing point of the water.

Linen Closets

- **Dial Soap.** To freshen the air in a linen closet, place a wrapped bar of Dial Soap on a shelf in the closet to keep the linens smelling fresh.

Lingerie

- **Johnson's Baby Shampoo.** To hand wash lingerie, mix one teaspoon Johnson's Baby Shampoo to a sink filled with warm water, let the lingerie soak in the sudsy solution for five minutes, and rinse clean without wringing the items. Lay the lingerie on a white towel, roll up the towel to absorb excess moisture, and then hang up the lingerie to drip dry.

Lint

- **Heinz White Vinegar.** To avoid generating lint, add one-half cup Heinz White Vinegar to the final rinse in the washing machine.

- **ReaLemon.** To prevent lint in the dryer, add one-quarter cup ReaLemon lemon juice in the final rinse cycle of the washing machine.

Lip Balm Stains

- **WD-40** and **Dawn Dishwashing Liquid.** Spray WD-40 on a lip balm stain, let sit for ten minutes, rub in a few drops of Dawn Dishwashing Liquid, and launder as usual. (Do not use WD-40 on silk.)

LIPSTICK STAINS

- **Alberto VO5 Hair Spray.** In a pinch, you can clean lipstick stains from clothes by spraying Alberto VO5 Hair Spray on the affected area. Let sit for a few minutes and blot with a paper towel until the stain comes up. The acetone in Alberto VO5 Hair Spray removes the oily dye found in lipstick from fabric. Launder as usual.

- **Colgate Regular Flavor Toothpaste.** Rub a dollop of Colgate Regular Flavor Toothpaste into the lipstick stain and launder as usual.

- **Crisco All-Vegetable Shortening** and **Dawn Dishwashing Liquid.** To clean a lipstick stain from washable fabric, rub a dab of Crisco All-Vegetable Shortening into the stain, let sit for thirty minutes, rub in a few drops of Dawn Dishwashing Liquid, and launder as usual.

- **Johnson's Baby Oil** and **Dawn Dishwashing Liquid.** Rub a few drops of Johnson's Baby Oil into the lipstick stain on washable fabrics, let sit for thirty minutes, rub in a few drops of Dawn Dishwashing Liquid, and launder as usual.

- **Johnson's Baby Shampoo.** Rub a few drops of Johnson's Baby Shampoo into the lipstick stain, and then launder the garment as usual.

- **Play-Doh.** If you accidentally get lipstick on your clothes while getting dressed, immediately rub the stain with a small ball of white Play-Doh. The modeling clay erases fresh lipstick stains before the oily dye gets a chance to settle.

- **Purell Instant Hand Sanitizer.** Saturate a lipstick stain on clothing with Purell Instant Hand Sanitizer and launder as usual.

- **Silly Putty.** To clean a lipstick stain from clothes, flatten a ball of Silly Putty into a pancake and use it to pat the lipstick stain, which will come up into the Silly Putty.

- **Spot Shot.** Saturate the stain with Spot Shot Instant Carpet Stain Remover, let sit for one minute, and launder as usual. (Do not use on dry-clean-only fabrics, non-colorfast garments, or silk.)

- **Star Olive Oil, Arm & Hammer Baking Soda,** and **Dawn Dishwashing Liquid.** Make a paste from Star Olive Oil and Arm & Hammer Baking Soda, rub the paste into the lipstick stain, rinse clean, and then add a few drops of Dawn Dishwashing Liquid and rinse out any residual olive oil stain. Launder as usual.

- **Vaseline Petroleum Jelly.** Rub a dab of Vaseline Petroleum Jelly into the lipstick stain, and then launder as usual.

- **WD-40** and **Dawn Dishwashing Liquid.** Spray WD-40 on a lipstick stain, let sit for ten minutes, and then rub in a few drops of Dawn Dishwashing Liquid and launder as usual. (Do not use WD-40 on silk.)

- **Wesson Oil** and **Dawn Dishwashing Liquid.** Rub a few drops of Wesson Oil into the lipstick stain on washable fabrics, let sit for thirty minutes, rub in a few drops of Dawn Dishwashing Liquid, and launder as usual in your regular wash.

- **Wonder Bread.** If you accidentally get lipstick on your clothes while getting dressed, immediately erase the stain with a slice of Wonder Bread before the oily dye gets a chance to soak into the fabric.

Liquor Stains

- **Canada Dry Club Soda.** To clean a fresh alcohol spill from a dry-clean-only garment, blot up as much liquid as possible and keep the stained area wet with Canada Dry Club Soda until you can get the garment to a dry cleaner.

- **Canada Dry Club Soda** and **Dawn Dishwashing Liquid.** To prevent an alcohol spill from drying and oxidizing to a brown color, blot up as much liquid as possible and saturate the affected area with Canada Dry Club Soda. Put a drop of Dawn Dishwashing Liquid on a slightly damp sponge and pat the spot. Rinse the spot with cool water and dry with a blow dryer on medium heat to prevent a yellow ring from forming.

- **Clorox 2.** To clean dried alcohol stains from clothes and prevent them oxidizing to a brown color, presoak the affected garment in Clorox 2 (a non-chlorine bleach) for thirty minutes, and then launder as usual.

- **Glycerin** and **Heinz White Vinegar.** To clean liquor stains from washable fabrics, mix three tablespoon Glycerin in a sink full of cold water and soak the garment in the solution. Add one-half cup Heinz White Vinegar to a new sink full of water and rinse the garment in the solution.

- **20 Mule Team Borax.** Immediately blot up as much liquid as possible, dissolve one teaspoon 20 Mule Team Borax in one cup warm water, sponge the solution on the stain, and launder as usual.

MAKEUP STAINS

- **Arm & Hammer Baking Soda.** To clean oily makeup stains from washable fabrics, sprinkle Arm & Hammer Baking Soda on the spot, let sit for ten minutes, and then brush with a clean, used toothbrush.

- **Colgate Regular Flavor Toothpaste.** Clean oily makeup stains from washable fabrics by squeezing a dab of Colgate Regular Flavor Toothpaste on a clean, used toothbrush and scrubbing the affected area.

- **Dawn Dishwashing Liquid.** Rub a few drops of Dawn Dishwashing Liquid into the makeup stain, and then launder the garment as usual.

- **Dove White Beauty Bar.** To clean blush, eye shadow, eyeliner, foundation, or mascara from washable fabrics, dampen the stain with water and rub it with a Dove White Beauty Bar, immersing the stain with soap. Rinse clean with warm water, repeat if necessary, and launder as usual.

- **Johnson's Baby Shampoo.** Rub a few drops of Johnson's Baby Shampoo into the makeup stain, and then launder the garment as usual.

- **20 Mule Team Borax.** Dissolve one teaspoon 20 Mule Team Borax in one cup warm water, sponge the solution on the makeup stain, and launder as usual.

MILDEW STAINS

- **Clorox Bleach.** If the fabric can withstand bleach, mix two tablespoons Clorox Bleach and one gallon cold water and soak the garment in the solution for five minutes. Launder as usual.

- **Fels-Naptha Soap.** To get rid of mildew stains on fabric, lather up a bar of Fels-Naptha Soap, work the lather into the spots, and launder.

- **Hydrogen Peroxide.** Saturate the mildew stain with Hydrogen Peroxide and launder as usual.

- **Nestlé Carnation NonFat Dry Milk** and **Morton Salt.** To clean a mildew stain from clothes, make a paste from two tablespoons Nestlé Carnation NonFat Dry Milk, one tablespoon Morton Salt, and water, rub the paste into the stain, let sit for fifteen minutes, then soak in a bucket of water overnight. Launder as usual.

- **Parsons' Ammonia.** Mix one tablespoon Parsons' Ammonia in one gallon water and soak the mildew-stained garment in the solution for fifteen minutes. Launder as usual.

- **ReaLemon** and **Morton Salt.** Mix equal parts ReaLemon lemon juice and Morton Salt and apply the paste to mildew stains, rubbing gently. Let sit for ten minutes and launder as usual.

- **20 Mule Team Borax** and **Dawn Dishwashing Liquid.** Mix one-quarter cup 20 Mule Team Borax, one tablespoon Dawn Dishwashing Liquid, and one gallon hot water in a bucket. Soak the stain and launder as usual.

MILK STAINS

- **Adolph's Original Meat Tenderizer.** Cover the milk stain with a paste made from Adolph's Original Meat Tenderizer and cool water. Wait twenty minutes and sponge off with cool water. The enzymes in the meat tenderizer break up the proteins in the milk.

- **Coca-Cola.** Saturate the milk stains with a can of Coca-Cola, let the garment sit for five minutes, and then launder in your regular wash.

- **Parsons' Ammonia** and **Dawn Dishwashing Liquid.** To eliminate milk stains on clothes, mix equal parts Parsons' Ammonia, Dawn Dishwashing Liquid, and water and apply the mixture to the spot. Let sit for five minutes and rinse thoroughly with water. (Do not use ammonia on acrylic, silk, spandex, or wool.)

MOLD

- **Heinz White Vinegar.** To clean mold from clothes, place the clothes in the washing machine, add one-quarter cup Heinz White Vinegar to the wash cycle along with your regular detergent, and launder as usual.

- **20 Mule Team Borax.** Mix one-quarter cup 20 Mule Team Borax with enough water to cover the moldy clothes and let soak in the solution until the mold vanishes.

MUD STAINS

- **Arm & Hammer Super Washing Soda** and **20 Mule Team Borax.** Let the mud dry, and then brush off as much of the dirt as possible. Pre-wash muddy clothes in the washing machine with the hottest water possible using one-half cup Arm & Hammer Super Washing Soda and one-half cup 20 Mule Team Borax. Run the items through the machine a second time with your regular laundry detergent.

- **Clorox 2.** To clean a mud stain from clothes, let the mud dry and shake it off. Then presoak the affected garment in Clorox 2 (a non-chlorine bleach) for thirty minutes, and then launder as usual.

- **Johnson's Baby Shampoo.** After you've let the mud dry and brushed off as much as possible, rub a few drops of Johnson's Baby Shampoo into the mud stain, and then launder the garment as usual.

- **Murphy Oil Soap.** Rub a few drops of Murphy Oil Soap into the dried mud stain, let sit for fifteen minutes, and rinse with cold water.

- **Parsons' Ammonia.** To clean stubborn dirt stains from clothes, add one ounce Parsons' Ammonia to the rinse water. (Never mix bleach and ammonia; the resulting fumes are deadly.)

- **Spot Shot.** Saturate the dried mud stain with Spot Shot Instant Carpet Stain Remover, let sit for one minute, and launder as usual. (Do not use on dry-clean-only fabrics, non-colorfast garments, or silk.)

- **20 Mule Team Borax.** Once you've let the mud dry, dampen the mud stain with water, rub 20 Mule Team Borax into the area, rinse clean, and launder as usual.

MUSTARD STAINS

- **Cascade.** To remove a mustard stain from a white garment, dissolve one-half cup Cascade dishwasher detergent powder in a bucket of very hot water, soak the garment overnight, and launder as usual.

- **Clorox 2.** To clean a mustard stain from a washable fabric, saturate the stain with water, apply Clorox 2 (a non-chlorine bleach) to the affected area, and rub in gently. Let sit for thirty minutes, and then launder as usual.

- **Efferdent.** To clean mustard from white fabric, dissolve two Efferdent denture cleansing tablets in one cup cool water and soak the stain in the solution for thirty minutes. Rinse clean and launder as usual.

- **Fels-Naptha Soap.** Fill a sink with cold water, soak the garment in the water, and rub the stain with Fels-Naptha Soap. Let the garment soak in the soapy water for twelve hours, and then launder as usual.

- **Glycerin.** After removing as much mustard as possible from the garment, apply Glycerin (available in drug stores) to the stain, let sit for one hour, and rinse clean. Treat with your regular stain remover and then launder as usual.

Mystery Stains

- **Arm & Hammer Super Washing Soda.** To clean a stain from clothes, make a paste from Arm & Hammer Super Washing Soda and water, apply the paste to the stain, let dry, and launder as usual.

- **Canada Dry Club Soda.** Dampen a paper towel with Canada Dry Club Soda, dab the stain with it, and then blot with a dry paper towel. The combination of the effervescence and sodium bicarbonate in the club soda seems to magically lift stains out of fabrics.

- **Colgate Regular Flavor Toothpaste.** If nothing else works to clean a stain from clothes, squeeze some Colgate Regular Flavor Toothpaste on a clean, old toothbrush and brush the stain.

- **Dawn Dishwashing Liquid.** Rub a few drops of Dawn Dishwashing Liquid into the stain, and then launder as usual. Dawn cuts through grease, dissolving many mystery stains.

- **Gillette Foamy.** Dampen the stain with cool water, spray a small dab of Gillette Foamy shaving cream on the spot, work it into the stain with your fingers, and then rinse well with cool water. The condensed soap in the shaving cream cleans away the offending stain.

- **McCormick Cream of Tartar.** Make a paste from McCormick Cream of Tartar and water, rub the paste into the stain, let dry, and launder as usual.

- **Purell Instant Hand Sanitizer.** Saturate a stain on clothing with Purell Instant Hand Sanitizer and launder as usual.

- **Spot Shot.** Saturate the stain with Spot Shot Instant Carpet Stain Remover, let sit for one minute, and launder as usual. (Do not use on dry-clean-only fabrics, non-colorfast garments, or silk.)

- **Windex.** Saturate the stain with Windex, blot well, and launder as usual with your regular detergent.

Nail Polish

- **Cutex Nail Polish Remover.** To clean nail polish from washable fabric, stretch the affected area over the top of a coffee mug and secure in place with a rubber band. Pour a few drops of Cutex Nail Polish Remover over the stain, allowing it to drip through the fabric, occasionally tapping the spot with clean, old toothbrush. Patiently repeat until the stain dissolves. Then launder as usual.

Odors

- **Heinz White Vinegar.** Add one-quarter cup Heinz White Vinegar to the final rinse to deodorize odors from clothing.

- **Morton Salt.** To deodorize persistent perspiration odor from clothes, dissolve one-half cup Morton Salt in bucket of warm water and soak the garment in the solution overnight. Launder as usual.

- **Odorzout.** To deodorize gasoline, garlic, pet odors, smoke, and urine from clothing, sprinkle Odorzout on the clothing, let sit overnight in a well-ventilated room, and launder as usual. Or add two teaspoons Odorzout to the wash load with your regular detergent. Odorzout absorbs odors rather than simply masking them with another fragrance.

- **20 Mule Team Borax.** Add one-half cup 20 Mule Team Borax to your regular wash load along with your regular detergent. Borax deodorizes laundry and also boosts the strength of the detergent.

Paint, Latex

- **Cascade.** To clean latex paint from clothes, treat the wet stain immediately by flushing the paint stain with warm water, and then rubbing in a few drops of Cascade Gel, rinsing until the stain dissolves. Repeat if necessary. Launder as usual.

- **Dawn Dishwashing Liquid.** To clean latex paint from clothes, treat the wet stain immediately by flushing the paint stain with warm water and then rubbing in a few drops of Dawn Dishwashing Liquid, rinsing until the stain dissolves. Repeat if necessary.

- **Easy-Off Oven Cleaner.** As a last resort to clean dried latex paint from cotton or polyester clothes, spray the paint stain with Easy-Off Oven Cleaner in a well-ventilated area, let sit for fifteen minutes on a surface that can withstand oven cleaner, and rinse thoroughly.

PAINT, OIL-BASED

- **Lestoil.** To clean oil paint from clothes, saturate the stain with Lestoil, let sit overnight, and launder as usual.

- **Purell Instant Hand Sanitizer.** After cleaning off the paint stain with turpentine, rub Purell Instant Hand Sanitizer into the resulting turpentine stain. Saturate the spot with your regular detergent, work it into the fabric well, and soak the garment overnight in a bucket of the hottest water possible for the fabric. Launder as usual.

- **Vaseline Petroleum Jelly.** Rub the oil paint stain with a dollop of Vaseline Petroleum Jelly, working it into the fabric, let sit for five minutes, and then launder as usual.

PANTY HOSE

- **Alberto VO5 Hair Spray.** To prolong the life of panty hose, spray the toe areas with Alberto VO5 Hair Spray every time before putting on the panty hose. The fixative in the hair spray strengthens the nylon netting so you're less likely to punch a hole through the hose with your toes.

- **Heinz White Vinegar.** To improve the elasticity in panty hose, add two tablespoons Heinz White Vinegar to the rinse water in your sink and let the panty hose soak for fifteen minutes before hanging them up to dry.

- **Johnson's Baby Shampoo.** To hand wash panty hose, mix one teaspoon Johnson's Baby Shampoo to a sink filled with warm water, let the panty hose soak in the sudsy solution for five minutes, rinse clean without wringing the panty hose, and hang to drip dry.

- **L'eggs Sheer Energy Panty Hose.** To make washing panty hose less cumbersome, cut off one leg from an old pair of clean, used L'eggs Sheer Energy Panty Hose, insert a pair of good panty hose into the leg, tie a loose knot in the end of the single panty hose leg, and toss it into your regular wash load.

- **Revlon Clear Nail Enamel.** To prevent a run in a pair of panty hose from getting bigger, glue the tear closed and seal the frays with Revlon Clear Nail Enamel.

- **Ziploc Freezer Bags.** To prolong the life of a brand-new pair of panty hose, saturate the panty hose with water in a sink, wring out the panty hose, place them in a Ziploc Freezer Bag, and put the bag in the freezer overnight. In the morning, remove the Ziploc Freezer Bag from the freezer, let the panty hose thaw, and let dry.

PENCIL MARKS

- **Pink Pearl Eraser.** To clean pencil marks from clothes, gently rub the marks with a Pink Pearl Eraser.

PERMANENT PRESS

- **Epsom Salt.** To give drooping permanent press garments a new life, launder as usual, and then add one cup Epsom Salt to the final rinse water and change the setting on the machine to the wash-and-wear cycle.

- **Nestlé Carnation NonFat Dry Milk.** To firm up lifeless permanent press garments, launder as usual, and then add one cup Nestlé Carnation NonFat Dry Milk to the final rinse water in the washing machine and change the setting on the machine to the wash-and-wear cycle.

PERSPIRATION STAINS

- **Arm & Hammer Baking Soda.** To eliminate perspiration stains and odor from clothes, rub a paste made from Arm & Hammer Baking Soda and water into the stain, let sit for thirty minutes, and launder as usual with your regular detergent.

- **Clorox 2.** Dampen the perspiration stain on the garment with water and pour some Clorox 2 (a non-chlorine bleach) on the spot. Let sit for five minutes, and then launder as usual.

- **Fels-Naptha Soap.** Saturate the perspiration stain on the garment with water, lather up a bar of Fels-Naptha Soap, and rub the lather into the perspiration stain. Launder as usual.

- **Heinz White Vinegar.** To clean existing perspiration stains from clothing, mix equal parts Heinz White Vinegar and water, saturate the stain with the solution, let sit for ten minutes, and launder as usual. Or fill the washing machine with enough water to cover the clothes, add one-quarter cup Heinz White Vinegar, let sit overnight, and launder as usual.

- **Morton Salt.** Mix four tablespoons Morton Salt and enough water to make a paste. Rub the paste into the perspiration stain, let sit for an hour, and launder as usual. Or fill the washing machine with enough water to cover the clothes, mix in one-half cup Morton Salt, let soak for one hour, and launder as usual.

- **Parsons' Ammonia** and **Dawn Dishwashing Liquid.** To get rid of perspiration stains on clothes, mix equal parts Parsons' Ammonia, Dawn Dishwashing Liquid, and water and apply the mixture to the spot. Let sit for five minutes, and then rinse thoroughly with water. (Do not use ammonia on acrylic, silk, spandex, or wool.)

- **Scotchgard Fabric Protector.** To avoid getting perspiration stains on clothes in the first place, spray the underarms of clean garments with Scotchgard Fabric Protector, which repels liquid.

- **Tide** and **Clorox 2.** To clean existing perspiration stains from clothes, dampen the stain with water, work in a few drops of liquid Tide, and then saturate the stain with Clorox 2 (a non-chlorine bleach). Let sit for thirty minutes, and then launder as usual.

- **20 Mule Team Borax** and **Heinz White Vinegar.** To clean existing perspiration stains from clothes, make a paste from equal parts 20 Mule Team Borax and Heinz White Vinegar and work it into the stain. Let sit for ten minutes, and then launder as usual.

PINK UNDERWEAR AND T-SHIRTS

- **Carbona Color Run Remover.** If you accidentally washed a red T-shirt with your white underwear and shirts, use Carbona Color Run Remover according to the directions on the box for a single garment or a full wash load. Do not use Carbona Color Run Remover on denim, khaki, synthetic materials, or silk.

- **Rit Color Remover.** If you accidentally washed a red T-shirt with your white underwear and shirts, use Rit Color Remover according to the directions on the box for a single garment or a full wash load.

RING-AROUND-THE-COLLAR

- **Arm & Hammer Baking Soda** and **Heinz White Vinegar.** To remove ring-around-the-collar, make a paste of Arm & Hammer Baking Soda and water. Rub the paste into the ring, and then pour Heinz White Vinegar on the baking soda. When the foaming subsides, launder the garment as usual.

- **Crayola Chalk.** Rub white Crayola Chalk over the ring stain, let sit for ten minutes, and then brush clean. Repeat if necessary. Chalk absorbs oil. Launder as usual.

- **Johnson's Baby Powder.** Rub Johnson's Baby Powder into the ring, and then launder as usual.

- **Johnson's Baby Shampoo.** Rub a few drops of Johnson's Baby Shampoo into ring-around-the-collar stains, using a clean, old toothbrush if necessary, and then launder the garment as usual.

- **Play-Doh.** Roll a ball of white Play-Doh over the ring-around-the-collar to erase the stain. Launder as usual.

- **Wonder Bread.** Rub a slice of Wonder Bread into the ring. The bread simultaneously absorbs and erases the stain. Launder as usual.

RUST STAINS

- **McCormick Cream of Tartar.** To clean rust stains from white clothes, make a paste from McCormick Cream of Tartar and hot water, apply to the stain, let sit for ten minutes, and rinse clean. Repeat if necessary, and then launder as usual. Or mix two tablespoons McCormick Cream of Tartar and one quart water in a pot, boil the garment in the solution for ten minutes, let cool, and rinse well.

- **ReaLemon** and **Morton Salt.** To clean rust stains from white fabrics, saturate the stain with ReaLemon lemon juice and sprinkle with Morton Salt, and then lay the garment in the sun. Launder as usual.

- **Zud Heavy Duty Cleanser.** To clean rust stains from clothes, saturate the stain with water, rub Zud Heavy Duty Cleanser into the stain, let sit for ten minutes, and rinse clean.

SAP

- **MasterCard, Bounty Paper Towels, Glycerin,** and **Dawn Dishwashing Liquid.** To clean wet sap from clothes, use the edge of an old MasterCard to scrape as much sap as possible from the fabric. Place the stained garment facedown on a stack of Bounty Paper Towels and saturate the back of the sap stain with Glycerin, pressing the fabric into the paper towels to absorb the sap stain. Repeat if necessary. Work Dawn Dishwashing Liquid into the remaining stain and launder as usual.

- **Star Olive Oil.** To clean dried sap from clothes, warm Star Olive Oil in a microwave oven and pour it over the stain and let soak to soften the sap. Then use the previous tip.

SEQUINED AND BEADED GOWNS

- **Smirnoff Vodka.** Freshen sequined and beaded gowns by putting Smirnoff Vodka in a trigger-spray bottle and lightly misting the neckline and underarms.

SHIRTS AND COLLARS

- **Kleenex Tissues.** To protect shirt and collars, fold a Kleenex Tissue into a one-inch-wide strip and place under the shirt or dress collar while on wire hangers.

SHOE POLISH STAINS

- **Purell Instant Hand Sanitizer.** Saturate a shoe polish stain on clothing with Purell Instant Hand Sanitizer and launder as usual.

- **Spot Shot.** Saturate the stain with Spot Shot Instant Carpet Stain Remover, let sit for one minute, and launder as usual. (Do not use on dry-clean-only fabrics, non-colorfast garments, or silk.)

- **Vaseline Petroleum Jelly** and **Dawn Dishwashing Liquid.** To clean a dry, thick shoe polish stain from clothes, cover the stain with Vaseline Petroleum Jelly, working it into the stain. Let sit for one hour. Scrape off as much of the shoe polish and petroleum jelly as possible, work in a few drops of Dawn Dishwashing Liquid, and launder as usual.

- **WD-40, Parsons' Ammonia,** and **Dawn Dishwashing Liquid.** Spray WD-40 on a shoe polish stain on clothes, let sit for fifteen minutes, sponge a few drops of Parsons' Ammonia into the stain, rub in a few drops of Dawn Dishwashing Liquid, and launder as usual.

SILKS

- **Johnson's Baby Shampoo.** To wash silks safely, fill the sink with tepid water, add a few drops of Johnson's Baby Shampoo, and gently wash silk garments in the soapy solution. Rinse clean, gently squeeze out excess water, and hang to dry.

- **Murphy Oil Soap.** Fill the sink with water, add two teaspoons Murphy Oil Soap, and gently wash the silks in the solution. Rinse clean and hang to dry.

SILLY PUTTY

- **MasterCard, WD-40** and **Dawn Dishwashing Liquid.** Scrape off as much Silly Putty as possible with the edge of an old MasterCard, spray WD-40 on the affected area, let sit for fifteen minutes, and scrape again. Rub in a few drops of Dawn Dishwashing Liquid and launder as usual.

SOCKS

- **Arm & Hammer Baking Soda.** To deodorize smelly socks, dissolve one-quarter cup Arm & Hammer Baking Soda in one gallon water in a bucket and soak the soaks in the solution overnight. Pluck the wet socks out of the bucket, toss them into your washing machine, and launder as usual with your regular detergent.

- **Calgon Water Softener.** Instead of washing socks using detergent, use one-half cup Calgon Water Softener in the washing machine.

- **ReaLemon.** To whiten white socks, mix two tablespoons ReaLemon lemon juice in a bucket of hot water and soak the socks in the solution for one hour. Launder as usual.

SOFT DRINK STAINS

- **Hydrogen Peroxide.** To clean a soft drink stain from washable clothes, blot up as much of the spill as possible, mix equal parts Hydrogen

Peroxide and water, and saturate the stain with the mixture. Let sit for twenty minutes and repeat if necessary. Launder as usual.

- **20 Mule Team Borax.** Immediately blot up as much liquid as possible, dissolve one teaspoon 20 Mule Team Borax in one cup warm water, sponge the solution on the stain, and launder as usual.

SOOT

- **Arm & Hammer Super Washing Soda** and **20 Mule Team Borax.** Toss the garment in your washing machine, add one-half cup Arm & Hammer Super Washing Soda, one-half cup 20 Mule Team Borax, and your regular detergent. Launder using the hottest water possible for that type of fabric.
- **Formula 409.** Wet the soot stain with water, saturate the stain with Formula 409, and launder as usual.

SORTING

- **Forster Clothespins.** To identify badly soiled clothes easily, keep a basket of Forster Clothespins near the laundry bin and instruct family members to clip one to any garment that needs special attention in the wash.

SPAGHETTI SAUCE STAINS

- **Heinz White Vinegar** and **Wine Away.** To clean spaghetti sauce stains from clothes, immediately rinse the stain from both sides of the fabric with cool water, saturate the affected area with Heinz White Vinegar, let sit for five minutes, and then rinse clean with cool water. Apply Wine Away Red Wine Stain Remover, wait until the stain disappears, and blot with a wet cloth.
- **Morton Salt.** The moment you spill spaghetti sauce on clothes, wet the spot, cover the stain with Morton Salt, let sit for five minutes, and launder as usual. The salt absorbs the spaghetti sauce from the fabric.

Stickers

- **Heinz White Vinegar.** To remove stickers from clothes, apply Heinz White Vinegar to the back side of the fabric behind the sticker, let sit for five minutes, and peel off the sticker.

Storage

- **Bounce.** To prevent musty smells when storing winter coats, sweaters, scarves, and mittens, place a sheet of Bounce on the bottom of the storage container and place sheets of Bounce between layers of clothes. When you open the storage container months later, you'll be greeted by a fresh, invigorating scent.

Suds

- **Morton Salt.** If you accidentally put too much detergent in the washing machine and end up with overflowing soap suds, sprinkle the suds with Morton Salt using a salt shaker. The shower of salt crystals pops the tiny soap bubbles, and the salt water depletes them as well.

Suede

- **Heinz White Vinegar.** To clean and condition suede, wipe the suede with a soft, cloth dampened with Heinz White Vinegar.

Sweaters

- **Hydrogen Peroxide.** To whiten a yellowing white sweater, mix two ounces Hydrogen Peroxide and one gallon warm water, soak the sweater in the solution for four hours, wash, and dry.
- **Johnson's Baby Shampoo.** Put a teaspoon of Johnson's Baby Shampoo in the water in the washing machine to launder sweaters so they dry feeling soft and smelling clean.

- **L'eggs Sheer Energy Panty Hose.** To prevent sweaters from getting points at the shoulders from hanging from clothespins on a clothes line, feed the legs of a clean, old pair of L'eggs Sheer Energy Panty Hose down the neck of the sweater and through the arms of the sweater. Clip the clothespins to the waist and feet of the panty hose, so the sweater is hanging from the nylon hose rather than the clothesline itself.

TAR

- **Crisco All-Vegetable Shortening.** To remove tar from clothes, rub a dollop of Crisco All-Vegetable Shortening into the stain, let sit for five minutes, and launder as usual.

- **MasterCard, Bounty Paper Towels, Glycerin,** and **Dawn Dishwashing Liquid.** To clean wet tar from clothes, use the edge of an old MasterCard to scrape as much tar as possible from the fabric. Place the stained garment facedown on a stack of Bounty Paper Towels and saturate the back of the tar stain with Glycerin, pressing the fabric into the paper towels to absorb the tar stain. Repeat if necessary. Work Dawn Dishwashing Liquid into the remaining stain and launder as usual.

- **Star Olive Oil.** To clean dried tar from clothes, warm Star Olive Oil in a microwave oven, pour it over the stain, and let soak to soften the tar. Then use the above tip.

TIES

- **Scotchgard Fabric Protector.** To avoid getting stains on a neck tie, spray the tie with Scotchgard Fabric Protector. Scotchgard effectively repels food and liquids.

TOMATO SAUCE STAINS

- **Heinz White Vinegar** and **Wine Away.** To clean tomato sauce stains from clothes, immediately rinse the stain from both sides of the fabric with cool water, saturate the affected area with Heinz White Vinegar, let sit for five minutes, and then rinse clean with cool water. Apply Wine Away Red Wine Stain Remover, wait until the stain disappears, and blot with a wet cloth.

TONER STAINS

- **Spot Shot.** To remove computer printer powdered toner or photocopy machine powdered toner from your clothes, lightly brush the powdered stain with a soft brush (not your fingers, which will add oil to the toner). Spray the stain with Spot Shot Instant Carpet Stain Remover, let sit for five to ten minutes, and launder with your regular detergent in the hottest water possible.

UNDERARM STAINS

- **Clorox 2** and **Glad Trash Bags.** To clean yellow underarm stains from clothes, saturate the stains with water, apply Clorox 2 (a non-chlorine bleach) on the affected spots, and rub in gently. Place the garment in a Glad Trash Bag, let sit overnight, and then launder in hot water. (For fabrics that cannot tolerate hot water, drape the garment over your sink, pour four cups of hot water through the stain, and then launder as usual.)

- **Fels-Naptha Soap.** To prevent underarm stains on clothes, lather up a bar of Fels-Naptha Soap and rub the lather into underarms of new clothes before laundering them for the first time. Launder with cool water and your regular detergent.

- **Heinz White Vinegar, 20 Mule Team Borax,** and **Glad Trash Bags.** Saturate yellow underarm stains with Heinz White Vinegar, rub in 20 Mule Team Borax, place in a Glad Trash Bag overnight, and then launder as usual.

- **Parsons' Ammonia.** To clean underarm stains caused by the aluminum chloride in antiperspirant, dampen the stain with full-strength Parsons'

Ammonia (unless the fabric is silk or wool, in which case use a mixture of equal parts ammonia and cold water), and then rinse thoroughly with cold water. The pH in the ammonia neutralizes the acid in the sodium chloride, dissolving the stain.

URINE STAINS

- **Clorox 2.** To clean urine stains from clothes, rinse well with cool water, soak the garment in Clorox 2 (a non-chlorine bleach) for thirty minutes, and launder as usual.

- **Heinz Vinegar.** Deodorize urine-stained sheets and clothes by adding one cup Heinz White Vinegar in the laundry water.

- **Morton Salt.** Dissolve one-half cup Morton Salt in a bucket of water, soak the garment in the salt water for one hour, and then launder as usual with your regular detergent.

- **Parsons' Ammonia** and **Dawn Dishwashing Liquid.** To remove urine stains on clothes, mix equal parts Parsons' Ammonia, Dawn Dishwashing Liquid, and water and apply the mixture to the spot. Let sit for five minutes, and then rinse thoroughly with water. (Do not use ammonia on acrylic, silk, spandex, or wool.)

- **Spot Shot.** Saturate the stain with Spot Shot Instant Carpet Stain Remover, let sit for one minute, and launder as usual. (Do not use on dry-clean-only fabrics, non-colorfast garments, or silk.)

VOMIT

- **20 Mule Team Borax, Dawn Dishwashing Liquid,** and **Morton Salt.** After scraping off as much solid chunks and excess liquid as possible and rinsing the garment under running cold water, make a paste from 20 Mule Team Borax and Dawn Dishwashing Liquid and scrub the stain with the paste. Dissolve one-half cup Morton Salt in a bucket of water and rinse the garment in the salt water. Launder as usual.

Water Softeners

- **Arm & Hammer Baking Soda.** If you have hard water, add one-half cup Arm & Hammer Baking Soda to a full load of laundry to boost the performance of the soap.

- **Arm & Hammer Super Washing Soda** and **20 Mule Team Borax.** To make your own water softener, mix one-half pound Arm & Hammer Super Washing Soda, one-quarter pound 20 Mule Team Borax, and one gallon water in a bucket. Add one cup of the mixture to your regular wash load along with your regular detergent. Store the homemade water softener in a one-gallon water jug, and be sure to label it to avoid any potential mishaps.

- **Heinz White Vinegar.** Increase the intensity of your laundry detergent in hard water by adding one-quarter cup Heinz White Vinegar to the wash cycle.

- **20 Mule Team Borax.** Boost the strength of your laundry detergent in hard water by adding one-quarter cup 20 Mule Team Borax to your wash load with your regular detergent.

White Socks

- **Cascade.** To whiten white socks, mix two tablespoons Cascade (powder or gel) and one gallon hot water in a bucket and soak the socks in the solution for one hour. Pour the entire contents of the bucket into your washing machine and launder as usual with your regular detergent.

- **ReaLemon.** To whiten white socks, mix one-half cup ReaLemon lemon juice and one gallon hot water, soak the socks in the lemony solution overnight, and then launder the socks (discarding the lemony liquid) as usual with your regular detergent.

Whiten Whites

- **Mrs. Stewart's Liquid Bluing.** Mix a few drops or up to one-quarter teaspoon Mrs. Stewart's Liquid Bluing in one quart water. Add the diluted bluing to either the wash water or the final rinse.

- **Nestlé Coffee-mate Original.** To whiten whites, use powdered Nestlé Coffee-mate Original creamer to whiten your clothes (cotton shirts, underwear, socks) just by mixing it with hot water and letting the clothes soak in it.

- **20 Mule Team Borax.** To whiten white garments, add one-quarter cup 20 Mule Team Borax to the wash cycle.

Wine Stains

- **Canada Dry Club Soda.** To clean a fresh wine stain from clothes, saturate the stain with Canada Dry Club Soda and launder as usual.

- **Heinz White Vinegar** and **Dawn Dishwashing Liquid.** To get rid of wine stains, mix equal amounts Heinz White Vinegar, Dawn Dishwashing Liquid, and water and work the mixture into the stain. Let sit for five minutes, and then toss in your regular wash load.

- **McCormick Cream of Tartar.** To clean a wine stain from fabric, blot up the liquid, make a paste from equal parts McCormick Cream of Tartar and water, spread the paste on the fabric, let sit for ten minutes, and wash in cold water with your regular detergent.

- **Morton Salt** and **Canada Dry Club Soda.** Cover a wine stain on clothes with Morton Salt. The salt absorbs the wine from the fabric. Rinse clean with Canada Dry Club Soda. Then launder as usual.

- **Nestlé Carnation NonFat Dry Milk.** In a pot, mix one-and-one-third cups Nestlé Carnation NonFat Dry Milk and seven-and-a-half cups water, place the wine-stained garment in the milky solution, and bring to a boil. Remove from the stove and let sit until the stain vanishes. Rinse clean and launder as usual.

- **Purell Instant Hand Sanitizer.** After blotting the wine stain, rub Purell Instant Hand Sanitizer into the spot and blot well. Repeat if necessary.

- **20 Mule Team Borax.** After blotting up as much of the wine stain as possible, make a paste from 20 Mule Team Borax and water and apply it to the stain. Let sit for ten minutes, and then launder as usual.

WOOL

- **Glycerin.** To soften woolens and lessen the scratchiness, add a few drops of Glycerin to the final rinse water after hand washing.

- **Johnson's Baby Shampoo.** If you accidentally launder a woolen sweater in the washing machine, pulling it out of shape, fill a sink with lukewarm water, mix in a few drops of Johnson's Baby Shampoo, and soak the garment for thirty minutes. Rinse clean and dry.

- **Murphy Oil Soap.** As you're filling the sink with cold water, add two teaspoons Murphy Oil Soap and wash the woolens in the soapy solution. Rinse clean, lay each woolen on a towel, roll up the towel to blot the water from the woolen, and then lay the woolen on an open towel to dry.

- **Pantene Pro-V Silkening Silk Transformation Crème.** After hand washing fine woolen clothes, add a few drops of Pantene Pro-V Silkening Silk Transformation Crème to the final rinse water to keep the wool silky soft.

- **Ziploc Freezer Bags.** After hand washing and rinsing your white woolens, place the garments in Ziploc Freezer Bags and place the bags in your freezer for ninety minutes. Remove, thaw to room temperature, and hang to dry. The cold bleaches the white wool.

YELLOW SPOTS AND STAINS

- **Colgate Regular Flavor Toothpaste.** To clean yellow spots from clothes, rub a dollop of Colgate Regular Flavor Toothpaste into the spot, and then launder in cold water.

- **Efferdent.** To remove random yellow spots and stains from linens and clothes, fill a sink with water, add two Efferdent denture cleansing tablets, and soak the affected garment until the stains vanish. Launder as usual.

ZIPPERS

- **Alberto VO5 Hair Spray.** If your zipper slides open of its own accord, spray the teeth of the zipper with Alberto VO5 Hair Spray to give them more traction.

- **ChapStick.** To make a stubborn zipper glide with greater ease, coat the teeth with some ChapStick lip balm. The wax lubricates the teeth and helps the zipper zip smoothly.

- **Crayola Crayons.** In a pinch, you can lubricate a stubborn zipper by rubbing an unwrapped Crayola Crayon (ideally white) along the teeth. The wax in the crayon makes the zipper slide nicely.

- **Faultless Spray Starch.** To make a sticky zipper zip properly again, spray the teeth with Faultless Spray Starch.

- **Ivory Soap.** Another way to make a zipper glide smoothly? Rub a bar of Ivory Soap along the teeth to lubricate them.

- **Vaseline Petroleum Jelly.** To make a stubborn zipper slide smoothly, coat the teeth with Vaseline Petroleum Jelly.

Leather and Suede

BLOODSTAINS

- **Hydrogen Peroxide.** To clean a bloodstain from leather, use a cotton ball to dab Hydrogen Peroxide on the spot. When the bubbling stops, blot the spot. Repeat if necessary. Wipe clean with a damp, soft cloth, and then dry thoroughly.

BOOTS

- **Endust.** To give boots a protective coating so water beads off the leather, polish the books with Endust.
- **Vaseline Petroleum Jelly.** To protect leather boots from water stains and salt marks, coat a soft, clean cloth with Vaseline Petroleum Jelly and gently rub your boots with the cloth before you wear them outside and whenever you return.

Dark Stains

- **ReaLemon** and **McCormick Cream of Tartar.** To remove dark stains from leather, make a paste from ReaLemon lemon juice and McCormick Cream of Tartar and rub it into the spot. Rinse well, and then clean with one of the methods listed below.

Furniture

- **Castor Oil.** Put a few drops of Castor Oil on a soft, clean cloth, rub it into dark leather upholstery, and use a second soft, clean cloth to absorb the excess oil and buff.

- **Dove White Beauty Bar.** Rub a Dove White Beauty Bar across a mildly damp, soft cloth and rub the cloth on the leather. Wipe dry with a fresh damp cloth and buff dry with a dry towel. After the leather dries, treat it with a leather conditioner.

- **Johnson's Baby Oil.** To clean and condition leather, use a soft, clean cloth to rub a few drops of Johnson's Baby Oil into the leather. Use a second soft, clean cloth to absorb the excess oil and buff.

- **Mr. Clean Magic Eraser.** To clean leather upholstery, saturate a Mr. Clean Magic Eraser with water, squeeze out the excess water, and gently rub the leather.

- **Murphy Oil Soap.** To clean leather upholstery, use a whisk to whip one-quarter cup Murphy Oil Soap and three tablespoons water in a bowl to create as much foam as possible. With a sponge, rub only the resulting foam into the upholstery. Rinse well, blot, and let dry. (For more ways to clean leather, see page 124.)

- **Star Olive Oil.** Put a few drops of Star Olive Oil on a soft, clean cloth and rub it into hardened leather upholstery to soften it.

- **Vaseline Petroleum Jelly.** To preserve light leather, apply a thick coat of Vaseline Petroleum Jelly, let sit for five hours, and then rub off using a clean, soft cloth.

Gloves

- **Alberto VO5 Conditioning Hairdressing.** Rub a few dabs of Alberto VO5 Conditioning Hairdressing into the leather and buff it dry with a paper towel or a soft, clean cloth.
- **Murphy Oil Soap.** To clean leather gloves, put the gloves on your hands and wash with a few drops of Murphy Oil Soap and water. Place the gloves flat on a countertop and let air dry.

Glue Stains

- **Zippo Lighter Fluid.** To clean glue from suede, saturate a cotton ball with Zippo Lighter Fluid, rub it over the glue stain, and wipe clean. Let dry and brush the suede to raise the nap.

Grass Stains

- **Grandma's Molasses.** To clean grass stains from white leather shoes, rub Grandma's Molasses on the stain and let sit overnight. In the morning, wash the molasses off the shoes with soap and water.

Grease Stains

- **Johnson's Baby Powder.** To clean a grease stain from leather, cover the stain with Johnson's Baby Powder, rub the powder into the stain, and brush clean.
- **Kingsford's Corn Starch.** Blot up the excess grease with a clean cloth. Sprinkle Kingsford's Corn Starch on the spot, let sit overnight, and then wipe clean. Cornstarch is highly absorbent.

GUM

- **Skippy Peanut Butter.** To clean gum from leather, apply a dab of Skippy Peanut Butter (creamy, not chunky) on the gum, let sit for five minutes, and wipe clean. The oils in the peanut butter dissolve the gum.

INK STAINS

- **Alberto VO5 Hair Spray.** Spray the ink stain with Alberto VO5 Hair Spray and blot up the ink stain with a clean cloth. Repeat if necessary. The acetone in the hair spray dissolves the ink.

- **Mr. Clean Magic Eraser.** To clean magic marker, permanent ink, and ballpoint ink from leather, gently rub the stains with a damp Mr. Clean Magic Eraser.

- **Revlon Gentle Cuticle Remover.** To clean a ballpoint ink stain from leather, brush Revlon Gentle Cuticle Remover on the marks. Let sit for ten minutes, and then wipe off with a clean cloth dampened with soapy water. Buff dry with a soft, clean cloth. (Be sure to test an inconspicuous spot on the leather beforehand for colorfastness.)

- **Vaseline Petroleum Jelly.** To remove a ballpoint ink stain, rub a dab of Vaseline Petroleum Jelly into the affected area, let sit overnight, and then wipe clean. Repeat for several days, if necessary.

MAKEUP STAINS

- **Wonder Bread.** Clean makeup stains from suede by rubbing the spot with a slice of Wonder Bread, which works like an eraser.

MILDEW

- **Listerine.** To clean mildew from leather, saturate a cotton ball with Listerine antiseptic mouthwash and apply to the affected area, let sit for five minutes, then buff clean with a soft cloth.

- **Vaseline Petroleum Jelly.** To remove mildew from leather, apply a thick coat of Vaseline Petroleum Jelly, let sit for five hours, and then rub off using a clean, soft cloth.

PATENT LEATHER

- **Nestlé Carnation NonFat Dry Milk.** To clean patent leather, mix one level teaspoon Nestlé Carnation NonFat Dry Milk with three teaspoons water. Apply the milky solution with a soft, clean cloth. Buff dry with a second soft, clean cloth.

- **Vaseline Petroleum Jelly.** Put a dab of Vaseline Petroleum Jelly on a soft, clean cloth and polish the patent leather. Buff with a clean, soft cloth to acheive a brilliant shine.

PURSES AND HANDBAGS

- **Alberto VO5 Conditioning Hairdressing.** Rub a few dabs of Alberto VO5 Conditioning Hairdressing into the leather and buff it dry with a paper towel or a soft, clean cloth.

- **Dove White Beauty Bar.** Dampen a soft, clean cloth with warm water, wring it out, and then lather with a Dove White Beauty Bar. Rub the cloth over the leather purse to remove the dirt, and then buff dry with a soft, clean cloth.

- **Kingsford's Corn Starch.** To clean grease stains from a leather pocketbook, sprinkle Kingsford's Corn Starch over the leather, wrap the bag in a towel, let sit for twenty-four hours, and gently brush clean.

- **Murphy Oil Soap.** Mix one-quarter cup Murphy Oil Soap and two quarts hot water in a bucket and use a soft, clean cloth to scrub the leather pocketbook with the solution. Dry with a second soft, clean cloth. Let air dry. Condition with Alberto VO5 Conditioning Hairdressing. (See above.)

SALT STAINS

- **Heinz White Vinegar.** To clean salt stains from leather, mix three teaspoons Heinz White Vinegar and one teaspoon water and dab the solution on the salt stain.

SHOES

- **Arm & Hammer Baking Soda.** To clean any scuffmarks off white leather shoes before polishing, apply a paste made from Arm & Hammer Baking Soda and water and scrub with a sponge. Rinse clean with a damp sponge. (For more ways to clean white leather shoes, see page 360.)

- **Dove White Beauty Bar.** Rub a Dove White Beauty Bar across a mildly damp, soft cloth and rub the cloth on the leather. Wipe dry with a fresh damp cloth and buff dry with a dry towel. After the leather dries, polish as usual. (For more ways to polish leather shoes, see page 355.)

SUEDE

- **Heinz White Vinegar.** To clean grease stains from suede, dampen a soft, clean cloth with Heinz White Vinegar and rub gently, and then brush the suede and let dry.

- **Pink Pearl Eraser.** To clean a spot from suede, rub the affected area with a Pink Pearl Eraser.

- **Quaker Oats.** To clean soiled suede, use a clean cloth to rub uncooked Quaker Oats into the stain in a circulation motion. Brush clean with a suede brush.

- **Resolve Carpet Cleaner.** To clean soiled suede, spray Resolve Carpet Cleaner on the stain, let sit for ten minutes, brush with a wet toothbrush, and let air dry.

- **Wonder Bread.** To clean stains from suede, rub the affected area with a slice of Wonder Bread, which works like a mild eraser.

Linens

BEDSPREADS AND COMFORTERS

- **Wilson Tennis Balls.** After washing a quilted bedspread or comforter according to the label instructions, place the bedspread or comforter in the dryer on a low setting and add two or three Wilson Tennis Balls to fluff up the stuffing.

BLANKETS

- **Heinz White Vinegar.** After washing a machine-washable blanket with mild soap and cold water, add one cup Heinz White Vinegar to the final rinse to remove soap residue and soften the blanket.

CANDLE WAX

- **Bounty Paper Towels.** To clean melted wax from a tablecloth, place a sheet of Bounty Paper Towels over the wax stain and press gently with a warm iron. The heat from the iron melts the wax, and the quicker-picker-upper absorbs it.

- **Wesson Oil.** To clean candle wax stains from linen, saturate the spot with Wesson Oil, blot up the excess oil with a paper towel, and launder as usual with your regular detergent.

COFFEE AND TEA STAINS

- **20 Mule Team Borax.** Drape the tablecloth over the kitchen sink, sprinkle 20 Mule Team Borax to cover the coffee or tea stain, and pour a pitcher full of hot water around the stain, working toward the center. Repeat if necessary, and then launder as usual.

FOOD STAINS

- **McCormick Cream of Tartar** and **ReaLemon.** Mix enough McCormick Cream of Tartar with ReaLemon lemon juice to make a paste, apply it to food stains on white tablecloths and napkins, let sit for thirty minutes, and then launder as usual. Together, cream of tartar and lemon juice work like bleach.

- **ReaLemon.** Saturate food stains on white tablecloths and napkins with ReaLemon lemon juice and set the garment in the sun to bleach the stain away. Apply more lemon juice to the stain before laundering as usual.

- **Spot Shot.** Saturate the food stain with Spot Shot Instant Carpet Stain Remover, let sit for one minute, and immediately launder as usual. (Do not use on dry-clean-only fabrics, non-colorfast garments, or silk.)

LACE TABLECLOTHS

- **Mrs. Stewart's Liquid Bluing.** To whiten a lace tablecloth, mix a few drops of Mrs. Stewart's Liquid Bluing in a quart or more of water. Add the mixture to the wash water or final rinse. (The water should appear light sky blue.)

BRUSHING UP ON CREST

In 1950, Procter & Gamble hired researchers at Indiana University (led by Dr. Joseph Muhler) to develop a toothpaste that could be proved effective in reducing tooth decay. By 1952, Muhler and his group created a therapeutic toothpaste containing stannous fluoride, a chemical believed to protect against cavities. Indiana University received a patent for the formula, but Procter & Gamble purchased the exclusive right to market and mass-produce the product.

In 1954, the results from clinical trials of Crest at Indiana University showed that the toothpaste reduced the number of cavities, but the American Dental Association (ADA) remained unconvinced of Procter & Gamble's claims. In 1960, after Procter & Gamble financed twenty-three separate group studies at Indiana University, the ADA's Council on Dental Therapeutics agreed that Crest had been shown to be "an effective anti-caries" agent, making Crest the first fluoride toothpaste clinically proven to be effective in preventing cavities and tooth decay. By advertising this designation, Crest became the market leader within two years, outselling Colgate toothpaste.

Procter & Gamble spent the next twenty-five years attempting to develop an improved version of Crest with better cavity protection, creating more than seventy toothpaste formulas, none of which surpassed Crest at fighting cavities. In 1980, the company finally succeeded in creating a superior Crest formula for cavity protection: Advanced Formula Crest with Fluoristat.

Strange Facts

- Industrial designer Donald Deskey designed the Art Deco interiors of Radio City Music Hall and the packaging for Crest toothpaste.

- In 1955, Crest began one of the most popular ad campaigns of the twentieth century, created by the Benton & Bowles advertising agency. Renowned illustrator Norman Rockwell created the first print ads for Crest, featuring a painting of a child and featuring the headline, "Look, Mom—No cavities!"

- Dick Wolf, producer of the *Law and Order* television series and spin-offs, began his career in advertising, writing copy for Crest toothpaste.

- **Nestlé Carnation NonFat Dry Milk** and **Heinz White Vinegar.** To whiten yellowed lace, mix three cups Nestlé Carnation NonFat Dry Milk, one cup Heinz White Vinegar, and one gallon water in a bucket and soak the lace tablecloth in the milky solution for one hour. Rinse clean and let dry.

LINEN CLOSETS

- **Dial Soap.** To freshen the air in a linen closet, place a wrapped bar of Dial Soap on a shelf in the closet to keep the linens smelling fresh.

LIPSTICK STAINS

- **Johnson's Baby Shampoo.** To clean lipstick stains from cloth napkins, rub a few drops of Johnson's Baby Shampoo into the lipstick stain, and then launder the garment as usual.

- **Purell Instant Hand Sanitizer.** Saturate a lipstick stain on a cloth napkin with Purell Instant Hand Sanitizer and launder as usual.

- **Spot Shot.** Saturate the lipstick stain with Spot Shot Instant Carpet Stain Remover, let sit for one minute, and launder as usual. (Do not use on dry-clean-only fabrics, non-colorfast garments, or silk.)

- **WD-40** and **Dawn Dishwashing Liquid.** To clean lipstick stains from cloth napkins, spray WD-40 on the stain, let sit for ten minutes, rub in a few drops of Dawn Dishwashing Liquid, and launder as usual. (Do not use WD-40 on silk.)

NAPKINS

- **Mr. Coffee Filters.** In a pinch, you can use a Mr. Coffee Filter as a substitute for a napkin or paper towel.

PILLOWS

- **Faultless Spray Starch.** To prevent hair oil and cold cream stains on pillow cases, spray the cases with a light mist of Faultless Spray Starch.

- **Wilson Tennis Balls.** After washing a pillow (whether filled with fiber or feathers) and letting it hang dry, place the pillow in the dryer on a low setting and add two or three Wilson Tennis Balls to fluff up the stuffing.

PLASTIC AND VINYL TABLECLOTHS

- **Arm & Hammer Baking Soda.** To eliminate the smell of vinyl or plastic, make a paste from Arm & Hammer Baking Soda and water, sponge the paste onto the vinyl or plastic tablecloth, and scrub. Rinse clean and dry.

- **Johnson's Baby Powder.** Before folding up plastic or vinyl table-cloths to store on a shelf, sprinkle the tablecloths with a small amount of Johnson's Baby Powder. The baby powder absorbs moisture and prevents the tablecloth from sticking together or getting mildew.

- **McCormick Cream of Tartar** and **ReaLemon.** Mix enough McCormick Cream of Tartar with ReaLemon lemon juice to make a paste, apply it to stubborn stains on plastic or vinyl tablecloths, let sit for thirty minutes, and then rinse clean. Let the tablecloth dry thoroughly before folding. Together, cream of tartar and lemon juice work like bleach.

SHEETS

- **Efferdent.** To remove random yellow spots and stains from sheets, fill a sink with water, add two Efferdent denture cleansing tablets, and soak the affected garment until the stains vanish. Launder as usual.

STAIN-PROOFING

- **Scotchgard Fabric Protector.** To make cleaning a fabric tablecloth easier, hang the tablecloth outdoors and spray it with Scotchgard Fabric Protector. (Never spray the tablecloth on top of a fine wood table, other-wise you risk ruining the finish.) Scotchgard Fabric Protector prevents spills from soaking into the fabric, so you can blot them up easily.

Towels

- **Epsom Salt.** If your towels lose their absorbency over time, fill the washing machine with cold water and one-quarter cup Epsom Salt and soak the towels in the solution for fifteen minutes. Add your regular detergent and launder as usual.

- **Heinz White Vinegar.** Add one-quarter cup Heinz White Vinegar in the final rinse of your washing machine as a fabric softener that deodorizes the towels at the same time.

- **Morton Salt.** To prevent colored towels from losing their color, add one cup Morton Salt to the wash water the first time you launder the towels. The salt water binds the dye into the towels.

- **Odorzout.** To eliminate mildew on towels, sprinkle the towels with Odorzout, let sit for twenty-four hours or longer, and then toss the powdered towels in the washing machine and launder as usual.

- **Parsons' Ammonia.** To stop colors from running, add one teaspoon Parsons' Ammonia to the wash water in the machine when laundering towels for the first time.

- **20 Mule Team Borax.** Presoak soiled towels in hot water and one-half cup 20 Mule Team Borax, which simultaneously deodorizes the fabric.

White Linens

- **Efferdent.** To clean food stains or random yellow spots from white linen tablecloths and napkins, dissolve two Efferdent denture cleansing tablets in one cup warm water and pour the fizzy blue mixture on the spot or stain. Let sit for fifteen minutes, and then launder as usual.

- **Heinz White Vinegar.** To clean coffee, tea, and wine stains from white linens, saturate the stain with Heinz White Vinegar, blot, and launder as usual.

- **Ivory Soap** and **Kingsford's Corn Starch.** To clean fruit juice stains from white linen, wet a bar of Ivory Soap and rub it into the stain on both sides of the fabric. Make a paste from Kingsford's Corn Starch and cold water and rub the paste into the stain. Let the linen air dry in the sun. Repeat if necessary.

WINE OR JUICE STAINS

- **Canada Dry Club Soda** and **Shout.** Drape the tablecloth over the kitchen sink and pour Canada Dry Club Soda on the stain so the carbonated beverage seeps through the fabric. Pretreat the stain with Shout stain remover and launder as usual.

- **Heinz White Vinegar.** To clean wine stains from white linens, saturate the stain with Heinz White Vinegar, blot, and launder as usual.

- **McCormick Cream of Tartar.** To clean a wine stain from a tablecloth, blot up the liquid, make a paste from equal parts McCormick Cream of Tartar and water, spread the paste on the fabric, let sit for ten minutes, and wash in cold water with your regular detergent.

- **Morton Salt** and **Canada Dry Club Soda.** Cover a wine stain on linen with Morton Salt. The salt absorbs the wine from the fabric. Rinse clean with Canada Dry Club Soda. Then launder as usual.

- **Purell Instant Hand Sanitizer.** After blotting the wine or juice stain, rub Purell Instant Hand Sanitizer into the spot and blot well. Repeat if necessary.

- **20 Mule Team Borax.** After blotting up as much of the wine stain as possible, make a paste from 20 Mule Team Borax and water and apply it to the stain. Let sit for ten minutes, and then launder as usual.

Luggage

Canvas Luggage and Tote Bags

- **Kingsford's Corn Starch.** Sprinkle Kingsford's Corn Starch on the canvas, rub the cornstarch into the fabric with a firm brush, and then brush clean. The cornstarch absorbs grease, oil, grime, and dirt.

Identifying

- **Con-Tact Paper.** Mark your suitcases with an easily identifiable mark made from brightly patterned Con-Tact Paper so you can quickly spot your luggage in airports.

Odors

- **Bounce.** Place sheets of Bounce in suitcases, backpacks, trunks, and duffle bags to keep them smelling fresh while they are tucked away in storage.

- **Ivory Soap.** To keep luggage smelling fresh, tuck a wrapped bar of Ivory Soap inside a suitcase before storing it. When you take out the suitcase to go traveling, leave the bar of soap inside to keep your clothes smelling fresh.

- *USA Today.* To deodorize musty luggage, fill a suitcase or trunk with crumpled pages of *USA Today*, shut closed, and let sit for two weeks. The newsprint absorbs foul odors.

- **Wonder Bread** and **Heinz White Vinegar.** To deodorize a musty old trunk, place a slice of Wonder Bread in a bowl, saturate the bread slice with Heinz White Vinegar, and place the bowl and bread inside the closed trunk. Let sit for twenty-four hours. Repeat if necessary.

PACKING

- **Ziploc Storage Bags.** Before traveling with children, select the number of outfits the child will bring, and place each outfit (along with socks and underwear) in its own Ziploc Storage Bag. This way, the child simply chooses a bag each morning, avoiding the hassle of picking out each individual item. You can also store bathing suits, flip-flops, and toiletry items in their own Ziploc Storage Bags.

VINYL BAGS

- **Arm & Hammer Baking Soda.** To eliminate the smell of vinyl, make a paste from Arm & Hammer Baking Soda and water, sponge the paste onto the vinyl item, and scrub. Rinse clean and dry.

- **Cutex Nail Polish Remover.** To remove the adhesive residue left by stickers or labels on vinyl, saturate a cotton ball with Cutex Nail Polish Remover and rub the glue until it comes off.

- **McCormick Pure Lemon Extract.** To clean vinyl purses, put a few drops of McCormick Pure Lemon Extract on a soft, clean cloth, and buff.

- **Nivea Creme.** To clean vinyl, apply Nivea Creme to a soft cloth and wipe down the vinyl surfaces.

Marble

CLEANING

- **Arm & Hammer Baking Soda.** To clean crusty grunge from marble, sprinkle Arm & Hammer Baking Soda on the spot and rub with a damp rag or sponge.

- **Crayola Chalk** and **Ziploc Storage Bags.** Place the twelve sticks from a box of white Crayola Chalk (or one stick of Crayola Sidewalk Chalk) in a Ziploc Storage Bag, roll up the bag to minimize the amount of air inside it, seal the bag shut, and use a hammer to pound the bag until the chalk becomes a fine powder. Empty the chalk powder into a bowl. Dip a damp sponge into the powdered chalk and rub the marble with it. Rinse clean and buff dry with a soft, clean cloth.

- **Downy Fabric Softener.** To clean marble, mix one-half cup Downy Fabric Softener and one-and-a-half cups water in a sixteen-ounce trigger-spray bottle. Spray the solution on a sponge and scrub. Rinse well and polish with a soft, clean cloth.

- **20 Mule Team Borax.** To clean gunk from marble, sprinkle 20 Mule Team Borax on the spot and rub with a damp rag or sponge.

FIXTURES

- **Arm & Hammer Baking Soda** and **ReaLemon.** To clean stains from marble fixtures, make a paste from Arm & Hammer Baking Soda and ReaLemon lemon juice, scrub the stain with the paste, rinse clean immediately, and dry. (Do not allow the paste to stay in contact with the marble for more than a minute or two; otherwise the acidic lemon juice may etch into the marble.)

GREASE STAINS

- **Parsons' Ammonia.** To clean grease stains from marble, wash the spot with Parsons' Ammonia (making sure the room is well ventilated), rinse thoroughly with water, and repeat if necessary. Dry thoroughly.

MINERAL DEPOSITS

- **Bounty Paper Towels, Hydrogen Peroxide,** and **Glad Trash Bags.** Cover the mineral deposits with a sheet of Bounty Paper Towels, saturate the paper towel with Hydrogen Peroxide, and cover the paper towel with a flat Glad Trash Bag. Let sit for fifteen minutes and rinse clean. Repeat if necessary.

Keep It Clean
WHY LOSE YOUR MARBLES?

- Use coasters under all drinking glasses, particularly those containing alcohol or citrus juices. The acids in many common foods and drinks will etch or dull marble.

- Do not place hot items directly on the marble surface. Use trivets or mats under hot dishes.

- Use placemats under china, ceramics, silver, or other objects that can scratch the surface.

- Dust mop interior floors frequently using a clean, non-treated, dry dust mop. Sand, dirt, and grit do the most damage to natural stone surfaces due to their abrasiveness.

- Place door mats or area rugs inside and outside doorways to marble floors to minimize the sand, dirt, and grit that will scratch the stone floor.

- Clean marble countertops or walls with a few drops of a mild liquid dishwashing detergent and warm water on a soft, clean cloth. Thoroughly rinse and dry the surface after washing.

- Protect floor surfaces with nonslip mats or area rugs and countertop surfaces with coasters, trivets, or placemats.

- Never use vinegar, lemon juice, or other cleaners containing acids on marble. They etch into the stone.

- Never use cleaners that contain acid, such as bathroom cleaners, grout cleaners, or tub and tile cleaners.

- Never use abrasive cleaners, scouring powders, or scouring creams on marble. The abrasives in these products may scratch the surface.

- Call a professional stone supplier, installer, or a restoration specialist for problems that appear too difficult to treat.

- To minimize water spotting on marble countertops in bathrooms, apply a good quality marble wax or Turtle Wax.

Protecting

- **Turtle Wax.** To protect marble countertops from getting scratched or stained, give the countertop a coat of Turtle Wax and buff well.

Soot

- **Arm & Hammer Baking Soda.** To clean soot from marble, make a paste from Arm & Hammer Baking Soda and water and scrub the paste into the affected areas. Rinse well.
- **Dawn Dishwashing Liquid.** Pour a few drops of Dawn Dishwashing Liquid on the spot, scrub with a wet scrub brush, and rinse clean.

Metals

ALUMINUM

- **McCormick Alum** and **Kingsford's Corn Starch.** To clean aluminum, mix equal parts McCormick Alum and Kingsford's Corn Starch and add enough water to make a paste. With a sponge, rub the paste on the aluminum. Let dry, rinse with hot water, and buff dry with a soft, clean cloth.

- **McCormick Cream of Tartar** and **Heinz White Vinegar.** Mix McCormick Cream of Tartar and Heinz White Vinegar to make a thick paste, use a sponge rub the paste on the aluminum, and let dry completely. Wash off the resulting powder with hot water and rub with a soft, clean cloth. The solution removes any grey discoloration from the aluminum, making it shiny again.

BRASS

- **Alberto VO5 Hair Spray.** After polishing a brass fixture, give the item a coat of Alberto VO5 Hair Spray. The fixative helps protect the brass from tarnish.

- **Campbell's Tomato Juice.** Place the brass items in a pan, pour in enough Campbell's Tomato Juice to cover the item, and simmer over low heat for one hour. Let cool, rinse clean, and dry.

- **Colgate Regular Flavor Toothpaste.** Squeeze a dollop of Colgate Regular Flavor Toothpaste on a clean, old toothbrush and scrub the brass. Rinse well and dry.

- **Gold Medal Flour, Morton Salt,** and **Heinz White Vinegar.** In a bowl, mix one tablespoon Gold Medal Flour, two teaspoons Morton Salt, and enough Heinz White Vinegar to make a thick paste. With a sponge, vigorously rub the paste on the brass item. Let dry thoroughly and rinse the item clean in hot water. Buff with a clean, soft cloth.

- **Heinz Ketchup.** Pour a generous amount of Heinz Ketchup on a clean sponge, rub the ketchup into the brass, let sit for an hour, rinse clean with soapy hot water, and dry.

- **Lea & Perrins Worcestershire Sauce.** Sprinkle a damp rag with Lea & Perrins Worcestershire Sauce and rub the brass item. Wipe with a clean, soft cloth and buff well.

- **McCormick Cream of Tartar.** Make a paste from two tablespoons McCormick Cream of Tartar and water, rub the paste onto the brass, and let dry. Rinse clean in hot water and polish dry with a soft, clean cloth.

- **Morton Salt, ReaLemon,** and **Heinz White Vinegar.** Mix two tablespoons Morton Salt, one tablespoon ReaLemon lemon juice, and one tablespoon Heinz White Vinegar, dampen a sponge with the mixture, and rub it on the brass. Let dry, rinse clean with hot water, and buff with a clean, soft cloth.

- **Nestlé Carnation NonFat Dry Milk.** Mix one-and-one-third cups Nestlé Carnation NonFat Dry Milk and seven-and-a-half cups water, place the brass items in a pan, and pour the milky solution over it. Simmer over low heat for one hour, let cool, rinse clean, and dry.

- **ReaLemon** and **Morton Salt.** To clean brass, mix equal parts ReaLemon lemon juice and Morton Salt. Wipe the solution on the brass until the metal comes clean. Rinse and dry.

- **Tabasco Pepper Sauce.** Sprinkle Tabasco Pepper Sauce directly on the brass item; rub with a soft, clean cloth; and rinse with warm water. Polish dry with another soft, clean cloth.

- **Wesson Oil.** To shine a clean brass item, pour a few drops of Wesson Oil on a soft, clean cloth and rub and buff the metal.

CHROME

- **Arm & Hammer Baking Soda.** Sprinkle Arm & Hammer Baking Soda on a damp sponge and rub the chrome. Rinse clean and dry.

- **Bounce.** After cleaning, polish chrome with a clean, used sheet of Bounce to give it a lustrous shine.

- **Cutex Nail Polish Remover.** To clean chrome, apply Cutex Nail Polish Remover and buff with a soft, clean cloth.

- **Gold Medal Flour.** To clean chrome faucets, sprinkle Gold Medal Flour on a damp sponge, scrub, rinse clean, and dry.

- **Heinz White Vinegar.** Dampen a soft, clean cloth with Heinz White Vinegar or Heinz Apple Cider Vinegar and wipe the chrome clean.

- **Lipton Tea Bags.** Use a Lipton Tea Bag to brew a strong cup of tea, let cool, and apply the tea to chrome with a soft, clean cloth.

- **Murphy Oil Soap.** To clean chrome, mix one teaspoon Murphy Oil Soap and two cups water in a sixteen-ounce trigger-spray bottle. Spray the chrome with the solution and wipe with a soft, clean cloth. Rinse and dry.

- **Parsons' Ammonia.** Dampen a soft, clean cloth with Parsons' Ammonia and wipe the chrome clean.

- **ReaLemon.** To clean chrome, apply ReaLemon lemon juice and buff with a soft, clean cloth.

- **Reynolds Wrap.** To clean rust from chrome, crumple up a sheet of Reynolds Wrap aluminum foil and rub the rust spot with the aluminum foil scrubber.

- **WD-40.** Spray WD-40 on a soft, clean cloth and rub the chrome until it shines like new.

- **Windex.** Spray the chrome with Windex and rub with a soft, clean cloth.

COPPER

- **Gold Medal Flour, Morton Salt,** and **Heinz White Vinegar.** In a bowl, mix one tablespoon Gold Medal Flour, two teaspoons Morton Salt, and enough Heinz White Vinegar to make a thick paste. With a sponge, vigorously rub the paste on the copper item. Let dry thoroughly and rinse the item clean in hot water. Buff with a clean, soft cloth.

- **Heinz Ketchup.** Cover the copper item with Heinz Ketchup, let sit for fifteen minutes, and then rub until the metal comes clean. Rinse and dry.

- **Lea & Perrins Worcestershire Sauce.** Cover the copper item with Lea & Perrins Worcestershire Sauce, let sit for fifteen minuets, and then rub until the metal comes clean. Rinse and dry.

- **Tabasco Pepper Sauce.** Sprinkle Tabasco Pepper Sauce directly on the copper; rub with a soft, clean cloth; and rinse with warm water. Polish dry with another soft, clean cloth.

Gold

- **Arm & Hammer Baking Soda.** Make a paste from Arm & Hammer Baking Soda and water, rub the paste on the gold with a sponge, rinse clean, and dry with a soft, clean cloth.

- **Colgate Regular Flavor Toothpaste.** Squeeze a dollop of Colgate Regular Flavor Toothpaste on a clean, old toothbrush and scrub the gold. Rinse well and dry.

- **Mr. Clean Magic Eraser.** To polish gold, gently rub the stains with a damp Mr. Clean Magic Eraser, wash the item thoroughly with soapy water, rinse clean, and dry.

- **Tabasco Pepper Sauce.** Sprinkle Tabasco Pepper Sauce directly on the gold item; rub with a soft, clean cloth; and rinse with warm water. Polish dry with another soft, clean cloth.

Silver

- **Arm & Hammer Baking Soda** and **ReaLemon.** To clean tarnish from silver jewelry, make a paste from Arm & Hammer Baking Soda and ReaLemon lemon juice. Brush the paste onto the jewelry with a clean, old toothbrush. Let dry thorughly and brush clean. Polish the jewelry with a clean, soft cloth.

- **Mr. Clean Magic Eraser.** To polish silver, gently rub the silver with a damp Mr. Clean Magic Eraser, wash the item thoroughly with soapy water, rinse clean, and dry.

- **Wesson Oil.** After cleaning silver, polish the item with a few drops of Wesson Oil on a soft, clean cloth.

Odors

AIR FRESHENERS

- **Arm & Hammer Baking Soda, Parsons' Ammonia,** and **McCormick Pure Vanilla Extract.** To make homemade air freshener, mix one-half ounce Arm & Hammer Baking Soda, one-half tablespoon Parsons' Ammonia, one-eighth teaspoon McCormick Pure Vanilla Extract, and two cups water in a sixteen-ounce trigger-spray bottle. Shake well.

- **Bounce.** Tape a fresh sheet of Bounce to the front of a fan or over an air-conditioning vent (or weave it through the louver slats in the vent) and turn it on to fill the area with the soothing scent of oleander. You can also place a Bounce sheet in a wastebasket, in a drawer, or behind books on the shelf.

- **Heinz White Vinegar** and **Arm & Hammer Baking Soda.** To make homemade air freshener, mix one tablespoon Heinz White Vinegar, one teaspoon Arm & Hammer Baking Soda, and two cups water in a sixteen-ounce trigger-spray bottle. Let the mixture finish foaming and then shake well before using.

- **Ivory Soap.** Unwrap a bar of Ivory Soap and place it on a desk, table, or countertop to freshen the air with the calming nostalgic scent of coconut oil, palm oil, and a light fragrance.

- **Lipton Chamomile Tea** and **L'eggs Sheer Energy Panty Hose.** Cut the foot off of a clean, used pair of L'eggs Sheer Energy Panty Hose, fill it with Lipton Chamomile Tea bags, and hang it as a sachet in your closet or place it in a drawer to leave a pleasant fragrance.

- **Maxwell House Coffee.** To freshen the air, place one-half cup fresh Maxwell House Coffee grounds in a bowl and set the bowl wherever odors are giving you problems. The coffee grounds absorb the foul smells.

- **McCormick Pure Vanilla Extract.** To freshen the air around the house, mix one teaspoon McCormick Pure Vanilla Extract and one cup water in a sixteen-ounce trigger-spray bottle and mist the air in your home.

- **ReaLemon** and **Arm & Hammer Baking Soda.** Mix one teaspoon ReaLemon lemon juice, one teaspoon Arm & Hammer Baking Soda, and two cups hot water in a sixteen-ounce trigger-spray bottle. Shake well.

- **Speed Stick.** To mask stale odors in your home, rub a Speed Stick on the incandescent light bulb of a prominent lamp in the room and turn on the lamp. The heat from the bulb spreads the mild smell of the deodorant throughout the room.

CAR SEATS

- **Bounce.** Place a sheet of Bounce under the front seats of your car to keep the car smelling fresh.

CLOSETS

- **Arm & Hammer Baking Soda.** To deodorize the air in a musty closet, place an open box of Arm & Hammer Baking Soda on a shelf.

- **Bounce.** Place a sheet of Bounce in a closet (hung from a hanger) to keep the closet smelling fresh.

- **Crayola Chalk.** Place an opened box of Crayola Chalk on the shelf in a damp closet to absorb moistness.

- **Dial Soap.** To freshen the air in closets, place a wrapped bar of Dial Soap on a shelf in the closet to keep it smelling fresh.

- **Jonny Cat Litter.** To eliminate musty smells in a closet, place a bowl filled with unused Jonny Cat Litter in a corner or on a shelf in the closet. The cat box filler absorbs odors.

- **Maxwell House Coffee** and **L'eggs Sheer Energy Panty Hose.** Cut the foot from a clean, used pair of L'eggs Sheer Energy Panty Hose, fill with fresh Maxwell House Coffee grounds, and tie a knot in the nylon. Hang the sachet from a hanger or the clothes rod in the closet. Coffee grounds absorb foul odors.

DEODORIZERS

- **Heinz White Vinegar.** Place a glass of Heinz White Vinegar on a table or countertop of any room in the house that needs deodorizing. The vinegar neutralizes odors.

- **Jonny Cat Litter.** To deodorize any confined space, such as a closet, laundry room, or any room in the house, place a tray filled with Jonny Cat Litter in the room and close the door. The cat box filler absorbs the unpleasant aroma.

DIAPER PAILS

- **Arm & Hammer Baking Soda.** To minimize odors exuding from a diaper pail, sprinkle some Arm & Hammer Baking Soda on top of the dirty diapers.

- **Odorzout.** To control odors emanating from diaper pails, sprinkle some safe, nontoxic Odorzout in the diaper pail.

ROLLING WITH SPEED STICK

In 1878, German immigrant Gerhard H. Mennen, a pharmacist working at a small drugstore in Newark, New Jersey, began selling "Corn Killer," his own remedy for corns. In 1889, he introduced "Mennen's Talcum Powder," featuring his portrait on every label. Mennen advertised heavily, and Mennen's Talcum Powder achieved widespread distribution.

After Mennen's death, his son, William Gerhard Mennen, a graduate of Cornell University with a degree in engineering, became president of the Mennen Company. In 1954, the Mennen Company moved to Morristown, New Jersey, and introduced Mennen Speed Stick, renowned for its wide translucent green deodorant stick and its fougère perfume. The Colgate-Palmolive Company acquired Mennen in 1992 and eventually dropped the name Mennen from the brand's name.

Strange Facts

- Speed Stick is named for the *speed* with which this translucent green deodorant *stick* can be used.

- G. Mennen Williams, the former governor of Michigan who later served as chief justice of the Michigan Supreme Court, was nicknamed Soapy because his grandfather founded the Mennen Company.

- Nirvana's 1991 hit song "Smells like Teen Spirit" boosted sales of Mennen's deodorant Teen Spirit, which quickly became the best-selling teenage girl's deodorant. Nirvana's lead singer Kurt Cobain had no idea that the Teen Spirit was the name of a deodorant. One of Cobain's friends, Kathleen Hanna, spray painted "Kurt smells like Teen Spirit" on his bedroom wall because Cobain's girlfriend at the time wore the deodorant.

- The slogan "By Mennen" and its simple three-note jingle used at the end of every television commercial for Mennen products became a highly successful advertising gimmicks.

- In an episode of the television sitcom *Seinfeld*, George Costanza (played by Jason Alexander) appropriates the Mennen three-note jingle to recite his last name.

DRAWERS

- **Bounce.** Place a sheet of Bounce in drawers to keep them smelling fresh.

- **Dial Soap**. To perfume the clothes in drawers, place a wrapped bar of Dial Soap in each drawer.

GARBAGE PAILS

- **Arm & Hammer Baking Soda.** To control odors wafting up from your garbage pail, sprinkle a handful of Arm & Hammer Baking Soda on top of the garbage.

- **Bounce.** Place a sheet of Bounce in the bottom of garbage pails to keep them smelling fresh in the kitchen, bathrooms, or bedrooms.

HAMPERS AND LAUNDRY BAGS

- **Arm & Hammer Baking Soda.** To deodorize smelly clothes in a hamper or laundry bag, toss a handful of Arm & Hammer Baking Soda in with the clothes.

- **Bounce.** Place a sheet of Bounce at the bottom of laundry baskets and laundry bags to mask the smell of the dirty laundry.

- **Dial Soap.** To eliminate odors in dirty laundry, place a wrapped bar of Dial Soap at the bottom of a laundry bag or hamper.

- **Odorzout.** Sprinkle Odorzout on the clothes in the hamper to absorb pungent odors.

HUMIDIFIERS

- **Clorox Bleach.** To perk up a foul smelling humidifier, pour one teaspoon Clorox Bleach in the humidifier water. The bleach kills any bacteria causing the stench.

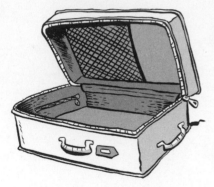

LUGGAGE

- **Bounce.** Place a sheet of Bounce in suitcases, backpacks, trunks, and duffle bags to keep them smelling springtime fresh while they are tucked away in storage.

- **Ivory Soap.** To keep luggage smelling fresh, place a wrapped bar of Ivory Soap inside each suitcase before storing it. When you take out the suitcase to go traveling, leave the bar of soap inside to keep your clothes smelling springtime fresh during your journey.

- *USA Today.* To deodorize musty luggage, fill a suitcase or trunk with crumpled pages of *USA Today,* shut closed, and let sit for two weeks. The newsprint absorbs foul odors.

- **Wonder Bread** and **Heinz White Vinegar.** To deodorize a musty old trunk, place a slice of Wonder Bread in a bowl, saturate the bread slice with Heinz White Vinegar, and place the bowl and bread inside the closed trunk. Let sit for twenty-four hours. Repeat if necessary.

SMOKE

- **Heinz White Vinegar.** To help eliminate the smell of tobacco smoke from a room, place a few drinking glasses filled with Heinz White Vinegar in a few spots about the room.

- **Jonny Cat Litter.** To neutralize the smell of cigarette smoke, fill ashtrays with Jonny Cat Litter to absorb the offensive odor and help extinguish lit cigarettes.

Offices

BACKPACKS

- **Scotchgard Fabric Protector.** To keep school books and supplies dry inside a student backpack, spray the outside of a student backpack with Scotchgard Fabric Protector.

BOOK COVERS

- **Con-Tact Paper.** Use clear Con-Tact Paper to make book covers and protect school books.

- **Reynolds Cut-Rite Wax Paper.** To protect a book cover from dirt, grime, and damage, use a sheet of Reynolds Cute-Rite Wax Paper to cover a dust jacket.

- **Scotch Packaging Tape.** To repair torn book covers, adhere the cover back to the binding with Scotch Packaging Tape.

BOOKS

- **Bounce** and **Ziploc Storage Bags.** To deodorize a book that smells like cigarette smoke, wrap two sheets of Bounce around the book, place it inside a Ziploc Storage Bag, seal, and let sit for three days.
- **Bounty Paper Towels.** To dry the pages of a waterlogged book, place a sheet of Bounty Paper Towels between each wet page, close the book, place a stack of heavy books on top of it, and let sit overnight. In the morning, remove the paper towels.
- **Johnson's Baby Powder.** To rescue the damp, moldy pages of a book, sprinkle Johnson's Baby Powder on the affected pages, close the book, and let sit for a week. Then brush clean. The baby powder absorbs the moisture, killing the mold, which brushes off easily.
- **Kingsford's Corn Starch.** To eliminate mildew from books, sprinkle Kingsford's Corn Starch on the affected pages, close the book, let sit for five hours, and brush clean. The cornstarch absorbs moisture, killing the mildew.
- **Wonder Bread.** To clean grease spots from the pages of a book, rub the affected pages with a slice of dry Wonder Bread.
- **Ziploc Freezer Bags.** To eliminate book lice from a book, place the book in a Ziploc Freezer Bag, seal, and store in the freezer for three days.

CALCULATORS AND CAMERAS

- **Huggies Baby Wipes.** To clean a calculator, wipe the device with a Huggies Baby Wipe.
- **Revlon Red Nail Enamel.** To remind yourself to turn off your calculator or camera flash attachment, paint the off button with Revlon Red Nail Enamel.

CHALKBOARDS

- **Arm & Hammer Baking Soda.** To clean a chalkboard, sprinkle Arm & Hammer Baking Soda on a damp, soft, clean cloth and wipe the board.

- **Murphy Oil Soap** and **Heinz White Vinegar.** To clean a chalkboard, mix one-quarter teaspoon Murphy Oil Soap, one-quarter cup Heinz White Vinegar, and one cup water. Saturate a sponge with the soapy solution and wash the chalkboard. Rinse well.

DRY-ERASE BOARDS

- **Nestlé Coffee-mate Original.** To clean indelible marker off a dry-erase board, dampen a sponge or paper towel with Nestlé Coffee-mate Original and wipe the indelible ink right off the dry-erase board. (If using the powder, simply mix with enough water to make a milky solution.)

ERASERS

- **Wonder Bread.** To erase pencil marks from paper, ball up a small piece of Wonder Bread (without the crust) and use it as you would an eraser.

FILES

- **Con-Tact Paper.** To organize your files cabinets, use different patterns of Con-Tact Paper to coordinate your files.

FINGER GRIPS

- **Playtex Living Gloves.** To make a finger grip for sorting through papers, cut off a fingertip from a clean, old Playtex Living Glove and slip it over your index or middle finger to sort through papers.

GLUE

- **Vaseline Petroleum Jelly.** To prevent the lid from sticking to a bottle of rubber cement or other glue, rub a dab of Vaseline Petroleum Jelly around the threads of the bottle.

IMPORTANT PAPERS

- **Ziploc Freezer Bags.** To organize and protect your important papers, place all of your vital papers (passports, birth certificates, immunization papers, stock certificates) in a gallon-size Ziploc Freezer Bag and put it in your freezer. Robbers rarely look in the freezer, and if a house catches on fire, the refrigerator is almost always left standing.

MAPS

- **Con-Tact Paper.** Cover those important maps with clean Con-Tact Paper. Trace your route with a dry-erasable marker that you can wipe off after the trip.

MEMO BOARD

- **Con-Tact Paper** and **Velcro.** To create an instant memo board, cover a sheet of white cardboard with Con-Tact Paper, adhere it to an office wall or refrigerator door with Velcro strips, and use a piece of string to hang an erasable marker from it.

PAPER CLIPS

- **Forster Clothespins.** Use a Forster Clothespin to organize and secure a pile of papers together.

PENCIL HOLDERS

- **Con-Tact Paper.** To make a pencil holder and organize your desk, wrap a clean, empty tin can with your favorite Con-Tact Paper.

PENS

- **Ziploc Storage Bags.** To prevent pens from leaking in a purse or backpack, keep pens in a Ziploc Storage Bag.

SCISSORS

- **Cutex Nail Polish Remover.** To clean scissors, soak a cotton ball in Cutex Nail Polish Remover and cautiously clean the scissor blades.

- **Reynolds Wrap.** To sharpen a dull pair of scissors, fold a sheet of Reynolds Wrap aluminum foil in half several times and cut through thicknesses.

- **3M Sandpaper.** To sharpen scissors or remove residue on blade edges, cut through a piece of 3M Sandpaper several times.

STAMPS

- **Reynolds Cut-Rite Wax Paper.** Keep stamps between sheets of Reynolds Cut-Rite Wax Paper to prevent them from sticking together.

Outdoors

AWNINGS

- **Arm & Hammer Super Washing Soda.** To clean dirty canvas awnings, sprinkle Arm & Hammer Super Washing Soda on the canvas and spray with a garden hose.
- **Fels-Naptha Soap.** To clean soiled canvas awnings, rub a wet scrub brush across a bar of Fels-Naptha Soap, scrub the canvas, and rinse well with a garden hose.

BIRD FEEDERS

- **Crisco All-Vegetable Shortening.** Keep squirrels away from a bird feeder by greasing the pole with Crisco All-Vegetable Shortening. The squirrels will try to climb up the pole and slide right back down, providing you with hours of free entertainment.

- **Efferdent.** Clean a hummingbird feeder by filling the bottle with hot water and dropping in one-half Efferdent denture cleansing tablet. Wait five minutes, and then rinse clean.

- **McCormick Ground (Cayenne) Red Pepper.** Keep squirrels out of your bird feeder by sprinkling the bird seed with McCormick Ground (Cayenne) Red Pepper. The birds cannot taste the cayenne pepper, but squirrels can and want nothing to do with it.

- **Vaseline Petroleum Jelly.** Prevent ants from climbing into a hummingbird feeder by rubbing Vaseline Petroleum Jelly on the chain or string from which you hang your hummingbird feeder.

BIRD POOP

- **Colgate Regular Flavor Toothpaste.** A dollop of Colgate Regular Flavor Toothpaste and a hard brush cleans bird droppings off any surface.

- **Heinz Apple Cider Vinegar.** To clean bird droppings, fill a trigger-spray bottle with Heinz Apple Cider Vinegar and spray the spot, wait a few moments, and then wipe off the droppings with a cloth.

- **Mr. Clean Magic Eraser.** To clean bird droppings from concrete, gently rub the stains with a damp Mr. Clean Magic Eraser, wash the item thoroughly with soapy water, and rinse clean.

BIRDBATHS

- **Heinz White Vinegar.** To keep cats away from birdbaths, fill a trigger-spray bottle with Heinz White Vinegar and spray around the base of the bird bath. The smell of vinegar repulses cats and neutralizes the smell of cat urine used to mark their territory.

- **Mrs. Stewart's Liquid Bluing.** Add a few drops of Mrs. Stewart's Liquid Bluing to the water in a birdbath to give the water a blue tinge that does not affect the clarity of the water. Reportedly, adding bluing to birdbaths also helps reduce algae buildup.

- **Reynolds Wrap.** Crumple up a sheet of Reynolds Wrap aluminum foil into a ball and use it as a scrubber for cleaning birdbaths.

DECKS

- **Aunt Jemima Corn Meal.** To give an icy wooden deck some traction so you can walk on it without slipping, sprinkle Aunt Jemima Corn Meal over the ice.

- **20 Mule Team Borax** and **Dawn Dishwashing Liquid.** To clean a wood deck, mix one-quarter cup 20 Mule Team Borax, one tablespoon Dawn Dishwashing Liquid, and one gallon hot water in a bucket. Mop the deck with the solution and rinse well.

- **Wilson Tennis Balls.** To prevent a deck chair from slipping through the cracks of a deck, slit four Wilson Tennis Balls and fit them on the feet of the deck chair.

FERTILIZER

- **Arm & Hammer Baking Soda, Epsom Salt,** and **Parsons' Ammonia.** To rejuvenate an ailing shrub, mix one teaspoon Arm & Hammer Baking Soda, one teaspoon Epsom Salt, and one-half teaspoon Parsons' Ammonia in a gallon of warm water. Apply one quart to each shrub the size of a rosebush.

- **Epsom Salt.** For every foot of a plant's height, sprinkle one teaspoon Epsom Salt evenly around the base for better blossoms and deeper greening. Adding Epson Salt to any plant food will also enrich the color of any flowering plants and aid in disease resistance. Or mix one tablespoon Epsom Salt in one gallon water and spray the mixture on the plant. Epsom Salt is calcium magnesium carbonate, which lowers the pH of the soil and provides magnesium.

- **Gatorade.** Watering ailing plants with Gatorade adds potassium to the soil, and the sugar feeds microorganisms, adding nitrogen.

- **Jell-O.** To give ailing plants additional nitrogen, mix an envelope of powdered Jell-O into one cup boiling water, stir until the gelatin powder dissolves, mix with three cups cold water, and then apply around the base of the plant.

- **Lipton Tea Bags.** Put Lipton Tea Bags (new or used) on the soil around ailing plants in garden beds and planters. Cover the tea bags with mulch. Every time you water the plants, the nutrients from the decomposing tea leaves work their way into the soil.

- **Maxwell House Coffee.** Maxwell House Coffee grounds are full of nutrients that plants love. Instead of throwing out the used coffee grounds after you make a pot of coffee, give them to your ailing plants in the garden. Just work the grounds into the soil. It may keep them up all night, but you can always use the decaf. If you're really ambitious, you can also use Maxwell House Coffee grounds to fertilize your entire lawn.

- **Nestea Iced Tea Mix.** Mix up a quart of unsweetened Nestea Iced Tea Mix according to the directions (without adding sugar or ice) and fertilize ailing plants with the solution. Or simply sprinkle the powdered mix directly on the soil. As the tea decomposes, the nutrients work their way into the soil.

Fishponds and Fountains

- **Mrs. Stewart's Liquid Bluing.** To brighten the water in fishponds and fountains, add a few drops of Mrs. Stewart's Liquid Bluing, which gives the water a pleasant blue tinge without affecting the clarity of the water or harming fish. Mrs. Stewart's Liquid Bluing contains a non-toxic amount of a pH balancer and a biocide to prevent the buildup of algae and bacteria.

Flowers

- **Epsom Salt.** To rejuvenate ailing flower bushes, sprinkle one teaspoon Epsom Salt for every foot of a plant's height evenly around the base for better blossoms and deeper greening. Adding Epson Salt to any plant food will also enrich the color of any flowering plants and aid in disease resistance. Or mix one tablespoon Epsom Salt in one gallon water and spray the mixture on the plant. Epsom Salt is calcium magnesium carbonate, which lowers the pH of the soil and provides magnesium.

- **Heinz White Vinegar.** To grow beautiful azaleas, camellias, cardinal flowers, gardenias, heather, and rhododendrons, occasionally water these acid-loving plants with a mixture of two tablespoons Heinz White Vinegar to one quart water.

- **Lipton Tea Bags.** To revive sickly flower bushes, put Lipton Tea Bags (new or used) on the soil around plants in flower beds and planters. Cover the tea bags with mulch. Every time you water the plants, the nutrients from the decomposing tea leaves work their way into the soil.

- **Maxwell House Coffee.** Fertilize azaleas, camellias, cardinal flowers, gardenias, heather, and rhododendrons with Maxwell House Coffee grounds by working used grounds around the base of these acid-loving plants once a month.

- **Nestea Iced Tea Mix.** To reinvigorate flowers, mix up a quart of unsweetened Nestea Iced Tea Mix according to the directions (without adding sugar or ice) and fertilize your flowerbeds with the solution. Or simply sprinkle the powdered mix directly on the soil. As the tea decomposes, the nutrients work their way into the soil.

GARBAGE CANS

- **Clorox Bleach.** Disinfect garbage cans by washing the trash receptacle with a solution made from three-quarters cup Clorox Bleach to one gallon water. Let stand for five minutes, and then rinse clean.

- **Jonny Cat Litter.** To deodorize a garbage can, cover the bottom of the bin with one inch of unused Jonny Cats to absorb grease and moisture.

- **L'eggs Sheer Energy Panty Hose.** To secure plastic garbage bags inside your trash can, cut off the elastic top from a pair of L'eggs Sheer

Energy Panty Hose and stretch the extra-large rubber band around the rim of the trash can to hold the lip of the plastic garbage bag in place.

HOSES

- **Forster Toothpicks** and **Scotch Packaging Tape.** To repair a punctured garden hose, insert a Forster Toothpick into the hole, snap it off flush with the hose's outer skin, then wrap Scotch Packaging Tape around the spot. The wood toothpick will absorb water, swelling to seal the hole.

- **Wrigley's Spearmint Gum.** Patch the holes in a garden hose with chewed Wrigley's Spearmint Gum.

LAWN

- **Arm & Hammer Baking Soda.** To repair yellow burn spots on a lawn caused by dog urine, dissolve one cup Arm & Hammer Baking Soda in one gallon water in a watering can and saturate the urine spots every three days. The baking soda neutralizes the acidity of the urine and simultaneously deodorizes the area, preventing the offending dog from recognizing the spot.

- **Maxwell House Coffee.** To restore brown patches on your lawn, fertilize your entire lawn with Maxwell House Coffee by simply sprinkling used coffee grounds (or fresh grounds if you want to be extravagant) over your yard. Coffee grounds are full of nutrients that boost the performance of grass. Coffee may keep your lawn up all night, but you can always use the decaf.

LAWN MOWERS

- **Pam Cooking Spray.** To prevent cut grass from sticking to lawn mower blades and making a mess, spray the underside of the lawnmower with Pam Cooking Spray before mowing the lawn.

- **Turtle Wax.** Prevent grass cuttings from building up underneath your lawn mower by waxing the underside of the lawn mower with Turtle Wax.

- **WD-40.** Prevent cut grass from sticking to the blades of a lawn mower by spraying WD-40 on the blade and the underside of the lawn mower housing before cutting the grass.

Lighting

- **Vaseline Petroleum Jelly.** To prevent outdoor light bulbs from sticking in fixtures when you go to change them, rub a thin coat of Vaseline Petroleum Jelly on the threads before inserting the bulbs.

Potted Plants

- **Bubble Wrap** and **Scotch Packaging Tape.** To protect plastic, wood, and fiberglass planters left outside during the winter months, wrap the planter with Bubble Wrap and secure in place with Scotch Packaging Tape. The extra insulation helps protect both the plant and the planter. Or before planting, cut a piece of Bubble Wrap to fit around the inside of a terra-cotta pot before filling with soil to insulate plant roots and prevent constant freezing and thawing. (Do not line the bottom of the planter to allow for drainage.)

- **Glad Trash Bags** and **Bubble Wrap.** To help outdoor potted plants survive the winter, place the pot inside a Glad Trash Bag, fill the bag with Bubble Wrap to insulate the plant roots and the pot (to prevent cracking). Seal the bag tightly around the trunk of the plant and set the pot on top of a wood block so it is raised off the ground.

Raking

- **Bubble Wrap** and **Scotch Packaging Tape.** If you have difficulty holding a rake when cleaning up fallen leaves, cut a strip of Bubble Wrap, wrap it around the handle of the rake, and secure it in place with a piece of Scotch Packaging Tape, creating a more convenient grip.

SAP

- **Crisco All-Vegetable Shortening.** Clean sap off garden tools and hands with a few dabs of Crisco All-Vegetable Shortening.

- **Johnson's Baby Oil.** If your tools or hands get covered with sap, Johnson's Baby Oil dissolves the sticky substance.

- **Miracle Whip.** A dollop of Miracle Whip removes sap from tools and hands. Apply and wipe clean with a cloth.

- **Pam Cooking Spray.** If you get sap stuck on your tools or hands, spray Pam Cooking Spray on the sticky spot, rub it in, and then wash in soapy water.

- **Skippy Peanut Butter.** Clean sap from garden tools or hands with a dollop of Skippy Peanut Butter. The peanut oil dissolves the gums in the sap.

SLIDING BOARDS

- **Reynolds Cut-Rite Wax Paper.** To resurface a metal sliding board, rub a sheet of Reynolds Cut-Rite Wax Paper on the metal slide.

- **Turtle Wax.** To resurface a metal or plastic sliding board, cover the sliding board with two coats of Turtle Wax, polishing between applications.

SWIMMING POOLS

- **Arm & Hammer Baking Soda.** To maintain the proper alkalinity in a swimming pool, add 1.5 pounds of Arm & Hammer Baking Soda for every 10,000 gallons of water in the pool to raise total alkalinity by 10 parts per million parts of pool water (ppm), keeping the total alkalinity of the pool within the range of 80 to 150 ppm of alkalinity. Maintaining a proper level of total alkalinity minimizes changes in pH when acidic or basic pool

THE STICKY STORY OF SKIPPY

In 1923, Joseph Rosefield perfected a process to prevent oil separation in peanut butter. Rosefield discovered that churning, rather than grinding, peanuts produced peanut butter with a much smoother consistency. After receiving the first patent for peanut butter that would stay fresh for up to a year, Rosefield joined forces with peanut butter manufacturer Swift & Company, known since 1928 as Peter Pan. A dispute prompted Rosefield to leave the company, and in 1932, he started Rosefield Packing Company, in Alameda, California, to produce his own brand of peanut butter, which he named Skippy. On February 1, 1932, Skippy Peanut Butter went on sale, and that same year, Rosefield added chopped peanuts to his product, introducing crunchy peanut butter.

Strange Facts

- Company founder Joseph Rosefield named his peanut butter after the popular cartoon character Skippy, created by Percy Crosby and syndicated in newspapers worldwide by Hearst Newspapers.

- The Skippy comic strip was adapted into the 1931 movie *Skippy*, which was nominated for the Academy Award for Best Picture. Written by Joseph L. Mankiewicz, Don Marquis, Norman Z. McLeod, and Sam Mintz, the movie starred Jackie Cooper and Robert Coogan.

- In 1945, King Features cancelled the syndication of Percy Crosby's Skippy comic strip. Three years later, Crosby attempted suicide. He was confined to the mental ward of Kings Park Veterans' Hospital, where he spent the rest of his life—classified as a paranoid schizophrenic for his assertions that Skippy Peanut Butter had infringed on his copyright.

- In 1960, Skippy Peanut Butter sponsored the television show *Dennis the Menace,* and three years later, artist Norman Rockwell created illustrations for Skippy Peanut Butter advertisements.

- The producers of the television show *Mr. Ed,* featuring a "talking" horse, used peanut butter to get the horse to move its lips and mouth.

- Over the years, television commercials for Skippy have featured former Mouseketeer Annette Funicello, Olympic speed skating champion Bonnie Blair, and New York Yankee Derek Jeter.

chemicals or contaminants enter the water, reducing chloramine formation and the corrosivity of water, consequently reducing eye irritation and unpleasant odors while improving bactericidal effectiveness.

- **Bon Ami.** Bon Ami, sprinkled on a sponge or scrub brush, can clean stains and scale deposits from pool plaster and tile.

- **Mr. Clean Magic Eraser**. To remove the mineral waterline mark from the tiles around a pool, dampen the Mr. Clean Magic Eraser with water from the pool and rub the mineral stains.

- **Mrs. Stewart's Liquid Bluing.** To give the water in a swimming pool an inviting blue appearance and prevent algae, for standard pools (20 × 40 feet), add one or two bottles of Mrs. Stewart's Liquid Bluing where water is re-circulated from the filter, being careful not to splash directly on pool surface. Do not use in aerated pools such as Jacuzzis or whirlpools because spotting can occur.

WEEDS

- **Heinz White Vinegar.** To prevent grass from growing in crevices, pour Heinz White Vinegar in sidewalk cracks and between bricks.
- **Morton Salt.** To kill weeds growing in the cracks of your front walkway, dissolve one-quarter cup Morton Salt in two quarts water, bring to a boil, and carefully pour the boiling salt water on the weeds.

Paintings and Pictures

CLEANING

- **Wonder Bread.** To clean blemishes from a painting, remove the crust from a slice of Wonder Bread and rub the bread over spots on the painting. The bread works like a mild eraser.

FRAMES

- **Kiwi Shoe Polish.** To stain unfinished picture or painting frames, apply one coat of Kiwi Shoe Polish, let dry, and repeat.

- **Nestlé Coffee-mate Original.** To clean gilt picture frames, rub the frame with a clean, soft cloth dampened with Nestlé Coffee-mate Original. The enzymes dissolve any grease and grime.

- **Old English Lemon Oil.** To polish a wood frame, put a few drops of Old English Lemon Oil on a soft, clean cloth and rub the frame gently.

Hanging

- **Scotch Transparent Tape.** To avoid cracking the plaster on the wall, adhere a small piece of Scotch Transparent Tape to the spot on the wall before driving the nail into it.

Glass

- **Bounce.** To collect dust and prevent more dust from settling, polish the glass over paintings and pictures with a clean, used sheet of Bounce.

Nail Holes

- **Arm & Hammer Baking Soda** and **Elmer's Glue-All.** If you're all out of plaster of Paris to fill a nail hole left in the wall, mix a paste from Arm & Hammer Baking Soda and Elmer's Glue-All and patch away.

- **Colgate Regular Flavor Toothpaste.** In a pinch, you can patch a nail hole in a white wall with Colgate Regular Flavor Toothpaste.

Newspaper Clippings

- **Phillips' Milk of Magnesia, Canada Dry Club Soda,** and **Bounty Paper Towels.** To preserve newspaper clippings, dissolve one Phillips' Milk of Magnesia tablet in one quart Canada Dry Club Soda. Let the mixture stand overnight. The next day, stir the mixture well, and then soak your clipping in the solution for one hour. Blot the newspaper clipping between two sheets of Bounty Paper Towels and place on a screen to dry.

Plexiglas

- **Cascade.** To clean Plexiglas, mix one-half teaspoon Cascade Gel in one gallon water in a bucket. Saturate a soft, clean cloth in the solution, wring well, and wipe the Plexiglas clean. Let air dry. (Do not dry Plexiglas with a dry cloth, which will scratch the surface.)

STICKERS

- **Conair 1875 Watt Hair Dryer.** To remove a price sticker from a picture frame, use a Conair 1875 Watt Hair Dryer aimed at the sticker to melt the adhesive backing, and then use a single-edge razor blade to peel up the sticker.

- **Cutex Nail Polish Remover.** To remove price tags, stickers, and labels from picture frames, saturate a cotton ball with Cutex Nail Polish Remover and rub it on the sticker until the adhesive dissolves.

- **Mr. Clean Magic Eraser.** To remove the adhesive residue from price-tag stickers, simply rub the remaining adhesive goo with a damp Mr. Clean Magic Eraser.

- **Nivea Creme.** To remove dried glue left from price tags and labels on glass, metals, and most plastics, apply Nivea Creme, let sit for five minutes, and wipe clean.

- **WD-40.** To remove a sticky price tag from glass, saturate the tag with WD-40, let sit for five minutes, and scrape clean.

- **Wesson Oil.** To remove price tags, stickers, and labels from picture frames, saturate the sticker with Wesson Oil, let sit for ten minutes, and then scrape off. The oil dissolves the gum in the adhesive.

Patio Furniture

ALUMINUM FURNITURE

- **Heinz White Vinegar.** To clean lightly oxidized aluminum patio furniture, mix equal parts Heinz White Vinegar and water and use a sponge to wipe the aluminum with the solution. Rinse clean and air dry.
- **S.O.S Steel Wool Soap Pads.** To clean unpainted aluminum patio furniture, scrub with a dampened S.O.S Steel Wool Soap Pad, rinse clean, and air dry.
- **Turtle Wax.** Giving aluminum garden furniture a coat of liquid Turtle Wax rejuvenates the luster of the metal.

CANVAS FURNITURE

- **Fels-Naptha Soap.** To clean soiled canvas patio furniture or awnings, rub a wet scrub brush across a bar of Fels-Naptha Soap, scrub the canvas, and rinse well.

CUSHIONS

- **Clorox Bleach.** To clean solid white patio furniture cushions, mix three-quarters cup Clorox Bleach and one gallon water, scrub the cushions with the solution, and rinse clean with a garden hose. Let air dry.

- **Dawn Dishwashing Liquid** and **20 Mule Team Borax.** To clean stains from patio furniture cushions, mix one-half teaspoon Dawn Dishwashing Liquid, one-half teaspoon 20 Mule Team Borax, and two cups warm water in a sixteen-ounce trigger-spray bottle. Spray this solution on the stained cushions, let sit for fifteen minutes, and rinse clean with a garden hose. Place the cushions back on the patio furniture and let dry in the sun.

- **Scotchgard Fabric Protector.** To make cleaning patio furniture cushions easier, spray clean cushions with Scotchgard Fabric Protector.

- **Spot Shot.** To clean stains from patio furniture cushions, spray the stains with Spot Shot Instant Carpet Stain Remover. Let sit for five minutes, rinse clean with a garden hose, and let dry.

- **Tide.** To clean patio furniture cushions, fill the bathtub with ten inches of water, add one cup liquid Tide, soak the cushions in the tub for ten minutes, and scrub with a brush. Rinse clean and let air dry.

DECK CHAIRS

- **Wilson Tennis Balls.** To prevent a deck chair from slipping through the cracks of a deck, slit four Wilson Tennis Balls and fit them on the feet of the deck chair.

ENAMELED ALUMINUM FURNITURE

- **Arm & Hammer Baking Soda.** To clean dulled enameled aluminum furniture, sprinkle Arm & Hammer Baking Soda on a damp sponge, scrub well, rinse clean, and air dry.

- **Bon Ami.** To clean enameled aluminum outdoor furniture, hose down the outdoor furniture and use Bon Ami to remove stubborn soil and stains by making a paste, rubbing gently, and rinsing.
- **Turtle Wax.** Apply a protective coating of Turtle Wax to cleaned aluminum patio furniture with a baked enamel finish. The car wax provides a shine and makes future cleaning easier.

HAMMOCKS

- **Dawn Dishwashing Liquid.** To clean a hammock, take down the hammock, lay it on a patio deck or a tarp, and saturate it with water using a garden hose. Mix one teaspoon Dawn Dishwashing Liquid in one gallon water in a bucket and scrub the soapy solution on the hammock with a soft brush. Rinse clean with the garden hose, turn the hammock over, and repeat on the other side. Hang the hammock in the sun to dry thoroughly.
- **Scotchgard Fabric Protector.** Before using a hammock for the first time (or after washing a used hammock), spray the clean, dry hammock with Scotchgard Fabric Protector to prevent the fabric from becoming saturated with water.

PATIO UMBRELLAS

- **Dawn Dishwashing Liquid.** To clean a canvas patio umbrella, saturate it with water using a garden hose. Mix one teaspoon Dawn Dishwashing Liquid in one gallon water in a bucket and scrub the soapy solution on the umbrella with a soft brush. Rinse clean and stand the open umbrella in the sun to dry.
- **L'eggs Sheer Energy Panty Hose.** To store a patio umbrella for the winter, insert the folded umbrella inside one leg of a pair of clean, old L'eggs Sheer Energy Panty Hose. Tie the other panty hose leg around the umbrella to hold it tightly together.

Plastic Patio Furniture

- **Bon Ami.** To clean plastic outdoor furniture, hose down the plastic furniture and use Bon Ami to remove stubborn soil and stains by making a paste, rubbing gently, and rinsing.

- **Cascade.** Mix three tablespoons Cascade Gel and one gallon warm water in a bucket and wash the plastic patio furniture with the solution. Let sit for fifteen minutes, rinse clean, and dry.

- **Clorox Bleach.** To clean plastic or resin patio furniture, pour two tablespoons Clorox Bleach into a sixteen-ounce trigger-spray bottle, fill the rest of the bottle with water, shake well, and spray the solution on the furniture. Let sit for ten minutes, rinse clean with a garden hose, and air dry.

- **Colgate Regular Flavor Toothpaste.** Squeeze a dollop of Colgate Regular Flavor Toothpaste on a damp, soft, clean cloth and rub it into the plastic furniture. Buff with another soft, clean cloth.

- **Mr. Clean Magic Eraser.** To clean mold and mildew from plastic patio furniture, gently rub the stains with a damp Mr. Clean Magic Eraser. Rinse clean.

- **Turtle Wax.** Apply a protective coating of Turtle Wax to clean plastic patio furniture. The car wax provides a lustrous shine and makes future cleaning easy and effortless.

Redwood Patio Furniture

- **Dawn Dishwashing Liquid** and **Clorox Bleach.** Mix one teaspoon Dawn Dishwashing Liquid, three-quarters cup Clorox Bleach, and one gallon water in a bucket and scrub the wooden outdoor furniture with a brush dipped in the solution. Rinse clean and air dry.

Storage

- **Glad Trash Bags.** To keep folding lawn chairs clean during winter storage, store each folding chair in a large Glad Trash Bag.

THE DIRT ON MR. CLEAN

In 1958, Lestoil dominated the liquid cleanser market, until Proctor & Gamble began running television commercials for Mr. Clean, created by Tatham-Laird, Inc. and starring a muscular, baldheaded, animated genie-like man, clad in a tight, white T-shirt and wearing a gold ring in his left earlobe. The first Mr. Clean commercials premiered on August 11, 1958.

In 2001, Procter & Gamble executives working in Japan discovered that grocery stores sold a block of melamine foam that locals used to erase the particles of dirt from surfaces. The soft, microporous foam works like extremely fine sandpaper. The German chemical company BASF, the largest chemical company in the world, manufactures melamine resin foam under the brand name Basotect, which has been used as insulation for pipes and ductwork; as soundproofing material for studios, sounds stages, and auditoriums; and to make ultraflame retardant airplane seating. In 2003, Procter & Gamble introduced the Mr. Clean Magic Eraser, made from Basotect.

Strange Facts

- Hal Mason, the animator who created the cartoon character Mr. Clean, originated the Pillsbury Dough Boy and the Frito Bandito; worked with cartoon producer Walter Lantz on the characters Woody Woodpecker, Andy Panda, and Oswald Rabbit; and wrote the 1982 television special *Chipmunks Christmas.*

- Thomas Scott Cadden wrote the Mr. Clean jingle, which was sung by Don Cherry (best known for his hit song "Band of Gold") and Betty Bryan. Cadden also wrote jingles for Head & Shoulders and Pringles.

- In 1998, *People* voted Mr. Clean as one of the "Sexiest Men Alive!"

- Mr. Clean's first name is Veritably.

- In 2006, Procter & Gamble held a Mr. Clean look-alike contest at the Mall of America, attracting more than a dozen participants. The winner received $5,000.

- Mr. Clean is named Monsieur Propre in France, Meister Proper in Germany, Mastro Lindo in Italy, Maestro Limpio in Mexico, Don Limpio in Spain, and M. Net in Quebec.

Pets

BATHING

- **Murphy Oil Soap.** To give a dog a bath, add a few drops of Murphy Oil Soap in your dog's bath water to moisturize and soften a dog's skin and coat. Murphy Oil Soap is pure vegetable oil soap that will not harm a dog's sensitive skin.

BIRD CAGES

- **Con-Tact Paper.** To clean a bird cage more easily, line the base of the bird cage with colorful Con-Tact Paper to create a water-resistant surface that's easier to wash clean.

- **Reynolds Cut-Rite Wax Paper.** Use Reynolds Cut-Rite Wax Paper on the bottom of a birdcage to catch foul matter.

Burrs

- **Johnson's Baby Oil.** To remove burrs from a dog or cat's fur (or a horse's mane and tail), wear work gloves (to avoid getting pricked by the burs), work Johnson's Baby Oil into the affected areas, and pry the burrs loose. Shampoo the animal to remove the mineral oil.

- **Kingsford's Corn Starch.** A less messy way to remove burrs from an animal's coat? Wearing work gloves, work Kingsford's Corn Starch into the cat or dog's coat, and then pluck the burrs free. Then brush out the cornstarch, which doubles as a dry shampoo.

Cat Litter Boxes

- **Arm & Hammer Baking Soda.** To help eliminate odors from a cat litter box, pour a thin layer of Arm & Hammer Baking Soda on the bottom of the box before adding the litter.

- **Glad Trash Bags.** To make a litter box liner, place the litter box inside a Glad Trash Bag. When you're ready to dispose of the used cat box filler, simply remove the litter box, turn the plastic trash bag inside out, and discard.

Dry Shampoo

- **Arm & Hammer Baking Soda.** To give your pet a dry shampoo, rub Arm & Hammer Baking Soda into the animal's coat and brush it clean. The baking soda absorbs dirt and grime, and it also deodorizes the animal.

- **Kingsford's Corn Starch.** Work Kingsford's Corn Stanch into your dog or cat's fur and brush it out for a dry shampoo. Corn starch absorbs dirt and grime from the animal's coat.

Electrical Cords

- **Fels-Naptha Soap.** To prevent cats or dogs from chewing electrical cords, rub the cords with Fels-Naptha Soap.

FLEAS

- **Heinz Apple Cider Vinegar** and **Dawn Dishwashing Liquid.**
To make flea shampoo for your dog, mix equal parts Heinz Apple Cider
Vinegar and Dawn Dishwashing Liquid. Lather up the dog with the solu-
tion and rinse clean.

- **Lipton Chamomile Tea.** To keep fleas away from your dog, place a
few open Lipton Chamomile Tea bags in the doghouse. Non-toxic chamomile repels fleas naturally.

- **Morton Salt.** To repel fleas in a doghouse, sprinkle Morton Salt into
the cracks and crevices inside the doghouse. Salt dehydrates fleas.

FURNITURE

- **Old Spice Aftershave Lotion.** To deter a cat from sharpening its
claws on furniture, pour a few drops of Old Spice Aftershave Lotion into
the palm of your hand and rub it on the wood or upholstery. The smell
repels cats.

- **Tabasco Pepper Sauce.** To prevent cats from scratching wood furniture, rub a few drops of Tabasco Pepper Sauce into the wood with a soft,
clean cloth. Cats have a keen sense of smell and are repulsed by the scent
of Tabasco Pepper Sauce.

HAIRBALLS

- **Arm & Hammer Baking Soda.** To clean a hairball from carpet,
scrape up the hairball and blot up as much of the excess liquid as possible,
and then cover the stain with a mountain of Arm & Hammer Baking
Soda. Let sit overnight, giving the baking soda enough time to absorb the
liquid, dry, and deodorize the stench, and then brush up the baking soda
and vacuum the spot.

- **Land O Lakes Butter.** To stop a cat from expelling hairballs and making a mess, add one-half teaspoon Land O Lakes Butter to the cat's food

once a week. The butter helps push the fur through the cat's digestive system, prevent hairballs from forming.

- **Star Olive Oil.** To prevent your cat from vomiting up hairballs, add one-half teaspoon Star Olive Oil to your cat's food once a week. The oil lubricates the cat's digestive system, allowing the fur to glide through.

- **20 Mule Team Borax.** Clean up as much of the hairball as possible, dissolve one tablespoon 20 Mule Team Borax in two cups water, apply the solution to the stain with a sponge, and blot clean.

- **Vaseline Petroleum Jelly.** Wipe a dab of Vaseline Petroleum Jelly on the bridge of your cat's nose. The cat will lick it off, and the petroleum jelly will smooth the animal's digestive tract, allowing the hair to glide along smoothly without forming hairballs.

HORSES

- **Bag Balm.** To soften hardened, dry, pinched, or contracted horse hoofs and quarter cracks, simply rub in Bag Balm.

- **Scope Cool Peppermint** and **Johnson's Baby Oil.** To keep flies off horses, mix equal parts Scope Cool Peppermint Mouthwash with Johnson's Baby Oil in a sixteen-ounce trigger-spray bottle and spray on your horses.

- **Simple Green.** To bathe a horse, mix one cup Simple Green All-Purpose Cleaner and ten cups water in a bucket. Wet the horse with water, and apply the solution with a cloth or soft scrub brush, working in sections so the Simple Green solution doesn't stay on the horse's skin for too long (and dry it out). Rinse the cleaned section thoroughly with water. (To treat stubborn stains, put a few drops of Simple Green on a damp cloth, rub the area, and rinse immediately.) When finished, rinse the horse with water and apply a coat conditioner. (Do not get the solution into the horse's eyes, nose, or mouth. If the solution does get in the horse's eyes by accident, rinse and flush the eyes with cool water, lifting upper and lower lids and rinsing for fifteen minutes. Also, do not leave buckets or puddles of Simple Green solution where horses or another animals might drink.)

Houseplants

- **Heinz White Vinegar.** To prevent cats from digging up houseplants and making a mess, add one teaspoon Heinz White Vinegar to two cups water in a sixteen-ounce trigger-spray bottle and mist the plants with the solution. The smell of the vinegar repels cats.

- **Maxwell House Coffee.** To keep cats from digging up the soil of houseplants, fertilize the houseplants with used Maxwell House Coffee grounds. The smell of the coffee grounds repels cats.

Odors

- **Arm & Hammer Baking Soda.** Sprinkle Arm & Hammer Baking Soda on pet bedding, let sit for three hours, and launder as usual.

Pet Food

- **Gatorade.** Pour an open box or bag of birdseed or pet food into a clean, empty Gatorade bottle and secure the lid to keep the pet food fresh and free from insects and mice.

Pet Hair

- **Bounce.** To remove pet hair from furniture, clothes, or bedding, simply wipe the affected area with a clean, used sheet of Bounce, which works like a magnet, attracting all the hairs.

- **Bounty Paper Towels.** To prevent a cat from shedding all over the house, dampen a sheet of Bounty Paper Towels and run it over the cat. The paper towel collects the loose hair.

- **Playtex Living Gloves.** To remove pet hair from clothes, furniture, and bedding, put on a pair of Playtex Living Gloves, fill a bucket halfway with water, dip the gloves in the water, wipe the area affected by the pet hair, and dip the gloves in the water again. The wet rubber attracts the pet hair, and the water in the bucket rinses it off.

- **Scotch Packaging Tape.** Wrap Scotch Packaging Tape around your hand with the sticky-side out and pat the furniture with the tape. The pet hairs will stick to the tape.

SKUNK ODORS

- **Arm & Hammer Baking Soda.** Make a thick paste from Arm & Hammer Baking Soda and warm water, apply the paste to the dog's fur, and let dry on the dog. The sodium bicarbonate absorbs the skunk smell.

- **Bausch & Lomb Sensitive Eyes Saline Solution.** Dogs generally approach a skunk face first and get sprayed in the eyes. To relieve the stinging from the skunk oil, flush your dog's eyes with Bausch & Lomb Sensitive Eyes Saline Solution. If your dog scratches its eyes or squints for more than an hour, take it to your veterinarian.

- **Campbell's Tomato Juice.** To get rid of the smell of skunk on a dog, wash the dog with its regular shampoo, pour Campbell's Tomato Juice over the dog, and work the tomato juice into the animal's coat. Let set for fifteen minutes or more, rinse well, and shampoo again.

- **Canada Dry Club Soda.** Another way to eliminate skunk odor on a dog? Pour Canada Dry Club Soda (ideally at room temperature) all over the dog, working it into the animal's coat. Let soak in for ten minutes, and then shampoo the dog as usual.

- **Heinz White Vinegar.** To deodorize skunk smell from a dog, saturate the dog's fur with Heinz White Vinegar, let sit for ten minute, and rinse clean with water.

- **Hydrogen Peroxide, Arm & Hammer Baking Soda,** and **Dawn Dishwashing Liquid.** To neutralize the stench of skunk oil on a dog, mix four cups Hydrogen Peroxide, one-quarter cup Arm & Hammer Baking Soda, and two teaspoons Dawn Dishwashing Liquid. Wearing Playtex Living Gloves (see next page), wash your dog with its regular shampoo, rinse clean, and then lather up the dog with the solution. Repeat as many times as necessary.

- **Massengill Disposable Douche.** Mix two ounces Massengill Disposable Douche in one gallon water, pour the diluted medicated douche over the dog, and let soak for fifteen minutes. Rinse clean with water and shampoo as usual.

- **McCormick Pure Vanilla Extract.** If you tried everything possible to get rid of the smell of skunk on your dog, but the smell still lingers, saturate a soft, clean cloth with McCormick Pure Vanilla Extract and wipe down your dog. The vanilla extract will help mask the skunk odor until it eventually wears off.

- **Playtex Living Gloves.** When washing skunk oil from your dog, wear a pair of Playtex Living Gloves to avoid getting the pungent skunk oil on your skin.

Keep It Clean
HOW TO CLEAN PET STAINS FROM CARPET

- Vacuum the carpet frequently to catch pet hair and dander.
- Clean up new pet messes immediately and then follow the steps for spot and stain removal opposite.
- Use cleaning products labeled with the CRI Seal of Approval that are specifically designed for pet stains and odors.
- Have your carpet professionally cleaned every twelve to eighteen months, or more frequently if necessary.
- Never use a steam cleaner on urine spots; the heat imbeds the stain and the smell into the carpet. Instead, use a wet-vacuum to suck the liquid from the carpet and rinse the spot with cool water to reduce the odor.
- If necessary, call in a certified carpet cleaning company that specializes in removing pet stains and odor permanently.

Urine Stains

- **Arm & Hammer Baking Soda.** To deodorize blotted-up urine stains in carpet, cover the stains with a mountain of Arm & Hammer Baking Soda. Let sit for forty-eight hours, giving the baking soda enough time to neutralize the odor, and then brush up the baking soda and vacuum the spot.

- **Canada Dry Club Soda.** Blot up as much of the liquid as possible, using paper towels or rags. Saturate the stain with Canada Dry Club Soda and blot with more paper towels or rags. Repeat until you have blotted up the urine from the carpet. The carbonation in the club soda brings the urine to the surface. Then treat the carpet with the tip below using Heinz White Vinegar.

- **Heinz White Vinegar.** To deodorize urine stains from carpet, mix equal parts Heinz White Vinegar and water in a trigger-spray bottle and spray the solution on the urine stain. (Be sure to first test an inconspicuous spot on the carpet for colorfastness.)

- **Hydrogen Peroxide, Arm & Hammer Baking Soda,** and **Ivory Dishwashing Liquid.** For stubborn urine odor in carpeting, mix one cup Hydrogen Peroxide, one tablespoon Arm & Hammer Baking Soda, and one-half teaspoon Ivory Dishwashing Liquid. Apply the solution to the stain with a damp sponge and let dry. Vacuum.

- **Listerine.** To deodorize urine stains from carpet, pour original Listerine antiseptic mouthwash on the stain and blot well. Rinse clean with water and blot again.

- **Parsons' Ammonia.** If a urine stain has lightened the color of the carpet, try sponging Parsons' Ammonia on the spot. Let sit for five minutes, rinse clean with water, and blot. Ammonia can sometimes restore the color of the carpeting.

- **Simple Green.** To clean cat or dog urine from cement or concrete, open all windows and doors to the room (if indoors) and set up fans to ventilate. In a bucket, mix one cup Simple Green All-Purpose Cleaner to ten cups hot water and scrub the cement or concrete surfaces down with the solution. After scrubbing, mop away as much moisture as possible. Run the fans with the windows and doors open until everything dries.

VOMIT

- **Arm & Hammer Baking Soda.** To clean vomit from carpet, scrape up all the chunks and blot up as much of the excess liquid as possible, and then cover the stain with a mountain of Arm & Hammer Baking Soda. Let sit overnight, giving the baking soda enough time to absorb the liquid, dry, and deodorize the stench, and then brush up the baking soda and vacuum the spot.

- **20 Mule Team Borax.** Clean up as much of the vomit as possible, dissolve one tablespoon 20 Mule Team Borax in two cups water, apply the solution to the stain with a sponge, and blot clean.

WHITENING

- **Mrs. Stewart's Liquid Bluing.** Pet owners use Mrs. Stewart's Liquid Bluing to whiten white pet fur—from a poodle being groomed for a show to a palomino's tail being readied for a parade. Just add a couple of drops of Mrs. Stewart's Liquid Bluing in the rinse water.

Sewing

BADGES

- **Elmer's Glue-All.** To hold a scouting badge in place to sew it on a uniform, glue the badge onto the fabric with Elmer's Glue-All and place a heavy book on top of the badge until it dries. Then sew on the badge. The glue will come off in the wash.

BASEBALL CAPS

- **Velcro.** When the plastic strap breaks on a baseball cap, replace it with strips of Velcro.

BUTTONHOLES

- **Revlon Clear Nail Enamel.** After sewing a buttonhole and before cutting it open, paint the spot in the fabric with Revlon Clear Nail

Enamel and let dry. The clear nail polish will prevent the fabric from fraying when you slice open the buttonhole with a single-edge razor blade.

BUTTONS

- **Elmer's Glue-All.** To fortify buttons on shirts, rub a tiny drop of Elmer's Glue-All on the thread around each button. This prevents the thread from coming loose and stops the buttons from falling off.

- **Gerber Applesauce.** To store buttons in your sewing basket, fill a clean, empty Gerber Applesauce baby food jar with your buttons.

- **Krazy Glue.** To prevent buttons from falling off, put a drop of Krazy Glue on the threads in the center of each button.

- **Oral-B Dental Floss.** To sew buttons on heavy coats, use Oral-B Dental Floss as a durable thread.

- **Revlon Clear Nail Enamel.** To prevent the threads on buttons from breaking, dab some Revlon Clear Nail Enamel on the threads in the center of each button to strengthen them.

- **Velcro.** Rather than replacing troublesome buttons, attach Velcro in place of the buttons.

EMBOSSING

- **Mr. Coffee Filters.** When embossing, pour the powder onto a Mr. Coffee Filter and then back into the jar without leaving any residue on the filter. The filter can be reused repeatedly, leaving plenty of money to buy more stamps.

Embroidery

- **Bounce.** To stabilize embroidery, place a clean, used sheet of Bounce on the back of T-shirts or sweat shirts when you cross-stitch or embroider designs on them—without the expense of purchasing interfacing.

Fraying

- **Revlon Clear Nail Enamel.** To prevent cut fabric from fraying, apply a thin coat of Revlon Clear Nail Enamel along seam edges to prevent the weave from unraveling.

Guide Strips

- **Con-Tact Paper.** To make sewing simple, cut a strip of brightly colored Con-Tact Paper and adhere it to your sewing machine as a guide strip.

Hand Cleaners

- **Huggies Baby Wipes.** Keep a box of Huggies Baby Wipes close by when working on needlecraft to periodically wash your hands. The wipes keep oils off the fabric and minimize the number of trips to the sink to wash with soap and water.

Hems

- **Forster Clothespins.** To hem fabric when sewing, instead of basting the fabric with pins, clip the hemline with Forster Clothespins.
- **Velcro.** Instead of continuously having to drop the hem on a child's pants or dress, sew two vertical strips of Velcro inside the bottom of each pant leg or under the dress. The Velcro allows you to adjust the pant legs or dress to the appropriate length.
- **Wrigley's Spearmint Gum.** Reattach a drooping hem temporarily with a dab of chewed Wrigley's Spearmint Gum.

KNITTING

- **Glad Flexible Straws.** To mark a stitch when knitting, cut a one-eighth inch length from a Glad Flexible Straw and use as a ring to mark a stitch on needles up to size ten.

- **Glad Flexible Straws.** To prevent wool from tangling when knitting with more than one ball of yarn, thread the end of each color yarn through a Glad Flexible Straw.

- **Pledge.** To speed up your knitting, spray Pledge furniture polish on the knitting needles so the yarn glides over them.

- **Revlon Red Nail Enamel.** To make a handy ruler for knitting, paint inch marks with Revlon Red Nail Enamel along the length of your knitting needles.

- **Reynolds Wrap.** An empty box of Reynolds Wrap aluminum foil makes an excellent storage container for knitting needles.

NEEDLES

- **Alberto VO5 Hair Spray.** To thread a needle easily, stiffen the end of the thread with Alberto VO5 Hair Spray so it can be easily poked through the eye of a needle.

- **Bounce.** Run your sewing needle through a sheet of Bounce before you begin sewing, and the needle will glide smoothly through your fabric.

- **Faultless Spray Starch.** Spray a little Faultless Spray Starch on the end of the thread to make it stiff enough to thread through the eye of a needle with ease.

- **Ivory Soap.** To thread a needle, pull the end of the thread over a bar of Ivory Soap to stiffen the thread.

- **Revlon Clear Nail Enamel.** Dip the end of the thread in Revlon Clear Nail Enamel. Let dry, and then thread.

OIL

- **Vaseline Petroleum Jelly.** If you need to oil your sewing machine and you're all out of machine oil, use a dab of Vaseline Petroleum Jelly.

PATTERNS

- **Faultless Sizing.** To make a fabric pattern last longer, spray the pattern with Faultless Sizing before pressing it.

- **Reynolds Cut-Rite Wax Paper.** To trace sewing patterns, use a sheet of Reynolds Cut-Rite Wax Paper as sturdy tracing paper.

- **Scotch Transparent Tape.** To attach a sewing pattern to fabric, use Scotch Transparent Tape to tape the pattern to the material, and then cut the pattern, leaving a reinforced edge.

- **Scotchgard Fabric Protector.** To preserve a sewing pattern, spray a new pattern with Scotchgard Fabric Protector to prevent rips, tears, and wrinkles in the paper.

- **Ziploc Storage Bags.** Store sewing patterns in Ziploc Storage Bags.

PINCUSHIONS

- **Ivory Soap.** Using a wrapped bar of Ivory Soap as a pincushion makes needles glide through fabric.

- **Pink Pearl Eraser.** To keep sewing areas clean, keep needles, pins, and safety pins stuck in a Pink Pearl Eraser.

- **S.O.S Steel Wool Soap Pads.** Stuff a homemade pin cushion with a clean, dry, used S.O.S Steel Wool Soap Pad. The steel wool will help keep pins and needles sharp.

QUILTING

- **Bounce.** Sew the right side of the fabric piece to a clean, used sheet of Bounce, leaving a place to turn the stitched piece. Turn the piece to the right side, and you have a pattern piece with raw edges already turned, ready to sew to your quilt block.

SCISSORS

- **Cutex Nail Polish Remover.** To clean scissors, soak a cotton ball in Cutex Nail Polish Remover and cautiously clean the scissor blades.

- **Reynolds Wrap.** To sharpen a dull pair of scissors, fold a sheet of Reynolds Wrap aluminum foil in half several times and cut through the thicknesses a few times.

- **3M Sandpaper.** To sharpen scissors, cut through a piece of 3M Sandpaper several times.

SEWING MACHINES

- **Bounty Paper Towels.** To absorb excess oil from a sewing machine after oiling it, stitch several rows on a sheet of Bounty Paper Towels before sewing any fabric.

- **Crayola Crayons.** To rewind a bobbin, mark the thread with a contrasting color Crayola Crayon a few yards after starting to wind it onto the bobbin. The crayon mark will alert you when the thread is coming to the end of the bobbin.

- **Forster Toothpicks.** To push fabrics through the pressure foot of a sewing machine, use a Forster Toothpick to free fabric that gets stuck under the pressure foot.

- **Glad Flexible Straws.** To extend the spout of an oil can, put a Glad Flexible Straw over the end of the spout to reach tight spots.

- **Johnson's Baby Oil.** To help vinyl fabric glide through a sewing machine, wipe the seam line with a cotton ball dipped in Johnson's Baby Oil before stitching.

- **Mr. Coffee Filters.** Mr. Coffee Filters make excellent stabilizers under fabric when sewing on a machine.

- **Vaseline Petroleum Jelly** and **Reynolds Cut-Rite Wax Paper.** When running tough material with sequins or beads through a sewing machine, the needle tends to get stuck and the thread constantly breaks. But if you rub Vaseline Petroleum Jelly on the presser foot every so often and place a sheet of Reynolds Cut-Rite Wax Paper under it, the fabric glides through easily.

SNAPS

- **Scotch Transparent Tape.** To make sewing snaps on clothing a snap, tape the snaps, hooks, and eyes to the garment, sew them on right along with the Scotch Transparent Tape, and then pull the tape off.

TAILOR'S CHALK

- **Ivory Soap.** When a bar of Ivory Soap in the shower or at the sink shrinks to a small piece, let it dry, and use it as tailor's chalk.

THIMBLES

- **Band-Aid Bandages.** To improvise a thimble, in a pinch, place a Band-Aid Bandage over your fingertip as a makeshift thimble when sewing.

THREAD

- **Bounce.** To prevent thread from tangling, run a threaded needle through a sheet of Bounce to eliminate the static cling on the thread before sewing.

- **Scotch Transparent Tape.** To keep a spool of thread from unwinding and tangling, secure the end of the thread in place with a piece of Scotch Transparent Tape.

YARN

- **Clorox Bleach.** Cut off the bottom of a clean, empty Clorox Bleach jug, place balls of yarn in the upside-down container, and thread the strands of yarn through the neck of the jug. The handle allows you to hang the jug from a chair or knob.

- **Gatorade.** Cut off the bottom of a clean, empty Gatorade bottle, place it over a ball of yarn, and thread the yarn through the neck of the bottle.

- **Pringles.** To store yarn or sting, run a strand of yarn through a hole punched in the plastic lid of a Pringles can and seal the yarn in the can.

- **Ziploc Storage Bags.** Store each ball of yarn in its own Ziploc Storage Bag, punch a hole in the bag, and run a strand of the yarn through it.

ZIPPERS

- **Oral-B Dental Floss.** If the teeth of a zipper on a winter coat, backpack, or tent break off at the bottom, sew the zipper together at the bottom with Oral-B Dental Floss, which is much more durable than thread.

- **Scotch Transparent Tape.** To sew in a zipper easily, baste the seam closed, press open, and tape the zipper face down along the basted seam on the wrong side of the fabric (allowing the tape to hold the zipper flat). Sew on a machine, and then remove the tape and basting.

- **Velcro.** Instead of sewing in a new zipper, attach a strip of Velcro as an easy replacement.

Shoes and Sneakers

BOOTS

- **Arm & Hammer Baking Soda.** To help your feet feel fresh and minimize foot odor, sprinkle some Arm & Hammer Baking Soda inside your hiking boots before wearing them on a hike.

- **Bounce.** To minimize foot odor in boots, insert a sheet of Bounce in each boot overnight (or until you wish to wear the boots).

- **Conair 1875 Watt Hair Dryer.** To dry the insides of wet boots, point the nose of a Conair 1875 Watt Hair Dryer inside the boots and blow in hot air until the inside of the boots are warm and cozy.

- **Endust.** To give boots a protective coating so water beads off the leather, polish the books with Endust.

- **Forster Clothespins.** Clip your left and right boots together with a Foster Clothespin so they stay together in the closet.

- **Pam Cooking Spray.** To clean caked-mud from the bottom of boots, spray the mud-encrusted soles with Pam Cooking Spray, let the mud dry, and knock the boots together outside. The mud falls right off.

- *USA Today.* To store boots, crumple up pages from *USA Today* and stuff them inside the boots. The newsprint absorbs moisture and odors, and the stuffing helps the boots retain their shape.

- **Vaseline Petroleum Jelly.** To protect leather boots from water stains and salt marks, coat a soft, clean cloth with Vaseline Petroleum Jelly and gently rub your boots with the cloth before you wear them outside and whenever you return.

CLEANING

- **Cutex Nail Polish Remover.** To clean grease or tar from white canvas shoes or sneakers, saturate a cotton ball with Cutex Nail Polish Remover and rub the stains.

- **Dawn Dishwashing Liquid** and **ReaLemon.** Scrub sneakers with a few drops of Dawn Dishwashing Liquid on a damp sponge or brush. Fill a sink or bucket with water, add two teaspoons ReaLemon lemon juice, and rinse the sneakers clean in the solution. Let air dry. The lemon juice simultaneously brightens and deodorizes the footwear.

- **Faultless Spray Starch.** Before wearing your new sneakers for the first time, give them a protective coat of Faultless Spray Starch, which impedes dirt from adhering to the canvas or leather.

- **Gillette Foamy.** To clean sneakers, spray them with Gillette Foamy shaving cream, scrub with a brush, let dry, and brush clean.

- **Resolve Carpet Cleaner.** Spray dirty sneakers with Resolve Carpet Cleaner, scrub with a brush, rinse clean, and let dry.

- **Scotchgard Fabric Protector.** When you bring home a new pair of sneakers from the store, spray them with a fine coat of Scotchgard Fabric Protector to shield the footwear from stains.

- **Spray 'n Wash.** A few squirts of Spray 'n Wash stain remover helps clean grease from leather shoes.

DEODORIZING

- **Bounce.** Place a sheet of Bounce inside your shoes and sneakers overnight to get your footwear to smell fresh and clean by morning.

- **Conair 1875 Watt Hair Dryer.** If your shoes, boots, or sneakers get wet from excessive perspiration, insert the nozzle of a Conair 1875 Watt Hair Dryer into the footwear and use on a low setting for five minutes. Drying out the moisture robs odor-causing bacteria of a hospitable environment to multiply.

- **Kingsford's Corn Starch.** To deodorize smelly shoes or sneakers, sprinkle Kingsford's Corn Starch inside the footwear to keep them dry and comfortable. Cornstarch absorbs moisture.

- **Lysol Disinfectant.** To deodorize smelly shoes, spray the inside of your shoes with Lysol Disinfectant spray to kill the fungus spores living inside.

- **Maxwell House Coffee.** To deodorize smelly footwear, sprinkle a pinch of unused Maxwell House Coffee grounds in each shoe every other day. The coffee grounds absorb the excess moisture and deodorize the footwear, which will smell like fresh-brewed coffee.

ESPADRILLES

- **Resolve Carpet Cleaner.** To clean ropey-soled espadrilles, spray Resolve Carpet Cleaner on a stiff brush and gently brush the rope.

- **Scotchgard Fabric Protector.** To protect the rope soles of espadrilles from water, give the soles two coats of Scotchgard Fabric Protector.

GRASS STAINS

- **Bon Ami.** Clean grass and mud stains from white shoes and sneakers. A sponge sprinkled with Bon Ami will uncover the original white and make shoes look new.

- **Grandma's Molasses.** To clean grass stains from white leather shoes, rub Grandma's Molasses on the stain and let sit overnight. In the morning, wash the molasses off the shoes with soap and water.

- **Simple Green.** Wet the grass stain with water and spray on a solution of equal parts Simple Green All-Purpose Cleaner and water. Rub with a sponge and rinse well.

MUD

- **Bon Ami.** To clean grass and mud stains from white shoes and sneakers, scrub the footware with a damp sponge sprinkled with Bon Ami. The cleansing powder will uncover the original white and make shoes look new.

ODORS

- **Arm & Hammer Baking Soda** and **Ziploc Freezer Bags.** To deodorize smelly sneakers or shoes, sprinkle some Arm & Hammer Baking Soda in the shoes, place each shoe inside a Ziploc Freezer Bag, secure the bags shut, and place the bags in the freezer overnight. Let the shoe thaw to room temperature and shake out the baking soda. Repeat if necessary.

- **Bounce.** Place a sheet of Bounce in each shoe or sneaker and let sit overnight. In the morning, they'll smell springtime fresh.

- **Ivory Soap.** Place a wrapped bar of Ivory Soap in each shoe or sneaker and let sit for several days. The soap absorbs the smells.

- **Maxwell House Coffee** and **L'eggs Sheer Energy Panty Hose.** Cut off the feet from a clean, used pair of L'eggs Sheer Energy Panty Hose, fill each foot with Maxwell House Coffee grounds, and tie a knot in the open end of each foot. Place a sachet in each shoe or sneaker and let sit overnight. The coffee grounds absorb the foul smells.

PATENT LEATHER

- **Balmex.** To remove scuffmarks from patent leather shoes, apply Balmex to a soft cloth and rub into the patent leather.

- **Liquid Paper** and **Revlon Clear Nail Enamel.** To hide a chip on white patent leather, paint over the nick with white Liquid Paper, let dry, and coat with Revlon Clear Nail Enamel.

- **Nestlé Carnation NonFat Dry Milk.** To clean patent leather shoes, mix one level teaspoon Nestlé Carnation NonFat Dry Milk with three teaspoons water; apply the milky solution with a soft, clean cloth; and buff dry with a second soft, clean cloth.

- **Nivea Creme.** To clean scuffmarks from patent leather shoes, apply a dab of Nivea Creme to the scuffmark and rub with a soft, clean cloth.

- **Vaseline Petroleum Jelly.** Put a dab of Vaseline Petroleum Jelly on a soft, clean cloth and shine the patent leather shoes. Buff with a clean, soft cloth to achieve a lustrous shine.

POLISHING

- **Bag Balm.** To shine leather shoes, just rub a dab of Bag Balm on the shoes and shine with a soft cloth.

- **Cool Whip.** Apply a tablespoon of Cool Whip to your leather shoes and shine with a soft, clean cloth. The various oils in the dessert topping polish the shoes.

- **Coppertone.** A few drops of Coppertone sunscreen rubbed into leather shoes with a soft cloth gives them a magnificent shine (and prevents your shoes from getting sunburned).

- **Huggies Baby Wipes.** In a pinch, rub leather shoes with Huggies Baby Wipes and buff dry.

- **L'eggs Sheer Energy Panty Hose.** When polishing shoes, buff with a clean, old pair of L'eggs Sheer Energy Panty Hose. The nylon is a mild abrasive that does an excellent job shining shoes.

- **Mop & Glo.** For shining shoes, Mop & Glo makes an excellent polish.

- **Nivea Creme.** Rub a dab of Nivea Cream into leather shoes and buff well for a terrific shine that keeps the leather soft and moisturized.

- **Pledge.** Spray a soft, clean rag with Pledge furniture polish, rub the leather shoes well, and buff.

- **Reynolds Cut-Rite Wax Paper.** After polishing your shoes, rub them with a sheet of Reynolds Cut-Rite Wax Paper. The wax paper shines the shoes while simultaneously giving them a fine wax coating.

- **SC Johnson Paste Wax.** In a pinch, you can polish light or dark leather shoes with SC Johnson Paste Wax. Rub the paste into the shoes and buff.

- **SPAM.** Rub a block of SPAM over leather shoes or boots and then buff. The animal oils in SPAM actually polish leather.

- **Tampax Tampons.** Many soldiers in the United States military buff their shoes and boots with Tampax Tampons to achieve an impressive shine for inspections.

- **Turtle Wax.** Dab Turtle Wax on shoes and buff with a soft cloth.

SALT

- **Heinz White Vinegar.** To clean winter salt from shoes and boots, mix equal parts Heinz White Vinegar and water, sponge the solution on the white marks, and wipe dry with a soft, clean cloth.

Keep It Clean

SHOE POLISH STEPS

- To prevent dirt and other debris from getting embedded into leather, wipe your shoes clean before you start polishing.

- Remove the shoelaces before you start polishing a pair of leather shoes. This way, you can clean the tongue and avoid staining the laces.

- Using a brush or soft cloth, apply the traditional paste shoe polish or cream evenly to leather shoes and boots and let dry. Buff to a shine using a natural bristle brush.

- If using liquid shoe polish, simply apply the liquid evenly to your shoes and let dry. The liquid dries to an instant shine with no buffing required.

- Store leather shoes with a shoetree (or stuff the shoes with newspaper or tissue) to help preserve the shape of the shoe.

- If suede shoes get wet, stuff them with newspaper while they dry naturally to keep their shape.

- Using a shoehorn to help you put on your shoes prevents the heel from losing its shape.

- When packing a suitcase, place your shoes inside a shoe bag or wrap them in soft material.

SCUFFMARKS

- **Balmex.** To remove scuffmarks from patent leather shoes, apply Balmex to a soft cloth and rub into the patent leather.

- **Colgate Regular Flavor Toothpaste.** To clean a scuffmark from gold, silver, or light-colored leather shoes, apply a dab of Colgate Regular Flavor Toothpaste to a clean, old toothbrush and brush off the scuffmark.

- **Cutex Nail Polish Remover.** To remove a black scuffmark from shoes, dampen a cotton ball with Cutex Nail Polish Remover and gently rub the spot.

- **Old Spice Aftershave Lotion.** To clean scuffmarks from shoes, saturate a cotton ball with Old Spice Aftershave Lotion and rub the scuffmarks until they vanish.

- **Sharpie Fine Point Permanent Marker.** To cover up a tear in the leather where the color has been removed from the shoe, touch up the spot with a Sharpie Fine Point Permanent Marker in a matching color. Wipe with a clean, soft cloth and polish as usual.

- **Zippo Lighter Fluid.** To clean a black scuffmark from shoes, dampen a cotton ball with Zippo Lighter Fluid and softly rub the spot.

SHOELACES

- **Elmer's Glue-All.** When the ends of shoelaces become frayed, dip the frayed end in Elmer's Glue-All, twist into a point, and let dry.

- **Revlon Clear Nail Enamel.** If the plastic tips fall off your shoelaces, twist the frayed end, dip it in Revlon Clear Nail Enamel, and let dry.

- **Revlon Clear Nail Enamel.** To prevent the metal eyelets on your sneakers from making black marks on your white shoelaces, remove the laces, give the eyelets a protective coat of Revlon Clear Nail Enamel, let dry, and replace the laces.

SNEAKERS

- **Cascade.** To clean dirty white sneakers, make a paste from Cascade Powder and hot water, apply the paste to the footwear, let sit for thirty minutes, and scrub with a clean, old toothbrush. Rinse well and let dry.

- **Faultless Spray Starch.** To keep white sneakers white, spray the clean sneakers with a few coats of Faultless Spray Starch.

- **Krazy Glue.** If the rubber sole of your sneaker is beginning to flap loose, reattach the sole with Krazy Glue.

- **Mr. Clean Magic Eraser.** To clean sneakers, saturate a Mr. Clean Magic Eraser with water, squeeze out the excess water, and rub the sneakers.
- **Play-Doh.** To clean grime from sneakers, roll a ball of white Play-Doh on the canvas to absorb and erase the stains. Noah and Joseph McVicker originally invented Play-Doh as a kneadable wallpaper cleaner.
- **Scotchgard Fabric Protector.** To prevent sneakers from getting soiled, spray the clean sneakers with a few coats of Scotchgard Fabric Protector.

STRETCHING

- **Ziploc Freezer Bags.** To stretch the toe area of a pair of shoes or boots that are too tight, slip a Ziploc Freezer Bag into each shoe, fill each bag with water making sure the toe area of the shoe is filled, and seal both bags securely shut. Place each shoe inside its own Ziploc Freezer Bag and secure the two outer bags shut. Place the pair of bagged shoes in the freezer for twenty-four hours. Let the shoes defrost to room temperature and remove all the plastic bags. As the water freezes to ice, the water molecules expand, stretching the leather shoes.

SUEDE

- **Quaker Oats.** To clean soiled suede shoes, use a clean cloth to rub Quaker Oats into the stain in a circulation motion. Brush clean with a suede brush.
- **Resolve Carpet Cleaner.** To clean soiled suede shoes, sprays Resolve Carpet Cleaner on the shoes, let sit for ten minutes, brush with a wet tooth-brush, and let air dry.

VINYL OR PLASTIC SHOES

- **Arm & Hammer Baking Soda** and **Murphy Oil Soap.** To clean vinyl or plastic shoes, mix one-quarter cup Arm & Hammer Baking Soda, one teaspoon Murphy Oil Soap, and one-quarter cup water in a bowl. Using a sponge, wash the vinyl or plastic with the solution, rinse well, and dry with a soft, clean cloth.

- **Zippo Lighter Fluid.** To clean a black scuffmark from vinyl or plastic shoes, dampen a cotton ball with Zippo Lighter Fluid and softly rub the spot until the marks disappear.

WHITE LEATHER

- **Arm & Hammer Baking Soda.** To clean any scuffmarks off white leather shoes before polishing, apply a paste made from Arm & Hammer Baking Soda and water and scrub with a sponge. Rinse clean with a damp sponge and dry.

- **Colgate Regular Flavor Toothpaste.** To clean a scuffmark from white leather shoes, apply a dab of Colgate Regular Flavor Toothpaste to a clean, old toothbrush and brush off the scuffmark.

- **Johnson's Baby Powder.** To remove excess shoe polish after polishing white shoes, sprinkle some Johnson's Baby Powder on the shoes and buff with a soft, clean cloth. The baby powder absorbs the surplus polish.

- **Liquid Paper.** Cover up stubborn scuffmarks on leather shoes with a little Liquid Paper. Let dry and polish the shoes as usual.

- **Murphy Oil Soap.** To keep white shoes white, scrub any stains with a few drops of Murphy Oil Soap and a clean, old toothbrush.

- **Sanford Art Gum Eraser.** Before polishing white leather shoes, clean any scuffmarks off the shoes by rubbing with a Sanford Art Gum Eraser.

- **Westley's Bleche-Wite Tire Cleaner.** To clean white leather shoes or sneakers, place the sneakers outside on a few sheets of newspaper, spray the sneakers with Westley's Bleche-Wite Tire Cleaner (a bleaching product for whitewall tires), let sit for five minutes, and wipe with a soft, clean rag. Rinse the shoes thoroughly (including the soles) to remove all the bleaching product and let dry.

Walls and Wallpaper

BRICK

- **Clorox Bleach.** To clean stains off a brick wall, mix three-quarters cup Clorox Bleach and one gallon water and (wearing rubber gloves) use a sponge to wipe the solution on the brick, making sure not to get any of the mixture on carpeting or furniture.
- **Pink Pearl Eraser.** Remove stray black marks from bricks by rubbing with a Pink Pearl Eraser.
- **Scrubbing Bubbles.** To clean stains from a brick wall, spray the bricks with Scrubbing Bubbles, let sit for ten minutes, and rinse clean.

CLEANSERS

- **Bon Ami.** Restore woodwork painted white to a brilliant white by applying dye-free Bon Ami with a sponge, brush, or cloth and a little water.

- **Parsons' Ammonia** and **Dawn Dishwashing Liquid.** Mix one cup Parsons' Ammonia, one teaspoon Dawn Dishwashing Liquid, and one gallon warm water in a bucket. Dampen a large natural sponge with this solution and wipe down the walls. Rinse with water and let dry.

- **Parsons' Ammonia, Heinz White Vinegar,** and **Arm & Hammer Super Washing Soda.** Mix one-half cup Parsons' Ammonia, one-quarter cup Heinz White Vinegar, one-quarter cup Arm & Hammer Super Washing Soda, and one gallon warm water in a bucket. Dampen a large natural sponge with this solution and wipe down the walls. Rinse with water and let dry.

- **ReaLemon, Dawn Dishwashing Liquid, Arm & Hammer Baking Soda,** and **20 Mule Team Borax.** For a great homemade cleanser for walls, mix two tablespoons ReaLemon lemon juice, one-half teaspoon Dawn Dishwashing Liquid, one tablespoon Arm & Hammer Baking Soda, one teaspoon 20 Mule Team Borax, and two cups water in a sixteen-ounce trigger-spray bottle. Shake well.

CRAYON

- **Arm & Hammer Baking Soda.** To clean crayon marks from walls or wallpaper, sprinkle some Arm & Hammer Baking Soda on a damp sponge and rub gently.

- **Colgate Regular Flavor Toothpaste.** To clean crayon marks from walls or wallpaper, squeeze a dollop of Colgate Regular Flavor Toothpaste on a damp, soft, clean cloth, and rub the marks.

- **Mr. Clean Magic Eraser.** To clean crayon marks from walls, dampen a Mr. Clean Magic Eraser with water and rub the crayon marks gently to avoid removing the shine from walls painted with semi-gloss, satin, and glossy paint.

- **Pledge.** Spritz crayon marks on wallpaper with Pledge furniture polish and wipe with a soft, clean cloth. The marks come right off.

- **S.O.S Steel Wool Soap Pad.** To clean crayon marks from wallpaper, gently rub the marks with a dry S.O.S. Steel Wool Soap Pad.

- **Spray 'n Wash.** Spray a little Spray 'n Wash stain remover on the crayon mark, let sit for five minutes, and wipe clean.

- **WD-40, Bounty Paper Towels,** and **Dawn Dishwashing Liquid.** Spray crayon marks on walls with WD-40 and wipe off with a sheet of Bounty Paper Towels. Then wash off the WD-40 with a soft, cloth dampened with soapy water made with a few drops of Dawn Dishwashing Liquid.

ELECTRICAL OUTLET COVERS

- **Scotch-Brite Heavy Duty Scrub Sponge.** To remove latex paint from electrical outlet covers, remove the outlet covers from the wall, soak in a sink full of water for one hour, and then scrub lightly with a Scotch-Brite Heavy Duty Scrub Sponge.

GREASE SPOTS

- **Bounty Paper Towels.** Place a sheet of Bounty Paper Towels over the grease stain and press gently with a warm iron. The heat from the iron melts the grease, and the quicker-picker-upper absorbs it.

- **Kingsford's Corn Starch.** To clean grease spots from walls, make a paste from Kingsford's Corn Starch and water, apply the paste to the grease stain, and let dry. Brush clean.

HAIR SPRAY BUILDUP

- **Mr. Clean Magic Eraser.** To clean hair spray buildup from walls, gently rub the fixative spray with a damp Mr. Clean Magic Eraser.

- **Parsons' Ammonia.** To clean hair spray from wallpaper, saturate a soft, clean cloth with Parsons' Ammonia and wipe the wallpaper.

INK AND MARKERS

- **Alberto VO5 Hair Spray.** To remove ink spots from walls, spray Alberto VO5 Hair Spray on the affected area and blot with a paper towel or cotton swab until the stain disappears. The acetone in Alberto VO5 Hair Spray removes indelible marker and ballpoint pen marks from walls.

- **Colgate Regular Flavor Toothpaste.** Some types of ink can be removed from walls by squeezing a dab of Colgate Regular Flavor Toothpaste on a clean, old toothbrush and briskly brushing the ink mark.

- **Mr. Clean Magic Eraser.** To clean magic marker, permanent ink, and ballpoint ink from virtually any surface, gently rub the stains with a damp Mr. Clean Magic Eraser.

- **Old Spice Aftershave Lotion.** To clean indelible ink from any hard surface, saturate a cotton ball with Old Spice Aftershave Lotion and wipe clean.

- **Purell Instant Hand Sanitizer.** Saturate an ink stain on the wall with Purell Instant Hand Sanitizer and blot with a paper towel or soft cloth. Repeat as many times as necessary until the ink stain vanishes.

- **Spray 'n Wash** and **Dawn Dishwashing Liquid.** Apply a little Spray 'n Wash stain remover to the ink stain, let sit for five minutes, rub gently with a few drops of Dawn Dishwashing Liquid on a damp sponge, rinse, and blot well.

KITCHEN WALLS

- **Con-Tact Paper.** To prevent stains on the wallpaper behind your oven range, clean the wallpaper thoroughly, let dry, and then paper over it with clear, washable Con-Tact Paper.

MARKS

- **Arm & Hammer Baking Soda.** To clean marks from walls, sprinkle some Arm & Hammer Baking Soda on a damp sponge and rub gently.

- **Bon Ami.** To clean scuffmarks from walls, sprinkle Bon Ami on a damp cloth or sponge and gently rub the spot clean.

- **Kiwi Shoe Polish.** Use a few dabs of white Kiwi Shoe Polish to cover up scuffmarks on a white wall.

- **Liquid Paper.** To cover up a scuffmark on a white wall, paint over the mark with Liquid Paper, also available in a wide range of colors.

- **Mr. Clean Magic Eraser.** To clean scuffmarks from walls, rub the scuffmark with a damp Mr. Clean Magic Eraser gently to avoid removing the shine from walls painted with semi-gloss, satin, and glossy paint.

- **Sanford Art Gum Eraser.** To clean marks from a wall, rub with a Sanford Art Gum Eraser. Gum erasers gently crumble as they work.

- **Wonder Bread.** Remove the crust from a slice of Wonder Bread and rub the bread over the smudges or marks on the wall. The dirt and grime falls off with the breadcrumbs.

MOLD AND MILDEW

- **Clorox Bleach.** To kill mold or mildew, mix five teaspoons Clorox Bleach and two cups warm water in a sixteen-ounce trigger-spray bottle. Wearing rubber gloves and protective eyewear (and making sure the room is well ventilated), spray the solution on the mold or mildew. Let sit until the color vanishes, rinse clean with water, and let dry. (Test on an inconspicuous spot first to make sure the bleach doesn't lighten the surface.)

- **Hydrogen Peroxide.** To kill mildew, mix two tablespoons Hydrogen Peroxide in one gallon water and wipe the surface with the solution. (Test on an inconspicuous spot first to make sure the Hydrogen Peroxide doesn't bleach the surface.)

NAIL HOLES

- **Arm & Hammer Baking Soda** and **Elmer's Glue-All.** If you're all out of plaster of Paris to fill a nail hole left in the wall, mix a paste from Arm & Hammer Baking Soda and Elmer's Glue-All and patch away.

- **Colgate Regular Flavor Toothpaste.** In a pinch, you can patch a nail hole in a white wall with Colgate Regular Flavor Toothpaste.

- **Marshmallow Fluff.** In a pinch, use a small dab of Marshmallow Fluff to spackle small holes in plaster walls. Let dry thoroughly before painting.

PANELING

- **Heinz White Vinegar** and **Star Olive Oil.** To wash wood paneling, mix one teaspoon Heinz White Vinegar, one teaspoon Star Olive Oil, and one quart water in a bucket. Saturate a soft, clean cloth in the solution, wring it out, and wipe the walls. Buff with a soft, clean cloth.

- **Kiwi Shoe Polish.** Touch up scratches and spots on paneling with a dab of a matching shade of Kiwi Shoe Polish. Buff.

- **Kraft Mayo.** To clean wood paneling discolored by water, cover the water stain with Kraft Mayo, let sit overnight, and wipe clean.

- **Lipton Tea Bags.** Brew two Lipton Tea Bags in one quart boiling water and let cool to room temperature. Dampen a soft, clean cloth in the tea, wring out well, and wipe the wood paneling, barely dampening it and keeping the cloth clean. Buff dry with a soft cloth.

- **ReaLemon.** After washing wood walls, mix three tablespoons ReaLemon lemon juice and one quart water and rinse the walls with the lemony solution. Lemon juice cleans grease and leaves a fresh scent.

WALLPAPER

- **Arm & Hammer Baking Soda.** To clean stains from wallpaper, sprinkle some Arm & Hammer Baking Soda on a damp sponge and rub gently.

- **Crayola Chalk.** Rub a stick of white Crayola Chalk over stains on wallpaper and wipe with a soft, clean cloth.

- **Kingsford's Corn Starch.** To clean grease stains from wallpaper, make a paste from Kingsford's Corn Starch and water, apply to the spot, let dry, and brush clean. Repeat if necessary. Cornstarch absorbs grease.

- **Murphy Oil Soap.** Mix one-quarter cup Murphy Oil Soap and two gallons water in a bucket, wash the walls with the sudsy solution, rinse clean, and dry.

- **Parsons' Ammonia.** Mix one-half cup Parsons' Ammonia and one gallon water, saturate a sponge in the solution, and wipe the wallpaper. Rinse well and dry.

- **Play-Doh.** Roll a ball of white Play-Doh over any stains or marks on wallpaper. The Play-Doh works like a gentle eraser.

- **Sanford Art Gum Eraser.** To clean marks from wallpaper, gently rub a Sanford Art Gum Eraser on the wallpaper. Gum erasers gently crumble as they work.

- **Wonder Bread.** Remove the crust from a slice of Wonder Bread and rub the bread over the smudges or marks on the wallpaper. The dirt and grime wipes falls off with the breadcrumbs.

WALLPAPER GLUE

- **Marshmallow Fluff.** If the corners of the wallpaper start peeling off the wall, adhere the wallpaper back in place with a small dab of Marshmallow Fluff, which works like glue.

- **Minute Rice.** To make a rice glue to adhere peeling corners of wallpaper back in place, mix one-half cup Minute Rice and one-half cup water, stirring until the mixture attains the consistency of glue.

Washing Machines

BLEACH DISPENSERS

- **Dawn Dishwashing Liquid.** Remove any removable parts from the bleach dispenser and wash clean with warm water and a few drops of Dawn Dishwashing Liquid.

CLEANING

- **Arm & Hammer Baking Soda.** To clean the outside of a washing machine, sprinkle Arm & Hammer Baking Soda on a damp sponge and wipe the surface.
- **Clorox Bleach** and **Heinz White Vinegar.** If your whites are coming out gray, clean the washing machine by filling it with hot water and adding one quart Clorox Bleach. Run the machine through the longest cycle, and immediately upon completion of that cycle, repeat with one quart Heinz White Vinegar (instead of the bleach).

- **Heinz White Vinegar.** If you don't have time to clean your washer thoroughly with Clorox Bleach followed by Heinz White Vinegar (see previous tip), fill the machine with hot water, add two cups Heinz White Vinegar, and run through the regular wash cycle. The vinegar cleans the soap scum from the hoses and shines the agitator and tub.

- **Pam Cooking Spray.** To move a washing machine without scratching up the vinyl, linoleum, or tile floor, spray the floor in front of the washing machine with a small amount of Pam Cooking Spray so it glides easily.

- **Turtle Wax.** To keep the exterior of your machine shiny clean, apply Turtle Wax and shine with a clean, soft cloth.

DETERGENT

- **Arm & Hammer Washing Super Soda.** To minimize detergent residue on clothes and the interior of your washing machine, use half the amount of detergent that you usually use and add one-half cup Arm & Hammer Super Washing Soda.

- **Heinz White Vinegar.** To eliminate detergent residue on clothes, add one-quarter cup Heinz White Vinegar to the final rinse cycle.

FABRIC SOFTENER DISPENSERS

- **Heinz White Vinegar.** Warm one cup Heinz White Vinegar and pour it into the washer's fabric softener dispenser (without any clothes in the machine). Run the machine through the regular cycle. The vinegar clears gunked-up fabric softener from the machine. If the fabric softener dispenser is hopelessly clogged, remove it from the machine and soak it in a bowl of Heinz White Vinegar overnight.

HARD WATER

- **Arm & Hammer Super Washing Soda.** To prevent soap scum from forming in the washing machine due to hard water, add one-half cup Arm & Hammer Super Washing Soda as the machine fills with water, and then add your regular detergent. Washing soda softens hard water, reducing the amount of detergent needed.

Powdered Laundry Detergent Scooper

- **Clorox Bleach** and **Revlon Red Nail Enamel.** To make a measuring scooper for adding the right amount of powdered laundry detergent to your wash load, avoiding a soapy mess, cut a clean, empty Clorox Bleach bottle in half diagonally toward the handle, add one cup of your regular powdered laundry detergent, gently shake the scooper to make the powder level, and mark the level with a line of Revlon Red Nail Enamel.

Sanitizing and Disinfecting

- **Clorox Bleach.** To sanitize the inside of a washing machine, run one cup Clorox Bleach through the regular rinse cycle without any clothes in the machine.

- **Listerine.** To disinfect the inside of a washing machine, run one cup Listerine antiseptic mouthwash through the regular cycle without any clothes in the machine.

Suds

- **Downy Fabric Softener.** If your washing machine is overflowing with suds because you accidentally added too much detergent, stop the  machine, add the typical amount of Downy Fabric Softener as directed on the bottle, and restart the machine. In a few minutes, the amount of suds will diminish.

- **Morton Salt.** If you put too much detergent in your washing machine, creating a tub full of suds, stop the machine, pour in one-half cup Morton Salt, and restart the machine. The suds will subside within a few minutes.

Windows and Curtains

Aerosol Snow

- **Heinz White Vinegar.** To remove aerosol snow from windows, use a sponge to apply Heinz White Vinegar to the snow, scrub with a firm brush, and wipe clean with a rag. Rinse well.

- **Parsons' Ammonia.** Mix one cup Parsons' Ammonia and three cups warm water, apply the solution with a sponge to the snow, scrub with a brush, and wipe clean. Rinse well.

Air Conditioners

- **Forster Clothespins.** To keep drapes from being blown in front of an air conditioner, clip several Forster Clothespins to the inside of the drapes to distance them from the air conditioner.

BLINDS

- **Bounce.** Wipe the dust from blinds with a clean, used sheet of Bounce. The antistatic elements in the Bounce sheet prevent the dust from resettling as quickly.

- **Glad Trash Bags** and **Resolve Carpet Cleaner.** To clean fabric blinds, slice open the sides of Glad Trash Bags to make long sheets and tape up the plastic behind the blinds and on the floor to protect the windows and the carpeting. Spray the blinds with Resolve Carpet Cleaner, let dry, and vacuum off any residue.

- **Huggies Baby Wipes.** To clean dust from blinds, use a Huggies Baby Wipe to wipe each slat.

- **Pledge.** To clean wood blinds, wipe each slat with a soft cloth sprayed with Pledge furniture polish and buff dry with a second soft, clean cloth to absorb any excess polish.

- **Scrubbing Bubbles.** To clean grease and grime from blinds, spray the blinds with Scrubbing Bubbles and wipe clean with a soft, clean cloth.

- **Tide.** To clean filthy metal, vinyl, or plastic blinds, remove the blinds from the window, lay them flat outside, and sponge them with a solution made from one-quarter cup liquid Tide and one gallon water. Hose the blinds clean and let air dry.

CHAMOIS

- **Star Olive Oil.** To soften a window chamois, fill a bucket with warm water, add one teaspoon Star Olive Oil, and soak the chamois in the solution for ten minutes, stirring occasionally.

CLEANING SOLUTIONS

- **Heinz White Vinegar.** To make homemade window cleaner, mix equal parts Heinz White Vinegar and water in a trigger-spray bottle.

Keep It Clean
WINDOW WASHING

- Buy a good quality squeegee.

- The best time to clean your windows is on a cool or cloudy day. If you clean windows in direct sunlight, you will get streaks on the windows.

- Fill a bucket with lukewarm water and add two tablespoons ammonia. Use a sponge with a white abrasive scrubber on one side (not green; they're too abrasive). Dip the sponge in the bucket, wet the window with the sponge side, and scrub the window with the white side to remove any film or rough patches.

- Using a clean, white cotton cloth, dry a one-inch vertical strip of glass along the top of the window. (The dry rubber blade of the squeegee must start on dry glass to avoid streaks.)

- Place the dry rubber blade of the squeegee now at the top of the window in the one-inch dry strip. Pull the squeegee down to the bottom of the glass in one smooth stroke.

- Dry the squeegee blade before starting the second stroke. Repeat until you finish the window.

- If necessary, complete the window with one last stroke from left to right at the bottom of the glass.

- Run a dry, clean cloth along the sides and bottom edge of the window.

- **Kingsford's Corn Starch.** Dissolve one cup Kingsford's Corn Starch in one gallon warm water. Dampen a sponge with the solution, wipe the window, and buff dry with a soft, clean, lint-free cloth.

- **Murphy Oil Soap** and **Heinz White Vinegar.** To make a powerful window cleanser, mix one-half teaspoon Murphy Oil Soap, three tablespoons Heinz White Vinegar, and two cups water in a sixteen-ounce trigger-spray bottle.

- **ReaLemon.** Saturate a soft, clean rag with ReaLemon lemon juice and rub it on the windows.

Cotton Curtains

- **Faultless Spray Starch.** To give cotton curtains body, spray them with Faultless Spray Starch.

Curtain Rods

- **Playtex Living Gloves.** To thread sheer curtains on a rod without continuously snagging the fabric, cut off one finger from a pair of clean, old Playtex Living Gloves and put it over the end of the curtain rod. The curtain will slide onto the rod with ease.

- **Turtle Wax.** To make curtains slide across the curtain rod with ease, give the curtain rod a coat of Turtle Wax.

Drapery Hooks

- **Ivory Soap.** To make drapery hooks easy to insert into fabric, push the pointed end of the hook into a bar of Ivory Soap and then insert it into the fabric. The soap lubricates the hook.

- **Revlon Red Nail Enamel.** Before removing drapery hooks from drapery to send the drapes to the dry cleaners, mark the spots on the fabric with Revlon Red Nail Enamel so you'll know exactly where to reinsert the hooks afterward.

Drying

- **USA Today.** To dry wet windows, crumple up a ball from a page of *USA Today* and wipe dry.

FINGERPRINTS

- **Coca-Cola.** To clean the oil from fingerprints and handprints from windows, saturate a sponge or soft, clean cloth with Coca-Cola and wipe the windows clean. Rinse and dry.

LUBRICATION

- **Ivory Soap.** To lubricate a window frame to allow the window to slide up and down easily, rub a bar of Ivory Soap along the tracks.

MINERAL DEPOSITS

- **Arm & Hammer Baking Soda.** To clean mineral deposits off windows, sprinkle Arm & Hammer Baking Soda on a wet rag and rub gently. Then wash the windows as usual.

- **Easy-Off Oven Cleaner.** To clean stubborn mineral deposits from the outsides of windows, spray with Easy-Off Oven Cleaner, let sit for five minutes, wipe clean, and rinse thoroughly.

- **McCormick Alum** and **Heinz White Vinegar.** Mix one teaspoon McCormick Alum and one-quarter cup Heinz White Vinegar; saturate a clean, soft cloth with the mixture; and rub the mineral deposits. Rinse well and dry.

- **Morton Salt.** To scrub mineral deposits off windows, dissolve six tablespoons Morton Salt in one cup cold water. Saturate a sponge with the salty water, scrub the mineral deposits, and wipe clean. Rinse thoroughly and dry.

NET CURTAINS

- **Revlon Clear Nail Enamel.** To repair tears in net curtains, paint some Revlon Clear Nail Enamel to rejoin the netting.

Paint

- **Cutex Nail Polish Remover.** To remove paint from window glass, saturate a cotton ball with Cutex Nail Polish Remover and rub it on the paint. Carefully scrape clean with a single-edge razor blade.

Scratches

- **Colgate Regular Flavor Toothpaste.** To remove superficial scratches from a picture window, rub a dab of Colgate Regular Flavor Toothpaste on the scratch and wipe clean with a soft cloth.

- **Turtle Wax Rubbing Compound.** Using a slightly dampened sponge, apply Turtle Wax Rubbing Compound to scratches on a picture window and wipe clean with a soft, clean cloth.

Screens

- **Parsons' Ammonia, Arm & Hammer Baking Soda,** and **Dawn Dishwashing Liquid.** To clean window screens, mix one-quarter cup Parsons' Ammonia, two tablespoons Arm & Hammer Baking Soda, and two tablespoons Dawn Dishwashing Liquid in a bucket of warm water. Using a sponge, wash the window screen with the solution, rinse the screen clean with a garden hose, and stand to dry in the sun.

- **Scrubbing Bubbles.** To clean wire screens (not nylon), spray Scrubbing Bubbles on the screens, let sit for five minutes, rinse clean with a garden hose, and let air dry.

- **Tide.** To clean window screens, remove the screens from the window, lay them flat outside, and sponge them with a solution made from one-quarter cup liquid Tide and one gallon water. Hose the screens clean and let air dry.

SHADES

- **Play-Doh.** Roll a ball of white Play-Doh over any stains or marks on a window shade. The Play-Doh works like a gentle eraser.

SHUTTERS

- **Bounce.** To clean plantation shutters, open up the shutter and wipe the louvers from the back side with a clean, used sheet of Bounce. The anti-static elements in the dryer sheet help collect the dust, and the residue will help prevent dust from adhering to the shutters.

WINDOW SILLS

- **Turtle Wax.** To hide nicks and pits in a wooden or an aluminum windowsill, wax the windowsill with Turtle Wax.

Workshops

CHISELS

- **Wilson Tennis Balls.** To store a chisel so the blades don't dull, cut a small slit in a Wilson Tennis Ball and insert the blade into the rubber ball.

CIRCULAR-SAW BLADES

- **Easy-Off Oven Cleaner.** To clean a saw blade gummed up with sap, put on rubber gloves and eye protection, spray the blade with Easy-Off Oven Cleaner in a well ventilated area, wait twenty minutes, rinse, and dry.

CLEANING

- **Colgate Regular Flavor Toothpaste.** To clean your tools, squeeze a dollop of Colgate Regular Flavor Toothpaste on a soft cloth, rub the tool, rinse, and dry.

- **Crisco All-Vegetable Shortening.** To clean and preserve the wooden handles of tools, rub a dab of Crisco All-Vegetable Shortening into the wood, and then buff with a soft, clean cloth.

FILES

- **Crayola Chalk.** To prevent the grooves in a metal file from getting blocked, rub a stick of white Crayola Chalk across the file.
- **Scotch Packaging Tape.** To clean metal shavings from a metal file, adhere a piece of Scotch Packaging Tape over the length of the file, press firmly, and then peel off. The shavings will stick to the tape.

FUNNELS

- **Clorox Bleach.** To create a homemade funnel and prevent a mess when pouring liquids, cut a clean, empty Clorox Bleach bottle in half and remove the cap.

GLUE

- **Vaseline Petroleum Jelly.** To prevent the cap from sticking to a tube of glue, rub a dab of Vaseline Petroleum Jelly around the threads on the rim of the tube.

GOGGLES

- **Bounce.** To prevent sawdust from sticking to safety goggles, wipe the goggles with a clean, used sheet of Bounce. The antistatic elements in Bounce eliminate the static electricity.

KNEE PADS

- **Bubble Wrap** and **Scotch Packaging Tape.** When cleaning up in the workshop, improvise knee pads by folding two sheets of Bubble

Wrap to form cushions and taping them around each knee with strips of Scotch Packaging Tape.

NAILS AND SCREWS

- **Cool Whip.** To store loose screws, bolt, nuts, and nails, use clean, empty Cool Whip canisters in the workshop.

- **Huggies Baby Wipes.** Use empty Huggies Baby Wipes boxes to hold loose screws, bolts, nuts, nails, drill bits, and spare parts.

- **Maxwell House Coffee.** A clean, empty Maxwell House Coffee can make an excellent storage container for nails, screws, and other loose parts.

- **Ziploc Storage Bags.** To pick up spilled nails or screws, place a magnet inside a Ziploc Storage Bag, hold the bag over the spill, and then turn the bag inside-out to capture them.

PAINTBRUSHES

- **Downy Fabric Softener.** To keep paintbrushes soft, after washing off the paint, rinse the paintbrush in a bucket of water mixed with one capful Downy Fabric Softener.

- **Heinz White Vinegar.** To clean hardened paint off a paintbrush, soak the paintbrush in Heinz White Vinegar overnight, and then soak the paintbrush in soapy water.

PLIERS

- **ChapStick.** To lubricate a pair of pliers, rub ChapStick lip balm over the pivot joint of the tool.

- **Crisco All-Vegetable Shortening.** A dab of Crisco All-Vegetable Shortening can be used to lubricate the pivot joint of pliers.

- **Vaseline Petroleum Jelly.** Lubricate the pin of your pliers with Vaseline Petroleum Jelly.

Rust

- **Arm & Hammer Baking Soda.** To clean rust from tools, mix a thick paste of Arm & Hammer Baking Soda and water and rub the paste on the tool with a damp sponge. Rinse and dry thoroughly.

- **Coca-Cola.** To clean rust from a tool, soak the tool in Coca-Cola overnight. In the morning, rinse clean and dry well.

- **Heinz White Vinegar.** To clean rust from tools, soak tools in Heinz White Vinegar overnight. In the morning, rinse and dry thoroughly. The acetic acid in vinegar dissolves rust.

- **Kool-Aid.** Soaking tools in Kool-Aid and then scrubbing well cleans rust.

- **Pam Cooking Spray.** To prevent tools from rusting, spray the clean tools with a light coat of Pam Cooking Spray, rub with a soft cloth, and wipe off the excess oil.

- **Turtle Wax.** To protect metal tools from rust, give the metal a coat of Turtle Wax and let dry.

Sawdust

- **Bounce.** Wipe up sawdust effortlessly with a clean, used sheet of Bounce. The antistatic elements in the dryer sheet attract sawdust with the efficiency of a tack cloth.

Saws

- **Ivory Soap.** Rub a bar of Ivory Soap across the sides and teeth of the handsaw to help the saw blade glide through wood and prevent sap from sticking to the blade.

Shop Aprons

- **Glad Trash Bags.** To make a shop apron, cut holes in a Glad Trash Bag for your head and arms and wear it.

Shop Vacuums

- **Glad Trash Bags.** To make emptying the debris from a shop vacuum easier, line the inside of the vacuum with a large Glad Trash Bag, folding the top edge of the bag over the rim to hold it in place.
- **L'eggs Sheer Energy Panty Hose.** To avoid having to clean the filter in a shop vacuum frequently, cut off one leg from a clean, used pair of L'eggs Sheer Energy Panty Hose and pull it securely over the pleated paper filter, creating a protective sheath.

Toolboxes

- **Bubble Wrap.** To cushion your tools and prevent them from getting damaged when you carry your toolbox, line the bottom of your toolbox with a sheet of Bubble Wrap.
- **Crayola Chalk.** To help prevent tools from rusting, place a few sticks of Crayola Chalk in your toolbox. The chalk absorbs moisture that would otherwise cause the tools to rust.
- **Kingsford Charcoal.** To prevent tools from rusting, place a couple of Kingsford Charcoal briquettes in your toolbox. The briquettes absorb excess moisture.

Acknowledgments

At Rodale, I am grateful to my editor, Karen Bolesta, for her passion, enthusiasm, and excitement for this book. I am also deeply indebted to my agent Stephanie Tade, researcher Debbie Green, expert copy editor Jennifer Bright Reich, project editor Lois Hazel, designer Christina Gaugler, layout designer Faith Hague, and ace illustrator and cartoonist Terry LaBan.

A very special thanks to my manager, Barb North, and the hundreds of people who have visited my website and taken the time to send me emails sharing their ingenious tips for brand-name products we all know and love.

Above all, all my love to Debbie, Ashley, and Julia.

The Fine Print

All-New Hints from Heloise by Heloise (New York: Perigee, 1989)

Another Use For by Vicki Lansky (Deephaven, Minnesota: Book Peddlers, 1991)

Ask Anne & Nan by Anne Adams and Nancy Walker (Brattleboro, Vermont: Whetstone, 1989)

The Bag Book by Vicki Lansky (Deephaven, Minnesota: Book Peddlers, 2000)

Baking Soda Bonanza by Peter A. Ciullo (New York: HarperPerrenial, 1995)

Bargain Beauty Secrets: Tips and Tricks for Looking Great and Feeling Fabulous by Diane Irons (Naperville, Illinois: Sourcebooks, 2002)

Beauty: The New Basics by Rona Berg, Anja Kroencke, and Deborah Jaffe (New York: Workman, 2001)

The Big Idea: How Business Innovators Get Great Ideas to Market by Steven D. Strauss (Chicago: Dearborn Trade, 2002)

"Cavity Protection or Cosmetic Perfection?" by Peter Miskell, *Business History Review*, Spring 2004

Clean & Green: The Complete Guide to Nontoxic and Environmentally Safe Housekeeping by Annie Berthold-Bond (Woodstock, New York: Ceres Press, 1990)

"Cleansing 'Triumphant Portal' Ceiling" by James Barron, *New York Times*, February 3, 1996

"Contraceptive Consumers: Gender and the Political Economy of Birth Control in the 1930s" by Andrea Tone, *Journal of Social History,* Volume 29, Number 3, Spring 1996, page 485

The Curse: A Cultural History of Menstruation by Janice Delaney, Mary Jane Lupton, and Emily Toth (Chicago: University of Illinois Press, 1998)

A Dash of Mustard by Katy Holder and Jane Newdick (London: Chartwell Books, 1995)

The Doctors Book of Home Remedies by Editors of *Prevention* Magazine (Emmaus, Pennsylvania: Rodale Press, 1990)

The Doctors Book of Home Remedies II by Sid Kirchheimer and the Editors of *Prevention* Magazine (Emmaus, Pennsylvania: Rodale Press, 1993)

Great Gardening Formulas, edited by Joan Benjamin and Deborah L. Martin (Emmaus, Pennsylvania: Rodale, 1998)

"Hal Mason, Animator, Dies; Created Famous Characters," *UPI*, October 13, 1986

Haley's Hints by Graham and Rosemary Haley (New York: New American Library, 1995)

"A Hand for Mr. Clean" by Judy Stark, *St. Petersburg Times*, July 24, 2004

Healing Home Spa: Soothe Your Symptoms, East Your Pain, and Age-Proof Your Body with Pleasure Remedies by Valerie Gennari Cooksley (New York: Prentice Hall, 2003)

Heinerman's Encyclopedia of Healing Herbs & Spices by John Heinerman (West Nyack, New York: Parker Publishing, 1996)

Hints from Heloise by Heloise (New York: Arbor House, 1980)

A History of the City of Newark by Frank John Urquhard (Newark: Lewis Historical Publishing, 1913)

Home Spa: Recipes and Techniques to Restore and Refresh by Manine Rosa Golden (New York: Abbeville Press, 1997)

Home Spa: Top-to-Toe Beauty Treatments for Total Well-Being by Stephanie Donaldson (New York: Lorenz Books, 2002)

The Home Spa: Creating a Personal Sanctuary by Carol Endler Sterbenz (Kansas City: Andrews McMeel, 1999)

Household Hints & Formulas by Erik Bruun (New York: Black Dog and Leventhal, 1994)

Household Hints & Handy Tips by *Reader's Digest* (Pleasantville, New York: Reader's Digest, 1988)

Household Hints for Upstairs, Downstairs, and All Around the House by Carol Reese (New York: Henry Holt and Company, 1982)

How to Clean Practically Anything, Fourth Edition by the editors of Consumer Reports Books with Edward Kippel (Yonkers, New York: Consumer Reports Books, 1996)

Killer Brands: Create and Market a Brand That Will Annihilate the Competition by Frank Lane (Cincinnati, Ohio: Adams, 2007)

Make It Yourself by Dolores Riccio and Joan Bingham (Radnor, Pennsylvania: Chilton, 1978)

Martha Stewart's Homekeeping Handbook: The Essential Guide to Caring for Everything in Your Home by Martha Stewart (New York: Clarkson Potter, 2006)

Mary Ellen's Best of Helpful Hints by Mary Ellen Pinkham (New York: Warner/B. Lansky, 1979)

Mary Ellen's Clean House! by Mary Ellen Pinkham with Dale Burg (New York: Crown, 1993)

Mary Ellen's Greatest Hints by Mary Ellen Pinkham (New York: Fawcett Crest, 1990)

Natural Home Spa by Sian Rees (New York: Sterling, 1999)

New Choices in Natural Healing: Over 1,800 of the Best Self-Help Remedies from the World of Alternative Medicine by Bill Gottlieb (Emmaus, Pennsylvania: Rodale Books, 1997)

911 Beauty Secrets: An Emergency Guide to Looking Great at Every Age, Size, and Budget by Diane Irons (Naperville, Illinois: Sourcebooks, 1999)

1001 Hints & Tips for Your Garden by the editors of *Reader's Digest* (Pleasantville, New York: Reader's Digest, 1996)

1001 Ingenious Gardening Ideas, edited by Deborah L. Martin (Emmaus, Pennsylvania: Rodale, 1998)

1,628 Country Shortcuts From 1,628 Country People by the editors of *Country* and *Country Woman* magazines (Greendale, Wisconsin: Reiman Publications, 1996)

Popular Mechanics Home Answer Book, edited by Steven Willson (New York: Hearst Books, 1991)

Practical Problem Solver by *Reader's Digest* (Pleasantville, New York: Reader's Digest, 1991)

The Resourceful Gardener's Guide, edited by Christine Bucks and Fern Marshall Bradley (Emmaus, Pennsylvania: Rodale Press, 2001)

Rodale's Book of Hints, Tips & Everyday Wisdom by Carol Hupping, Cheryl Winters Tetreau, and Roger B. Yepsen, Jr. (Emmaus, Pennsylvania: Rodale Press, 1985)

The Spa Encyclopedia: A Guide to Treatments and Their Benefits for Health and Healing by Hannelore R. Leavy and Reinhard R. Bergel, Ph.D. (Clifton Park, New York: Delmar Learning, 2003)

Strange Stories, Amazing Facts by the Editors of *Reader's Digest* (Pleasantville, New York: Reader's Digest, 1976)

Sunset Western Garden Book by the editors of *Sunset* magazine (Menlo Park, California: Sunset, 1995)

Talking Dirty with the Queen of Clean by Linda Cobb (New York: Pocket Books, 1999)

Talking Dirty Laundry with the Queen of Clean by Linda Cobb (New York: Pocket Books, 2001)

Time Almanac Reference Edition 1994 by the Editors of *Time* magazine, (Washington, D.C.: Compact Publishing, 1994)

"Toothpaste Tempest," *Chemical Week*, August 22, 1964, pages 53-4.

"Turkish Barbers" by Sergeant William Treseder, *San Diego Reader*, June 4, 2008

"Under My Skin" by D.T. Max, *New York Times*, January 13, 2008

Vet on Call: The Best Home Remedies for Keeping Your Dog Healthy by Pets Part of the Family (Emmaus, Pennsylvania: Rodale, 1999)

What Really Matters: Service, Leadership, People, and Values by John Pepper (New Haven, Connecticut: Yale University Press, 2007)

The Woman's Day Help Book by Geraldine Rhoads and Edna Paradis (New York: Viking, 1988)

The World's Best-Kept Beauty Secrets by Diane Irons (Naperville, Illinois: Sourcebooks, 1997)

Trademark Information

"Adolph's" is a registered trademark of Unilever.

"Alberto VO5" is a registered trademark of Alberto-Culver USA, Inc.

"Arm & Hammer" and "Clean Shower" are registered trademarks of Church & Dwight Co, Inc.

"Aunt Jemima" is a registered trademark of the Quaker Oats Company.

"Bag Balm" is a registered trademark of Dairy Association Co., Inc.

"Balmex" is a registered trademark of Chattem, Inc.

"Band-Aid" is a registered trademark of Johnson & Johnson.

"Bar Keepers Friend" is a registered trademark of SerVaas Laboratories.

"Bausch & Lomb" is a registered trademark of Bausch & Lomb.

"Bayer" is a registered trademark of Bayer Corporation.

"Blue Bonnet" is a registered trademark of ConAgra Foods, Inc.

"Bon Ami" is a registered trademark of Bon Ami Company.

"Bounce" is a registered trademark of Procter & Gamble.

"Bounty" is a registered trademark of Procter & Gamble.

"Bubble Wrap" is a registered trademark of Sealed Air Corporation.

"Budweiser" is a registered trademark of Anheuser-Busch, Inc.

"Calgon" is a registered trademark of Reckitt Benckiser Inc.

"Campbell" is a registered trademark of Campbell Soup Company.

"Canada Dry" is a registered trademark of Cadbury Beverages Inc.

"Carbona" is a registered trademark of Delta Carbona, L.P.

"Carnation" and "Nestlé" are registered trademarks of Société des Produits Nestlé S.A., Vevey, Switzerland.

"Cascade" is a registered trademark of Procter & Gamble.

"ChapStick" is a registered trademark of A. H. Robbins Company.

"Cheerios" is a registered trademark of General Mills.

"Chicken of the Sea" is a registered trademark of Chicken of the Sea International.

"Clabber Girl" is a registered trademark of Clabber Girl Corporation.

"Clorox" is a registered trademark of the Clorox Company.

"Coca-Cola" and "Coke" are registered trademarks of the Coca-Cola Company.

"Coffee-mate" is a registered trademark of Nestlé.

"Colgate" is a registered trademark of Colgate-Palmolive.

"Colman's" is a registered trademark of World Finer Foods Inc.

"Comet" is a registered trademark of Procter & Gamble.

"Conair" is a registered trademarks of Conair Corporation.

"Con-Tact" is a registered trademark of Rubbermaid, Incorporated.

"Cool Whip" is a registered trademark of Kraft Foods.

"Coppertone" is a registered trademark of Schering-Plough HealthCare Products, Inc.

"Country Time" and "Country Time Lemonade" are registered trademarks of Kraft Foods.

"Crayola" is a registered trademark of Binney & Smith Inc.

"Crest" is a registered trademark of Procter & Gamble.

"Crisco" is a registered trademark of the J. M. Smucker Co.

"Cutex" is a registered trademark of MedTech.

"Dannon" is a registered trademark of the Dannon Company.

"Dawn" is a registered trademark of Procter & Gamble.

"Dial" is a registered trademark of Dial Corp.

"Dickinson's" is a registered trademark of Dickinson's Brands, Inc.

"Dixie" is a registered trademark of James River Corporation.

"Domino" is a registered trademark of Domino Foods, Inc.

"Dove" and "White Beauty" are registered trademarks of Unilever.

"Downy" is a registered trademark of Procter & Gamble.

"Dr Pepper" is a registered trademark of Dr Pepper/Seven Up, Inc.

"Easy-Off" is a registered trademark of Reckitt Benckiser Inc.

"Efferdent" is a registered trademark of Warner-Lambert.

"Elmer's Glue-All" and Elmer the Bull are registered trademarks of Borden.

"Endust" is a registered trademark of the Sara Lee Corporation.

"Ex-Lax" is a registered trademark of Novartis Consumer Health, Inc.

"Fantastik" is a registered trademark of S.C. Johnson & Son, Inc.

"Faultless" is a registered trademark of Faultless Starch/Bon Ami Company.

"Fels-Naptha" is a registered trademark of the Dial Corp.

"Formula 409" is a registered trademark of the Clorox Company.

"Forster" is a registered trademark of Diamond Brands, Inc.

"Frisbee" is a registered trademark of Mattel, Inc.

"Fruit of the Earth" is a registered trademark of Fruit of the Earth, Inc.

"Gatorade" is a registered trademark of the Gatorade Company.

"Gerber" is a registered trademark of Gerber Products Company.

"Gillette" is a registered trademark of Procter & Gamble.

"Glad" is a registered trademark of First Brands Corporation.

"Glade" is a registered trademark of S.C. Johnson & Son, Inc.

"Gold Medal" is a registered trademark of General Mills, Inc.

"Grandma's Molasses" is a registered trademark of B&G Foods, Inc.

"Hartz" is a registered trademark of Hartz Mountain Company.

"Heinz" is a registered trademark of H.J. Heinz Company.

"Hidden Valley" and "Original Ranch" are registered trademarks of the Clorox Company.

"Huggies" is a registered trademark of Kimberly-Clark Corporation.

"Hula Hoop" is a registered trademark of Wham-O Inc.

"Ivory" is a registered trademark of Procter & Gamble.

"Jell-O" is a registered trademark of Kraft Foods.

"Jet-Dry" is a registered trademark of Reckitt Benckiser, Inc.

"Jet-Puffed" is a registered trademark of Kraft Foods.

"Jonny Cat" is a registered trademark of Oil-Dri Corporation of America.

"Johnson's," "Johnson & Johnson," and "No More Tears" are registered trademarks of Johnson & Johnson.

"Joy" is a registered trademark of Procter & Gamble.

"Kingsford" is a registered trademark of Kingsford Products Company.

"Kingsford's" is a registered trademark of ACH Food Companies.

"Kiwi" is a registered trademark of Sara Lee Corporation.

"Kleenex" is a registered trademark of Kimberly-Clark Corporation.

"Kool-Aid" is a registered trademark of Kraft Foods.

"Kraft" is a registered trademark of Kraft Foods.

"Krazy" is a registered trademark of Borden, Inc.

"L'eggs" and "Sheer Energy" are registered trademarks of Hanesbrands, Inc.

"Land O Lakes" is a registered trademark of Land O Lakes, Inc.

"Lea & Perrins" is a registered trademark of H. J. Heinz Company.

"Lestoil" is a registered trademark of the Clorox Corporation.

"Lipton," "The 'Brisk' Tea," and "Flo-Thru" are registered trademarks of Unilever.

"Liquid Paper" is a registered trademark of Liquid Paper Corporation.

"Listerine" is a registered trademark of Warner-Lambert.

"Lysol" is a registered trademark of Reckitt Benckiser Inc.

"Marshmallow Fluff" is a registered trademark of Durkee-Mower Inc.

"Massengill" is a registered trademark of SmithKlein Beecham.

"MasterCard" is a registered trademark of MasterCard International Incorporated.

"Maxwell House" and "Good to the Last Drop" are registered trademarks of Kraft Foods.

"McCormick" is a registered trademark of McCormick & Company, Inc.

"Minute" is a registered trademark of Riviana Foods Inc.

"Miracle Whip" is a registered trademark of Kraft Foods.

"Mop & Glo" is a registered trademark of Reckitt Benckiser, Inc.

"Morton" is a registered trademark of Morton International, Inc.

"Mott's" is a registered trademark of Mott's Inc.

"Mr. Bubble" is a registered trademark of The Village Company, LLC.

"Mr. Clean" and "Magic Eraser" are registered trademarks of Procter & Gamble.

"Mr. Coffee" is a registered trademark of Mr. Coffee, Inc.

"Mrs. Stewart's" is a registered trademark of Luther & Ford, Company.

"Murphy" is a registered trademark of Colgate-Palmolive Company.

"Nabisco" is a registered trademark of Kraft Foods.

"Nestea" and "Nestlé" are registered trademarks of Société des Produits Nestlé S.A., Vevey, Switzerland.

"Nivea" is a registered trademark of Beiersdorf AG.

"Noxzema" is a registered trademark of Procter & Gamble.

"Odorzout" is a registered trademark of No Stink, Inc.

"Old English" is a registered trademark of Reckitt Benckiser, Inc.

"Old Spice" is a registered trademark of Procter & Gamble.

"Oral-B" is a registered trademark of Oral-B Laboratories.

"Palmolive" is a registered trademark of Colgate-Palmolive.

"Pam" is a registered trademark of American Home Foods.

"Pampers" is a registered trademark of Procter & Gamble.

"Pantene" and "Pro-V" are registered trademarks of Procter & Gamble.

"Parsons'" is a registered trademark of Church & Dwight Co., Inc.

"Phillips'" is a registered trademark of Bayer HealthCare LLC.

"Pine-Sol" is a registered trademark of the Clorox Company.

"Pink Pearl" is a registered trademark of Sanford.

"Play-Doh" is a registered trademark of Hasbro, Inc.

"Playtex" and "Living" are registered trademarks of Playtex Products, Inc.

"Pledge" is a registered trademark of S.C. Johnson & Sons, Inc.

"Post-it" is a registered trademark of 3M.

"Preparation H" is a registered trademark of Whitehall-Robbins.

"Pringles" and "Potato Crisps" are registered trademarks of Procter & Gamble.

"Purell" is a registered trademark of Johnson & Johnson Consumer Companies, Inc.

"Q-tips" is a registered trademark of Chesebrough-Pond's USA Co.

"Quaker Oats" is a registered trademark of the Quaker Oats Company.

"ReaLemon" and "ReaLime" are registered trademarks of Borden.

"Resolve" is a registered trademark of Reckitt Benckiser Inc.

"Revlon" is a registered trademark of Revlon Consumer Products Corporation.

"Reynolds," "Reynolds Wrap," and "Cut-Rite" are registered trademarks of Reynolds Metals.

"Rit" is a registered trademark of BestFoods.

"SC Johnson" is a registered trademark of S.C. Johnson & Sons. Inc.

"S.O.S" is a registered trademark of the Clorox Company.

"Sanford" is a registered trademark of Sanford, a Newell Rubbermaid Company.

"Saran" and "Saran Wrap" are registered trademarks of S.C. Johnson & Sons, Inc.

"Scope" is a registered trademark of Procter & Gamble.

"Scotch," "Scotch-Brite," and "Scotchgard" are registered trademarks of 3M.

"Scrubbing Bubbles" is a registered trademark of S.C. Johnson & Sons, Inc.

"Sea Breeze" is a registered trademark of Sea Breeze.

"Sharpie" is a registered trademark of Sanford L.P.

"Shout" is a registered trademark of S.C. Johnson & Sons, Inc.

"Silly Putty" is a registered trademark of Binney & Smith Inc.

"Simple Green" is a registered trademark of Sunshine Makers, Inc.

"Skippy" is a registered trademark of Unilever.

"Slinky" is a registered trademark of James Industries.

"Smirnoff" is a registered trademark of United Vintners & Distributors.

"Sno Bol" is a registered trademark of Church & Dwight Co., Inc.

"Soft Scrub" is a registered trademark of the Dial Corp.

"SPAM" is a registered trademark of Hormel Foods Corporation.

"Speed Stick" is a registered trademark of Colgate-Palmolive.

"Spic and Span" is a registered trademark of Procter & Gamble.

"Spot Shot" is a registered trademark of the WD-40 Company.

"Spray 'n Wash" is a registered trademark of Reckitt Benckiser Inc.

"Sprite" is a registered trademark of the Coca-Cola Company.

"Star" is a registered trademark of Star Fine Foods.

"Stayfree" is a registered trademark of McNeil-PPC, Inc.

"SueBee is a registered trademark of Sioux Honey Association.

"Tabasco" is a registered trademark of McIlhenny Company.

"Tampax" is a registered trademark of Tambrands, Inc.

"Tang" is a registered trademark of Kraft Foods.

"3M" is a registered trademark of 3M.

"Tide" is a registered trademark of Procter & Gamble.

"Turtle Wax" is a registered trademark of Turtle Wax, Inc.

"20 Mule Team" and "Borax" are registered trademarks of United States Borax & Chemical Corporation.

"Uncle Ben's" and "Converted" are registered trademarks of Uncle Ben's, Inc.

"USA Today" is a registered trademark of Gannett News Service.

"Vaseline" is a registered trademark of the Chesebrough-Pond's USA.

"Velcro" is a registered trademark of Velcro Industries.

"Vicks" and "VapoRub" are registered trademarks of Procter & Gamble.

"WD-40" is a registered trademark of the WD-40 Company.

"Wesson" is a registered trademark of Hunt-Wesson, Inc.

"Westley's" and "Bleche-Wite" are registered trademarks of Blue-Coral Sick 50, Ltd.

"Wilson" is a registered trademark of Wilson Sporting Goods Co.

"Windex" is a registered trademark of S. C. Johnson & Son, Inc.

"Wine Away" is a registered trademark of Evergreen Labs, Inc.

"Wish-Bone" is a registered trademark of Unilever.

"Wonder" is a registered trademark of Interstate Brands Corporation.

"Woolite" is a registered trademark of Reckitt Benckiser, Inc.

"Wrigley's," "Doublemint," "Juicy Fruit," and "Wrigley's Spearmint" are registered trademarks of Wm. Wrigley Jr. Company.

"Ziploc" is a registered trademark of S.C. Johnson & Son, Inc.

"Zippo" is a registered trademark of Zippo Manufacturing Company.

"Zud" is a registered trademark of Reckitt Benckiser, Inc.

Index

Boldface page references indicate illustrations. <u>Underscored</u> references indicate boxed text.

Starch, making, 177
Static cling, preventing, 76–77
Static electricity, preventing, 61, 63
Steaming clothing, tip for, 177
Steel wool pads, storing, 222–23
Steering wheels, cleaning car, 7
Stems of flowers, tips for lengthening and
    straightening, 101
Sticker removal
    from artwork, 328
    from car bumper, 2
    from car windshield, 7
    from clothing, 273
    from wood furniture, 130
Sticky messes, avoiding, 103, 107
Storage containers for food, tip for recycled, 117
Stove knobs, cleaning, 223
Stoves. *See* Ovens and stoves, cleaning
Strainers, improvised, 224
Strawberries, hulling and storing, 117, **117**
Stretching shoes, tip for, 359
Stripping furniture tip, 130–31
Stuffed animals, cleaning, 18, 20
Suede items, cleaning, 273, 286, 359
Sugar, tips for storing, 118
Sweaters, laundering, 273–74
Sweat stain removal, 267–68, 275–76
Sweeping tips, 72, 82–83, **83**, 90–91, 95
Swimming pool tips, 323, 325

Tablecloths
    candle wax removal from, 287–88
    food stain removal from, 292 93, **292**
    lace, cleaning, 288, 290
    picnic, tips for, 45
    plastic, cleaning, 291
    stain-proofing, 291
    vinyl, cleaning, 291
    white, 292, **292**
Tables, dusting glass, 81
Taco holders, improvised, 118
Tailor's chalk, improvised, 349
Tar removal
    from carpets and rugs, 64
    from cars, 8
    from clothing, 274
    from dryers, 77, **77**
    from skin, 49
    from vinyl floors, 95
Tea, tip for making, 118
Tea cups, cleaning, 188–89

Tea kettles, cleaning, 224–25
Teapots, cleaning, 225
Tea stain removal
    from carpets and rugs, 54–55
    from clothing, 239–40
    from linens, 288, 292–93
Teething rings, cleaning, 17
Telephones, cleaning, 86
Televisions, cleaning, 83, 86
Television screens, dusting, 83
Tents, repairing camping, 49
Thanksgiving holiday tip, 153
Thermos bottles, cleaning, 49, 225
Thimbles, improvised, 349
Thread, tips for storing sewing, 349–50
Ties, laundering, 274
Tile, cleaning
    bathroom, 30, 37, 39
    ceramic floor, 91–92
Tires, cleaning car, 8–10, **10**
Tissues in laundry, managing, 77
Toasters, cleaning, 225–26
Toilet brush holder, making, 38
Toilets, cleaning, 40–41
Tomato sauce stain removal, 272, 274–75
Toners, making, 145
Toner stain removal, 275
Toolbox tips, 382
Tools. *See* Garden tools; Workshop tools
Tote bag, tips for using, 294–95
Towels, cleaning, 292
Toys, cleaning, 20, 47
Training pants, cleaning and deodorizing, 20
Travel bags, Ziploc bags for, 20
Trunks
    car, preventing freezing of, 8
    deodorizing wooden, 127, **127**
T-shirts, laundering red, 266
Turkeys, trussing, 118, 153

Umbrellas
    patio, cleaning and storing patio, 331
    personal, repairing, 49–50
Underarm stain removal, 275–76
Upholstery cleaning
    car, 5, 8
    furniture, 122–24
    vinyl, cleaning and deodorizing, 131
Urine stain removal
    from carpets and rugs, 64–65, 340, 341–42
    from clothing, 276

About the Author

Joey Green—author of *Polish Your Furniture with Panty Hose, Paint Your House with Powdered Milk, Wash Your Hair with Whipped Cream,* and *Clean Your Clothes with Cheez Wiz*—got Jay Leno to shave with peanut butter on *The Tonight Show,* Rosie O'Donnell to mousse her hair with Jell-O on *The Rosie O'Donnell Show,* and had Katie Couric drop her diamond engagement ring in a glass of Efferdent on *Today.* He has been seen polishing furniture with SPAM on *NBC Dateline,* cleaning a toilet with Coca-Cola in the *New York Times,* and washing his hair with Reddi-wip in *People.*

Green, a former contributing editor to *National Lampoon* and a former advertising copywriter at J. Walter Thompson, is the author of more than forty books, including *Marx & Lennon: The Parallel Sayings, Weird Christmas,* and *The Zen of Oz Ten Spiritual Lessons from Over the Rainbow.* A native of Miami, Florida, and a graduate of Cornell University, he wrote television commercials for Burger King and Walt Disney World and won a Clio Award for a print ad he created for Eastman Kodak. He backpacked around the world for two years on his honeymoon and lives in Los Angeles with his wife, Debbie, and their two daughters, Ashley and Julia.

**For more alternative uses for brand-name products,
visit www.wackyuses.com**
